North Korea
a country study

Federal Research Division
Library of Congress
Edited by
Robert L. Worden

On the cover: Statues of a worker, a peasant, and a party intellectual in
   front of Chuch'e Tower in P'yŏngyang
Courtesy *Pulmyŏl ŭi t'ap* (Tower of Immortality), P'yŏngyang: Munye
   Ch'ulpansa, 1985, 325

Fifth Edition, First Printing, 2008.

Library of Congress Cataloging-in-Publication Data

North Korea: a country study / Federal Research Division, Library of
Congress; edited by Robert L. Worden. -- 5th ed.
   p. cm. -- (Area handbook series) (DA Pam ; 550-81)
"Research completed October 2007."
Includes bibliographical references and index.

   1. Korea (North). I. Worden, Robert L. II. Library of Congress. Federal
Research Division.
   DS932.N662 2008
   951.93--dc22

                 2008028547

Foreword

This volume is one in a continuing series of books prepared by the Federal Research Divison of the Library of Congress under the Country Studies/Area Handbook Program, formerly sponsored by the Department of the Army and revived in FY 2004 with congressionally mandated funding under the sponsorship of the Joint Chiefs of Staff, Strategic Plans and Policy Directorate (J–5).

Most books in the series deal with a particular foreign country, describing and analyzing its political, economic, social, and national security systems and institutions, and examining the interrelationships of those systems and the ways they are shaped by historical and cultural factors. Each study is written by a multidisciplinary team of social scientists. The authors seek to provide a basic understanding of the observed society, striving for a dynamic rather than a static portrayal. Particular attention is devoted to the people who make up the society, their origins, dominant beliefs and values, their common interests and the issues on which they are divided, the nature and extent of their involvement with national institutions, and their attitudes toward each other and toward their social system and political order.

The books represent the analysis of the authors and should not be construed as an expression of an official U.S. government position, policy, or decision. The authors have sought to adhere to accepted standards of scholarly objectivity. Corrections, additions, and suggestions for changes from readers will be welcomed for use in future editions.

David L. Osborne
Chief
Federal Research Division
Library of Congress
Washington, DC 20540–4840
E-mail: frds@loc.gov

Acknowledgments

This edition supercedes *North Korea: A Country Study*, published in 1994. The authors wish to acknowledge their use of portions of that edition in the preparation of the current book.

Various members of the staff of the Federal Research Division of the Library of Congress assisted in the preparation of the book. Sandra W. Meditz made many helpful suggestions during her review of all parts of the book and managed the editing, indexing, and production of the book. Catherine Schwartzstein edited the manuscript, made many very useful suggestions, and helped clarify obscure points. She also performed the final prepublication editorial review and compiled the index. Sarah Ji-Young Kim provided valuable assistance in checking facts, reviewing and revising maps and figures, collecting illustrations, and assisting with the preparation of the Country Profile and Bibliography. Margaret L. Park, a Library of Congress intern from Rutgers University, prepared the preliminary drafts of the maps for the book. Janie L. Gilchrist performed word processing.

The authors also are grateful to other individuals in the Library of Congress who contributed to the book. Foremost was Sonya Sungeui Lee, Korea Reference Specialist in the Asian Division, who gave important advice and clarified many points. She also helped identify illustrations from the Library of Congress collections to use in the book. Paul Dukyong Park of the Asian Division assisted in locating and providing copies of North Korean publications. Youngsim Leigh of the African/Asian Acquisitions and Overseas Operations Division provided various sources and contact information for photographs and other information on North Korea. Sarah Byun, Elaine Hyojoung Kim, and Young-ki Lee of the Regional and Cooperative Cataloging Division clarified points on the romanization of Korean-language words. Suk-Young Kim, a fellow in the John W. Kluge Center of the Library of Congress, on sabbatical from the University of California Santa Barbara, read parts of the manuscript and made valuable suggestions both on the text and on North Korean propaganda posters that could be used for illustrations. The extensive research assistance on Chapter 4 by Lucia Selvaggi of Boston University must be acknowledged as well.

Christopher S. Robinson prepared the book's maps and charts and also performed the photocomposition and preparation of the final digital manuscript for the printer. Both he and Katarina David of the Federal Research Division performed digital conversion of photographs and illustrations used in the study.

Finally, the authors acknowledge the generosity of individuals and public and private organizations that allowed their photographs to be used in this study; they have been acknowledged in the illustration captions. Additionally, thanks goes to Boon-hee Jung and Chan-ho Lee of the Ministry of Unification of South Korea and to Jung-woo Lee of the Overseas Pan-Korean Center in Washington, DC, for providing recent photographs of North Korea.

Contents

List of Figures

Preface

This edition of *North Korea: A Country Study* replaces the previous edition, published in 1994. Like its predecessor, this study attempts to review the history and treat in a concise manner the dominant social, political, economic, and military aspects of contemporary North Korea. Sources of information included books, scholarly journals, foreign and domestic newspapers, official reports of governments and international organizations, and numerous periodicals and Web sites on Korean and East Asian affairs. A word of caution is necessary, however. Even though more information is forthcoming from and about North Korea since it became a member of the United Nations in 1991, the government of a closed society such as that of North Korea controls information for internal and external consumption, limiting both the scope of coverage and its dissemination.

A chronology of major historical events is provided at the front of the book (see table A). Chapter bibliographies appear at the end of the book, and brief comments on some of the more valuable and enduring sources recommended for further reading appear at the end of each chapter. A glossary also is included.

Spellings of place-names in the book are in most cases those approved by the U.S. Board on Geographic Names (BGN); spellings of some of the names, however, cannot be verified, as the BGN itself notes. Readers of this book are alerted that because the BGN recognizes the Sea of Japan as the formal name of the body of water to the east of the Korean Peninsula, this book also uses that term. However, Koreans themselves call this body of water the East Sea; thus, that term also is given at each first use. Similarly, the Yellow Sea is identified as the West Sea. The generic parts appended to some geographic names have been dropped and their English equivalents substituted: for example, Mayang Island, not Mayang-do, Mount Paektu, not Paektu-san, and South P'yŏngan Province, not P'yŏngan-namdo. In some cases, variant names have been introduced: for example, Amnok for the river as it is known in North Korea and Yalu as the same river is known in China. The name North Korea has been used where appropriate in place of the official name, Democratic People's Republic of Korea. The McCune–Reischauer system of transliteration has been employed except for the names of some prominent national and historical figures. Thus, Kim Il-sŏng is rendered as Kim Il Sung, and Kim Chŏng-il is rendered as Kim Jong Il. The names of Korean authors writing in English are spelled as given in the original publication.

Measurements are given in the metric system. A conversion table (see table B) is provided to assist readers who are unfamiliar with metric measurements.

The body of the text reflects information available as of August 1, 2007. Certain other parts of the text, however, have been updated: the Chronology and Introduction discuss significant events that have occurred since the completion of research, and the Country Profile and portions of some chapters include updated information as available.

Table A. Chronology of Important Events

2333–ca. 194 B.C.	Old Chosŏn kingdom.
2000 B.C.	Pottery culture introduced.
Fourth century B.C.	Walled-town states noted.
ca. 194–108 B.C.	Wiman Chosŏn state; iron culture emerges.
A.D. 246–668	Three Kingdoms period.
246–660	Paekche kingdom.
312–671	Koguryŏ kingdom.
356–935	Silla kingdom.
384	Buddhism adopted as state religion in Paekche.
ca. 535	Buddhism adopted as state religion in Silla.
668	Korea unified under Silla, Koguryŏ pushed to the north.
698–926	Parhae state rises as successor to Koguryŏ.
751	Dharani Sutra, oldest example of woodblock printing in the world.
892–935	Later Paekche kingdom.
918–1392	Koryŏ Dynasty.
1231	Koryŏ army defeated by invading Mongols.
1254	Second Mongol invasion.
1274 and 1281	Korean forces join Mongols in abortive invasions of Japan.
1392–1910	Chosŏn Dynasty.
1418–50	Reign of King Sejong, who introduces hangul (or *chosŏn'gul*) alphabet.
1592 and 1597	Armor-clad "turtle ships" under Yi Sun-sin defeat Japanese invaders.
1627 and 1636	Manchu invasions of Korea.
August 1866	Koreans attack armed American ship, the *General Sherman*, in Taedong River, destroying the ship and killing crew.
1864–73	Yi Ha-ung introduces institutional reforms.
1876	Unequal treaty imposed by Japan; China seeks to reassert traditional influence.
1885	Chinese general Yuan Shikai blocks Korean reforms and nationalism.
1894	Tonghak (Eastern Learning) rebellion.
1894–95	Using pretext of Sino-Japanese War, Japan moves troops into Korea.
1905–10	Japanese protectorate established over Korea.
1910–45	Korea becomes a colony of Japan.
April 15, 1912	Kim Il Sung born.
1919	Nationwide protests demand independence from Japan.
1925	Korean Communist Party established in Seoul.
1931	Japan annexes Manchuria; Chinese and Korean joint resistance forces emerge; heavy industrialization in northern Korea follows.
1937–45	World War II in East Asia; Koreans involved in both sides of the war.
February 16, 1941	Kim Jong Il born (but later his official birth date is proclaimed as February 16, 1942).
1943	Allied powers (United States, United Kingdom, and Soviet Union) define postwar period of tutelage for Korea.
August 11, 1945	United States sets thirty-eighth parallel as dividing line between Soviet and U.S. zones.
September 1945	Kim Il Sung arrives in North Korea.
October 10, 1945	North Korean Communist Party established.

Table A. Chronology of Important Events (Continued)

February 8, 1946	Interim People's Committee, led by Kim Il Sung, becomes first North Korean central government.
August 28–30, 1946	Korean Workers' Party (KWP) founded, First KWP Congress held.
February 8, 1948	Korean People's Army (KPA) formally established.
March 27–30, 1948	Second KWP Congress.
August 15, 1948	Republic of Korea established in South Korea with its capital at Seoul.
September 2, 1948	First Supreme People's Assembly (SPA) held.
September 9, 1948	Democratic People's Republic of Korea (DPRK) established in North Korea with its capital at P'yŏngyang; constitution adopted.
December 26, 1948	Soviet forces withdrawn from northern half of Korean Peninsula.
June 25, 1950	Korean War ("Fatherland Liberation War") breaks out.
October 25, 1950	Chinese forces enter Korean War.
February 7, 1953	SPA gives Kim Il Sung title of marshal.
July 27, 1953	Armistice signed by United States (for the United Nations), North Korea, Soviet Union, and China (but not South Korea).
1954–56	Three-Year Postwar Reconstruction Plan.
December 1955	Kim Il Sung proclaims *chuch'e* political ideology of autonomy and self-reliance.
April 23–29, 1956	Third KWP Congress.
August 27, 1957	Second SPA election.
1957–61	Five-Year Plan.
October 26, 1958	Withdrawal of Chinese forces from Korea completed.
September 6–18, 1961	Fourth KWP Congress.
1961–67	First Seven-Year Plan.
October 8, 1962	Third SPA election.
1964	Nuclear research facility established at Yŏngbyŏn.
October 5–12, 1966	Kim Il Sung elected KWP general secretary.
November 25, 1967	Fourth SPA election.
January 23, 1968	North Korean patrol boats capture U.S. intelligence ship *Pueblo*.
November 2–13, 1970	Fifth KWP Congress held.
July 4, 1972	High-level talks between North Korea and South Korea end with announcement that unification will be sought peacefully.
December 25, 1972	State constitution revised; Kim Il Sung elected president.
August 25, 1975	North Korea joins Nonaligned Movement.
October 10–14, 1980	Sixth KWP Congress held.
February 28, 1982	Seventh SPA election.
September 8, 1984	SPA adopts joint-venture law.
December 12, 1985	North Korea signs Treaty on the Non-Proliferation of Nuclear Weapons.
November 2, 1986	Eighth SPA election.
March 13, 1987	North Korea becomes party to 1972 Biological Weapons Convention.
January 1989	South Korea's Hyundai founder tours North Korea, announces joint venture in tourism.
April 22, 1990	Ninth SPA election.
September 1990	First of series of prime minister–level meetings between North Korean and South Korean officials takes place in Seoul.
September 17, 1991	North Korea becomes member of the United Nations.
December 1991	Kim Jong Il appointed KPA supreme commander.

Table A. Chronology of Important Events (Continued)

December 13, 1991	Agreement on Reconciliation, Nonaggression, Exchanges, and Cooperation (Basic Agreement) signed between North Korea and South Korea calls for reconciliation and nonaggression and establishes four joint commissions; joint declaration on denuclearization initialed.
January 20, 1992	Joint Declaration on the Denuclearization of the Korean Peninsula signed; both sides agree not to "test, manufacture, produce, receive, possess, store, deploy or use nuclear weapons" or to "possess nuclear reprocessing and uranium enrichment facilities"; agreement takes effect on February 19, 1992.
January 30, 1992	P'yŏngyang signs full-scope Safeguards Agreement with the International Atomic Energy Agency (IAEA), having pledged to do so in 1985.
April 1992	State constitution amended, emphasizes *chuch'e* instead of Marxism-Leninism.
January 1993	North Korea refuses IAEA access to two suspected nuclear waste sites.
March 12, 1993	P'yŏngyang announces intent to withdraw from Treaty on the Non-Proliferation of Nuclear Weapons.
April 1993	National Defense Commission chairmanship passes from Kim Il Sung to Kim Jong Il.
June 15, 1994	Former U.S. president Jimmy Carter visits P'yŏngyang.
July 8, 1994	Kim Il Sung dies unexpectedly.
October 1994	Bilateral talks held with United States starting in June lead to Agreed Framework freezing North Korea's nuclear facilities.
1995–98	Devastating floods followed by famine.
July 8, 1997	The end of three years of mourning for Kim Il Sung.
October 8, 1997	Kim Jong Il appointed general secretary of KWP.
July 26, 1998	Tenth SPA election.
September 1998	State constitution revised, Kim Jong Il's power consolidated as he is reconfirmed as chairman of the National Defense Commission, the "highest office of state."
June 13–15, 2000	First inter-Korean summit, emanating from "Sunshine Policy" announced by South Korea in 1998, held in P'yŏngyang.
July 2000	North Korea begins participating in the ASEAN Regional Forum (ARF).
October 9–12, 2000	Vice Marshal Cho Myŏng-nok visits President William J. Clinton in Washington, DC.
October 23, 2000	U.S. Secretary of State Madeleine Albright hosted in P'yŏngyang for talks on North Korea's missile program.
October 2002	North Korea admits developing nuclear weapons technology.
December 2002	North Korea removes United Nations seals and cameras from Yŏngbyŏn nuclear facility, moves fresh fuel to reactor.
August 3, 2003	Eleventh SPA election.
August 27–29, 2003	Six-Party Talks initiated in Beijing, involving North Korea, South Korea, the United States, China, Russia, and Japan.
February 25–28, 2004	In second round of Six-Party Talks, North Korea proposes it be provided "compensation" in return for freezing its nuclear weapons program.
June 23–25, 2004	In third round of Six-Party Talks, U.S. proposal to resolve nuclear issue discussed.
February 10, 2005	P'yŏngyang announces it has nuclear weapons and is suspending its participation in the Six-Party Talks.
July 26–August 7, 2005	First session of fourth round of Six-Party Talks held in Beijing.
September 13–19, 2005	In Joint Statement of Principles, at second session of fourth round of Six-Party Talks, all parties unanimously reaffirm goal of denuclearization of the Korean Peninsula in a verifiable manner.

Table A. Chronology of Important Events (Continued)

November 9–11, 2005	At first session of fifth round, North Korea begins boycott of Six-Party Talks, citing the "U.S.'s hostile policy" and U.S. law enforcement action that led in September to a freeze of North Korean accounts in Macau's Banco Delta Asia.
July 4–5, 2006	North Korea launches seven ballistic missiles over Sea of Japan (East Sea).
October 9, 2006	North Korea announces that six days earlier it conducted an underground nuclear weapon test, with the statement that the test will "contribute to defending the peace and stability on the Korean Peninsula and in the area around it."
December 18–22, 2006	Second session of fifth round of Six-Party Talks held in Beijing, with all parties reaffirming commitment to Joint Statement of September 19, 2005, but left deadlocked over financial dispute with the United States.
February 8–13, 2007	Third session of fifth round of Six-Party Talks held in Beijing; joint document on initial steps toward denuclearization of the Korean Peninsula, with a 60-day timetable for North Korea to shut down its main nuclear reactor, signed on February 13.
March 19–22, 2007	First session of sixth round of Six-Party Talks held in Beijing.
June 25, 2007	North Korea acknowledges transfer of funds frozen by United States at Banco Delta Asia in Macau, confirms it will take next step in implementing February 13, 2007, agreement.
July 16, 2007	IAEA confirms Yŏngbyŏn nuclear reactor has been shut down.
July 18–20, 2007	First session of sixth round of Six-Party Talks resumes in Beijing; joint communiqué signed on July 20 stating parties' commitment to the September 19, 2005, joint statement and the February 13, 2007, agreement and a tentative date for the next round of negotiations.
September 27–30, 2007	Second session of sixth round of Six-Party Talks held in Beijing; implementation of February 13, 2007, agreement confirmed.
October 2–4, 2007	Second North–South summit held in P'yŏngyang; Kim Jong Il and South Korean president Roh Moo Hyun issue joint declaration on North–South cooperation to oppose war on the Korean Peninsula and to abide by nonaggression.
November 14–16, 2007	North Korean prime minister Kim Yong-il holds talks in Seoul with South Korean prime minister Han Duck-soo.
December 11, 2007	Cross-border freight-train service reestablished for first time since Korean War.
January 4, 2008	North Korea declares it has disclosed all nuclear developments; United States disagrees.
February 26–27, 2008	New York Philharmonic Orchestra performs in P'yŏngyang.
March 28, 2008	North Korea test fires missiles over the sea and warns that it might stop disabling its nuclear facilities.
May 16, 2008	United States agrees to restart deliveries of food aid to North Korea.
June 26, 2008	North Korea submits declaration of its nuclear inventory to China, as chair of the Six-Party Talks.
June 27, 2008	United States announces intent to remove North Korea from list of state terrorism sponsors and to lift some trade sanctions. North Korea destroys cooling tower at Yŏngbyŏn Scientific Research Center.
June 30, 2008	First renewed U.S. food aid delivery arrives in North Korea.
August 11, 2008	United States announces decision not to remove North Korea from state-sponsored terrorism list until P'yŏngyang allows independent verification of its declared nuclear programs.
October 11, 2008	United States formally removes North Korea from its list of state terrorism sponsors.

Table B. Metric Conversion Coefficients and Factors

When you know	Multiply by	To find
Millimeters............................	0.04	inches
Centimeters...........................	0.39	inches
Meters................................	3.3	feet
Kilometers	0.62	miles
Hectares	2.47	acres
Square kilometers......................	0.39	square miles
Cubic meters..........................	35.3	cubic feet
Liters................................	0.26	gallons
Kilograms.............................	2.2	pounds
Metric tons	0.98	long tons
	1.1	short tons
....	2,204	pounds
....		
Degrees Celsius (Centigrade).............	1.8 and add 32	degrees Fahrenheit

Country Profile

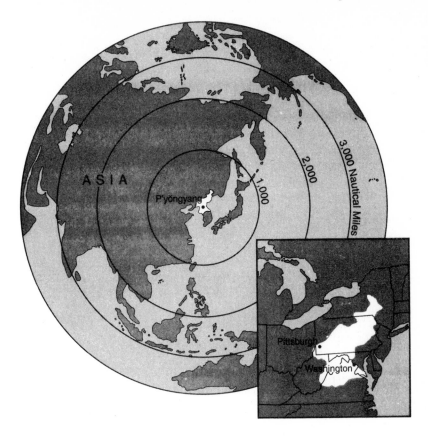

Country

Formal Name: Democratic People's Republic of Korea
(DPRK—Chosŏn Minjujuŭi Inmin Konghwaguk).

Short Form: North Korea (Chosŏn).

Term for Citizen(s): Korean(s).

Capital: P'yŏngyang.

Date of Independence: August 15, 1945, from Japan; Democratic
People's Republic of Korea founded September 9, 1948.

Geography

Size: Total 120,410 square kilometers land area, 130 square kilometers water area.

Topography: Approximately 80 percent mountain ranges separated by deep, narrow valleys; wide coastal plains on west coast, discontinuous coastal plains on east coast. The highest peak Mount Paektu, 2,744 meters above sea level. Only 22.4 percent of land arable. Major rivers are Amnok (Yalu) and Tuman (Tumen) in north, Taedong in south.

Climate: Long, cold, dry winters; short, hot, humid summers.

Society

Population: 23,479,089 estimated in July 2008. In 2008, birthrate 14.6 births per 1,000; death rate 7.3 per 1,000; sex ratio 0.95 male to each female as of 2008 estimate. Approximately 60 percent of population living in urban areas, about 14 percent in P'yŏngyang in 2005. In 2008 estimated population density per square kilometer 194.

Ethnic Groups: Almost all ethnic Koreans, a few Chinese and Japanese.

Language: Korean, some dialects not mutually intelligible; written language uses phonetic-based hangul (or *chosŏn'gul*) alphabet.

Religion: Traditionally Buddhist, now about 10,000 practicing; about 10,000 Protestants, 4,000 Roman Catholics, indeterminate number of native Ch'ŏndogyo (Heavenly Way) adherents. Organized religious activity except officially supervised is strongly discouraged. Personality cult of Kim Il Sung promoted by state as sole appropriate belief.

Health: Life expectancy estimated in 2008 at 69.4 years for males, 75 for females. Infant mortality 21.9 per 1,000; one doctor for every 700 inhabitants and one hospital bed for every 350 inhabitants. Estimated famine deaths in 1990s vary from 500,000 to 3 million people. In 1998 an estimated 60 percent of children suffered malnutrition, 16 percent acutely malnourished.

Education and Literacy: Eleven years free, compulsory, universal primary and secondary education. Higher education offered in 300 colleges and universities. In 2000 primary and secondary education included: 27,017 nursery schools, 14,167 kindergartens, 4,886 four-year primary schools, and 4,772 six-year secondary schools, enrolling 5.9 million students. Nearly 1.9 million students attended postsecondary institutions. Literacy rate 99 percent.

Economy

Major Features: Traditionally socialized, centrally planned, and primarily industrialized command economy isolated from rest of world; prior to 1991 heavily dependent on Soviet aid. Since 2002 "economic improvement measures" practiced to create incentives, increase salaries, and improve flow of products to cash-paying consumers; increased economic cooperation with South Korea.

Gross Domestic Product (GDP): In 2007 estimated at US$40 billion, possibly as low as US$10 billion; per capita income based on GDP (purchasing parity power) estimated in 2007 was $1,900. GDP by sector, based on 2002 estimates, is agriculture 30 percent, industry 34 percent, and services 36 percent.

Agriculture: Principal crops include rice, potatoes, corn, cabbages, apples, soybeans, pulses, and sweet potatoes; other vegetables, fruits, and berries also important. Livestock includes pigs, poultry, rabbits, horses, cattle, sheep, and goats. Fishing provides important dietary supplement, including freshwater and saltwater fish, shellfish, and mollusks; about 63,700 tons produced using aquaculture in 2002.

Industry and Manufacturing: Machine building, armaments, electric power, chemicals, metallurgy, textiles, and food processing.

Natural Resources: Coal, iron ore, cement, nonferrous metals (copper, lead, and zinc), precious metals (gold and silver), also magnesite.

Exports: Estimated US$1.4 billion free on board, 2006. Major commodities: minerals, metallurgical products, manufactures (including armaments), textiles, fishery products. South Korea, China, and Thailand are largest trading partners.

Imports: Totaled US$2.8 billion cost, insurance, and freight, 2006. Major imports: petroleum, coking coal, machinery and equipment, textiles, and grain. China, South Korea, Thailand, and Russia are main trading partners.

Exchange Rate: Officially US$1=140.00 wŏn in late October 2008; internal black market rate 2,500–3,000 wŏn to US$1.

Fiscal Year: Calendar year.

Transportation and Telecommunications

Inland Waterways and Ports: 2,250 kilometers, most used only by small boats; Amnok (Yalu), Tuman (Tumen), and Taedong most important navigable rivers. Major port facilities—all ice-free—at Namp'o and Haeju on west coast and Najin, Ch'ŏngjin, Hŭngnam, and Wŏnsan on east coast; merchant fleet 171 ships of gross-registered tons or more in 2007.

Roads: In 2006 total road network estimated at 25,554 kilometers; 724 kilometers paved, 24,830 kilometers unpaved. Major expressway links Wŏnsan on east coast with P'yŏngyang inland and Namp'o on west coast.

Railroads: In 2006 total rail network approximately 5,235 kilometers, although officially claimed to total 8,500 kilometers, 1.435-meter standard gauge roadbeds located primarily along east and west coasts; 3,500 kilometers electrified. Rolling stock includes about 300 electric and numerous diesel locomotives; great majority of freight carried by rail. Subway system opened in P'yŏngyang in 1973.

Civil Aviation: In 2007 estimated 77 usable airports, 36 with permanent-surface runways and 41 with unpaved runways. Sunan International Airport north of P'yŏngyang offers about 20 flights per week on North Korean, Chinese, and Russian carriers; other airports at Ch'ŏngjin, Hamhŭng, Najin, and Wŏnsan. State-run airline Air Koryo, uses 15 Soviet-made planes, provides domestic service to three airports and foreign service to eight cities in China, Thailand, Germany, and Russia. In 2001 only 5 tons per kilometer freight carried by air.

Pipelines: 154 kilometers of oil pipelines in 2007.

Telecommunications: 17 AM, 14 FM, and 14 shortwave government-controlled radio stations in 2006. Nearly all households have access to broadcasts from radios (4.7 million in 2001) or public loudspeakers. Four main television stations, 55 television sets per 1,000 population; in 2005 estimate, 980,000 telephones in use; e-mail service introduced in 2001, but public Internet access restricted.

Print Media: Twelve principal newspapers, 20 major periodicals; electronic and print media controlled by state.

Government and Politics

Party and Government: Communist state under one-man dynastic leadership. Party, state, and military structures consolidated under the leadership of Kim Jong Il; National Defense Commission, which he chairs, nation's "highest administrative authority." Position of president conferred posthumously on Kim Il Sung after his death in 1994. Premier and cabinet appointed by unicameral Supreme People's Assembly (SPA), except minister of the People's Armed Forces, who answers directly to Kim Jong Il. President of SPA Presidium is titular head of state. Constitution adopted in 1948, revised in 1972, 1992, and 1998. Korean Workers' Party (KWP) ruling party under general secretary Kim Jong Il. Last full party congress was 1980; Central Committee last met in 1994. With KWP, Chongu (Friends) Party and Korean Social Democratic Party provide nominal multiparty system.

Administrative Divisions: Nine provinces (*do*), two provincial-level municipalities (*chikalsi* or *jikhalsi*—P'yŏngyang and Najin–Sŏnbong), one special city (*t'ukpyŏlsi*)—Namp'o. The second level includes ordinary cities (*si* or *shi*), urban districts (*kuyŏk*), and counties (*gun* or *kun*). Third level made up of traditional villages (*ri*, or *ni*); cities subdivided into wards (*gu*); some cities and wards subdivided into neighborhoods (*dong*), the lowest level of urban government to have its own office and staff.

Judicial System: Three-level judicial system patterned on Soviet model. Central Court highest court and accountable to Supreme People's Assembly (SPA); also provincial courts at intermediate level and "people's courts" at lowest level; special courts try cases involving armed forces personnel and crimes related to railroads and rail employees.

Foreign Relations: Once heavily dependent on traditional close allies, Soviet Union and China; diplomatic relations expanded significantly since early 1990s. North Korea now has diplomatic relations with 150 nations; maintains full embassies in 27 nations. Nuclear weapons proliferation and missile sales major issues shaping relations with neighbors and United States. Three-Party Talks (North Korea, United States, and China) in 2003 discussed nuclear weapons and economic aid issues; Six-Party Talks (United States, North Korea, South Korea, China, Japan, and Russia) held 2003–7. Improved relations with South Korea aimed at eventual peaceful reunification of Korean Peninsula.

National Security

Armed Forces: Korean People's Army—1,106,000 personnel in 2005, world's fourth largest after China, United States, and India. Army—approximately 950,000 (including at least 87,000 special operations troops); navy—46,000; air force—110,000.

Military Budget: According to North Korea, US$1.8 billion, or 15.7 percent of government budget (2003). External sources believe more likely around US$5 billion, or 44.4 percent of government budget.

Military Units: Army—nine infantry, four mechanized, one tank, and one artillery corps; P'yŏngyang Defense Command; Border Security Command; Missile Guidance Bureau; and Light Infantry Training Bureau. Navy—two fleets, 19 naval bases. Air force—four air divisions, three air combat divisions stationed at 11 airbases.

Military Equipment: Main battle tanks, light tanks, armored personnel carriers, towed artillery, self-propelled artillery, multiple rocket launchers, mortars, surface-to-surface rockets and missiles, antitank guided weapons, recoilless launchers, and air defense guns; submarines, frigates, corvettes, missile craft, large patrol craft, fast torpedo craft, patrol force craft, amphibious ships, coastal defense missile batteries, hovercraft, minesweepers, depot ship, midget ships, and survey vessels; bombers, fighters and ground attack fighters, transports, transport helicopters and armed helicopters, training aircraft, unmanned air vehicle, and air-to-air missiles and surface-to-air missiles.

Auxiliary Forces: Border guards and police under Ministry of People's Security—189,000; reservists and paramilitaries—7.7 million.

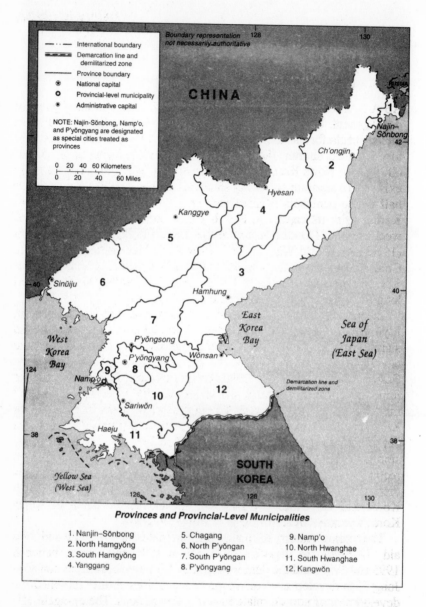

Figure 1. Administrative Divisions of North Korea, 2007

Provinces and Provincial-Level Municipalities

1. Nanjin–Sŏnbong
2. North Hamgyŏng
3. South Hamgyŏng
4. Yanggang
5. Chagang
6. North P'yŏngan
7. South P'yŏngan
8. P'yŏngyang
9. Namp'o
10. North Hwanghae
11. South Hwanghae
12. Kangwŏn

Introduction

AS A NATION, KOREA HAS a long history of cultural and political development. Uniquely Korean characteristics have been in place on the peninsula for more than 4,000 years. As a divided nation, that history is much shorter. The Democratic People's Republic of Korea (DPRK), or North Korea, with its capital in P'yŏngyang, has formally existed as a separate state only since September 9, 1948. The southern half of the peninsula is governed by the Republic of Korea (South Korea), with its capital in Seoul, which came into being just three weeks earlier. Divided Korea is the legacy of Japanese colonialism (1910– 45), World War II (1937–45 in Asia, 1939–45 in Europe), the Cold War between the United States and its allies and the former Soviet Union and its allies (1948–91), the Korean War (1950–53), and long-term intransigence between the two Koreas.

Events that took place within China and the Soviet Union, P'yŏngyang's staunchest supporters, in the late twentieth century had significant effects on North Korea. Economic reforms in China in the late 1970s and the demise of the Soviet Union and the communist Eastern bloc in the early 1990s resulted in market-based costs for imports from these partners and lesser amounts of economic aid and moral support. These realities, plus improved relations between North Korea and Japan, coincided with the gradual improvement of relations between P'yŏngyang and Seoul, leading in 1991 to their joint admission to the United Nations and an agreement between the two sides on reconciliation and nonaggression. Prospects appeared positive for further rapprochement between North and South and between North Korea and the United States until the unexpected death of North Korea's paramount leader, Kim Il Sung (1912–94).

The regime's ability to manipulate international economic and food aid, following the disasters of floods in 1995 and famine between 1995 and 1998, and the determination of Kim's successor, his son Kim Jong Il, to develop nuclear weapons capabilities further inhibited the development of normal relations with other nations. The on-again-off-again Six-Party Talks—held in Beijing among North Korea, South Korea, China, Russia, Japan, and the United States—between 2003 and 2007 have produced many reassurances and moderate expectations but few tangible results.

The Korean Peninsula is strategically situated in the northeast corner of the Asian landmass. The northern half of the peninsula borders the People's Republic of China and Russia to the north and South Korea to the south. The Yellow Sea (or West Sea as preferred by Koreans) washes the western shore of the peninsula, and the Sea of Japan (or East Sea as preferred by Koreans) is off the east coast. The peninsula is a salient pointing at Japan and has, for millennia, been a crossroads of cultural exchange and military invasions between mainland and insular Northeast Asia. Long an area of interest to imperial China, Korea has been fought over by all of its neighbors and, most recently, was the focal point of major conflict during the Korean War. In the decades since an armistice was signed in 1953, the peninsula—both north and south—has been transformed by internal and external political, military, and economic forces, and the societies of the two halves of the peninsula have been continually reshaped. North Korea is notable for being largely mountainous—more than 80 percent of the land is mountain ranges, divided by deep, steep valleys relieved only on the west coast by wide plains and more sporadic plains on the east coast. The climate can be harsh, bitterly cold in the winter and hot and humid in the summer.

The origins of Korean civilization, like any ancient culture, emerge from legends and myths, some of which are bolstered by archaeology and historical analyses. Paleolithic and neolithic societies populated the peninsula between 500,000 and 7,000 years ago, respectively. But it is the pottery culture that emerged around 2000 B.C. and the development of walled-town states in the fourth century B.C. that historians of Korea see as the origins of Korean culture. The northern advance of Korean culture and influence was met by a similar advance from China and the establishment of a Chinese presence in what today are North Korea and northern parts of South Korea. Temporarily blocked in the north, Korean—or Chosŏn—culture was concentrated in the south. Three kingdoms—Silla, Paekche, and Koguryŏ—developed there during the third century to the seventh century A.D. When Koguryŏ became ascendant for a time, it pushed its control deep into what is today northeastern China. Silla eventually became supreme, and a centralized government emerged by the fifth century A.D. Buddhism was introduced from China by the fourth century, a legal code was established in the sixth century, and cultural borrowing from Tang Dynasty (614–906) China, especially Confucianism, took hold. As Silla declined, the new state of Koryŏ arose and established its own dynasty (924–1392) and flourishing culture until its demise in the late fourteenth century in the wake of invasions by the Mongols from Inner Asia.

The Chosŏn Dynasty (1392–1910) followed Koryŏ, and Korea enjoyed a long period of cultural development and relative peace. Neo-Confucian doctrines introduced from China swept away old practices, resulting in the emergence of a well-educated secular society, an agrarian majority, and scholar-officials imbued with Neo-Confucian principles that prescribed the hierarchical position of every member of society. A Chosŏn king is credited with inventing the modern Korean hangul alphabet (which the North Koreans call *chosŏn'gul*). Korean printers were using movable metal type two centuries before the Europeans. Korea's deployment of the world's first armor-clad ships, so-called "turtle ships," repulsed devastating invasions from Japan in the late sixteenth century, but they were followed in the mid-seventeenth century by Manchu invasions from the north that debilitated Chosŏn.

Revival from foreign invasions engendered increasing isolation and, by the nineteenth century, dynastic decline. The arrival of the Western powers in East Asia brought new problems and differing degrees of success at modernization and reform by Korea and its neighbors, China and Japan. Imperialist rivalries among China, Japan, and Russia resulted in direct interference in Korea's affairs. Despite attempts by reformers to strengthen Korea, Russian and Japanese competition over a disintegrating China spilled over into Korea. Following the Russo–Japanese War (1904–5), Japan solidified its control over Korea by making it a protectorate, then a colony and part of the Japanese Empire.

Japanese rule over Korea differed from that imposed by other colonial powers. Rather than just extract resources and labor from Korea, Japan allowed manufacturing to take root (primarily in the north) and agriculture to flourish (primarily in the south). Korean economic growth sometimes outstripped that in Japan. Nonetheless, the experience was humiliating for Koreans, and nationalism and political activism emerged. The North Koreans' legacy of guerrilla warfare against Japan during World War II would later give legitimacy to the P'yŏngyang regime. The end of World War II brought independence from Japan but also division of the peninsula into two parts and eventually a devastating war.

North Korea's contemporary society is under the regimentation of one-party rule and controlled by the world's first communist dynasty, that of the Kim family. Despite claims of socialism by the leadership, society is as structured today as in premodern times. After 1948 the new leadership began to build a rigid class structure that emphasized Confucian hierarchical values, the cult of Kim Il Sung, and a thought-controlled, thoroughly militarized society. Members of the ruling Korean Workers' Party (KWP) and the military establishment are pre-eminent in society and favored with housing, food, education, and creature comforts. For others, life has been impoverished, with limited education, a poor health-care system, no open religious institutions or spiritual teaching, and few basic human rights.

The economy of North Korea has gone through tremendous change since 1948. Before World War II, the northern half of the Korean Peninsula was an industrial heartland supporting Japan. Rather than ship raw materials or semifinished products back to Japan, colonial entrepreneurs built mines to exploit the raw materials and factories to produce the finished products. As North Korea developed following the destruction of the Korean War, it did quite well for a time. Within four years, most parts of the economy had returned to 1949 levels of production. All sectors of the economy reportedly experienced high growth rates. Central economic development plans were imposed, but competition to fulfill plan targets by various parts of the economy caused imbalances between light and heavy industries and between industry and agriculture. Nevertheless, until 1960 the North's reconstructed economy grew faster than that of the South. During the 1960s, in sharp contrast to the growth during the previous plans, the economy experienced slowdowns and reverses. Despite a desire to modernize, the regime's 1955 declaration of national self-reliance (*chuch'e*) had become a central focus of economic planning. Most trade was with China and the Soviet Union, which provided North Korea with needed industrial, military, and technological assistance at bargain rates. Then the Cold War ended, the Soviet Union collapsed, China had reformed its economy and opened it to the world, and North Korea was left in a state of shock. South Korea, which had not recovered as quickly from the Korean War, had eventually surged past the North and built an economy with vast international implications. Gradual rapprochement with the South led to joint economic ventures and infusions of investment and aid from the South. Flood and famine in the mid-1990s, however, caused grievous harm to the economy and between 500,000 and 3 million deaths. "Adjustments" to the economy were in order, and the regime cautiously allowed changes to the public distribution system, adopted monetized economic transactions, and changed the incentives for labor and companies in 2002. The centrally planned economy was shelved, but the economy itself continues in transition and is barely functional.

The North Korean state is tightly controlled by a small group of elites led by Kim Il Sung from 1948 to 1994 and, since 1994, by his son and successor, Kim Jong Il. The cult of personality and the nepotism of the Kim family are special features of North Korean politics. Kim Il Sung's wife, daughter, son-in-law, a cousin by marriage, a brother-in-law, and his son all held high-level positions in the regime during the elder Kim's lifetime. Kim Jong Il was groomed as a successor well in advance of his father's unexpected death in 1994. After three years of official mourning, the younger Kim assumed control of the state, party, and military. And he set out to groom one of his own sons to succeed him. The cult status built around the father has been retained and enhanced by the son. Whether it will pass on to a third generation is yet to be seen.

As the ubiquitous Kim cult is a beacon for society, the concept of *chuch'e* is a guiding principle for politics. Marxism–Leninism, once a hallowed principle in North Korea, was not included when the state constitution was amended in 1992. By 1998, when the constitution was revised again, the concept of private ownership was added, and technocrats and local light-industry managers were granted some autonomy from central party control. Nevertheless, *chuch'e*, in the words of this book's authors, is "inextricably intertwined" with the cult of Kim, and the regime could be imperiled by further economic disasters.

In the North Korean regime, the party, the state, and the military also are inextricably intertwined, with the top leadership positions of all three held by Kim Jong Il. However, the "military-first" (*sŏngun*) policy, which was formalized in 1995, has meant a slippage in the control the party bureaucracy has over the state. To control the state, political and moral suasion are insufficient for Kim; instead, he exercises tight military control to fill this apparent gap. Constitutionally, the highest military organ of state authority is the National Defense Commission, and Kim Jong Il is its chairman. The presidency is held posthumously by Kim Il Sung, and the titular head of state is the chairman of the Presidium of the Supreme People's Assembly, North Korea's nominal legislature. The National Defense Commission is accountable on paper to the Supreme People's Assembly. But with Kim as chairman of the commission, as well as supreme commander of the Korean People's Army, chairman of the KWP's Central Military Commission, and general secretary of the KWP, there is no room for doubt about who is in charge and which organ of state is predominant. The KWP has not held a national party congress since 1980, and the KWP Central Committee, which is supposed to hold plenary sessions every six months, has not met since 1994. Nevertheless, the KWP continues to play a critical role in supervising its own members and controlling mass organizations, such as those for children, youth, women, workers, loyal opposition parties, and even Koreans living overseas, regimenting civilian society in general.

Society also is controlled by the civilian bureaucracy. Through officials from the central government down to the ward level and through control exercised over the media and all forms of communication, the government plays an important part in the day-to-day regimentation of society. Mirroring the Supreme People's Assembly are provincial and local people's assemblies, which provide an appearance of popular support and involvement, at least by local elites, in the governance of the country.

Kim Jong Il also controls the all-powerful military establishment. North Korea has, after China, the United States, and India, the fourth largest combat force in the world. There are more than 1.2 million personnel on active duty and an additional 7.7 million personnel in paramilitary and reserve forces. With a forward deployment of its forces near the demilitarized zone (DMZ—see Glossary) that divides North and South, North Korea helps keep the Cold War legacy alive. This deployment is bolstered by the world's largest artillery force—some 13,500 artillery pieces and rocket launchers. Members of the armed forces are among the best fed, housed, educated, and trained in North Korean society. The intent is to keep them at a high state of readiness against the perceived threat from U.S. forces stationed in South Korea and patrolling the adjacent seas and in the air in Northeast Asia. North Korea has developed and tested long-range missiles and nuclear weapons capabilities to counter the specter of a remilitarized Japan and the perennial fear of the United States. The Ministry of People's Armed Forces, which provides administrative direction to the military, is not subordinate to the cabinet but instead answers directly to the chairman of the National Defense Commission.

North Korea's military capabilities are designed to support the goals of the state and the party, namely to reunify and communize the peninsula. These goals influence military strategic planning, cadre training, and force modernization. The Korean People's Army has a three-part strategy of surprise attack; quick, decisive war; and mixed tactics to carry out the nation's defense policy. The tactics include plans to launch massive conventional, chemical artillery, and missile attacks and simultaneous insertion of special operations forces. The development of a nuclear weapons capability has been part of the overall strategy. So too is the long-term construction of North Korea's large defense industry, which also is closely managed by the National Defense Commission. The *sŏngun* policy ensures that defense, industry, and the military establishment in general have all they need or want.

August 24, 2007

*   *   *

As the manuscript for this book was being completed, a number of significant events occurred in or concerning North Korea. North Korea reported on October 9, 2006, that it had conducted its first nuclear test—a "historic event that brought happiness to our military and people," according to the Korean Central News Agency. Amidst skepticism about the size and success of the test, independent sources revealed that a low-yield (estimated between a half-kiloton and five-kiloton) device had been detonated. As North Korea apparently joined the world's nuclear club, it received international condemnation, from the United States, Japan, South Korea, and the United Nations, and even from its close ally, China. Even as sanctions were discussed, a North Korean official suggested that his country could launch a nuclear missile if the United States did not resume negotiations. However, Kim Jong Il himself reportedly apologized for the test and said there were no plans for additional tests.

Despite the tensions caused by the North Korean test, on December 18, 2006, the Six-Party Talks resumed in Beijing among representatives of North Korea, South Korea, the United States, Japan, Russia, and China. After protracted negotiations, an agreement was finally signed on February 13, 2007, by which North Korea agreed to shut down its main, Soviet-built nuclear reactor capable of producing weapons-grade plutonium and to allow inspections by the International Atomic Energy Agency (IAEA). In return, the United States agreed to release US$25 million of North Korean (allegedly money-laundered) funds frozen in 2005 by the U.S. Department of the Treasury at Banco Delta Asia, a Macau-based bank owned by the Delta Asia Financial Group, and to provide economic aid and improve diplomatic relations. P'yŏngyang did not shut down the aging nuclear reactor at Yŏngbyŏn as promised by April 14 but gave assurances that it would do so soon after the United States released the Banco Delta Asia funds via the Federal Reserve Bank in New York on June 25, 2007, to a North Korean account at a commercial bank in Russia near the border with North Korea. Just before the announcement, Assistant Secretary of State Christopher R. Hill made an unannounced two-day trip to P'yŏngyang on June 21–22. The trip was made despite there being no U.S. demand for concessions as a condition of the visit, which was requested by North Korea. Following Hill's meetings with Ministry of Foreign Affairs officials, the Six-Party Talks resumed two days later on July 18–20 and continued on September 27–30 in Beijing. At the latter session, the six parties agreed to implement the February 17, 2007, agreement. In subsequent months, the United States agreed on May 16, 2008, to restart deliveries of food aid and in June 2008 to remove North Korea from its list of countries sponsoring terrorism.

On June 27, 2008, North Korea submitted to the Chinese, as the host nation of the Six-Party Talks, a 60-page declaration of its nuclear inventory, including a list of its nuclear facilities, the amount of produced and extracted plutonium and how it is used, and the volume of its uranium stocks. The next day, Washington reciprocated with the announcement that it would remove North Korea from its list of states that sponsor terrorism, and North Korea dramatically destroyed a cooling tower at the Yŏngbyŏn facility. Despite these breakthroughs, the North Koreans rejected the U.S. suggestion of on-the-spot inspections of their nuclear facilities and sampling of nuclear material. The Bush administration responded on August 11 by announcing that it would not remove North Korea from the state-sponsored terrorism list until P'yŏngyang established a mechanism that allowed international inspectors to verify the claims of its June 27 nuclear declaration.

Other momentous events included the April 11, 2007, appointment of Kim Yong-il as North Korea's premier, replacing Pak Pong-ju, who had held the office since September 2003. Kim had been the long-time deputy bureau director and minister of land and marine transport before becoming premier. In May 2007, the railroad crossing the western DMZ was reconnected between North Korea and South Korea for the first time since 1950. On May 17, two five-car passenger test trains ran between Kaesŏng in North Korea and Munson, in South Korea, across the DMZ and back. Freight service on the same 25-kilometer route was inaugurated on December 11, 2007.

North Korea reportedly suffered its heaviest-ever rainfall in August 2007 and the worst since the devastating floods of 1995. About 10 percent, or 450,000 tons, of the country's crops were destroyed in the August floods; hundreds of people died, and some 300,000 were left homeless. A summit conference planned for August 28–30 in P'yŏngyang between Kim Jong Il and South Korean president Roh Moo Hyun was postponed until October 2–4 because of the floods. At the conclusion of their cordial summit, Kim and Roh signed a joint declaration calling for permanent peace and economic prosperity on the Korean Peninsula. Despite follow-up prime ministerial talks in Seoul in November, political realities in South Korea compelled Roh to take a stronger stance on North Korea, and inter-Korean relations, like the Six-Party Talks, continued to fluctuate.

More serious developments occurred in September 2008. On September 9, Kim Jong Il failed to appear at public celebrations for the sixtieth anniversary of the founding of the DPRK. The condition of Kim's health, as he recovered from a reported cerebral hemorrhage, was subject to silence within North Korea and considerable speculation outside the country. Regional and more distant observers expressed concern about the sustainability of the P'yŏngyang regime. The nuclear dispute with the United States and other nations took a serious turn on September 24 when North Korea asked IAEA officials to remove their seals and surveillance equipment at the Yŏngbyŏn nuclear reprocessing plant and then denied them access. P'yŏngyang sought more concessions—and removal from Washington's state-sponsored terrorism list—as it threatened to resume processing nuclear fuel. However, on October 11, the United States formally removed North Korea from its terrorism list, and the North agreed to resume its denuclearization procedures.

Amidst ostensibly improved international relations between North Korea and other nations, bilateral ties between P'yŏngyang and Seoul became more tense. The North objected to South Korea's emerging, more conservative policies concerning nuclear, human rights, and other issues. On October 7, North Korean units tested two ship-to-ship missiles in the Yellow Sea, which was seen as a provocation by the South. On October 17, P'yŏngyang threatened to cut off all civilian relations if the conservative policies of the South—which the North viewed as provocative—continued. In the meantime, the North continued to deny reports concerning Kim Jong Il's poor health, and foreign sources began to reveal new famine conditions emerging in various parts of the DPRK.

November 5, 2008   Robert L. Worden

Chapter 1. Historical Setting

Statue of Kim Il Sung as a young man preaching revolution, a part of Wangjae-san Grand Monument, Onsŏng, North Hamgyŏng Province Courtesy Pulmyŏl ŭi t'ap *(Tower of Immortality), P'yŏngyang: Munye Ch'ulpansa, 1985, 137*

THE INTERNAL AND EXTERNAL SITUATION of the Democratic People's Republic of Korea (DPRK), or North Korea, was relatively stable and predictable from the end of the Korean War in
1953 to the fall of the Berlin Wall in 1989. The first-generation revolutionaries who built and directed the political system after 1948 still
held power as the 1990s began. Kim Il Sung, the founder of the state
and the center of its politics, continued to hold ultimate power. But·
the collapse of the Soviet Union in 1991, the emergence of a major
crisis in relations with the United States in 1993 over North Korean
nuclear policy, and Kim's unexpected death in 1994 put North Korea
on a much less stable and predictable footing. A general collapse of
its energy system and massive flooding followed in 1995, leading to
famine that claimed the lives of somewhere between 300,000 and
800,000 people annually through 1998. A new generation led by, and
beholden to, Kim's son—Kim Jong Il—took over at the highest echelons in the late 1990s and attempted to respond to the watershed
changes of the previous decade, on the Korean Peninsula and in the
world.

North Korea responded to a dynamically shifting set of political,
economic, and diplomatic opportunities and constraints with a stark
survival strategy and sporadic reform. The nation held far-reaching
negotiations with the United States that led in October 1994 to the ces-
sation of further development at its nuclear complex at Yŏngbyŏn.
After former dissident Kim Dae Jung came to power in the Republic
of Korea (South Korea) in 1998, his policy of engagement led to the
first-ever summit meeting between the leaders of the two Koreas in
June 2000, and to a host of agreements on South Korean investment,
trade, and tourism in or with the North. Kim Jong Il also broadened
the North's diplomatic ties by opening relations with Australia, Canada, and most countries in the European Union. The fate of the entire
North Korean system hinged on its success in adaptation to this new
environment: whether the state survived as a separate entity, an equal
partner in some sort of federation with the South, or went the way of
many other communist systems and simply disappeared still was a
very open question in the early twenty-first century.

However the new leaders respond, the legacies of the past weigh
heavily on them. More than most communist systems, North Korea
has molded Marxism–Leninism to the requisites of an indigenous
political culture and a continuous tradition going back to antiquity.
Furthermore, the deep-seated continuity of leadership and national

structure since the late 1940s means that North Korea continues to work within long-established foundations of politics, economics, and diplomacy. It is essential to grasp the evolution of North Korean history in order to understand the developments since the mid-1980s.

The DPRK originated with the national division in 1945 and in the midst of the post–World War II confrontation between the United States and the Soviet Union. North Korea was, and in some ways still is, a classic Cold War state, driven by reference to the long-running conflict with South Korea and the United States. It was founded in the heyday of Stalinism, which had particular influence on the North's heavy-industry-first economic program. The regime's Korean origins traced to a harsh guerrilla struggle against Japan in the 1930s. Here is a state perhaps uniquely forged in warfare, in Manchuria (as Northeast China was then commonly known) against Japan, in a civil struggle fought by unconventional means at the inception of the regime, and through vicious fratricidal war while national structures were still in infancy. Out of that war came one of the world's most remarkable garrison states, with most of the adult population having military experience. All these influences combined to produce a hardened leadership that, whatever else one might think of it, knew how to hold onto power. But North Korea also accomplished a rare synthesis between foreign models and domestic sources of politics; the political system is deeply rooted in native soil, drawing upon Korea's long history of unitary existence on a small peninsula surrounded by greater powers.

The Origins of the Korean Nation

Koreans inhabit a mountainous peninsula protruding southward from Northeast Asia and surrounded on three sides by water (see fig. 1; The Physical Environment, ch. 2). The peninsula, for most of its recorded history, was surrounded on three sides by other peoples: Chinese to the west, Japanese to the east, and an assortment of "barbarian" tribes, aggressive invaders, and, in the twentieth century, an expanding and deepening Russian presence to the north. Although Japan exercised decisive influence by the late sixteenth century, in ancient times the peoples and civilizations on the contiguous Asian continent were far more important.

The northern border between Korea and China formed by the Amnok (known as the Yalu in China) and Tuman (Tumen as it is called in China) rivers has been recognized for centuries. These rivers did not always constitute Korea's northern limits, as Koreans ranged far beyond this barrier well into Northeast China and Siberia, and neither Koreans nor the ancient tribes that occupied the plains of Manchuria regarded these riverine obstacles as sacrosanct borders.

The harsh winter climate also turned the rivers into frozen pathways for many months, facilitating the back and forth migration from which, over time, the Korean people were formed.

Paleolithic excavations show that human beings inhabited the Korean Peninsula 500,000 years ago, but most scholars assume that present-day Koreans are not descended ethnically from these early inhabitants. Neolithic humans were there 7,000 or 8,000 years ago, their presence affirmed by the ground and polished stone tools and pottery they left to posterity. Around 2000 B.C., a new pottery culture spread into Korea from China, leaving evidence of prominent painted designs. These neolithic people practiced agriculture in a settled communal life and were widely supposed to have had consanguineous clans as their basic social grouping. Korean historians in modern times sometimes assume that clan leadership systems characterized by councils of nobles (*hwabaek*) that emerged in the subsequent Silla period traced back to these neolithic peoples. There is no hard evidence, however, to support such imagined beginnings for the Korean people.

A mythical figure, Tan'gun, is said to have founded the Korean nation in 2333 B.C. (a date set by the South Korean government), the year he built his royal palace near modern-day P'yŏngyang and established the Old Chosŏn kingdom. Although his origins are obscure, the Tan'gun legend has existed since before the second century A.D. and has had influence ever since. The North Korean regime's Foundation Day on October 3 relates to Tan'gun, and the government claimed in 1993 to have found and excavated his tomb near P'yŏngyang.

By the fourth century B.C., a number of walled-town states on the peninsula had survived long enough to come to the attention of China. The most illustrious state was Old Chosŏn, which had established itself along the banks of the Liao and the Taedong rivers in southern Manchuria and northwestern Korea. Old Chosŏn prospered into a civilization based on bronze culture and a political federation of many walled towns, which, judging from Chinese accounts, was formidable to the point of arrogance. Riding horses and using bronze weapons, the Chosŏn people extended their influence to the north, taking most of the Liaodong Basin. But the rising power of the north China state of Yan (also known as Eastern Zhou) checked Chosŏn's growth and eventually pushed it back to territory south of the Ch'ŏngch'ŏn River, located midway between the Yalu and Taedong rivers. As Yan gave way in China to the Qin (221–207 B.C.) and the Han (206 B.C.–A.D. 220) dynasties, Chosŏn declined, and refugee populations migrated eastward. Out of this mileu emerged Wiman, a man who assumed the kingship of Chosŏn sometime between 194 and 180 B.C. Wiman Chosŏn melded Chinese influence and the Old Chosŏn federated structure; apparently reinvigorated under Wiman, this state again expanded over hundreds of kilometers of territory. Its ambitions ran up against a Han invasion, however, and Wiman Chosŏn fell in 108 B.C.

These developments coincided with the emergence of iron culture, enabling a sophisticated agriculture based on implements such as hoes, plowshares, and sickles. Cultivation of rice and other grains increased markedly, allowing the population to expand. There was an unquestioned continuity in agrarian society from this time until the emergence of a unified Korean state many centuries later, even if the peoples of the peninsula could not be called *Korean*.

Han Chinese built four commanderies to rule the peninsula as far south as the Han River, with a core area at Lolang (Nangnang in Korean), near present-day P'yŏngyang. It is illustrative of the relentlessly different historiography practiced in North Korea and South Korea, as well as both countries' dubious projection backward of Korean nationalism, that North Korean historians denied that the Lolang district was centered in Korea and placed it northwest of the peninsula, possibly near Beijing. Perhaps this was because Lolang was clearly a Chinese city, as demonstrated by the many burial objects showing the affluent lives of Chinese overlords and merchants.

The Three Kingdoms Period

Paekche

For about four centuries, from the second century B.C. to the second century A.D., Lolang was a great center of Chinese statecraft, art, industry (including the mining of iron ore), and commerce. Its influence was far-reaching, attracting immigrants from China and exacting tribute from several states south of the Han River, which patterned their civilization and government after Lolang. In the first three centuries A.D., a large number of walled-town states in southern Korea had grouped into three federations known as Chinhan, Mahan, and Pyŏnhan; rice agriculture had developed in the rich alluvial valleys and plains to the point of establishing reservoirs for irrigation.

Chinhan was situated in the middle part of the southern peninsula, Mahan in the southwest, and Pyŏnhan in the southeast. The state of Paekche, which soon came to exercise great influence on Korean history, emerged first in the Mahan area; it is not certain when this happened, but Paekche certainly existed by A.D. 246 because Lolang mounted a large attack on it in that year. That Paekche was a centralized, aristocratic state melding Chinese and indigenous influence was not in doubt, nor was its growing power: within a century, Paekche had demolished Mahan and continued expanding northward into what today is the core area of Korea, around Seoul. It is thought that the Korean custom of father-to-son royal succession began with King Kŭn Ch'ogo (reigned ca. 346–75) of Paekche. His grandson inaugurated another long tradition by adopting Buddhism as the state religion in 384.

Koguryŏ

Meanwhile, two other powerful states had emerged north of the peninsula around the time of Christ—Puyŏ in the Sungari River Basin in Manchuria, and Koguryŏ, Puyŏ's frequent enemy to its south, near the Yalu River. Koguryŏ, which also exercised a lasting influence on Korean history, developed in confrontation with the Chinese. Puyŏ was weaker and sought alliances with China to counter Koguryŏ but eventually succumbed around A.D. 312. Koguryŏ was expanding in all directions, in particular toward the Liao River in the west and toward the Taedong River in the south. In 313 Koguryŏ occupied the territory of Lolang and came into conflict with Paekche.

Peninsular geography shaped the political space of Paekche and Koguryŏ, and a third kingdom, Silla. In the central part of Korea, the main mountain range, the T'aebaek, runs north to south along the edge of the Sea of Japan (or, as Koreans prefer, the East Sea). Approximately three-quarters of the way down the peninsula, however, roughly at the thirty-seventh parallel, the mountain range veers to the southwest, dividing the peninsula almost in the middle. This southwest extension, the Sŏbaek Range, shielded peoples to the east of it from the Chinese-occupied portion of the peninsula but placed no serious barrier in the way of expansion into or out of the southwestern portion of the peninsula. This was Paekche's historical territory.

Koguryŏ, however, extended over a wild region of northwestern Korea and eastern Manchuria subjected to extremes of temperature and structured by towering mountain ranges, broad plains, and life-giving rivers. The highest peak, known as Paektu-san (Mount Paektu, or White Head Mountain), is situated on the contemporary North Korea–China border and has a beautiful, crystal-pure lake at its summit. Kim Il Sung and his guerrilla band utilized associations with this mountain as part of the founding myth of North Korea, just as Kim Jong Il was said to have been born on the slopes of the mountain in 1942. Unsurprisingly, North Korea claimed the Koguryŏ legacy as the mainstream of Korean history.

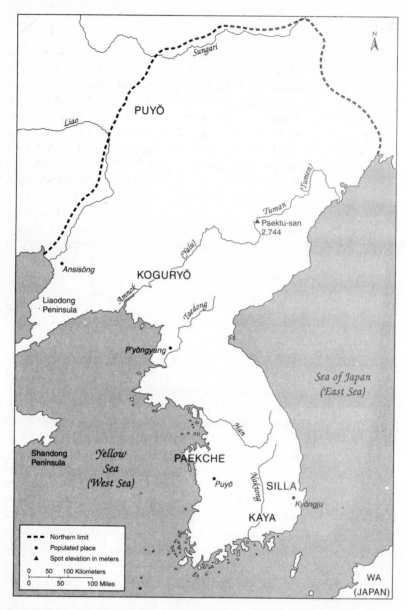

Source: Based on information from Ki-baik Lee, *A New History of Korea*, Seoul, 1984, 39;
Republic of Korea, Government Information Agency, Korean Overseas Information
Service, *Facts About Korea*, Seoul, 2006, 17; and Suh Cheong-Soo, ed., *An Encyclo-
pedia of Korean Culture*, Seoul, 2004, 219.

Figure 2. Korea in the Fifth Century A.D.

Silla

According to South Korean historiography, however, it was the glories of a third kingdom that were most important in founding the nation. Silla eventually became the repository of a rich and cultured ruling elite, with its capital at Kyŏngju in the southeast, north of the modern port of Pusan. The military men who ruled South Korea, either as dictators or elected leaders beginning in 1961, all came from this region, and most South Korean historians consider Silla's historical lineage as predominant. It was the Paekche legacy that suffered in divided Korea, as Koreans of other regions and historians in both North Korea and South Korea discriminated against the people of the Chŏlla provinces in the southwest of the peninsula. But taken together, the Three Kingdoms continued to infuence Korean history and political culture. Koreans often assumed that regional traits that they liked or disliked went back to the Three Kingdoms period.

Silla evolved from a walled town called Saro. Silla chroniclers are said to have traced its origins to 57 B.C., but contemporary historians have regarded King Naemul (r. A.D. 356–402) as the ruler who first consolidated a large confederated kingdom and established a hereditary monarchy. His domain was east of the Naktong River in today's North Kyŏngsang Province. A small number of states located along the south-central tip of the peninsula facing the Korea Strait did not join either Silla or Paekche but instead formed a Kaya League, which maintained close ties with states in Japan. Silla eventually absorbed the neighboring Kaya states in spite of an attack by Wa forces from Japan on behalf of Kaya in A.D. 399, which Silla repelled with help from Koguryŏ. Centralized government probably emerged in Silla in the second half of the fifth century, as the capital became both an administrative and a marketing center (see fig. 2). In the early sixth century, Silla's leaders introduced plowing by oxen and built extensive irrigation facilities. Increased agricultural output presumably ensued, allowing further political and cultural development, including an administrative code in 520, a hereditary caste structure known as the bone-rank system to regulate membership of the elite, and the adoption of Buddhism as the state religion around 535. Status in Silla society was so much influenced by birth and lineage that the bone-rank system led each family and clan to maintain extensive genealogical records with meticulous care. Because only male offspring prolonged the family and clan lines and were the only names registered in the genealogical tables, the birth of a son was greeted with great felicitation. The elite, of course, was most conscious of family pedigree.

Silla was weaker militarily than Koguryŏ, however, and sought to fend off its rival through an alliance with Paekche. By the beginning of the fifth century, Koguryŏ had achieved undisputed control of all of Manchuria east of the Liao River as well as the northern and central regions of the Korean Peninsula. At this time, Koguryŏ had a famous leader appropriately named King Kwanggaet'o (r. 391–412), whose name translates as "wide open land." Reigning from the age of 18, he conquered 65 walled towns and 1,400 villages, in addition to assisting Silla when the Wa forces from Japan attacked. But as Koguryŏ's domain increased, it confronted China's Sui Dynasty (589–618) in the west and Silla and Paekche to the south.

Silla attacked Koguryŏ in 551 in concert with King Sŏng (r. 523–54) of Paekche. After conquering the upper reaches of the Han River, Silla then turned on Paekche forces and drove them out of the lower Han area. While a tattered Paekche kingdom nursed its wounds in the southwest, Silla allied with Chinese forces of the Sui and the successor Tang (618–906) dynasties in combined attacks against Koguryŏ. The Sui emperor, Yang Di, launched an invasion of Koguryŏ in 612, marshalling more than 1 million soldiers, only to be lured into a trap by the revered Koguryŏ commander, Ŭlchi Mundŏk, who destroyed the Sui forces. Perhaps as few as 3,000 Sui soldiers survived their eclipse, thus contributing to the fall of the dynasty in 618. Tang emperor Tai Zong launched another huge invasion in 645, but Koguryŏ forces won another striking victory in the siege of the Ansisŏng (An Si Fortress), forcing him to withdraw.

Koreans have always viewed these victories as sterling examples of resistance to foreign aggression. Had Koguryŏ not beaten back the invaders, all the states of the peninsula might have fallen under long-term Chinese domination. Thus commanders such as Ŭlchi Mundŏk became models for emulation thereafter, especially during the Korean War (1950–53). Paekche could not hold out under combined Silla and Tang attack, however. The latter landed an invasion fleet in 660, and Paekche quickly fell. Tang pressure also had weakened Koguryŏ, which, after eight successive years of battle, succumbed to a combination of external attack, internal strife, and several famines. Koguryŏ retreated to the north, enabling Silla forces to advance and consolidate their control up to the Taedong River, which flows through P'yŏngyang.

Silla emerged victorious in 668. It is from this famous date that South Korean historians speak of a unified Korea. The period of the Three Kingdoms thus ended, but not before all of them had come under the long-term sway of Chinese civilization by introducing Chinese statecraft, Buddhist and Confucian philosophy, Confucian practices of educating the young, and the Chinese written language

(Koreans adapted the characters to their own language through a system known as *idu*). The Three Kingdoms also introduced Buddhism, the various rulers seeing, in a body of believers devoted to Buddha but serving one king, a valuable political device for unity. Artists from Koguryŏ and Paekche perfected a mural art found on the walls of tombs and took it to Japan where it deeply influenced Japan's temple and burial art. Indeed, many Korean historians have come to believe that the wall murals in royal tombs in Japan indicated that the imperial house lineage may have Korean origins.

Korea under Silla

Silla and Paekche had sought to use Chinese power against Koguryŏ, inaugurating another tradition of involving foreign powers in Korean internal disputes. Silla's reliance on Tang forces to consolidate its control had its price, however, because Silla had to resist encroaching Tang forces, which limited its sway to the area south of the Taedong River. But Silla's military force, bolstered by an ideal of the youthful warrior (*hwarang*), was formidable, and it seized Paekche territories by 671 and by 676 pushed Koguryŏ northward and the Tang commanderies off the peninsula, thereby guaranteeing that the development of the Korean people would take independent form.

The broad territories of Koguryŏ were not conquered, however, and a Koguryŏ general named Tae Cho-yŏng established a successor state called Parhae that extended to both sides of the Amnok and Tuman rivers. Parhae forced Silla to build a northern wall in 721 and kept Silla forces below a line running from present-day P'yŏngyang to Wŏnsan. By the eighth century, Parhae controlled the northern part of Korea, all of northeastern Manchuria, and the Liaodong Peninsula. Both Silla and Parhae continued to be influenced deeply by Tang civilization.

There were many contacts between Silla and Tang China, as large numbers of students, officials, and monks traveled to China for study. In 682 Silla set up a national Confucian academy to train high officials and later instituted a civil-service examination system modeled on that of the Tang. Parhae modeled its central government even more directly on Tang systems than did Silla and sent many students to Tang schools. Parhae culture melded indigenous and Tang influences, and its level of civilization was high enough to merit the Chinese designation as a "flourishing land in the East."

Silla in particular, however, developed a flourishing indigenous civilization that was among the most advanced in the world. Its capital at Kyŏngju was renowned as the "city of gold," where the aristocracy pursued a high culture and extravagant pleasures. Tang historians wrote that elite officials possessed thousands of slaves, with like numbers of horses, cattle, and pigs. The wives of such senior officials wore gold tiaras and earrings of delicate and intricate filigree. Silla scholars studied the Confucian and Buddhist classics, advanced state administration, and developed sophisticated methods for astronomy and calendrical science. The Dharani Sutra, recovered in Kyŏngju, dates as far back as 751 and is the oldest example of woodblock printing yet found in the world. "Pure Land" Buddhism united the mass of common people, who could become adherents through the repetition of simple chants. The crowning glories of this "city of gold" are the Pulguksa Temple in Kyŏngju and the nearby Sŏkkuram Grotto, both built around 750 and home to some of the finest Buddhist sculpture in the world. The grotto, atop a coastal bluff near Kyŏngju, boasts a great stone Sakyamuni Buddha in the cave's inner sanctum, poised such that the rising sun over the sea strikes him in the middle of the forehead.

Ethnic differences between Koguryŏ and the Malgal people native to Manchuria weakened Parhae by the early tenth century, however, just as Silla's power had begun to dissipate a century earlier when regional castle lords splintered central power and rebellions shook Silla's foundations. While Parhae came under severe pressure from Qidan (or Kitan) warriors from Inner Asia (the region west and north of China proper), Silla's decline encouraged a resurgent Paekche under a leader named Kyŏnhwŏn to found Later Paekche at Chŏnju in 892, and another restorationist, named Kungye, to found Later Koguryŏ at Kaesŏng in central Korea. Wang Kŏn, the son of Kungye, who succeeded to the throne in 918, shortened the name to Koryŏ and became the founder of a new dynasty (918–1392) by that name, whence came the modern term "Korea."

Unification by Koryŏ

Wang Kŏn's army fought ceaselessly with Later Paekche for the next decade, with Silla in retreat. After a crushing victory over Paekche forces at present-day Andong in 930, Koryŏ received a formal surrender from Silla and proceeded to conquer Later Paekche by 935—amazingly, with troops led by the former Paekche king, Kyŏnhwŏn, whose son had treacherously cast him aside. After this accomplishment, Wang Kŏn became a magnanimous unifier. Regarding himself as the proper successor to Koguryŏ, he embraced survivors of the Koguryŏ lineage who were fleeing the dying Parhae state, which had been conquered by Qidan warriors in 926. He then took a Silla princess as his wife and treated the Silla aristocracy with unexampled generosity. Wang Kŏn established a regime embodying the last remnants of the Three Kingdoms and accomplished a true unification of the peninsula.

Pulguksa Temple, built between 751 and 774, is a masterpiece of the golden age of Buddhist art in the Silla kingdom and is on the UNESCO World Heritage List. The temple is in Kyŏngju, North Kyŏngsang Province, South Korea.
Courtesy Korea Tourism Organization, New York

With its capital at Kaesŏng, the Koryŏ Dynasty's composite elite forged a tradition of aristocratic continuity that lasted down to the modern era. The elite combined aristocratic privilege and political power through marriage alliances, control of land and central political office, and making class position hereditary. This established a pattern for Korea, in which landed gentry mingled with a Confucian- or Buddhist-educated stratum of scholar-officials; often scholars and landlords were one and the same person, but in any case landed wealth and bureaucratic position were powerfully fused. Thus at the center a strong bureaucracy influenced by Confucian statecraft emerged, which thereafter sought to dominate local power and militated against the Japanese or European feudal pattern of small-scale sovereignty, castle domains, and military tradition. By the thirteenth century, there were two dominant government groupings—those of the civil officials and the military officials—known thereafter as *yangban* (the two orders—see Glossary).

The Koryŏ elite admired the splendid civilization that emerged during China's Song Dynasty (960–1279). Official delegations and ordinary merchants brought Koryŏ gold, silver, and ginseng to China in exchange for Song silks, porcelains, and woodblock books. The treasured Song porcelains stimulated Koryŏ artisans to produce an even finer type of inlaid celadon porcelain. Unmatched in the world before or since for the pristine clarity of its blue-green glaze and the delicate art of its inlaid portraits (usually of flowers or animals), Koryŏ celadon displayed the refined taste of aristocrats and later had great influence on potters in Japan.

Buddhism coexisted with Confucianism throughout the Koryŏ period, deeply influencing the daily life of society and perhaps bequeathing to modern Korea its eclecticism of religious belief. Koryŏ Buddhist priests systematized religious practice by rendering the Chinese version of the Buddhist canon into mammoth wood-block print editions, known as the *Tripitaka Koreana*. The first edition was completed in 1087 after a lifetime of work but was lost; another, completed in 1251 and still extant, was located at the Haein Temple. Its accuracy, combined with the exquisite calligraphic carvings, made it the finest of some 20 *Tripitaka* editions created in East Asia. By 1234, if not earlier, Koryŏ had also invented movable iron type, two centuries before its use in Europe.

This high point of Koryŏ culture coincided with internal disorder and the rise of the Mongols, whose power swept most of the known world during the thirteenth century. Koryŏ was no exception, as Khubilai Khan's forces invaded and demolished Koryŏ's army in 1231, forcing the Koryŏ government to retreat to Kanghwa Island (off modern-day Inch'ŏn), a ploy that exploited the Mongol horsemen's fear of water. But after a more devastating invasion in 1254, in which countless people died and some 200,000 people were made captives, Koryŏ succumbed to Mongol domination, and its kings married Mongol princesses. The Mongols then enlisted thousands of Koreans in ill-fated invasions of Japan in 1274 and 1281, using Korean-made ships. The Kamakura shogunate (1185–1333) turned back both invasions with aid, as legend has it, from opportune typhoons known as the "divine wind" or *kamikaze*. The last period of Mongol influence was marked by the appearance of a strong bureaucratic stratum of scholar-officials or literati (*sadaebu* in Korean). Many of them lived in exile outside the capital, and they used their superior knowledge of the Confucian classics to condemn the excesses of the ruling families, who were backed by Mongol power.

The overthrow of the Mongols by the Ming Dynasty (1368–1644) in China gave an opportunity to a rising group of military men, steeled in battle against coastal pirates from Japan, to contest power in Koryŏ. When the Ming claimed suzerainty over former Mongol domains in Korea, the Koryŏ court was divided between pro-Mongol and pro-Ming forces. Two generals marshaled their forces for an assault on Ming armies on the Liaodong Peninsula. One of the generals, Yi Sŏng-gye, was pro-Ming. When he reached the Amnok

One of the 81,200 wood printing blocks of the Tripitaka Koreana, *completed in 1251 following the destruction of the originals during the Mongol invasions*
Courtesy Korean Collection, Asian Division, Library of Congress, Washington, DC

More than 6,500 volumes of the Tripitaka Koreana *are housed at Haein Temple in South Kyŏngsang Province, South Korea.*
Courtesy Korea Tourism Organization, New York

River, he abruptly turned back and marched on the Koryŏ capital, which he subdued quickly. He thus became the founder of Korea's longest-lasting dynasty, the Chosŏn (1392–1910). The new state was named Chosŏn, harking back to Old Chosŏn 16 centuries earlier, and its capital was built at Seoul.

The Chosŏn Dynasty

Florescence

One of Yi Sŏng-gye's first acts was to carry out a sweeping land reform long advocated by literati reformers. After a national cadastral survey, all old land registers were destroyed. Except for estates doled out to loyalists called "merit subjects," Yi declared all other land to be owned by the state, thus undercutting Buddhist temples (which held sizable tracts of farmland) and locally powerful clans—both of which had exacted high rents from peasants, leading to social distress in the late Koryŏ period. These reforms also greatly enhanced the taxation revenue of the central government.

Buddhist influence in and complicity with the old system made it easier for the literati to urge an extirpation of Buddhist economic and political influence, and exile in the mountains for monks and their disciples. Indeed, the literati accomplished a deep Confucianization of Chosŏn society, which particularly affected the position of women. Often prominent in Koryŏ society, they were relegated to domestic chores of child rearing and housekeeping, as so-called "inside people."

As Neo-Confucian doctrines swept the old order away, Korea effectively developed a secular society. Common people, however, retained attachments to folk religions, shamanism, geomancy, and fortune-telling, influences condemned by Confucianism. This Korean mass culture created remarkably lively and diverse art forms: uniquely colorful and unpretentiously naturalistic folk paintings of animals, popular novels in Korean vernacular, and characters such as the *mudang* (shamans who summon spirits and perform exorcisms). In this way, women frequently found expression for their artistic creativity.

For more than a century after its founding, Chosŏn flourished as an exemplary agrarian bureaucracy deeply influenced by a cadre of learned scholar-officials, steeped in the doctrines of Neo-Confucianism. Like Koryŏ, the Chosŏn Dynasty did not manifest the typical features of a feudal society. Chosŏn possessed an elaborate procedure for entry to the civil service, which was highly developed, and a practice of administering the country from the top down and from the center.

The system rested upon an agrarian base, making it different from modern bureaucratic systems; the particular character of agrarian-bureaucratic interaction also provided one of Korea's departures from the typical Chinese experience.

The leading Western historian of the Chosŏn Dynasty, James B. Palais, has shown that conflict between bureaucrats seeking revenues for government coffers and landowners hoping to control tenants and harvests was a constant during the Chosŏn, and that in this conflict over resources the landowners often won out. Despite theoretical state land ownership, private landed power soon came to be stronger and more persistent in Korea than in China. Korea had centralized administration, to be sure, but the ostensibly strong center was more often a façade concealing the reality of aristocratic power.

Thus Korea's agrarian bureaucracy was superficially strong but actually rather weak at the center. The state ostensibly dominated the society, but in fact landed aristocratic families kept the state at bay and perpetuated local power for centuries. This pattern persisted until the late 1940s, when landed dominance was obliterated in a northern revolution and attenuated in southern land reform; since then the balance has shifted toward strong central power and top-down administration of the whole country in both Koreas (see The New Socialist Society, ch. 2; The Economy after World War II, ch. 3).

Confucianism began with the family and an ideal model of relations between family members. It generalized this family model to the state, and to an international system—the Chinese world order. The principle was hierarchy within a reciprocal web of duties and obligations: the son obeyed the father by following the dictates of filial piety; the father provided for and educated the son. Daughters obeyed mothers and mothers-in-law, younger siblings followed older siblings, wives were subordinate to husbands. The superior prestige and privileges of older adults made longevity a prime virtue. The rest of society viewed transgressors of these rules as uncultured beings not fit to be members of their community. When generalized to politics, a village followed the leadership of venerated elders, and citizens revered a king or emperor who was thought of as the father of the state. Generalized to international affairs, China's emperor was the big brother of the Korean king.

The glue holding the system together was education, meaning socialization into Confucian norms and virtues that began in early childhood with the reading of the Confucian classics. The model figure was the so-called true gentleman, the virtuous and learned scholar-official who was equally adept at poetry or statecraft. Education started very early, as Korean students had to master the extraordinarily difficult classical Chinese language—tens of thousands of written characters and their many meanings; rote memorization was the typical method. Throughout the Chosŏn Dynasty, all official records, all formal education, and most written discourse was in classical Chinese. With Chinese language and philosophy, of course, came a profound cultural penetration of Korea, such that most Chosŏn arts and literature came to use Chinese models.

The Korean written alphabet, hangul (see Glossary), was systematized in the fifteenth century under the greatest of Korean kings, Sejong (r. 1418–50), who also greatly increased the use of metal moveable type for book publications of all sorts. Some scholars consider Korean to be part of the Ural–Altaic group of languages, including Turkish, Hungarian, Finnish, and Japanese; others believe it may be a language isolate. In spite of the long influence of written Chinese, Korean remains very different in lexicon, phonology, and grammar. The hangul alphabet did not come into general use until the twentieth century, however; since 1948 the North Koreans have used the Korean alphabet—which they call *chosŏn'gul*—exclusively, while South Koreans retained usage of a mixed Sino–Korean script until the 1990s, at which time Chinese characters became less used.

Confucianism is often thought to be a conservative philosophy, stressing tradition, veneration of a past golden age, obedience to superiors, careful attention to the performance of ritual, disdain for material things, commerce, the remaking of nature, and a preference for relatively frozen social hierarchies. Much commentary on contemporary Korea focuses on the alleged authoritarian, antidemocratic character of this Confucian legacy. Yet a one-sided emphasis on these aspects would never explain the extraordinary commercial bustle of South Korea, the materialism and conspicuous consumption of new elites, or the determined struggles for democratization put up by Korean workers and students. On the other hand, the assumption that North Korean communism broke completely with the past would blind one to continuing Confucian legacies there: its family-based politics, the succession to rule of the leader's son, and the extraordinary veneration of Kim Il Sung (see The Cult of Kim Il Sung, ch. 2).

The Chosŏn Dynasty had a traditional class structure that departed from the Chinese Confucian example, providing an important legacy for the modern period. *Yangban* was still the Korean term for this aristocracy, but it no longer connoted simply two official orders. Its key features were its virtual monopoly on education and official position, possession of land, and the requirement of hereditary lineage for entry to *yangban* status. Unlike in China, commoners could

Korean movable-type specimens made of brass, iron, copper, and wood, ca. thirteenth century. Korea advanced the technology of printing by developing movable cast-metal type, from the 1230s.
Courtesy Korean Collection, Asian Division, Library of Congress, Washington, DC
King Sejong (r. 1418–50), the fourth king of the Chosŏn Dynasty, to whom is attributed the development of the Korean hangul alphabet
Courtesy Korea Tourism Organization, New York

not sit for state-run examinations leading to official position. Koreans had to prove that they belonged to a *yangban* family, which in practice meant a forebear having sat for exams within the past four generations. In Korea, as in China, the majority of peasant families could not spare a son to study for the exams, so that upward social mobility was sharply limited. But in Korea the limit also was specifically hereditary, leading to less mobility than in China and attitudes toward class distinction that often seemed indistinguishable from castes. A major study of all successful exam candidates in the Chosŏn Dynasty (some 14,000) showed remarkable persistence in those elite families producing students to sit for the exams; other studies have documented the persistence of this pattern into the early twentieth century. Even in 1945, one could say that this aristocracy was substantially intact, although its effective demise came soon thereafter.

Korea's traditional class system also included a peasant majority, and minorities of petty clerks, merchants, and so-called "base" classes, caste-like hereditary groups (*paekchŏng*) such as butchers, leather tanners, and beggars. Although merchants ranked higher than low-born classes, Confucian elites frowned on commercial activity and squelched it as much as possible right down to the twentieth century. Peasants ranked higher than merchants because they worked the life-giving land, but the life of the peasantry was almost always difficult during the Chosŏn period, although more so in the later centuries. Most peasants were tenants, required to give up at least half of their crop to landlords as tax, and subject to various additional exactions. The low-born classes were probably worse off, however, given the very high rates of slavery for much of the Chosŏn period. One source reported more than 200,000 government slaves in Seoul alone in 1462, and recent academic study has suggested that as much as 60 percent of Seoul's population may have been slaves. In spite of slavery being hereditary, rates of escape from slavery and manumission also were unusually high. Class and status hierarchies also are inherent in the Korean language and have persisted into the contemporary period. The correct form of address to superiors and inferiors was quite different, and elders could be addressed only using elaborate honorifics. Even verb endings and conjugations differed according to station.

Chosŏn-period Confucian doctrines did not stop at the nation's boundary but also informed a foreign policy known as "serving the great" (*sadae*), meaning China. Chosŏn lived within China's world order, radiating outward from Zhongguo (the Middle Kingdom) to associated states, of which Korea was the most important. It was China's little brother, a model tributary state, and in many ways the most important of China's allies. Koreans revered things Chinese, and China responded by being for the most part a good neighbor, giving more than it took away. Exercising a light-handed suzerainty, China assumed that enlightened Koreans would follow it without being forced. Absolutely convinced of its own superiority, China indulged in a policy that might be called benign neglect of things Korean, thereby allowing Korea substantive autonomy as a nation.

This sophisticated world order was broken up and laid low by the Western impact in the late nineteenth century, but there were important legacies for the twentieth century. As dwellers within a small power, Koreans had to learn to be shrewd in foreign policy, and they had a good example of that in China. Koreans cultivated the sophisticated art of "low determines high" diplomacy, seeking to use foreign power for their own ends, wagging the dog with its tail. Thus both South Korea and North Korea often struck foreign observers as rather dependent on big-power support, yet both not only claimed but also strongly asserted their absolute autonomy and independence as nation-states, and both were adept at manipulating their big-power clients. Until the mid-1980s, North Korea was masterful, both in getting big powers to fight its battles and in maneuvering between the two communist giants, the Soviet Union and China, to get something from each and to prevent either from dominating it. Much as in the traditional period, P'yŏngyang's heart was with China.

The soft spot that Koreans had in their hearts for China was not, however, the main characteristic of Korea's traditional diplomacy: that was isolationism, even what scholar Kim Key-hiuk has called exclusionism (see Glossary). For three centuries after the Japanese invasions of the 1590s, Korea isolated itself from Japan, dealt harshly with errant Westerners washing up on its shores, and kept the Chinese at arm's length. Thus Westerners called Korea the "hermit kingdom," the term expressing the pronounced streak of obstinate hostility toward foreign power and the deep desire for independence that marked traditional Korea. Ethnocentric and obnoxious to foreigners, a self-contained, autonomous Korea not besmirched by things foreign has remained an ideal for many Koreans. North Korea has exercised a "hermit kingdom" option by remaining one of the more isolated states in the world; it was really South Korea that, since 1960, was revolutionary in the Korean context by pursuing an open-door policy toward world markets and seeking a multilateral, varied diplomacy.

Dynastic Decline

A combination of literati purges in the early sixteenth century, Japanese invasions at the end of the century, and Manchu invasions in the middle of the next century severely debilitated the Chosŏn state, which never again reached the heights of the fifteenth century. This period also saw the Manchus sweep away the Ming Dynasty in China, ending a remarkable period when Korean society seemed to develop apace with China, while making many independent innovations.

The doctrinaire version of Confucianism that was dominant during the Chosŏn made squabbles between elites particularly nasty. The literati were grounded in Neo-Confucian metaphysics, which reached sublime heights virtually unmatched elsewhere in East Asia in the writings of Yi T'oegye, known as "Korea's Zhu Xi" after the Chinese twelfth-century founder of the Neo-Confucian school. For many other scholar-officials, however, the doctrine rewarded arid scholasticism and obstinate orthodoxy. First, they had to commit their minds to one or another side of abstruse philosophical debate, and only then could the practical affairs of state be put in order. This situation quickly led to so-called literati purges, a series of upheavals beginning in the mid-fifteenth century and lasting more than 100 years, with the losers finding their persons, their property, their families, and even their graves at risk from victors determined to extirpate their influence—always in the name of a higher morality. Later in the dynasty, the concern with ideological correctness exacerbated more mundane factional conflicts that debilitated central power. But such thinking also expressed the pronounced Korean concern with the power of ideas, still visible in Kim Il Sung's doctrine of *chuch'e* (see Glossary; Political Ideology, ch. 4), which has assumed that rectification of the mind precedes correct action, even to the point of Marxist heresy in which ideas determine material reality. At any rate, by the end of the sixteenth century the ruling elite had so homogenized its ideology that there were few heterodox miscreants left: all were presumably united in one idea.

At the end of the sixteenth century, Korea suffered devastating foreign invasions. The first came shortly after Toyotomi Hideyoshi ended Japan's internal disorder and unified the islands. His eventual goal was to put China under his control, and he launched an invasion that put some 160,000 Japanese soldiers at Pusan in 1592. At this, the Chosŏn court took flight to the Yalu River, infuriating ordinary Koreans and leading slaves to revolt and burn the registries. Japanese forces marched through the peninsula at will. In the nick of time, however, Korean admiral Yi Sun-sin built the world's first armor-clad ships, so-called "turtle ships" encased in thick plating with cannons sticking out at every point on their circular shape, which destroyed Japanese fleets wherever they were found. The Korean ships cut Japan's supply routes, and, combined with the dispatch of Ming forces and so-called "righteous armies" that rose up in guerrilla warfare (even Buddhist monks participated), caused the Japanese to retreat to a narrow redoubt near Pusan.

After desultory negotiations and delay, Hideyoshi launched a second invasion in 1597. The Korean and Ming armies were ready this time. Yi Sun-sin, with a mere dozen warships, demolished the Japanese forces in Yellow Sea battles near the port of Mokp'o. The would-be conqueror Hideyoshi died, and Japanese forces withdrew to their home islands where they nursed an isolationist policy for the next 250 years. In spite of the Chosŏn victory, the peninsula had been devastated. Refugees wandered its length, famine and disease were rampant, and even the basic land relationships were overturned by the widespread destruction of the registers. Korea had paid a terrible price for turning back invasions that otherwise would have substantially redirected East Asian history.

Chosŏn had barely recovered when the Manchus invaded from the north, fighting on all fronts to oust the Ming Dynasty. Invasions

*Admiral Yi Sun-sin (1545–98), the Korean
naval hero who is best known for his
innovative armored "turtle ships"
Courtesy Korea Tourism Organization,
New York*

in 1627 and 1636 established tributary relations between Korea and
the Manchus' Qing Dynasty (1644–1911), but they were less delete-
rious than the Japanese invasions, except in the northwest, where
Manchu forces wreaked havoc. Thereafter, the Chosŏn Dynasty had
a period of revival, which, had it continued, might have left Korea
much better prepared for its encounter with the West.

The Confucian literati were particularly reinvigorated by an intellectual movement advocating that philosophy be geared to solving
real problems of the society. Known as the Sirhak (Practical Learning) Movement, it produced some remarkable people, such as Yu
Hyŏng-wŏn (1622–73), who sat in a small farming village and pored
over the classics seeking reform solutions to social problems. He
developed a thorough, detailed critique of nearly all the institutional
aspects of Chosŏn politics and society and a set of concrete reforms
to invigorate it. Chŏng Yag-yong (1762–1836), thought to be the
greatest of the Sirhak scholars, wrote several books that offered his
views on administration, justice, and the structure of politics. Still
others, such as Yi Su-kwang (1563–1628), traveled to China and
returned with the new Western learning then spreading in Beijing,
while Yi Ik (1681–1763) wrote a treatise entitled *Record of Concern
for the Underprivileged.*

A new vernacular fiction also developed in the seventeenth and eighteenth centuries, much of it taking the form of social criticism. The best known example is *Ch'unhyang chŏn* (The Tale of Ch'unhyang), which argues for the common human qualities of low-born, commoners, and *yangban* alike. Often rendered as a play, it has been a great favorite in both North Korea and South Korea. An older poetic form, made up of short stanzas and called *sijo*, became another vehicle for free expression of distaste for the caste-like inequities of Korean society. Meanwhile, Pak Chi-wŏn (1737–1805) journeyed to Beijing in 1780 and wrote *Jehol Diary*, which compared Korean social conditions unfavorably with those he observed in China.

The economy was differentiating, as the transplanting of rice seedlings boosted harvests and some peasants became enterprising small landlords. Commercial crops developed, including tobacco, ginseng, and cotton, and merchants proliferated at big markets, such as those in Seoul at Dongdaemun (East Gate) and Namdaemun (South Gate), and at the way stops to China at Ŭiju, or Japan at Tongnae, near Pusan. The use of coins for commerce and for paying wages became more widespread, and handicraft production increased beyond government control. The old Koryŏ city of Kaesŏng became a strong center of merchant commerce and conspicuous wealth. Finally, throughout the seventeenth century Western learning filtered into Korea, often through the auspices of a spreading Roman Catholic movement—which attracted commoners above all by its creed of equality.

Korea in the Nineteenth-Century World Order

Unfortunately for Korea, the early nineteenth century witnessed a period of sharp decline in which most of Chosŏn's new developments were extinguished. Harsh persecution of Catholics began in 1801, and agricultural production declined, resulting in an agrarian state of rank poverty, with many peasants pursuing slash-and-burn agriculture in the mountains. Popular uprisings began in 1811 and occurred sporadically through the rest of the century, culminating in the Tonghak (Eastern Learning—see Glossary) Movement of the 1860s, which led to a major peasant rebellion in the 1890s.

Korean leaders were aware that China's position had been transformed by the arrival of powerful Western gunboats and traders, but they reacted to the First Anglo-Chinese War, better known as the Opium War (1839–42), by reinforcing Korea's isolation. When U.S. Navy Commodore Matthew C. Perry and his "black ships" forced Japan to open its ports in the mid-1850s, stimulating drastic reform of Japanese institutions—the Meiji Restoration of 1868—and subsequent industrialization, Korean literati attributed this change to Japan's inferior grasp of Confucian doctrine. There were French and American attempts to "open" Korea, including an August 1866 incident when an armed American-owned merchant ship, the *General Sherman* (the former U.S. gunboat USS *Princess Royal*), steamed up the Taedong River almost to P'yŏngyang, whereupon locals burned it and killed all its crew (an event in which Kim Il Sung claimed his great-grandfather was involved). Korea's success in rebuffing such intrusions encouraged the regime to think it could hold out indefinitely against external pressure.

Developments from 1864 to 1873 under a powerful leader named the Taewŏn'gun, or Grand Prince, Yi Ha-ung (1821–98) offered further evidence of Korean resilience, because he was able to reform the bureaucracy, bring in new talent, extract new taxes from both the *yangban* and commoners, and keep the foreign imperialists at bay. Korea's descent into the maelstrom of imperial rivalry was quick after this time, however, as Japan succeeded in imposing a Western-style unequal treaty in February 1876, giving its nationals extraterritorial rights and opening three Korean ports to Japanese commerce. China sought to reassert its traditional position in Korea by playing the imperial powers off against each other, leading to unequal treaties between Korea and the United States, Britain, Russia, Italy, and other nations. The Chinese even gave the Koreans the design of their national flag during this period. These activities split the Korean court into pro-Chinese, pro-Japanese, pro-American, and pro-Russian factions, each of which influenced policy down to the final annexation of Korea by Japan in 1910. Meanwhile, various Korean reform movements, influenced either by Japanese or American progressives, attempted to gain momentum.

Although Korean historians have postulated an "enlightenment movement," this phase of sporadic Westernization cannot remotely be compared to the Enlightenment in Europe and was constantly thwarted by reactionary scholars and officials. A number of individuals, including Kim Hong-jip, Kim Ok-kyun, Yun Ch'i-ho, and Yu Kil-chun, were very impressed by what they witnessed in Japan in the early 1880s, as that country industrialized quickly. Yun went on to become an influential modernizer in the twentieth century, and Yu became the first Korean to study in the United States—at the Governor Dummer Academy in Byfield, Massachusetts. Meanwhile, Kim Ok-kyun, impressed by the Meiji Restoration, sought to pull off a coup d'état in 1884 with a handful of progressives and about 200

Japanese Legation soldiers. Resident Chinese troops quickly suppressed the coup, however, and Kim fled to Japan.

For a decade thereafter, China reasserted a rare direct influence, when General Yuan Shikai established his residency in 1885 and momentarily made China first among the foreign powers then resident in Korea. A conservative reformer in China, he had no use for Korean reformers and instead blocked the slightest sign of Korean nationalism. Japan put a definitive end to Chinese influence in the Sino–Japanese War (1894–95), seizing on the reinvigorated Tonghak Movement, which led to widespread rebellion in 1894. Uniting peasants against Western pressure, growing Japanese economic penetration, and Chosŏn's corrupt and ineffectual government, the rebellion spread from the southwest into the center of the peninsula, thus threatening Seoul. The hapless court invited China to send troops to put the rebellion down, whereupon Japan had the pretext it wanted to send troops to Korea. After defeating Chinese forces, Japan declared Korea independent, thus breaking its long tributary relationship with China. Thereafter, Japan pushed through epochal reforms that ended the old civil service exam system, abolished traditional class distinctions, ended slavery, and established modern fiscal and judicial mechanisms.

Korean reformers influenced by the West, such as Phillip Jaisohn (Sŏ Chae-p'il, 1866–1948) who had studied in the United States, launched an Independence Club in 1896 to promote Westernization and used the vernacular hangul in its newspaper, the *Tongnip Sinmun* (The Independent), alternating pages in Korean with English. The club included many Koreans who had studied Western learning in Protestant missionary schools and, for a while, influenced not only young reformers but also elements of the Korean court. One of the reformers was Yi Sŭngman, otherwise known as Syngman Rhee (1875–1965), who became the first president of the Republic of Korea (South Korea) in 1948. The club was repressed and collapsed after two years.

In 1897 King Kojong (r. 1864–1907), when confronted with Japanese plots, fled to the Russian Legation, where he conducted the nation's business for a year and shortly thereafter declared Korea to be the "Great Han (Korean) Empire," from which came the later name Taehan Min'guk, or Republic of Korea. It was the futile last gasp of the Chosŏn; the only question was which imperial power would colonize Korea. Japan found a champion in U.S. president Theodore Roosevelt. In 1902 Britain established an alliance with Japan, and both London and Washington gave Japan a free hand in Korea.

The widow Myong-su shows her faithfulness to her late husband by spurning an
wanted suitor (upper left) and giving all her belongings to her servants to take care
her stepson (lower right). Woodcut from volume 3 of Oryun haengsilto *(Five Rules*
of Conduct), a 1775 Korean book on Confucian ethics.
Courtesy Korean Collection, Asian Division, Library of
Congress, Washington, DC

To the north, Russia also was expanding into Manchuria and Korea and, in alliance with France and Germany, had forced Japan to return the Liaodong Peninsula, acquired from China as a result of the Japanese victory in 1895. Japan promptly leased the region from China and continued to develop it. Shortly thereafter, in 1900, Japanese forces intervened with the other foreign powers to suppress the Boxer Uprising in China. Russia continued to develop the railroad system in Manchuria and to exploit forests and gold mines in the northern part of Korea. During this period, Americans, too, were given concessions for railroad and streetcar lines, waterworks, Seoul's new telephone network, and mines.

Russia and Japan sought to divide their interests in Korea, suggesting at one point that the thirty-eighth parallel be the dividing line between their spheres of influence. The rivalry devolved into the Russo–Japanese War (1904–5), however, when Japan launched a successful surprise attack on the Russian fleet at Dalian (Port Arthur) in Northeast China. Japan then electrified all of Asia by becoming the first nonwhite people to subdue one of the "great powers"; thereafter many Asian progressives, Sun Yatsen of China and many young Koreans included, went to study in Japan. Under the peace treaty signed in 1905, brokered by Theodore Roosevelt in a conference at Portsmouth, New Hampshire, Russia recognized Japan's paramount rights in Korea. Diplomatic notes exchanged between the United States and Japan acknowledged a trade-off between the Philippines and Korea. Japan would not question American rights in its colony, and the United States would not challenge Japan's new protectorate, which it established in 1905. Japan thus controlled Korea's foreign policy, installed a resident general, and, in 1907, deposed King Kojong. Kojong was succeeded by his son Sunjong (r. 1907–10), the second and last emperor of Korea. Significant Korean resistance followed on this deposition, spreading through several provinces as local *yangban* organized militias for guerrilla warfare against Japan. In 1909 a Korean assassin named An Chung-gŭn killed Itō Hirobumi, the Japanese statesman who had concluded the protectorate agreement. An expatriate Korean in San Francisco also gunned down Durham Stevens, a foreign affairs adviser to the Japanese who had lauded their efforts in Korea. Such opposition was too little and too late. In 1910 Japan turned Korea into its colony, thus extinguishing Korea's hard-fought independence, which had first emerged with Silla and Koguryŏ resistance to Chinese pressures.

The Chosŏn Dynasty faltered under the impact of Korea's opening in 1876 and then collapsed in a few decades. Despite its extraordinary five-century longevity, while the traditional system was adaptable, even supple in the marginal adjustments and incremental

King Sunjong (1874–1926; r. 1907–10), second and last emperor of the Great Han (Korean) Empire, ca. 1907 Courtesy George Grantham Bain Collection, LC–USZ62–72799, Lot 11148, Prints and Photographs Division, Library of Congress, Washington, DC

responses necessary to forestall or accommodate domestic or internal conflict and change, it could not withstand the full foreign onslaught of technically advanced imperial powers with strong armies. The old agrarian bureaucracy managed the interplay of different and competing interests by having a system of checks and balances that tended over time to equilibrate the interests of different parties. The king and the bureaucracy kept watch on each other, the royal clans watched both, scholars could criticize or remonstrate from the moral position of Confucian doctrine, secret inspectors and censors went around the country to watch for rebellion and assure accurate reporting, landed aristocrats sent sons into the bureaucracy to protect family interests, and local potentates influenced the county magistrates sent down from the central administration. The Chosŏn Dynasty was not a system that modern Koreans would wish to restore or live under, but in its time it was a sophisticated political apparatus, sufficiently adaptable and persistent to give unified rule to Korea for half a millennium.

Japanese Colonialism, 1910–45

Korea did not escape the Japanese grip until 1945, when Japan lay prostrate under the U.S. and Soviet onslaught that brought World

War II to a close. The colonial experience that shaped postwar Korea was intense and bitter. It brought development and underdevelopment, agrarian growth and an impoverished peasant tenancy, industrialization and extraordinary dislocation, and political mobilization and deactivation. The colonial period also resulted in a new role for the central state, new sets of Korean political leaders, communism and nationalism, and armed resistance and treacherous collaboration. Above all, it left deep fissures and conflicts that have gnawed at the Korean national identity ever since.

Colonialism was often thought to have created new nations where none existed before, to have drawn national boundaries, brought diverse tribes and peoples together, tutored the natives in self-government, and prepared for the day when the imperialist powers decided to grant independence; but all such advantages existed in Korea for centuries before 1910. Furthermore, by virtue of their relative proximity to China, Koreans had always felt superior to Japan and blamed Japan's devastating sixteenth-century invasions for hindering Korean wealth and power in subsequent centuries.

Thus the Japanese engaged not in creation, but in substitution after 1910: substituting a Japanese ruling elite for the Korean *yangban* scholar-officials, colonial imperative coordination for the old central state administration, Japanese modern education for Confucian classics, Japanese capital and expertise for the budding Korean versions, Japanese talent for Korean talent, and eventually even the Japanese language for Korean. Koreans never thanked the Japanese for these substitutions, did not credit Japan with creations, and instead saw Japan as snatching away the ancien régime, Korea's sovereignty and independence, its indigenous if incipient modernization, and above all its national dignity. Unlike some other colonial peoples, therefore, Koreans never saw Japanese rule as anything but illegitimate and humiliating. Furthermore, the very closeness of the two nations—in geography, in common Chinese cultural influences, and in levels of development until the nineteenth century—made Japanese dominance all the more galling to Koreans and gave a peculiar intensity to the relationship, a dynamic that suggested to Koreans that "there but for accidents of history go we."

The Japanese built bureaucracies in Korea, all of which were centralized and all of them big by colonial standards. Unlike the relatively small British colonial cadre in India, the Japanese came in large numbers (700,000 by the 1940s), and the majority of colonizers worked in government service. For the first time in history, Korea had a national police, responsive to the center and possessing its own communications and transportation facilities. The huge Oriental Development Company organized and funded industrial and

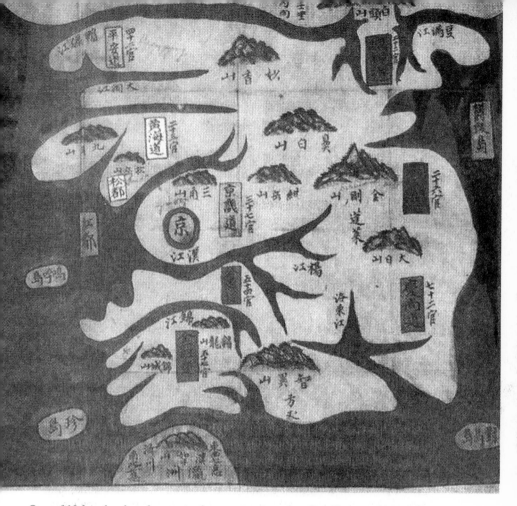

One of 12 hand-colored maps in the manuscript atlas, Tae Chosŏn chido *(Great Korean Map); the atlas, dating to ca. 1874, has individual maps of the provinces of Korea, China, Japan, and the world.*
Courtesy Geography and Map Division, Library of Congress, Washington, DC

agricultural projects, and came to own more than 20 percent of Korea's arable land; it employed an army of officials who fanned out through the countryside to supervise agricultural production. The official Bank of Korea performed central banking functions, such as regulating interest rates and providing credit to firms and entrepreneurs—almost all of them, of course, Japanese. Central judicial bodies wrote new laws establishing an extensive, "legalized" system of racial discrimination against Koreans, making them second-class citizens in their own country. Bureaucratic departments proliferated at the Government General Headquarters in Seoul, turning it into the nerve center of the country. Semi-official companies and conglomerates, including the big *zaibatsu* (business empires) such as Mitsubishi and Mitsui, laid railroads, built ports, installed modern factories, and ultimately remade the face of old Korea.

Japan held Korea tightly, watched it closely, and pursued an organized, architectonic colonialism in which the planner and administrator was the model, not the swashbuckling conqueror. The strong, highly centralized colonial state mimicked the role that the Japanese state had come to play in Japan—intervening in the economy, creating markets, spawning new industries, and suppressing dissent. Politically, Koreans could barely breathe, but economically there was significant—if unevenly distributed—growth. Agricultural output rose substantially in the 1920s, and a hothouse industrialization took place in the 1930s. Growth rates in the Korean economy often outstripped those in Japan itself; one estimate suggested an annual growth rate for Korea of nearly 3.6 percent in the 1911–38 period, compared to a rate of 3.4 percent for Japan itself.

Koreans have always thought that the benefits of this growth went entirely to Japan, and that Korea would have developed rapidly without Japanese help anyway. Nonetheless, the strong colonial state, the multiplicity of bureaucracies, the policy of administrative guidance of the economy, the use of the state to found new industries, and the repression of labor unions and dissidents that went with it provided a surreptitious model for both North and South Korea in the postwar period. Japan showed them an early version of the "bureaucratic-authoritarian" path to industrialization, and it was a lesson that seemed well learned by the 1970s.

The Rise of Korean Nationalism and Communism

The colonial period brought forth an entirely new set of Korean political leaders encouraged both by the resistance to, and the opportunities of, Japanese colonialism. The emergence of nationalist and communist groups dates back to the 1920s; it was in this period that the left–right splits of postwar Korea began. The transformation of the *yangban* aristocracy also began at this time. In the 1930s, new groups of armed resisters, bureaucrats, and, for the first time, military leaders emerged. Both North Korea and South Korea have been profoundly influenced by the political elites and the political conflicts generated during colonial rule.

One thing from the Chosŏn Dynasty that the Japanese were not able to destroy was the *yangban* aristocracy. Although the higher scholar-officials were pensioned off and replaced by Japanese, landlords were allowed to retain their holdings and encouraged to continue disciplining peasants and extracting rice as in-kind tax payments from them. The traditional landholding system was put on a different basis through new legal measures and a full property survey shortly after the Japanese took over, but tenancy continued and was systematically extended throughout the colonial period. By 1945 Korea had an agricultural tenancy system with few parallels in the world. More-traditional landlords were content to sit back and let Japanese officials increase output; by 1945 such people were widely viewed as treacherous collaborators with the Japanese, and strong demands emerged to share out their land to the tenants. During the 1920s, however, another trend began as landlords became entrepreneurs.

In 1919 mass movements swept many colonial and semicolonial countries, including Korea. Drawing on U.S. president Woodrow Wilson's promises of self-determination, a group of 33 intellectuals on March 1, 1919, petitioned for independence from Japan and touched off nationwide mass protests that continued for months. The Japanese fiercely crushed these protests, causing many younger Koreans to become militant opponents of colonial rule. The year 1919 was a watershed for the anti-imperialist movement in Korea. The leaders of the movement were moderate intellectuals and students who sought independence through nonviolent means and support from progressive elements in the West. Their courageous witness and the nationwide demonstrations that they provoked remained a touchstone of Korean nationalism. The movement succeeded in provoking reforms in Japan's administration, but its failure to realize independence also stimulated radical forms of anticolonial resistance.

Some Korean militants went into exile in China and the Soviet Union and founded early communist and nationalist resistance groups. The Korean Communist Party was established in Seoul in 1925. One of the organizers was Pak Hŏn-yŏng, who became the leader of the Korean communist movement in southern Korea after 1945. Various nationalist groups also emerged during this period, including the exiled Korean Provisional Government in Shanghai, which included Syngman Rhee and another famous nationalist, Kim Ku, among its members.

Sharp police repression and internal factionalism made it impossible to sustain radical groups over time. Many nationalist and communist leaders were jailed in the early 1930s, only to reemerge in 1945. When Japan invaded and then annexed Manchuria in 1931, however, a strong guerrilla resistance embracing Chinese and Koreans emerged. There were more than 200,000 guerrillas—all loosely connected, and including bandits and secret societies—fighting the Japanese in the early 1930s. After murderous but effective counter-
bers declined to a few thousand by
th.
milieu that Kim Il Sung (originally

named Kim Sŏng-ju, 1912–94; the name Il Sung means "become the sun") emerged. He was a significant guerrilla leader by the mid-1930s, considered by the Japanese as one of the most effective and dangerous of guerrillas. The Japanese formed a special counterinsurgent unit to track Kim down and assigned Koreans to it as part of their divide-and-rule tactics.

Both Koreas created myths about this guerrilla resistance: North Korea claimed that Kim single-handedly defeated the Japanese, and South Korea claimed that Kim was an imposter who stole the name of a revered patriot. Nonetheless, this experience was important for understanding postwar Korea: the resistance to the Japanese became the main legitimating doctrine of North Korea; North Koreans traced the origin of the army, the leadership, and their ideology back to this founding moment. For the next five decades, the top North Korean leadership was dominated by a core group that fought the Japanese in Manchuria.

Japan went to war against China in 1937 and the United States in 1941, and as World War II took on global dimensions, Koreans for the first time had military careers opened to them. Although most were conscripted foot soldiers, a small number achieved officer status, and a few even attained high rank. Virtually the entire officer corps of the Republic of Korea army during the Rhee period (1948–61) was drawn from Koreans with experience in the Japanese Imperial Army. At least in part, the Korean War (1950–53) became a matter of Japanese-trained military officers fighting Japanese-spawned resistance leaders.

Japan's far-flung war effort also caused a labor shortage throughout the empire, including Korea, where it meant that bureaucratic position was more available to Koreans than at any previous time. Thus, a substantial cadre of Koreans obtained administrative experience in government, local administration, police and judicial work, economic planning agencies, banks, and the like. That this development occurred in the last decade of colonialism created a divisive legacy, however, for this also was the harshest period of Japanese rule, the time Koreans remember with greatest bitterness. Korean culture was squashed, and Koreans were required to speak Japanese and to take Japanese names. The majority suffered badly at the precise time that a minority was doing well. This minority acquired the taint of collaboration and never successfully shucked it off. Korea from 1937 to 1945 was much like Vichy France in the early 1940s. Bitter experiences and memories of the period continue to divide people, even within the same family, and as they have been too painful to confront directly, they have become buried history. Nonetheless, the memory continues to play upon the national identity.

Perhaps the most important characteristic of Korea's colonial experience was the manner in which it ended: the last decade of a four-decade imperium was a pressure cooker, building up tensions that exploded in the postwar period. The colonial period built to a crescendo, abruptly collapsed, and left the Korean people and two different great powers to deal with the results. There had been some fighting against Japan along the Korea–China border in the late 1930s, including forays into Korea by Kim Il Sung's force, but no sustained armed resistance within Korea itself.

In the mid-1930s, Japan entered a phase of heavy industrialization that embraced all of Northeast Asia. Unlike most colonial powers, Japan located heavy industry in its colonies and brought the means of production to the labor and raw materials. Manchuria and northern Korea acquired steel mills, automotive plants, petrochemical complexes, and enormous hydroelectric facilities. The region was held exclusively by Japan and tied into the home market to the degree that national boundaries became less important than the new transnational, integrated production. To facilitate this production Japan also built railroads, highways, cities, ports, and other modern transportation and communication facilities. By 1945 Korea proportionally had more kilometers of railroads than any other Asian country except Japan, leaving only remote parts of the central east coast and the wild Northeast China–Korea border region untouched by modern means of conveyance. These changes were externally induced and served Japanese, not Korean, interests. Thus, they represented a kind of overdevelopment.

The same changes fostered underdevelopment in Korean society as a whole. Because the changes were exogenous, the Korean upper and managerial classes did not blossom; instead, their development was retarded or ballooned suddenly at Japanese behest. Among the majority peasant class, change was considerable. Koreans became the mobile human capital used to work the new factories in northern Korea and Manchuria, mines and other enterprises in Japan, and urban factories in southern Korea. From 1935 to 1945, Korea began its industrial revolution, with many of the usual characteristics: uprooting of peasants from the land, the emergence of a working class, urbanization, and population mobility. In Korea the process was telescoped, giving rise to remarkable population movements when considered comparatively. By 1945 about 11 percent of the entire Korean population was living abroad (mostly in Japan and Manchuria), and fully 20 percent of all Koreans were either abroad or in a province other than that in which they were born (with most of the interprovincial movement being southern peasants moving

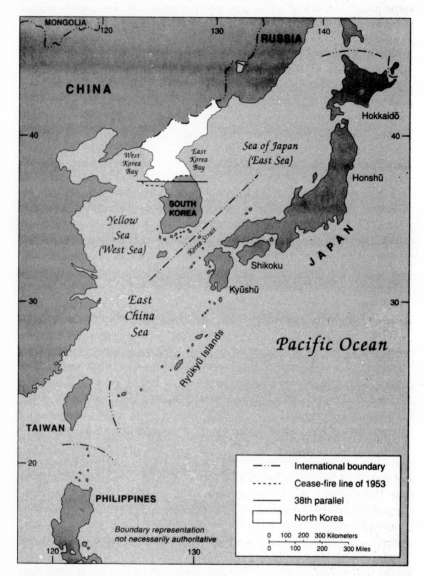

Figure 3. North Korea in Its Asian Setting

into northern industry). This was, by and large, a forced or mobilized movement; by 1942 it often meant drafted and conscripted labor. Peasants lost land or rights to work land only to end up working in unfamiliar factory settings, doing the dirty work for a pittance.

When the colonial system abruptly terminated in August 1945, millions of Koreans sought to return to their native villages from these far-flung mobilization details. But they were no longer the same people: they had grievances against those who remained secure at home, they had suffered material and status losses, they often had come into contact with new ideologies, they all had seen a broader world beyond the villages. It was this intense final decade that loosed upon postwar Korea a mass of changed and disgruntled people who greatly disrupted the early postwar period and the plans of the United States and the Soviet Union.

National Division in the1940s

Tensions in the 1940s

The crucible of the period of national division and opposing states in Korea was the decade from 1943 to 1953. The politics of contemporary Korea cannot be understood without comprehending the events of this decade. It was the breeding ground of the two Koreas, of war, and of a reordering of international politics in Northeast Asia (see fig. 3).

From the time of the tsars, Korea was a concern of Russian security. The Russo–Japanese War was fought in part over the disposition of the Korean Peninsula. It was often surmised that the Russians saw Korea as a gateway to the Pacific, and especially to warm-water ports. Furthermore, Korea had one of Asia's oldest communist movements. Thus, it would appear that postwar Korea was of great interest to the Soviet Union; many have thought that its policy was a simple matter of Sovietizing northern Korea, setting up a puppet state, and then, in 1950, directing Kim Il Sung to unify Korea by force. There was greater complexity than this in Soviet policy, however, as historian Andrei Lankov's scholarship has demonstrated. The Soviets did not get a warm-water port out of their involvement in Korea, and they did not have an effective relationship with Korean communists. Communist Party of the Soviet Union general secretary Joseph V. Stalin purged and even shot many of the Koreans who had functioned in the Comintern (see Glossary), and he did not help Kim Il Sung and other guerrillas in their struggle against the Japanese.

The United States took the initiative in big-power deliberations on Korea during World War II, suggesting a multilateral trusteeship for postwar Korea to the British in March 1943, and to the Soviets at the end of the same year. President Franklin D. Roosevelt, worried about the disposition of enemy-held colonial territories and aware of colonial demands for independence, sought a gradualist, tutelary policy of preparing colonials (like the Koreans) for self-government and independence. At the Cairo Conference in December 1943, the Allies, at the urging of the United States, declared that after Japan was defeated,

Korea would become independent "in due course," a phrase consistent with Roosevelt's ideas. At about the same time, planners in the U.S. Department of State drastically altered the traditional U.S. policy of noninvolvement toward Korea by defining the security of the peninsula as important to the security of the postwar Pacific, which was, in turn, important to U.S. national security.

At a midnight meeting in Washington on August 10–11, 1945, U.S. War Department officials, including John J. McCloy and Dean Rusk, decided to make the thirty-eighth parallel—roughly the half-way point between the northern and southern extremities of Korea—the dividing line between Soviet and U.S. zones in Korea. Neither the Soviets nor the Koreans were consulted. The day following Japan's surrender—August 15, 1945—was designated as the date of Korean independence from Japan. Then, when 25,000 U.S. soldiers occupied southern Korea in early September 1945, they found themselves up against a strong Korean impulse for independence and for thorough reform of colonial legacies. By and large, Koreans wished to solve their problems themselves and resented any implication that they were not ready for self-government.

During World War II, Stalin usually did not voice an opinion in his discussions with Roosevelt about Korea. From 1941 to 1945, Kim Il Sung and other guerrillas were given sanctuary in Sino–Soviet border towns near Khabarovsk, trained at a small school, and dispatched as agents into Japanese-held territory. Recent research by Japanese historian Wada Haruki suggests that Chinese communists controlled the border camps, not Russians. Although the U.S. Department of State suspected that as many as 30,000 Koreans were being trained as Soviet guerrilla agents, postwar North Korean documents, captured by forces led by General Douglas MacArthur, show that there could not have been more than a few hundred guerrilla agents. When the Soviets occupied Korea north of the thirty-eighth parallel in August 1945, they brought these Koreans (often termed Soviet–Koreans, even though most of them were not Soviet citizens) with them. Although this group was not large, several of them became prominent in the regime, for example Hŏ Ka-i, an experienced party organizer, and Nam Il, whom Americans came to know during the Korean War when he led the North Korean delegation in peace talks. The Soviets acquiesced to the thirty-eighth parallel decision without saying a word about it and then accepted the U.S. plan for a multilateral trusteeship at a foreign ministers' meeting in December 1945. Over the succeeding two years, the two powers held so-called joint commission meetings trying to resolve their differences and establish a provisional government for Korea.

U.S. and Soviet Occupations

The U.S. military command, along with emissaries dispatched from Washington, tended to interpret resistance to U.S. desires in the South as radical and pro-Soviet. When Korean resistance leaders set up an interim "People's Republic" and so-called "people's committees" throughout southern Korea in September 1945, the United States saw this fundamentally indigenous movement as part of a Soviet master plan to dominate all of Korea. Radical activity, such as the ousting of landlords and attacks on Koreans who had served in the colonial police, usually was a matter of settling scores left over from the colonial period, or of demands by Koreans to run their own affairs. But it immediately became wrapped up with U.S.–Soviet rivalry, such that the Cold War arrived early in Korea—in the last months of 1945. Once the U.S. occupation chose to bolster the status quo and resist radical reform of colonial legacies, it immediately ran into monumental opposition to its policies from the mass of South Koreans.

Most of the first year of the occupation (1945–46) was given over to suppression of the many people's committees that had emerged, which provoked a massive rebellion that spread over four provinces in the fall of 1946. After it was suppressed, radical activists developed a significant guerrilla movement in 1948 and 1949. They also ignited a major rebellion at the port of Yŏsu in southern South Korea in October 1948. Much of this disorder stemmed from the unresolved land problem, as conservative landed elements used their bureaucratic power to block redistribution of land to peasant tenants. The North Koreans sought to take advantage of this discontent, but the best evidence shows that most of the dissidents and guerrillas were southerners, upset about southern policies. Indeed, the strength of the left wing was in those provinces farthest from the thirty-eighth parallel, in the southwest, which historically had been rebellious (the Tonghaks came from there), and in the southeast, which had felt the greatest impact from Japanese colonialism.

By 1947 Washington was willing to acknowledge formally that the Cold War had begun in Korea and abandoned attempts to negotiate with the Soviets toward a unified, multilateral administration. The Soviets also had determined that the postwar world would be one of two blocs, and they exercised broad administrative control in North Korea. According to declassified documents, when President Harry S. Truman announced the Truman Doctrine and the containment policy in the spring of 1947, Korea was very nearly included along with Greece and Turkey as a key containment country; U.S. Department of State planners foresaw a whopping US$600 million package of economic and military aid for southern Korea, backing away only when the U.S. Congress and the War Department balked at such a huge sum. The decision was then made to seek United Nations (UN) backing for U.S. policy in Korea, and to hold UN-sponsored elections in all of Korea if the Soviets would go along, in southern Korea alone if they did not. The elections were held in the South in May 1948, and they resulted in the establishment of the Republic of Korea on August 15 that year.

The Arrival of Kim Il Sung

Kim Il Sung did not appear in North Korea until late September 1945. What he did in the weeks after the Japanese surrender is not known. The Soviets presented Kim to the Korean people as a guerrilla hero. From August 1945 to January 1946, the Soviets worked with a coalition of communists and nationalists, the latter headed by a Protestant leader named Cho Man-sik. The coalition did not set up a central administration, nor did it establish an army. In retrospect, their policy was more tentative and reactive than U.S. policy in South Korea, which moved forward with plans for a separate administration and army. Soviet power in East Asia was flexible and resulted in the withdrawal of Soviet troops from Manchuria in early 1946.

Whether in response to U.S. initiatives or because most Koreans despised the trusteeship agreement that had been negotiated at the end of 1945, separate institutions began to emerge in North Korea in early 1946. In February 1946, an Interim People's Committee led by Kim Il Sung became the first central government in the North. The next month, a revolutionary land reform ensued, dispossessing landlords without compensation. In August 1946, a powerful political party (called the Korean Workers' Party—KWP) quickly filled the political vacuum and dominated politics; and in the fall, the first rudiments of a northern army appeared. Central agencies nationalized major industries (previously mostly owned by the Japanese) and began a two-year economic program based on the Soviet model of central planning and the priority of heavy industry. Nationalists and Christian leaders were ousted from all but pro forma participation in politics, and Cho Man-sik was held under house arrest. Kim Il Sung and his allies dominated all the political parties, ousting people who resisted them.

Within a year of the liberation from Japan, North Korea had a powerful political party, a growing economy, and a single leader named Kim Il Sung. Although Kim had rivals, his emergence—and that of the Kim system—dated from mid-1946. By then he had placed close, loyal allies at the heart of power. His prime assets were his background, his skills at organization, and his ideology. Although Kim was only 34 years old when he came to power, few other Koreans who were still alive could match his record of resistance to the Japanese. He was fortunate to emerge in the last decade of a 40-year resistance that had killed off many leaders of the older generation. North Korea absurdly claimed that Kim was the leader of all Korean resisters, when in fact there were many more besides him. But Kim was able to win the support and firm loyalty of several hundred people like him: young, tough, nationalistic guerrillas who had fought in Manchuria. The prime test of legitimacy in postwar Korea was one's record under the hated Japanese regime, and so Kim and his core allies possessed nationalist credentials that were superior to those of the South Korean leadership. Furthermore, Kim's backers had military force at their disposal and used it to advantage against rivals with no military experience.

Kim's organizational skills probably came from his experience in the Chinese Communist Party in the 1930s. Unlike traditional Korean leaders—and many more intellectual or theoretical communists, such as Pak Hŏn-yŏng—Kim pursued a style of mass leadership, using his considerable charisma and the practice of visiting factories and farms for "on-the-spot guidance," and he encouraged his allies to do the same. The North Koreans went against Soviet orthodoxy by including masses of poor peasants in the KWP, indeed terming it a "mass" rather than a class or vanguard party.

Since the 1940s, North Korea has enrolled 12 to 14 percent of the population in the dominant party, compared to 1 to 3 percent for most communist parties. The vast majority of party members have been poor peasants with no previous political experience. Membership in the party gave them position, prestige, privileges, and a rudimentary form of political participation. Kim's ideology tended to be revolutionary-nationalist rather than communist. The *chuch'e* ideology had its beginnings in the late 1940s (although the term *chuch'e* was not used until 1955), a doctrine that stressed self-reliance and independence but also drew upon the Neo-Confucian emphasis on rectification of the mind prior to action in the real world. Soon after Kim took power, virtually all North Koreans were required to participate in study groups and "re-education" meetings, where regime ideology was inculcated.

In the 1940s, Kim faced factional power struggles among his group (those guerrillas who operated in Manchuria), communists who had remained in Korea during the colonial period (the domestic faction), Koreans associated with Chinese communism (the Yan'an faction), and Koreans from or close to the Soviet Union (the Soviet faction). In the aftermath of the Korean War, amid much false scapegoating for the disasters of the war, Kim purged the domestic faction, many of whose leaders were from southern Korea; Pak Hŏn-yŏng and 12 of his associates were pilloried in show trials under ridiculous charges that they were American spies. Ten of them subsequently were executed. In the mid-1950s, Kim eliminated key leaders of the Soviet faction, including Hŏ Ka-i, and overcame an apparent coup attempt by members of the Yan'an faction—whereupon he purged many of them. Some, like the guerrilla hero Mu Chŏng, reportedly escaped to China. These power struggles ensued during only the first decade of the regime and were not repeated. There were of course conflicts within the leadership later on, but they were relatively minor and did not successfully challenge Kim's power.

In the 1946–48 period, there was much evidence that the Soviets hoped to dominate North Korea. In particular, they sought to involve North Korea in a quasicolonial relationship in which Korean raw materials, such as tungsten and gold, were exchanged for Soviet manufactures. Although the Soviets also sought to keep Chinese communist influence out of Korea, in the late 1940s Maoism was quietly introduced into Korean newspapers and books by a Yan'an-trained Korean agent. Soviet influence was especially strong in the media, where major organs were staffed by Koreans from the Soviet Union, and in the security bureaus. Nonetheless, the Korean guerrillas who fought in Manchuria were not easily molded and dominated. They were tough, highly nationalistic, and determined to have Korea for themselves. This was especially so for the Korean People's Army (KPA), which was an important base for Kim Il Sung and which was led by another Manchurian guerrilla, Ch'oe Yŏng-gŏn, when it was founded on February 8, 1948. At the founding ceremony, Kim urged his soldiers to carry forward the tradition of the Manchurian guerrillas.

The Establishment of the Democratic People's Republic of Korea

The Democratic People's Republic of Korea was established on September 9, 1948, three weeks after the Republic of Korea was formed in Seoul on August 15. Kim Il Sung was named premier, a title he retained until 1972, when, under a new constitution, he was named president. At the end of 1948, the Soviets withdrew their occupation forces from North Korea. This decision contrasted strongly with Soviet policies in Eastern Europe. Tens of thousands of Korean soldiers who fought in the Chinese civil war (1946–49) also filtered back into Korea. All through 1949, tough, crack troops with Chinese, not Soviet, experience returned to be integrated with the KPA; the return of these Korean troops inevitably skewed North Korea toward China. It enhanced Kim's bargaining power and enabled him to maneuver between the two communist giants. The Soviets kept advisers in the Korean government and military, although far fewer than the thousands claimed by South Korean sources. There were probably 300 to 400 advisers assigned to North Korea, although many of those were experienced military and security people. Both countries continued to trade, and the Soviets sold World War II–vintage weaponry to North Korea.

In 1949 Kim Il Sung had himself named *suryŏng* (see Glossary) an old Koguryŏ term for "leader" that the Koreans always modified by the adjective "great" (as in Great Leader). The KPA was built up with recruiting campaigns for soldiers and bond drives to purchase Soviet tanks; meanwhile, the tradition of the Manchurian guerrillas was burnished in the party newspaper, *Nodong Shinmun* (Workers' Daily), perhaps to offset the influence of powerful Korean officers who fought with the Chinese communists, such Mu Chŏng and Pang Ho-san.

The Korean War, 1950–53

North Korea seemed almost to be on a war footing in early 1949. Kim's New Year's speech—analogous to a "state of the union" address in spelling out guidelines—was bellicose and excoriated South Korea as a puppet state. The army expanded rapidly, soldiers drilled in war maneuvers, and war-bond-purchasing drives continued for the purchase of Soviet weaponry. North Korea fortified the thirty-eighth parallel, and soon border incidents began breaking out. Neither side recognized the parallel as a legitimate boundary; the Rhee regime also wanted to unify Korea under its rule, by force if necessary. Rhee often referred to a "northern expedition" to "recover the lost territory," and in the summer of 1949 his army provoked the majority of the fighting along the thirty-eighth parallel (according to declassified U.S. documents), fighting that sometimes took hundreds of lives.

This belligerent attitude was a prime reason why the United States refused to supply tanks and airplanes to South Korea: it feared that they would be used to attack the North. When U.S. secretary of state Dean Acheson made a speech in January 1950, in which he appeared to place South Korea outside the U.S. defense perimeter in Asia, he was mainly seeking to remind Rhee that he could not count on automatic U.S. backing, regardless of how he behaved.

Although there remain murky aspects to the start of the Korean War, it now seems that the opening of conventional war on June 25, 1950 (thus, the term "6–25 War" that is used in South Korea; the North refers to the war as the Fatherland Liberation War), was mainly Kim's decision, resisted by Stalin for many months and then acquiesced to in early 1950, and that the key enabling factor was the existence of as many as 100,000 troops with battle experience in China. When the Rhee regime, with help from U.S. military advisers, severely reduced the guerrilla threat in the South in the winter of 1949–50, the civil war moved into a conventional phase. Kim clearly sought backing from Stalin for his assault, but documents from the Soviet and Chinese sides, which have appeared sporadically since the 1990s, suggest that he got more backing from China. The key meetings appear to have occurred in April 1950, when Kim made secret trips, first to Moscow and then to Beijing.

Had U.S. forces not entered the war, the northern regime would have won easily; the southern army and state collapsed in a few days. As eventually occurred, however, it was Kim's regime that the war nearly extinguished. The key year in which formal U.S. policy moved from multilateral internationalism to unilateral containment in Korea was 1947. There were at this time severe global limits on U.S. power, and the Truman administration could not publicly commit arms and money to Korea on the same scale as to Greece and Turkey. But in secret U.S. congressional testimony in early 1947, Acheson said that the United States had drawn the line in Korea, and he meant it. It was in pursuit of this basic containment policy that Acheson, by then secretary of state, urged Truman to commit military forces to save South Korea in June 1950. But, as the fighting wore on in the summer of 1950, U.S. policy changed once again. Had the United States simply sought to contain the communist thrust into the South, it would have restored the thirty-eighth parallel when it crushed the North Korean army. Instead, UN forces led by the United States under General Douglas MacArthur marched into North Korea and sought to destroy the northern regime and unify the peninsula under Syng-man Rhee's rule. Again, declassified documentation now shows that this action reflected a change from containment to a new policy called rollback: as policy planners described it, the United States for the first time had the chance to displace and transform some communist real estate.

This thrust by UN forces in the fall of 1950, however, brought Chinese forces in on the northern side; these "volunteers" and a reinvigorated North Korean army pushed UN and South Korean forces out of the North within a month and caused a crisis in American domestic politics as backers of Truman fought with backers of MacArthur over the administration's unwillingness to carry the war to China. Although the war lasted another two years, until an armistice was signed on July 27, 1953, the outcome of early 1951 was definitive: a stalemate and a U.S. commitment to containment that accepted the de facto reality of two Koreas—and that explains why U.S. troops remain in South Korea today.

When the war finally ended, the North had been devastated by three years of bombing attacks that hardly left a modern building standing. Both Koreas had watched as a virtual holocaust ravaged their country and turned the vibrant expectations of 1945 into a nightmare. Furthermore, when Kim's regime was nearly extinguished in the fall of 1950, the Soviets did very little to save it. China picked up the pieces, which the North Koreans have never forgotten. From this moment on, it was clear that North Korea valued its relationship with China, whereas it dealt with the Soviet Union because it had to, not because it wanted to. And, in the end, South Korea did not sign the armistice agreement as a sign of disagreement over the decision not to pursue the war to the final defeat of the communist forces in the North.

The point to remember is that this was a civil war. The true tragedy was not the war itself, for a civil conflict solely among Koreans might have resolved the extraordinary tensions generated by colonialism and national division. The tragedy was that the war solved nothing: only the status quo ante was restored. Today, the tensions and the problems remain.

The Postwar Period

The Economy

North Korea long had a socialist command economy with multiyear plans (as much as seven to 10 years) and a bias toward heavy industry. It allowed only a sharply limited role for market allocation, mainly in the rural sector, where peasants sold produce from small private plots. There was almost no small business. The North also sought a self-reliant, independent national economy; therefore, it would seem to be a typical socialist system on the Stalinist model, and certainly it was in the emphasis on heavy industry.

The Three-Year Postwar Reconstruction Plan (1954–56), which began after the Korean War, and the Five-Year Plan (1957–61), which succeeded it, both stressed the reconstruction and development of major industries, with consumer goods at the bottom of priorities (see North Korea's Development Strategy, ch. 3). This bias toward major industries, however, pushed the economy forward at world-beating growth rates in the 1950s and 1960s. Official sources put the average annual growth rate in industry at 41.7 percent for the Three-Year Plan and 36.6 percent during the Five-Year Plan. The First Seven-Year Plan (1961–67) projected an average rate of 18 percent, but stoppages of aid from the Soviet Union in the early 1960s, owing to North Korean support for China in the Sino–Soviet dispute, caused the plan to be extended for three years.

By the early 1970s, North Korea clearly had exhausted extensive development of its industries based on its own, prewar Japanese or new Soviet technologies, and it therefore turned to the West and Japan to purchase advanced technology and turnkey plants. These included a French petrochemical complex in 1971, a cement plant in 1973, and, in 1977, a request that Japan sell an integrated steel mill (which was denied). Even a complete pantyhose factory was imported, suggesting more attention to consumer items. Ultimately, these purchases caused North Korea to run into problems servicing its external debt, which ran to US$2 billion and US$3 billion by the late 1970s.

Later seven- and 10-year plans failed to reach projected growth rates; still, a U.S. Central Intelligence Agency (CIA) study published in 1978 estimated that North Korea's per capita gross national product (GNP—see Glossary) was the same as South Korea's as late as 1976. In 1979 Kim Il Sung claimed a per capita income in the North of US$1,900, and later North Korea put the figure at more than US$2,500, but it is not known if the figure was accurate, or how it was derived. Since the early 1980s, North Korea has fallen badly behind South Korea as transportation bottlenecks and fuel resource problems have plagued the economy. Published CIA figures for the 1980s and 1990s place North Korea at around US$1,000 in per capita GNP. The North did not do badly in producing goods of the second industrial revolution: steel, chemicals, hydroelectric power, internal combustion engines, locomotives, motorcycles, and various sorts of machine-building items. But it lagged far behind in the "communications" technologies of the third industrial revolution: electronics, computers, and semiconductor chips, for example.

There were innovations, however, which suggested significant North Korean differences from the Stalinist model of industrialization. The delivery of goods and services was decentralized to the neighborhood or village level, and several provinces were claimed to be self-reliant in food and consumer goods. Foreign visitors saw few long lines at stores and restaurants, although resident diplomats found that little was available in the stores. Clearly the morale of the population was better than in the former Soviet Union until the mid-1990s, as both the cities and the factories give an appearance of efficiency and hard work.

North Korea had reasonably successful socialist agricultural systems until the collapse of the economy in the mid-1990s (see Collapse in the 1990s, ch. 3). Agriculture was collectivized after the

Korean War, in stages that went from mutual aid teams to second-stage cooperatives but stopped short of building huge state farms as in the Soviet Union or the communes of Maoist China. Relying mostly on cooperative farms corresponding to the old natural villages rather than state farms, and using material incentives with little apparent ideological bias against them, North Korea pushed agricultural production ahead rapidly. World Health Organization officials who visited in 1980 reported that "miracle" strains of rice were in wide use, and the CIA reported in a published study in 1978 that grain production had grown more rapidly in the North than in the South, that living standards in rural areas "have probably improved faster than in the South," and that North Korean agriculture was quite highly mechanized, fertilizer application was perhaps among the highest in the world, and irrigation projects were extensive.

Up until the late 1980s, North Korea claimed to have the highest per hectare rice output in the world; although that claim cannot be proved, experts did not question the North's general agricultural success, and published CIA figures put North Korea's per capita grain output among the highest in the world in around 1980. Subsequently, North Korea failed to reach projected targets, however, such as the grand goal of producing 10 million tons of grain annually by 1986. By the 1990s, South Korea's rural population lived much better than its northern counterpart, and with accumulated disasters, by the late 1990s the North was producing barely more than 4 million tons of grain per year.

North Korea became a significant participant in international arms trafficking, selling missiles, machine guns, artillery, light tanks, and other items to friendly countries such as Pakistan, Syria, and Iran. North Korea traded weaponry for oil with Iran, accounting for as much as 40 percent of Iranian arms imports during the long Iran–Iraq War (1980–88; see Defense Industry, ch. 5).

Foreign observers discount North Korea's claims of nearly complete self-reliance. Until the Soviet collapse in 1991, the Soviet Union and China had provided petroleum, coking coal, and many other critical resources and competed for influence with aid and technicians. (Now Russia and China compete to have economic relations with South Korea.) North Korea has done well in using indigenous coal and hydroelectric resources to minimize oil use; only 10 percent of its energy regime is dependent on imported petroleum. The pursuit of self-reliance is, of course, primarily a matter of anti-Western politics and foreign relations; it sacrifices efficiencies of scale and comparative advantage.

Until the 1970s, North Korea's foreign trade was almost wholly with the socialist bloc, but then it diversified imports and exports toward Japan, Western Europe, and various developing nations. By the mid-1970s, some 40 percent of its trade was with noncommunist countries, and within the bloc only half was with the Soviet Union; but, by the late 1980s, foreign exchange and other difficulties left North Korea once again dependent on trade with the Soviet Union, and the Russian demand for payment in hard currency for oil and other items drastically hurt North Korea's economy in the early 1990s. Exporting has been a priority for several years, although the North in no sense has an export-led economy like the South. The focus on exports is to garner foreign exchange to import advanced technologies needed for further industrial growth and to pay for imported oil; the exporting policy has not been particularly success-ful. (North Korea's total trade with Russia and China was far less than South Korea's in the early 2000s.)

In spite of these difficulties, American visitors to North Korea in the 1980s tended to come away impressed by what they saw. Crossing into North Korea from China made people think they had left a poor country for a moderately well-off one. The fields were deep green, and every meter of land was carefully tended; construction projects had round-the-clock shifts; people bustled through the streets to work at all hours; the cities suggested a clean, sparsely populated, diligent, and efficient system.

The country still has an isolated, antiquarian, even bucolic atmo-sphere, as if one were thrown back to the 1950s; at the same time, it has a few world-class facilities, such as the P'yŏngyang Maternity Hospital, which is replete with German and Hungarian technology, or the fleet of Mercedes put at the disposal of officialdom (see Health Care, ch. 2). Until the famine period of the mid- to late 1990s, the mass of the people were well fed and plainly dressed, with little access to consumer goods beyond basic clothing and household items (see Effects of the Famine, ch. 3).

Quite apart from the shocks it has received from abroad since 1989, North Korea faces its own set of structural problems in the economy. Its ponderous bureaucracy is impenetrable and exasperating to foreign business executives—and to its own officials, who find it hard to com-municate with other bureaucracies. Its dogged desire for self-reliance has alienated foreigners and placed many obstacles in the way of trade with the West, not least the relative lack of foreign exchange. Techno-logical obsolescence means the North must import newer technologies if it ever hopes to compete with the South, and since 2000 it has begun to adopt the new policies necessary to gain access to such technology, for example, revaluing its currency, enacting new tax and profit laws for foreigners, and permitting limited space for market mechanisms (see Legal and Administrative Reforms, ch. 3). As long as North Korea maintains its hostility toward the United States and its military force commitments aligned against the South, it will not get the trade and technology that it claims to want and certainly needs.

Both Koreas are industrial and urbanized nations, but on entirely different models of political economy. A unified Korea would thus be a formidable industrial state. What would permit this unlikely marriage of divergent systems? Perhaps the stress on education in both Koreas, strong backing from big-power allies, effective use of state intervention in promoting economic development, and, above all, the simple fact that neither are "new" states but rather grow out of an ancient and proud nation that began its modernization a century ago, not just in the postwar period.

Corporatism and the *Chuch'e* Idea

Marxism presented no political model for achieving socialism, only an opaque set of prescriptions. This political vacuum opened the way to an assertion of indigenous political culture and could even be said to demand it by virtue of the very paucity of political models. The strongest foreign influence on the North Korean leadership was the Chinese communist model, and so Kim Il Sung was very much a "mass line" leader like Mao Zedong, making frequent visits to factories and the countryside, sending cadres "down" to local levels to help policy implementation and to solicit local opinion, requiring small-group political study and so-called "criticism and self-criticism," using periodic campaigns to mobilize people for production or education, and encouraging soldiers also to engage in production in good "people's army" fashion. The Ch'ŏllima (see Glossary) or "flying horse" Movement inaugurated in the late 1950s was a typical example of a Chinese-inspired strategy. North Korea, like China but unlike the Soviet Union, also maintained a "united front" policy toward noncommunist groups, so that in addition to the ruling KWP there were much smaller parties—the Korean Social Democratic Party and the native Ch'ŏndogyo (see Glossary) religion's Chongu (Friends) Party—with mainly symbolic functions (see The Korean Workers' Party, ch. 4).

There are many differences from China and the Soviet Union, however, and many of them have been there from the beginning. The symbol of the KWP, for example, is a hammer and sickle with a writing brush superimposed, symbolizing the "three-class alliance" of workers, peasants, and intellectuals. Unlike Mao's China, North Korea has never excoriated intellectuals as a potential "new class" of exploiters; instead, it has followed an inclusive policy toward them, perhaps because postwar Korea was so short of intellectuals and experts, and because so many left the North for the South in the 1945–50 period. The term intellectual, of course, refers to experts and technocrats, not dissenters and critics, of which there are exceedingly few in North Korea, even when compared to China and the former Soviet Union. The relatively sophisticated industrial structure that North Korea began in 1945 also required a higher proportion of experts and created labor shortages in agriculture, thereby stimulating mechanization of farming, another difference from China. In contrast to the typical Marxist–Leninist model, the KWP is less a tiny vanguard than a big "mass party," as mentioned earlier, which then raises the question, what is the vanguard? It is what Kim Il Sung called the "core" or "nucleus" at the commanding heights of the regime, consisting of himself and his closest associates. All "good things" emanate in top-down fashion from this core, in sharp departure from Maoist dicta about the source of good ideas being the mass of peasants and workers.

North Korea's political system is therefore a mix of Marxism–Leninism, Korean nationalism, and indigenous political culture. The term that perhaps best captures this system is *socialist corporatism*. Although corporatism historically is associated with conservative, even fascist regimes, since the 1920s there has been a particular strain of leftist corporatism, which argued that in the twentieth-century nation-state, conflict replaced class conflict as the motive force of history. Romanian Marxists were among the first to spell this out as a type of socialism particularly appropriate to colonial or less-developed countries, now usually called developing nations. North Korea was the first example of postcolonial socialism; the colonial heritage of dependency and underdevelopment deeply affected North Korean politics and still does so today. If nation-state conflict is the point, then you would emphasize masses rather than classes, that is, national unity rather than workers fighting bourgeois intellectuals; you would have a mass party, not a class party of proletarians. North Korean ideology has followed suit, burying Marxism–Leninism under the ubiquitous, always-trumpeted *chuch'e* idea. One cannot open a North Korean newspaper or listen to a single speech without hearing about *chuch'e*. The term was first used in a 1955 speech in which Kim castigated some of his comrades for being too pro-Soviet—thinking that if the Soviets eat fish on Monday, Koreans should, too, and so forth. But *chuch'e* really means keeping all foreigners at arm's length, which resonates deeply with Korea's "hermit kingdom" past.

Chuch'e has no meaning for a Marxist, but much for East Asians. It shares a first Chinese character with the *ti-yong* (essence and practical use) phrase popular in late nineteenth-century China and a second character with the Japanese *kokutai* (national polity) of the 1930s. The *ti-yong* concept built on Chinese learning as the basis of the ideology and Western learning or technology for its utility. *Kokutai* was a somewhat mystical term meant to distinguish all that was uniquely Japanese from all that was alien and foreign. *Chuch'e* combines both meanings, taking Korean ideas as central, foreign ideas as secondary; it also suggests putting Korean things first at all times, being ever "subjective" where Korea is concerned. By the 1970s, *chuch'e* had triumphed fundamentally over Marxism–Leninism as the basic ideology of the regime, but the emphases have been there from the beginning.

Corporatist doctrine has always preferred an organic politics to the liberal, pluralist conception: a corporeal body politic, not a set of diverse groups and interests. North Korea's goal of tight unity at home produced a remarkable organicism, unprecedented in any existing communist regime. Kim was not just the "iron-willed, ever-victorious commander," the "respected and beloved Great Leader;" he was also the "head and heart" of the body politic (even "the supreme brain of the nation"). The flavor of this politics can only be realized through quotation from Korean Central News Agency releases:

> Kim Il Sung ... is the great father of our people .... Long is the history of the word father being used as a word representing love and reverence ... expressing the unbreakable blood ties between the people and the leader. Father. This familiar word represents our people's single heart of boundless respect and loyalty .... The love shown by the Great Leader for our people is the love of kinship. Our respected and beloved Leader is the tender-hearted father of all the people .... Love of paternity ... is the noblest ideological sentiment possessed only by our people ....

> His heart is a traction power attracting the hearts of all people and a centripetal force uniting them as one .... Kim Il Sung is the great sun and great man ... thanks to this, great heart national independence is firmly guaranteed.

This verbiage was especially strong when the succession to Kim's son was publicly announced at the Sixth KWP Congress in 1980. The KWP was often referred to as the "mother" party, the mass line was said to provide "blood ties," the leader was always "fatherly," and the country was presumably one big "family." Kim was said to be paternal, devoted, and benevolent, and the people were said to respond with loyalty, obedience, and mutual love. Unlike the Maoists, the regime has never tampered with the families of citizens per se, and indeed the family is termed the core unit of society in the constitution, and the society is called a "great integrated entity" (see Family Life, ch. 2).

North Korean socialism demonstrates an apparent volunteerism, something also redolent of corporate politics. North Korean propagandists say that "everything is decided by idea," directly contradicting the materialism at the heart of Marxism. And, of course, the leader's ideas are the best, compounded by his firm "will," always described as "iron-like," or "steel-like." Kim Il Sung invented *chuch'e*, and all Koreans "must have *chuch'e* firm in mind and spirit," and only then can they be good "Kimilsungists," and only then can the revolution be successful. The more one seeks to understand *chuch'e*, the embodiment of Kim's rule and will, the more the meaning recedes. It is a state of mind, not an idea, and one that is unavailable to the non-Korean. It is the opaque core of North Korean national solipsism (see Glossary).

The North Korean system is not simply a hierarchical structure of party, military, and state bureaucracies, but also a hierarchy of ever-widening concentric circles. At the center is Kim Jong Il. The next circle is his family, followed by the now-elderly guerrillas who fought with Kim Il Sung, and then the KWP elite. These individuals form the core circle, which controls everything at the highest echelon of the regime. Here politics is primarily personalistic, resting on something akin to oaths of fealty and obligation. The core must constantly be steeled and hardened, while moving outward and downward concentrically to encompass other elements of the population, and to provide the glue holding the system together. As the penumbra of workers and peasants is reached, trust gives way to control on a bureaucratic basis, and to a mixture of normative and remunerative incentives. Nonetheless, the family remains the model for societal organization. An outer circle marks off that which is Korean from that which is foreign, a reflection of the extraordinary ethnic and linguistic unity of Koreans and the country's history of exclusionism.

This corporate system is instinctively repellent to anyone who identifies with the modern liberal idea, or indeed with the modern Marxist idea. North Korea's simple adherence to its corporatism would be one thing, but by trumpeting the system's worth far and wide, it has earned widespread disbelief and ridicule. Nonetheless, the system is different. In 1990, when many Marxist–Leninist regimes had collapsed, the North Koreans proudly stated that they were still hewing to their well-worn path, of "nation-first-ism," placing the nation first in everything.

Kim Jong Il with his parents, ca. 1943
Courtesy Kŭmsukangsan *(P'yŏngyang), February 2002, 8*

The North Korean difference can be explained only by reference to the tradition and the political culture from which it derives. It is a mixture of Confucian holdovers, Korean traditionalism, and socialist corporatism.

The strength and stability of the system rest on marrying traditional forms of legitimacy to modern bureaucratic structures, with the peculiar charisma of Kim Il Sung providing the transition and the glue between the two. The weakness is that core political power seems still to rest upon personalistic ties, with trust barely extending beyond the leader's family and his long-time guerrilla associates. This is the reason that Kim Jong Il was deeply involved in party and government activities for at least 25 years before he took power, and an entire generation of party faithful and government bureaucrats was rewarded over these same years for supporting his succession. Nor is father-to-son succession in any way alien to East Asian political culture: many huge South Korean firms are headed by the founder's son.

This look inside North Korea may or may not explain why North Korea is so reviled in the West. In any case, its external policies frequently give good reasons for abhorring it. In October 1983, a bomb blast in Rangoon, Burma, decimated South Korean president Chun Doo Hwan's cabinet and very nearly killed Chun himself. A Burmese court determined that North Korean terrorists carried out this despicable act. The North Koreans presumably acted on the assumption that killing Chun would have an effect similar to the 1979 assassination of South Korean president Park Chung-hee: that is, the removal of the maximum leader causes deep disorders to the political system; they were probably right. In 1987 another terrorist blew a South Korean airliner apart, an act also linked to North Korea. The motive for that act was more murky, perhaps intended to dissuade foreigners from coming to the 1988 Olympics in Seoul. If so, it bespoke desperation and a purely malicious and gratuitous terrorism emanating from P'yŏngyang. The Olympics went off without widely predicted terrorist activity, however, and to date there has been no further evidence of North Korean terrorism. In the early twenty-first century, the North reportedly has trafficked in illegal narcotics and counterfeit currency.

With its external reputation for worst-case socialism, in the 1990s most observers thought North Korea would go the way of the Stalinist states of Eastern Europe and collapse. Some thought East Germany would be the model, with North Korea folding up and embracing a new unity with the South. Others suggested the example of Romania, where Nikolae Ceauşescu had modeled his dictatorial rule on Kim Il Sung's. The "revolution of 1989" was so unexpected as to breed humility into all observers of socialist states, but, so far, North Korea has not followed the East German path. It was Mikhail Gorbachev who reined in the military there; amid the widespread demonstrations against Erich Honnecker's regime, Gorbachev kept the 360,000 Soviet Army troops in their barracks. North Korea, however, has an independently controlled army estimated at 1.2 million strong, and most of the pressure the Soviets could exert had been applied (overall Soviet aid to P'yŏngyang declined precipitously after Gorbachev took power, although military aid continued).

Korea's main difference from Eastern Europe is that it suffered a terrible civil war, with some 4.5 million killed, in recent memory. The North probably suffered nearly 2 million casualties. There also were 1 million Chinese casualties. It is very hard to believe that military commanders who fought the South in a bloody civil war would allow South Korea to overwhelm North Korea, by whatever means. If North Korea's socialist system collapses under the intense international pressures of our time, probably the apparatchiks will declare themselves to have been nationalists all along (with some measure of truth) and try to keep their hold on power.

International Relations

It is a mark of some kind of failure that, more than half a century after the Korean War ended, the two Koreas still face each other across the bleak Demilitarized Zone (DMZ—see Glossary), engaged most of the time in unremitting hostility, punctuated by occasional brief thaws and increasing North–South exchanges. Huge armies are still poised to fight at a moment's notice. This has been true since the Korean War, which really solved nothing, except to solidify armed bulwarks of containment, to which the United States, South Korea, and North Korea remain committed, even in the post–Cold War world. Both Koreas continue to be deeply deformed by the necessity to maintain this unrelenting struggle. Yet, around the peninsula much has changed.

Watershed changes in world politics in the 1970s altered the Cold War logic that had governed East Asia. With U.S. president Richard M. Nixon's opening to China in 1971–72, both North Korea and South Korea watched helplessly as their great-power benefactors cozied up to each other. With the conclusion of the Second Indochina War (1954–75), obstacles to ending the Cold War throughout Asia were even fewer. The new strategic logic of the 1970s had an immediate and beneficial impact on the Korean Peninsula. The Nixon administration withdrew a division of U.S. troops without heightening tension. The North Koreans responded by virtually halting attempts at infiltration (compared to 1968, when more than 100 soldiers died along the DMZ and the spy ship USS *Pueblo* was seized) and by significantly reducing their defense budget. Henry Kissinger revealed in his memoirs that Kim Il Sung was in Beijing during Kissinger's famous "secret visit" in July 1971; although it is not known whether they talked, it is likely that Nixon and Kissinger encouraged South Korea to talk with the North and indicated to the North various benefits that might come their way if North Korea took a moderate path. In what seemed to be a miraculous development, in early 1972 both Koreas held talks at a high level (between the director of the Korean Central Intelligence Agency and Kim Il Sung's younger brother), culminating in a stunning July 4, 1972, announcement that both would seek reunification peacefully, independently of outside forces, and with common efforts toward creating a "great national unity" that would transcend the many differences between the two systems. Within a year, this initiative had effectively failed, but it was a reminder of what can be accomplished through enlightened diplomacy and of the continuing importance of the unification issue.

Later on, the policies of the United States and China shifted again, if less dramatically. When the Carter administration announced plans for a gradual but complete withdrawal of U.S. ground forces from Korea (air and naval units would remain deployed in or near Korea), a prolonged period of North Korean courting of Americans began. In 1977 Kim referred to President Jimmy Carter as "a man of justice," and the North Korean press momentarily dropped its calumnies against the United States, including use of the term "U.S. imperialism." Kim gave interviews saying he was knocking on the American door, wanted diplomatic relations and trade, and would not interfere with American business interests in the South once Korea was reunified. The North Koreans also began using a term of opprobrium for Soviet imperialism, *chibaejuŭi* ("dominationism"), a term akin to the Chinese usage, "hegemonism." By and large, P'yŏngyang stayed close to China's foreign policy line during the Carter years, while taking care not to antagonize the Soviets needlessly. When Vietnam invaded Cambodia in 1978, the North Koreans forcefully and publicly condemned the act, while maintaining a studied silence when China responded by invading Vietnam.

Civil disorders in South Korea in 1979–80 and the emergence of a new Cold War atmosphere on a world scale froze the Korean situation for much of the 1980s. The Carter administration dropped its program of troop withdrawal in 1979. The Reagan administration invited President Chun Doo Hwan to visit Washington as its first foreign policy act, a move designed to bolster South Korean stability. The United States committed itself to a modest but significant buildup of force and equipment levels in the South. In the early 1980s, the United States added some 4,000 personnel to the 40,000 already in South Korea, sold Seoul advanced F–16 fighters, and with the South mounted huge "Team Spirit" military exercises involving upwards of 200,000 troops of the two nations toward the beginning of each year.

Sino–American relations warmed considerably in 1983, and for the first time China said publicly that it wished to play a role in reducing tension on the Korean Peninsula; this announcement was followed by a major North Korean initiative in January 1984, which called for the first time for three-way talks among the United States, South Korea, and North Korea. Previously, North Korea had never been willing to sit down with both nations at the same time. (The Carter administration had made a similar proposal for three-way talks in 1979.) Through most of the 1980s, China sought to sponsor talks between Washington and P'yŏngyang (talks that occasionally took place in Beijing between low-level diplomats) and encouraged Kim Il Sung to take the path of diplomacy. By the early 1990s, China had a much larger trade with South Korea than with North Korea, with freighters going back and forth directly across the Yellow Sea, and in 1992 China and South Korea normalized diplomatic relations. South Korea pursued an active diplomacy toward China, the Soviet Union and then Russia, and various East European countries, saying it would favor trade and diplomatic relations with "friendly" communist regimes. This policy bore fruit in 1988, when most communist countries attended the Seoul Olympics, with only Cuba honoring the North Korean "boycott." The collapse of East European communism grievously damaged North Korean diplomacy, as Hungary, Poland, Yugoslavia, and other states opened diplomatic relations with Seoul.

North–South Relations in the Twenty-first Century

The two Koreas made sporadic progress in relations with each other in the late 1980s. The founder of the Hyundai conglomerate toured North Korea in January 1989 and announced a joint venture in tourism, which was the seed of a program whereby tens of thousands of South Koreans tour the scenic Mount Kŭmgang (Mount Diamond) in the North (see Special Economic Zones, ch. 3). As 1991 ended, a watershed breakthrough seemed to occur when the two prime ministers signed a nonaggression pact, which committed both sides to substituting a real peace for the Korean War armistice, reducing troops and mutual vilification, and engaging in wide-ranging exchanges. This progress was followed up at the end of 1991 by an agreement to make the Korean Peninsula nuclear-free. This particular agreement was facilitated by a key American decision in 1991 to withdraw its nuclear weapons from South Korea.

The 1994 Agreed Framework freezing North Korea's nuclear facilities opened up eight years of wide-ranging diplomacy on the Korean Peninsula. Four-Power Talks (the two Koreas, the United States, and China) sought to bring a final conclusion to the Korean War. President Kim Dae Jung's "Sunshine Policy" of engagement opened the way to many joint ventures with the North, including a project in Kaesŏng that envisions operating hundreds of factories in which South Korean firms would employ North Korean labor, and reconnecting roads and railroad lines across the DMZ. In June 2000, Kim Dae Jung traveled to P'yŏngyang for a summit to meet Kim Jong Il, the first time that the two heads of state shook hands since the country was divided in 1945. The administration of President William J. Clinton exchanged high-level visits in late 2000, with Secretary of State Madeleine Albright traveling to P'yŏngyang to meet Kim Jong Il, coming very close to a major deal that indirectly would have bought out the North's medium- and long-range missiles. The administration of President George W. Bush did not concur with that agreement, however, and its concerns about a second nuclear program involving highly enriched uranium derailed the substantial détente that had occurred in the previous decade. Relations between Washington and P'yŏngyang deteriorated in a low-key crisis that began in October 2002 and lasted into the second Bush administration. Unfortunately, the Agreed Framework unraveled, ending the freeze on the North's plutonium facilities and giving the North the fuel to build several nuclear weapons. North Korea declared itself to be a nuclear-weapons state on February 10, 2005, thus confirming a new and dangerous element in the balance of forces on the Korean Peninsula (see Strategic Weapons, ch. 5).

*   *   *

For additional reading on history prior to the twentieth century, the best sources are Carter J. Eckert, Ki-baik Lee, Young Ick Lew, Michael Robinson, and Edward W. Wagner's *Korea Old and New: A History*; Han Woo-Keun's *The History of Korea*; and James B. Palais's *Politics and Policy in Traditional Korea*. For the Japanese period, Carter J. Eckert's *Offspring of Empire: The Koch'ang Kims and the Colonial Origins of Korean Capitalism*; Sang Chul Suh's *Growth and Structural Changes in the Korean Economy, 1910–1940*; and Michael Robinson's *Cultural Nationalism in Korea, 1920–25* provide sound information. *The Politics of Korean Nationalism* by Chong-Sik Lee; *Communism in Korea* by Robert A. Scalapino and Chong-Sik Lee; *The Korean Communist Movement, 1918–1948* by Dae-Sook Suh; and Suh's *Kim Il Sung: A Biography* are good books on the origins of Korean nationalism and communism. The Korean War and its origins are covered in Bruce Cumings, *The Origins of the Korean War*; Rosemary Foote, *The Wrong War*; and Peter Lowe, *The Origins of the Korean War*. *Communism in Korea* by Scalapino and Chong-Sik Lee, Ellen Brun and Jacques Hersh's *Socialist Korea: A Case Study in the Strategy of Economic Development*, and a study of North Korea's agrarian socialism by Mun Woong Lee, *Rural North Korea under Communism: A Study in Sociocultural Chang*, offer a thorough grounding in North Korean history. A survey of North Korea's international relations and U.S. policy toward North Korea can be found in Selig S. Harrison's *Korean Endgame: A Strategy for Reunification and U.S. Disengagement*. (For further information and complete citations, see Bibliography.)

Chapter 2. The Society and Its Environment

Bas-relief on P'yŏngyang's Arch of Triumph. The inscription on the flag reads "The world's one and only patriot. Long live Kim Il Sung." Courtesy Pulmyŏl ŭi t'ap *(Tower of Immortality), P'yŏngyang: Munye Ch'ulpansa, 1985, 283*

BEFORE ITS DIVISION IN 1945, Korea had been culturally and linguistically distinct for more than 5,000 years and a sovereign nation-state under the Chosŏn Dynasty (1392–1910) for more than 500 years. Traditional culture and social structure during this long period of independent rule were deeply influenced by Chinese civilization, and high value was placed on Confucian ideals of social harmony, loyalty, orthodoxy, authority, and filial piety.

The years of colonization by imperial Japan (1910–45) humiliated Korea, depriving it of freedom and creating a skewed economy, but left the country ethnically and culturally distinct and little changed socially. Much more damaging to the ancient culture and society has been the division in 1945 into North Korea and South Korea, two independent nations with 10 million separated families that had hoped to reestablish a sovereign nation under traditional Korean values, beliefs, and behavior. The Democratic People's Republic of Korea (North Korea), the larger of the two countries and historically the more industrially developed, had a population of 9.1 million in 1945, only slightly more than half that of the traditionally more agrarian Republic of Korea (South Korea), which had 16 million people in 1945.

The two peoples that have emerged since 1945—the socialist society in the North and the pluralistic society in the South—live at opposite ends of the spectrum of world societies. Previously, it would have been almost unthinkable that two such different systems as the Koreas at the beginning of the twenty-first century could have emerged from the traditional Korean society that 100 years earlier had remained mostly unchanged for more than a millennium.

The Physical Environment

North Korea is located in the northern half of the Korean Peninsula, which extends about 1,000 kilometers southward from Northeast Asia. The nation occupies about 55 percent of the total land area of the peninsula, or approximately 120,410 square kilometers, and water covers 130 square kilometers.

North Korea lies between South Korea to the south, China to the north and northwest, and Russia to the northeast. The northern borders with China and Russia extend for 1,435 kilometers, with 1,416 kilometers separating North Korea from the Chinese provinces of Jilin and Liaoning and the remaining 19 kilometers separating it

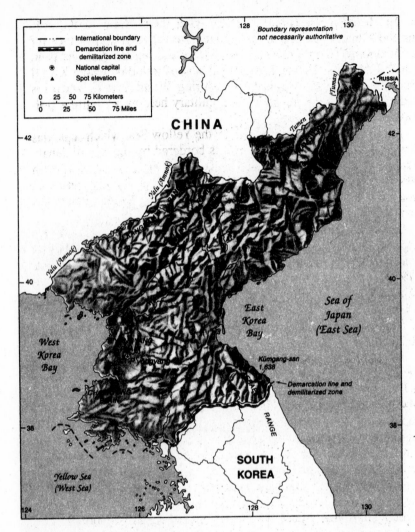

Figure 4. Topography and Drainage

from Russia's Primorskiy Territory. This northern border is formed
by the Amnok (or Yalu, as it is known in China) and Tuman (Tumen,
as it is known in China) rivers, which have their sources in the
region around Mount Paektu (Paektu-san or White Head Mountain),
an extinct volcano and Korea's highest mountain (see fig. 4). The
Amnok flows in a southwesterly direction into the Yellow Sea (or
West Sea as it is known to Koreans), and the Tuman flows in a north-
easterly direction into the Sea of Japan (or East Sea as it is known to
Koreans). Part of the border with China near Mount Paektu has yet

to be clearly demarcated. Koreans trace their origin to the area around Mount Paektu, and the mountain has special significance for contemporary North Koreans because of the legend that has been created that their leader, Kim Jong Il, son of founding leader Kim Il Sung, was born on Mount Paektu during World War II, when his father was attaining the status of a military hero as a longtime anti-Japanese guerrilla fighter.

Korea's west coast is bordered by the Yellow Sea, which separates Korea from China. The east coast is bordered by the Sea of Japan. The 8,460-kilometer seacoast of Korea is highly irregular, with North Korea's half of the peninsula having 2,495 kilometers of coastline. Some 3,579 islands lie adjacent to the Korean Peninsula, most of them along the south coast.

North Korea's southern border with South Korea is at the thirty-eighth parallel, an unnatural division of the Korean Peninsula that was roughly the point where the opposing armies in the Korean War (1950–53) faced one another at the time of the cease-fire and signing of an armistice marking the end of the fighting on July 27, 1953. It is a border that was hastily agreed upon at the end of World War II by U.S. and Soviet leaders, with no particular reference to natural land features.

Known since 1953 as the Demarcation Line (see Glossary), the border between North Korea and South Korea at the thirty-eighth parallel is the most heavily guarded border in the world and the last flashpoint of the Cold War. The so-called Demilitarized Zone (DMZ—see Glossary), a 4,000-meter-wide strip of land that straddles the Demarcation Line, runs east and west for a distance of 238 kilometers over land and three kilometers over the sea. North Korea claims a 12-nautical-mile territorial sea and an exclusive economic zone of 200 nautical miles. It also has established a military boundary line of 50 nautical miles on its east coast and the exclusive economic zone on the west coast in which foreign ships and aircraft without permission from the North Korean government are officially banned.

Topography and Drainage

Approximately 80 percent of North Korea's land area is made up of mountain ranges separated by deep, narrow valleys. All mountains on the Korean Peninsula higher than 2,000 meters above sea level are in North Korea, the highest one being Mount Paektu on the northern border with China at 2,744 meters above sea level. There are wide coastal plains on the west coast, the most extensive being the P'yŏngyang and Chaeryŏng plains, each covering about 500 square kilometers. Because the mountains on the east coast drop abruptly to the sea, the discontinuous coastal plains in the east are much smaller than those on the west coast. The majority of the population lives in the plains and lowlands, which constitute less than 25 percent of the country, providing North Korea only a small amount of arable land.

The mountain ranges in the north and east form the watershed for most of the country's rivers, which run in a westerly direction and empty into the Yellow Sea. The longest of these is the Amnok, 790 kilometers in length and navigable for 678 kilometers. The second largest river, the Tuman, which is navigable for only 81 of its 521 kilometers, is one of the few major rivers to flow into the Sea of Japan. The third longest river, the Taedong, which flows through P'yŏngyang and is largely responsible for the natural beauty of North Korea's capital city, is navigable for 245 of its 397 kilometers.

There is no east–west waterway crossing the Korean Peninsula. Ships in eastern ports of North Korea can reach western ports only by going around the southern tip of South Korea. Outside observers of isolated and secretive North Korea were astonished when, in 1999, the captured intelligence ship USS *Pueblo,* which had been taken to the east coast port of Wŏnsan after its seizure by North Korea in January 1968, appeared in P'yŏngyang as a much-acclaimed tourist attraction. Apparently, North Korea had disguised the ship, officially still a commissioned vessel of the U.S. Navy, and sailed it around the peninsula, up the west coast and along the Taedong to P'yŏngyang.

There are relatively few lakes in North Korea, and they tend to be small because of the lack of glacial activity and the stability of the earth's crust in the region. Unlike neighboring Japan and China, North Korea has experienced few severe earthquakes.

Climate

North Korea has long, cold, dry winters and short, hot, humid summers. Temperatures range between –8° C in December and 27° C in August. Approximately 60 percent of the annual rainfall occurs between June and September, the main rice-growing period. August is the wettest month of the year with an average rainfall of 317 millimeters. Typhoons can be expected on an average of at least once every summer. Since the mid-1990s, erratic weather conditions, particularly devastating floods in 1995 followed by a prolonged drought, have contributed to a precipitous drop in agricultural production (caused by serious failures of government agricultural policies as well as poor weather, deforestation, and soil erosion) and led to one of the worst famines of the late twentieth century, resulting in the death of more than 1 million North Koreans.

*Peaks of the North Korean side of Mount Paektu,
as seen from the Chinese side across Lake Chunji
Courtesy Sarah Ji-young Kim*

Environmental Factors

After the Korean War, North Korea embarked on an ambitious but ill-fated program of industrialization. Industry used generally obsolete technology and outmoded equipment transferred from the Soviet Union and China that in other communist-bloc nations eventually produced air, water, and soil pollution. The passage of an environmental protection law by the Supreme People's Assembly in April 1986 suggests that North Korea had a serious pollution problem, probably most particularly in the industrial cities of Namp'o, Hamhŭng, and Ch'ŏngjin.

Air pollution, alleviated somewhat by the absence of private automobiles and restrictions on the use of gasoline-powered vehicles because of the critical shortage of oil, has long been severe because of the heavy reliance on coal as the major source of energy. The major causes of pollution have been industrial boilers and kilns and household heating and cooking. According to a United Nations Environment Programme (UNEP) report published in 2003, data on air pollution are very limited and confined mainly to P'yŏngyang, where there is almost no industry and hydroelectric power rather than coal is more commonly used to meet energy demands, giving an atypical picture of air quality throughout the rest of the country. However, in 1990 boilers and industrial kilns in P'yŏngyang consumed nearly 3.4 million tons of coal, and household consumption for heating and cooking amounted to another nearly 358,000 tons of coal. The government has given priority to the prevention of air pollution in P'yŏngyang, where the government elite live, and to other major cities, with policies aimed at reducing coal consumption in the household sector, enhancing combustion efficiency, and employing gas purification devices on boilers and kilns. For sustainable management of air quality, however, the government will need to introduce advanced technologies, such as clean coal technology, high-efficiency purification of exhaust gas, and renewable energy options for environmentally sound energy development.

North Korea is richly endowed with forests, which are distributed throughout the country with highest cover in the northern area. However, the majority of the forests are mountain forest cover, more than 70 percent of which stands on slopes greater than 20 degrees. In 1945 the forested area of North Korea was estimated at 9.7 million hectares. War and industrial use greatly depleted this resource. Forest stock per hectare increased from 53.6 cubic meters in 1978 to 55.9 cubic meters in 1990, at which time afforested and reforested areas totaled 1.1 million hectares. Thereafter, however, socioeconomic and industrial development led to a decrease in forested areas to 986,000 hectares by 1996. This degradation in forest resources, which play an important role in economic development as well as human well-being, has continued. At least part of the decline is the result of the excessive use of firewood during the energy crisis of the late 1990s brought about by the cut-off of exports of petroleum from Russia and the flooding of North Korea's coal mines. Deforestation for firewood occurred simultaneously with the destruction of huge areas of forests in the devastating floods and droughts that plagued North Korea in the 1995–97 period. Forest fires, landslides, and noxious insect damage have further decreased forest area and stocks. This trend has been accentuated by conversion of forest into farmland since the mid-1990s, during the years of decreasing food imports. The government has undertaken initiatives to restore forests damaged by the recent flooding, droughts, forest fires and illegal deforestation, including the 1999 promulgation of the Law on the Forest, which established an annual Tree-Planting Day on March 2, and the inauguration of a 10-year plan for afforestation/reforestation to restore and rehabilitate 2 million hectares of degraded forests. The proposed measures, if successful, will restore only recent damage, however, rather than augment traditional forest resources.

North Korea is rich in water resources, including rainfall, rivers, and underground water, but there is wide fluctuation in precipitation across the country and a short outflow time of rainfall because of the steep slopes of catchments. There were severe shortages of water during the period of high temperatures and continued drought in the mid-1990s. One of the world's worst famines was a direct result of the shortage of water, the contamination of the water due to flooding and drought, and the decrease in agricultural production due to the natural disasters of those years (see Effects of the Famine, ch. 3). Discharges from some urban settlements and industries have subjected certain bodies of water to severe eutrophication, and some water-quality indices do not meet environmental standards. With water contamination and lack of investment in disinfections in storage reservoirs, water-borne diseases have led to numerous deaths, including 300,000 to 800,000 annually during the drought and famine in the mid-1990s. The government adopted the Law on Water Resources in June 1997, amended in January 1999, establishing a basis for water-resources protection and strengthening government control on effluents and sewage from factories, enterprises, and purification plants. Television, radio, newspapers, and newsletters were directed to inform the public frequently about the need for water conservation, which is now viewed as a critical issue in the country.

Floods in the mid-1990s inflicted an estimated US$925 million in damage to North Korea's arable land. Forest degradation in hilly forest areas adjacent to agricultural land contributed to land erosion. North Korea's mountainous terrain means that its agriculture is heavily dependent on chemical fertilizers, and the acidification of arable land by fertilizer application has brought about a decline in both soil humus content and crop output. In order to protect land resources from acidification and to enhance fertility, treated sewage and coal ash from urban centers are applied to the land. Again, P'yŏngyang is given priority over other parts of the country in the processing of municipal solid waste into fertilizer. There have been continuous efforts by the government to increase pubic awareness about the importance of land quality as the basis of their livelihood and national prosperity.

Population

North Korea's population, estimated in July 2007 to be 23,301,725, is slightly less than half that of South Korea. The North's 2007 estimated birthrate is 15.0 births per 1,000 and the death rate 7.2 per 1,000. The country is highly urbanized. Only about 40 percent of its citizens live in rural areas, a low percentage for a less-developed country and a reflection of the mountainous terrain and limited arable land. Population density is estimated at 188 persons per square kilometer. The inability of the rural population to produce enough food to feed the urban society would normally lead

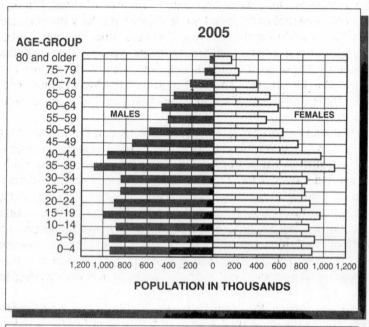

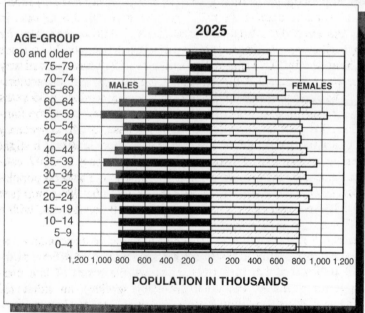

Source: Based on information from United States, Department of Commerce, Census Bureau, International Programs Center, *International Data Base Population Pyramids (North Korea)*, Washington, DC, 2007, http://www.census.gov/ipc/www/idbpyr.html.

Figure 5. Population by Age and Sex, 2005, and Estimated for 2025

any government to finance necessary imports of food through exports of industrial and mineral products, which is how the northern half of Korea traditionally survived. However, since the mid-1990s, when agricultural production began falling precipitously and the demands for imported food have risen dramatically, the regime has not been able to increase exports of industrial products because of a simultaneous decline in industrial production (see Post-Famine Situation, ch. 3).

With plausible policy adjustments, an earlier call for international assistance, and less interference with the humanitarian aid organizations' established norms for food distribution, North Korea could have averted the great famine of the mid- and late 1990s. As it was, the country suffered the worst famine in the late twentieth century, the only one in a country not at war, and one of the most devastating famines of the last century, which left at least 1 million people—5 percent of North Korea's population—dead. Most of the deaths were among the young and the elderly who, as is typical in famines, succumbed to diseases such as tuberculosis before actually starving to death.

Since the famine, the population growth rate has slowed significantly. The estimated annual growth of 0.9 percent (2002–5) represents a dramatic decline from 2.7 percent in 1960, 3.6 percent in 1970, and even the 1.9 percent rate in 1975. Earlier estimates by demographic experts that North Korea's population would increase to 25.5 million by 2000 and to 28.5 million in 2010 have proved way off the mark because of the effects of the unexpected, devastating famine. In 1990 life expectancy at birth was approximately 66 years for males and almost 73 for females. Despite the effects of the famine, the 2007 estimate showed a slight increase in life expectancy (69.2 years for males and 74.8 for females). There also was a slight imbalance in the male:female sex ratio. According to 2007 estimates, there were 0.94 males for every female in the general population and 0.98 males for every female in the 15 to 64 age-group (see fig. 5). The population is almost completely ethnic Korean, with a few Chinese and Japanese.

The North Korean government seems to perceive its population as too small in relation to that of South Korea. There is no official birth-control policy, but falling growth rates are the result of late marriages (after a man's compulsory military service), an exhausted population as a result of long hours of work and political study, families' limited resources and housing space, and, now more so than in earlier years, the deterioration in health conditions because of chronic food shortages (see Family Life, this ch.).

Social Structure and Values

Creating a New Society

In the relatively short span of 60 years, North Korea has developed a unique society that is, in the opinion of many observers, the world's most oppressive, heading the list of countries having atrocious human rights records. The society can best be described as a distinctively Korean version of socialism, mixing Marxist–Leninist ideas with the rigid hierarchical social structure and authoritarianism of Confucianism, enforced by an extreme totalitarian regime that rules with a mixture of terror and the world's most intense personality cult. Despite mounting economic failures and horrific human rights abuses, the leadership has remained firmly in control of a compliant society in a well-armed but impoverished nation.

Perhaps more than can be said of any other country, North Korea is the creation of one man—Kim Il Sung—one of the most intriguing figures of the twentieth century, dominating his country during his lifetime and afterward as few individuals in history have done. From the late 1950s until his death in 1994, Kim's power was nearly unlimited, and he ruled his country longer than any other leader of the twentieth century. American political scientist Donald Oberdorfer pointed out in *The Two Koreas* that when Kim died in July 1994, he had outlived Joseph Stalin for four decades and Mao Zedong by almost two decades and had remained in power during the terms of office of six South Korean presidents, nine U.S. presidents, and 21 Japanese prime ministers. No leader has ever had so free a hand in shaping the destiny of his country, and it is fair to say that none has had greater success in creating a national society of his own design, quite unlike any other society, communist or otherwise. It is remarkable that such a man should have become the architect of a modern state and society almost single-handedly. He had only eight years of formal education (the last two of which were in schools in Northeast China before he was expelled for revolutionary activities). Kim was an anti-Japanese guerrilla fighter who served for a decade in a unit attached to the Chinese Communist Party's guerrilla army, then for four years with a Soviet military unit during World War II, being thereafter installed by the Soviets as the new leader of North Korea in 1945.

Kim Il Sung does not appear to have had a coherent philosophic construct guiding his life or planning for North Korean society. He was not an intellectual and not well read. He was reported to have known a lot of Confucianism and a smattering of Marx, Lenin, and Hegel. Christian influences in Kim's early life had not been well known until the serial publication in 1992–95 of his six-volume memoir *With the Century*. He was born in P'yŏngyang in 1912 to the daughter of a Presbyterian elder and a father who had been a student at a missionary school in P'yŏngyang. He claimed, later in life, not to have "been affected by religion" despite his youthful connections with the church but acknowledged that he "received a great deal of humanitarian assistance from Christians." But Kim Jong Il, unlike his father, has never had anything favorable to say about religion, having had no personal familiarity with religious beliefs and practices (see Religion, this ch.).

Whereas South Korea's society was shaped by myriad influences, the North's is Kim Il Sung's creation. It reflects his genius and limitations, his restricted experience of the world and his deeply held convictions and, perhaps most important of all, his nationalistic doctrine of *chuch'e* (see Glossary), doing things his way, being independent, not following foreign example or advice but rather his own idea of what was best for North Korea (see Political Ideology; The Role of *Chuch'e*, ch. 4). Just as he personally laid out the streets of the rebuilt P'yŏngyang (his "dream city") after the devastation of the Korean War and decided which buildings would go where and which architects would design which buildings in which style (Soviet or Korean), he planned and enforced the daily life of his people from their waking up until their going to bed, from the cradle to the grave. His role in the everyday life of the people may have been somewhat exaggerated, especially in later years when the cult of Kim Il Sung reached dazzling proportions, but there is abundant evidence that no other leader has ever had a greater hand in planning, directing, and boasting about a society that he created.

It is difficult to describe the mix of ideas and influences that came to bear on the creation of North Korea's unique society. It is a rigid class society emphasizing Confucian hierarchal values, a fanatical cult society extolling Kim Il Sung as a demigod, an Orwellian thought-controlled society, a thoroughly militarized society, an impoverished socialist economy with a limited education system and woefully poor health-care system, no free religious institutions or spiritual teaching, and few, if any, basic human rights (see Education; Health Care, this ch.).

The Cult of Kim Il Sung

What matters most in North Korea is loyalty to the "Great Leader" Kim Il Sung and his teachings and, since 1994, their interpretation by his son and heir, the "Dear Leader," Kim Jong Il. This is immediately apparent upon one's first meeting with a North Korean, whose every sentence is peppered with references to "the thought of Kim Il Sung," "dedication to Kim Il Sung," being a "Kim Il Sung man," or just "Kim Il Sung."

The Kim cult has flourished in the special conditions of a relatively small country with a homogeneous population, a tradition of social harmony, authoritarian rule and loyalty of the people to the ruler, and, in this case, a charismatic leader with a unique style of leadership who ruled for an unusually long time. For nearly 50 years, Kim Il Sung traveled around his country for more than 150 days and sometimes as many as 225 days a year. From 1954 to 1961, he reportedly made more than 1,300 on-the-spot inspections of collective farms, factories, mines, highways, housing complexes, childcare facilities, museums, and other public buildings. In the 30 years from 1950 to 1980, he reportedly traveled more than 513,000 kilometers, averaging approximately 52 kilometers a day. He was personally familiar with every town and village, every farm and factory, visiting many of them repeatedly. Over the years, most North Koreans saw him close at hand on one or another of his visits to their provinces.

While the relatively small size of North Korea made it easier for him to establish a personal relationship with his people than it was for Stalin or Mao, who were remote by comparison, Kim's particular personality and skills in establishing personal rapport, especially with children, cannot be denied. One of his effective leadership practices, for example, which won the hearts of both children and their parents, was his custom on his endless visits to nursery and elementary schools of taking a Polaroid camera and having each child's picture taken with him. The children would then take the photographs home and hang them in their homes, where only images of Kim were allowed to be displayed. For many years, North Koreans have begun and ended their day with a bow to Kim's portrait in their home.

From available evidence, it seems that the cult of personality in North Korea rests on a genuine belief of the vast majority of the people in the greatness and goodness of Kim Il Sung. Visitors to North Korea often remark on the depth of the people's feelings for Kim. Whatever criticism there is, it is rarely voiced, even in private; people are afraid to criticize the regime, especially Kim. Some defectors have admitted to having secret doubts about his infallibility, but they would never have voiced these doubts in public or, for that matter, in private. The most convincing reason for accepting the genuineness of the people's love for Kim actually comes from defectors who have absolutely no reason to exaggerate their true feelings for Kim after having made the highly dangerous decision to defect and having no fear of being returned to the dreadful existence from which

Parade celebrating the fiftieth anniversary of the North Korean Communist Party (later the Korean Workers' Party), P'yŏngyang, October 11, 1995; Kim Il Sung is featured in the large circular portrait.
Courtesy Korea Today *(P'yŏngyang), November 1995, 1*

they have so narrowly escaped. In spite of any reservations they may have about the excesses of the cult, they still express a certain reverence for Kim Il Sung as a person and as a leader. Their admiration seems deep-seated, genuine, and unshakeable. Studied at a distance as an abstraction, the cult may appear ludicrous, almost unbelievable, but, up close, its hold over the perception and thought patterns of North Koreans is awe inspiring.

When Kim Il Sung died suddenly and unexpectedly of a heart attack in July 1994 at the age of 82, the nation was shocked and overcome with grief on a scale that few outsiders comprehended at the time. Kim had been their leader during all or most of their lifetimes; the people had seen him at close range on many occasions. They felt they had lost a father, as well as the "Great Leader," who in 1998 was officially proclaimed the "Eternal President" of North Korea. More than that, they had lost a cult leader whom they revered as a demigod.

It would be hard to exaggerate the mood of vulnerability, confusion, and uncertainty, on top of grief, that engulfed the nation in 1995, at the time when the first of a series of natural calamities, floods, droughts, famines, and starvation, gripped the nation, bringing it to near economic collapse (see Collapse in the 1990s, ch. 3). Many North Koreans attributed the severe problems then afflicting the country to the loss of the "Great Leader," as if there had been some disastrous world reordering.

The handling of Kim's funeral reflected the country's state of mind. No foreign dignitaries were invited to attend the funeral ceremonies, despite the fact that a head of state for almost half a century was being honored. Kim's *chuch'e* philosophy of national independence may have played some role in the decision to ban outsiders, but the simple explanation seems to have been the people's feeling of a loss too personal and too private to share with others. Perhaps the moral superiority and defiant aloofness that cult members typically feel toward nonbelievers militated against the inclusion of outsiders at such a painful time. The limited glimpse that the outside world was afforded of the national outpouring of grief, with hundreds of thousands of North Koreans weeping for days, bespoke an honest desire to grieve in private, with no play for international sympathy or support. There is no reason to think that their tears at this time were anything but genuine.

After the funeral, at which the designated heir, Kim Jong Il, appeared but did not speak, he did not appear again in public for many months. When asked why, he said simply that he was still grieving for his father, an unusual admission for a head of state. Observers of the scene wondered why he had not moved more quickly to assume the mantel of leadership. While there may well have been overriding political considerations involving the need to consolidate his own political position, there was a sense that he, too, was almost paralyzed by grief over his father's death and sensitive to the country's need for time and space to absorb the loss (see Leadership Succession, ch. 4). His state of mind over his father's death is often cited as a major reason for his slowness in responding to the natural disasters that befell North Korea in the mid-1990s.

Since the elder Kim's death, the cult has grown to even greater proportions. It continues to dominate every aspect of North Korean life. In this regard, it should be emphasized that it still is—as it always has been—the cult of Kim Il Sung. Kim Jong Il succeeded to power as the son of Kim Il Sung in the tradition of the Chosŏn monarchy. One might assume that, as his son, Kim Jong Il would be elevated to the same godlike status. However, that does not seem to be the case. He is more the apostle or high priest of his father's cult, and a very zealous one at that. As the chief beneficiary of the cult, he has every reason to maintain and promote the cult to ever higher excesses. For a period of time in his career, the younger Kim's main responsibility in the Ministry of Culture actually seems to have been the promotion of the cult. He has proven expertise in that area. Among Kim Il Sung's children, Kim Jong Il "was the one who got his father's trust. He supported Kim Il Sung's deification," according to Hwang Jang-yop, Korean Workers' Party (KWP) secretary for ideology. The younger Kim is credited with coining the term *Kimilsungism*, with its specific connotation of one-man rule, and during the 1960s and 1970s he presided over the elevation of Kim Il Sung from national hero and "Great Leader" to official deity.

It would have been far riskier for Kim Jong Il to have tried to replace his father in the people's affections, which he is not likely to have accomplished in any case, than to co-opt his father's cult for his own purposes. In this way, he has avoided any comparison to his father in which he would inevitably be found wanting. At the same time, he has capitalized on the benefits of being the son of a cult demigod, a position that no one else can challenge and that is compatible with traditional Confucian thinking, which holds high the father-son relationship of the five personal connections (ruler and subject, father and son, elder brother and younger brother, husband and wife, and friend and friend) that contribute to the perfect harmony of society.

It would be a mistake, however, to assume that Kim Jong Il's political power is any less than his father's because the younger Kim is not the object of a comparable cult of personality. He is the present-day leader of a cult society, with all the powers associated with being the leader, as distinct from the object of worship. It is doubtful that he could ever have created so intense and enduring a cult built around his persona. He is not the charismatic man his father was. He has inherited total political power, which he reinforces by reinvigorating the cult worship of his father, without himself having the stature of his father as a demigod in what is essentially a secular religious state.

Foreign visitors to North Korea are often stunned by the omnipresence of Kim Il Sung in the lives of North Koreans, not only in their view all the time but constantly in their thoughts as well. There are photographs of Kim hanging in people's homes; gigantic posters of Kim hanging from the roofs of huge public buildings; state-issued portraits of Kim in offices, classrooms, shops, public halls, factories, hospitals, and other indoor locations, as well as on the front of trains and the decks of ships; mosaics of Kim with his band of anti-Japanese guerrilla fighters on the walls of the elaborately decorated P'yŏngyang subway system; and statues and sculptures, some of them gold-plated, and the most impressive of all a huge, illuminated white marble statue of Kim seated at one end of the magnificent International Friendship Exhibition Hall in a pose reminiscent of Abraham Lincoln's statue in the Lincoln Memorial in Washington, DC. By one count, there were more than 500 life-size statues of Kim in 1980, and by the time of his death in 1994 that number had increased many times over. There are elaborately staged theatrical productions of his life story, some of them reportedly produced by Kim Jong Il, who is known to have taken a personal interest and role in the development of North Korea's movie and theater industries.

Kim Il Sung's birthplace at Man'gyŏngdae and his burial site in P'yŏngyang are shrines, and North Korean students and workers go on annual pilgrimages to them from all over the country, often walking many kilometers to get there. On a typical day, Man'gyŏngdae is visited by some 10,000 people, including foreign visitors who are taken there as a routine first stop on their tour of P'yŏngyang and the vicinity. There are raised plaques at spots in the middle of roads where Kim stopped to give on-the-spot guidance. Subway seats where he sat are roped off as memorials. There are signs over the doors of factories and day-care nurseries marking the date that Kim visited. Objects that he touched on these visits are covered with glass or draped with a veil and often set aside in a special room. North Korea's only four-year civilian university is named after him, as is the four-year military university (see Higher Education, this ch.; Officer Corps Professional Education and Training, ch. 5). Kim's birthday (April 15) is celebrated as the most important national holiday of the year. There is a photograph of Kim on the identification card that hangs from the neck of every North Korean. People are not required to bow down to all his portraits in public locations, but North Koreans have been known to take out the picture of Kim that they carry and bow to it, sometimes ostentatiously, as when a North Korean diplomat returns home from an overseas assignment. Kim Il Sung is literally everywhere in North Korea. In P'yŏngyang, one cannot walk 100 meters without encountering his likeness.

Kim Il Sung's tomb is also an indicator of the level of cult development. Reconstruction of the Kŭmsusan Assembly Hall in P'yŏngyang started in 1995 and reportedly cost US$8.9 billion. Referred to by foreign media as a "tomb palace," the nearly 35,000-square-meter, five-story memorial houses Kim's embalmed body and a typical larger-than life statue of the deceased president. Some

200,000 people can assemble on the square in front of the complex. Male visitors to the hall where Kim lies in view are required to wear suits, and women are required to wear *hanbok* (traditional Korean dress). The tomb is connected to the P'yŏngyang subway and has people-mover walkways, escalators, air purification systems, automatic shoe cleaners, and granite and marble construction throughout.

If this were not suffocating enough, there is the more psychologically stifling pressure of how much Kim Il Sung is constantly on the minds of the North Korean people, not just forever in their sight. Beginning in nursery school, children memorize poems about Kim's early life and make up their own poems and drawings in his memory. In later years, they act out stories of his life, and in middle and high school they memorize long passages from his teachings. Farmers can recite his writings about agriculture from memory; workers know other passages from his treatises on industry; women memorize his words about the family; foreign affairs students memorize his lectures on *chuch'e* and other international subjects; and everyone learns what it means to be "a Kim Il Sung man." Every morning they hear the regime's political message for the day taken from Kim's writings, and at weekly political meetings and self-criticism sessions, they study these writings in much greater detail, beginning and ending with patriotic songs glorifying Kim. The only movies and theater productions that they see are variations on the theme of Kim's life. Whether working or relaxing, Kim Il Sung is always in the forefront.

The most distinguishing feature about North Korean society, then, is the intensity of the Kim cult, not just its more extreme outward manifestations, but the hold that it has over the people's minds and feelings. North Korea is, above all else, the world's most intense, cult society with all the trappings of a nation-state.

As members of a cult society, North Koreans are trained not to think but to follow. They may be rational on most issues, but on sensitive issues touching on the cult or Kim's life and teachings, they are totally intransigent. Their unshakable faith in the correctness of Kim's teachings and confidence in his way of doing things, according to *chuch'e* doctrine, can make them closed to negotiation and resistant to compromise, even at the sacrifice of their own best interests. The strong belief in the rightness of their cause and their faith in better times to come, which true believers often have and take heart from, can see them through difficulties that nonbelievers might not weather as well. Some analysts consider that North Korea has been able to survive the natural calamities and adverse international pressure since the mid-1990s—which forecasters predicted would bring the nation to the point of national collapse—only because of the internal strength of a people bound together in an irrational but unifying national cult.

A Class Society

Two phrases are likely to dominate any conversation with a North Korean, regardless of the subject under discussion, just as they dominate every aspect of life in North Korea. They are *Kim Il Sung sanga* (Kim Il Sung's thoughts) and *sŏngbun* (see Glossary), meaning socioeconomic or class background.

In North Korea, a person's *sŏngbun* is either good or bad, and detailed records are kept by KWP cadre and government security officials of the degree of goodness or badness of everyone's *sŏngbun*. The records are continually updated. It is easy for one's *sŏngbun* to be downgraded for lack of ideological fervor, laziness, incompetence, or for more serious reasons, such as marrying someone with bad *sŏngbun*, committing a crime, or simply being related to someone who commits an offense. It is very difficult to improve one's *sŏngbun*, however, particularly if the stigma derives from the prerevolutionary class status or behavior of one's parents or relatives.

In the early days of the regime, *sŏngbun* records were sketchy, and some people survived by concealing the fact that their father, uncle, or grandfather had owned land or was a physician, merchant, or lawyer. However, in the late 1960s, the state made a major effort to conduct exhaustive secret investigations of the background of all North Koreans. Periodically after that, additional investigations were carried out by the public security apparatus whenever Kim Il Sung had reason to believe there was opposition to his rule in a certain area of the country, town, or factory.

During the Chosŏn Dynasty, four distinct Confucian-based social strata developed: the scholar-officials (or nobility), the "middle people" (technicians and administrators subordinate to the scholar-officials), the commoners (a large group comprising about 75 percent of the total population, including farmers, craftsmen, and merchants), and the "despised" or base people at the bottom of society. To ensure stability, the government devised a system of personal tallies kept by the scholar-officials to identify people according to their status.

Kim Il Sung borrowed heavily from this Confucian system but upset the social hierarchy in a radical remaking of society, more in keeping with communist teachings and his personal experience as a guerrilla fighter. Because the only "good" people in the pre-1945 period, in Kim's view, were factory workers, laborers, and farmers, they and their descendants were accorded privileged status. The highest distinction went to the anti-Japanese guerrillas who had fought with him in Northeast China (Manchuria) prior to and during World War II, and then to veterans of the Korean War and their descendants. Next came the descendants of the prerevolutionary working people and the poor, small farmers.

The regime also recognized the essential roles of intellectuals and professional workers in society. The symbolism of this is seen in the KWP's insignia, which depicts a pen in the middle of the traditional socialist hammer and sickle to emphasize the relationship among the physical labor of workers and farmers and intellectual activities of the well educated. Kim realized that an educated population and skilled technicians were needed to rebuild the industrial bases that had been established in North Korea during the Japanese colonial period and destroyed during the Korean War. However, the knowledgeable people Kim favored were not the precommunist period literati but rather educated technologists who were useful to reconstruction and who were completely trustworthy and loyal to the regime. Education in the new Korea was supposed to remove the distinctions between intellectuals and the working class through, according to Charles K. Armstrong, "the political conversion of the former and the intellectual uplifting of the latter."

Ranked below the former guerrillas, working people and farmers, and intellectuals, in descending order were—and still are—some 50 distinct groups. The only touch of humor in this otherwise deadly business of ranking people according to their *sŏngbun* is the terminology some defectors say refers to the chosen versus the neglected: "tomatoes" versus "apples" versus "grapes." Tomatoes, which are red to the core, are worthy communists; "apples," which are red only on the surface, need ideological improvement; and "grapes" are hopeless.

Based on their *sŏngbun* ranking, North Korea's population can be divided into three main groups. The preferred class, consisting of some 10 to 15 percent of the population, is given every advantage. Its members receive better schooling, including the possibility of attending Kim Il Sung University, better jobs (in foreign affairs work or in the military), better housing, better clothing, better food and more of it, and better medical care. The middle 40 to 50 percent of the population—ordinary people—can hope for a lucky break, such as a good assignment in the military that will bring them to the attention of KWP cades and may get them a better job afterward. There is no hope, however, of a college education or a professional career. And finally, there is the bottom 40 percent of the population—the "undesirables"—to whom all doors to advancement are closed. They can expect little except assignment to a collective farm or factory, just like their parents. This group includes a high percentage of women, who generally do not have the military as a way to improvement and are usually assigned immediately after middle school to a farm or to a factory job in the neighborhood in which they grew up. For them, travel to another town or region is out of the question.

In this total reorganization of society that Kim Il Sung wrought with amazing success, and relatively little terror compared to the wholesale purges of Stalin and Mao, today's privileged, educated class are the children of the precommunist working class, while those discriminated against are the former privileged and educated class and their descendants. Thus, North Korean leaders of Kim Il Sung's generation were not likely to have been educated beyond middle school, and their children—the leaders of today who have received a privileged education through college and a few through university—are a first-generation elite, schooled in Kimilsungism, with no family history of intellectual or professional achievement, untraveled and inexperienced in the ways of the world, owing everything to Kim Il Sung and his social revolution.

In this respect, the society that Kim created represents a significant break from traditional Korean society, where the privileged class, the scholar-officials, were a meritocratic elite who gained their positions through educational achievement. Talent was a necessary, although not always a sufficient, prerequisite for getting into the core elite. Influential family connections also helped to obtain high official positions but not to the same extent as in contemporary North Korea.

The new social system has created a tight, cohesive leadership, bound not only by an intense loyalty to Kim Il Sung and Kim Jong Il but also by lifetime bonds to one another. In North Korea, one lives in housing provided by a father's work unit, grows up with children of other fathers who work with one's father, goes to school with those children, takes vacations with them, and eventually goes to work with them in the same career for the rest of one's life. Sociologists who contend that the complexity of an individual's personality derives from the number of social groups to which an individual belongs could only conclude that the personality of most North Koreans is not that complex. They know fewer people in their lifetimes than the average person does in most other countries, and the people they know all share basically the same life experience in the same collective farm or factory or, in the case of the elite, in the same military ranks or foreign service or administrative work.

Another limiting feature of a class society based on *sŏngbun* is its effect on the morale of the people, both the privileged and underprivileged. One source, a defector interviewed by this author in 1980, had been given every advantage in life, schooled in the finest schools including Kim Il Sung University, trained for the Ministry of Foreign Affairs, and given overseas assignments. This defector, however, was preoccupied with the unfairness of a system that allowed his friends, sons of higher-ranking party officials like his father, to escape volunteer labor, vacation at seaside resorts, and obtain choice assignments abroad despite their poorer grades and oftentimes lack of motivation and hard work. It would seem that the system breeds discontent at all levels, except perhaps at the very highest level. Competent people constantly "find themselves working for people who are their inferiors in knowledge and intelligence. They see incompetent people, trusted by the party because of their good *sŏngbun*, getting ahead while the more competent are blocked from advancement on account of their *sŏngbun*. People may be secretly admired for their own worth despite their lower status in life, but being held in good repute by others is no substitute for being deemed politically reliable by the party."

In the final analysis, the system hurts more than just the people themselves. As one North Korean defector noted: "workers with a good family background neglect their work but are still promoted while workers with a poor family background do not work hard because there is no hope for promotion." Thus, among its other evils, the *sŏngbun* system is, by its very nature, antithetical to the industrialization process, which prospers when people are promoted on the basis of merit, rather than class background or ideology. The ever-widening economic disparity between North Korea and South Korea would seem to bear this out. The economic boom of South Korea, where much less importance is attached to class background and more emphasis is given to education and ability, has left North Korea far behind. In the North, where loyalty to Kim and a good family background are all that matter, ideological considerations have seriously interfered with good economic policy, and the results have been disastrous.

In short, Kim Il Sung managed nothing less than the complete remaking of the social structure without the terror associated with Stalin's and Mao's creation of communist societies in the Soviet Union and China, respectively. Kim's success in effecting fundamental social change was much greater than that of other communist regimes as a result of both the much smaller, more homogeneous population of North Korea, and also his particular skills. By any standard, he must be judged to have accomplished one of the most successful and intensely coercive social engineering feats of modern times.

The New Socialist Society

Kim Il Sung's vision of a new socialist North Korean society developed from ideas that influenced him during his 15 years with China's communists and later with Soviet military units in the 1930s and 1940s. The idea of centering life, including the provision of social services, around an individual's basic work or school unit was a revolutionary break with traditional Confucian thinking, which envisioned society as a great family living in perfect harmony, with each individual family being the primary social unit.

Many observers in the late 1940s and 1950s believed that Kim and his cohorts were out to destroy family life. There is enough evidence to convince some that the family is no longer the basic social unit of North Korea, that it has been supplanted by the work unit, which controls virtually every aspect of an individual's life. However, the family has proved remarkably resilient in North Korea, as in China and the republics of the former Soviet Union. It may be that the family never really was as threatened as many Western observers thought, because it is not at all clear that Kim intended to destroy family ties in his remaking of society. He seems to have planned to reinforce the bonds of family while constructing a new socialist command structure that would better ensure his control over every aspect of the people's lives, thinking perhaps that the two were not in conflict. The family remains strong in North Korea, despite the radical changes introduced by Kim Il Sung that limit the time that family members spend together.

The Work Unit as the Basic Social Unit

In North Korea, everyone over the age of six is a member of some sort of a unit outside the family. It can be the school one attends; the factory, collective farm, or government office where one works; or the military unit to which one is assigned. The unit provides housing, as well as food, clothing, and medical care. Normally, it is the father's work unit that provides housing for his family. Thus, wives and children do not usually live with the people they work with or go to school with, although some students, mainly those in college or at Kim Il Sung University, live on campus. With the exception of domestic chores, women and children perform all their daily tasks with their work or school unit.

People apply to the unit for permission to travel, to stay at out-of-town hotels, or to eat at public restaurants. It is the unit that authorizes vacation time and arranges for one's stay at government-owned vacation retreats. The individual must apply to the unit for permission to see a doctor or have an operation. If a person has saved enough money to buy a watch, bicycle, or other major consumer good, he or she must first get the unit's permission to make the purchase. He or she must also get its approval to marry. Finally, it is with fellow unit members that a person attends all party meetings, militia training, self-criticism sessions, morning and evening study sessions, and cultural events, such as concerts and museum visits, and social events, such as movies and dances and day trips to Kim's birthplace at Man'gyŏngdae or tourist sites in P'yŏngyang. The fact that a person can be tied to the same unit for years, sometimes for a lifetime, suggests the importance of personal relationships with others in the unit. It is easy to imagine the frustrations and unhappiness that people endure when those relations are not good and there is no hope of changing work units. The leader of the unit has a greater hold over a person than his or her spouse or parent when it comes to the everyday decisions discussed above, including some of the most important decisions of a lifetime, such as whom one will marry. It is also easy to see how the regime can control nearly every aspect of a person's life through the leader of his or her work unit, the individual who makes almost every decision affecting the lives of the people in that unit.

The totalitarian regime came into being with the division of the population into these socialist work units, a feat that Kim Il Sung accomplished soon after coming to power in 1946 with virtually no resistance and no use of force. This charismatic leader, who extolled traditional Confucian beliefs in filial piety, love of family, and loyalty to the state, disarmed many people. They were not well informed about communist doctrine and social organization.

The grouping of people into work units applies to all North Koreans from the age of six to 60 (for women) or 65 (for men), when they can retire. Thus, unless husbands and wives belong to the same work unit—a common occurrence—they do not share many of the experiences that families in other countries normally share. Nor do they do as much with their children as parents in other countries. For instance, children visit Kim's birthplace and museums in P'yŏngyang on outings arranged by their schools. They go to the theater and concerts with their classmates. Meanwhile, their parents go to these same events, at different times, in the company of fellow members of their work units. Tickets are distributed to members of a work unit as a group; they are not given separately to individuals or families at a time of their choosing. Thus, although family members may be exposed to many of the same experiences, they do not share these experiences with their parents or siblings.

Parents are much less directly involved than Western parents in other aspects of their children's upbringing, such as their education and medical care. Family vacations are very rare. Children see physicians assigned to their school; parents consult physicians assigned to their work units. School authorities, working with local party officials, arrange the volunteer labor schedules of students during vacation times, with little or no coordination with parents' volunteer labor schedules. Teachers accompany students to collective farms, where they help with rice transplanting and rice harvesting; parents are likely to be assigned to different collective farms for the same or different two-week stints of volunteer labor.

The only time that parents and children are regularly together after 7:30 to 8:30 AM and before 10:00 or 10:30 PM is on Sunday, the one family day in North Korea. Generally, families spend the day together at home, most often doing household chores or resting. They may go for a walk in the park or visit an amusement center or the zoo. Often one sees fathers out with their children on Sunday afternoons, while mothers are at home catching up on the week's laundry and cleaning. The more affluent might eat Sunday dinner at a local restaurant as a special treat, not a common occurrence, something they would probably do no more than a few times each year. There is a simple joy in being at home together as a family. Engaged in work, study sessions, self-criticism sessions, militia training, and other activities for most of their waking hours, six days a week, North Koreans long for leisure moments at home with their families. Women, especially those in the cities, are reported to especially resent the activities that keep them away from home in the evenings and separated from their children most of the week.

There is much in this description of family life in North Korea to suggest that the family is no longer the basic social unit of society, that it has been supplanted by the work unit, which controls nearly every aspect of an individual's life. At the same time, one of the distinguishing features about the North Korean leadership has been its strong familial aspects, including Kim Il Sung's blatant nepotism in giving his relatives high party and government posts and his even more extraordinary and eventually successful efforts in promoting his son as his successor, a Confucian rather than communist practice. Kim's sense of family was always central to his life and leadership. North Korean propaganda constantly stresses the importance of the family. Concerned that separating babies of only a few months of age from their working mothers and putting them in daytime nurseries—a practical solution to the pressing need to keep women in the workforce—might be interpreted as a move against the family, officials have been at pains to deny any such intention.

Some observers have suggested that the Kim cult, with Kim as the father figure, was meant to substitute for a sense of family—that of all North Koreans belonging to one big family, an old Confucian idea. Both Kim regimes have placed similarly high value on traditional ideas of close familial bonds together with loyalty to the state.

In short, Kim Il Sung does not appear to have viewed the work unit and family as competing social units. As he envisaged it, the work unit was the best way of providing equal services to the population and getting equal work from the people, a communist ideal that appealed to him. He probably did not see that goal as threatening the strong Korean sense of family, even though in practice it would mean much less time for the family to be together and a major loss in the family's control over decision making. One can conclude that family life and the prerogatives of the family have suffered, to the dismay of the people. But whatever discontent this has caused has certainly not lessened the people's strong feelings of family and may actually have fostered closer family ties as the one bulwark against the state's total control over people's lives. If the family is not the main social unit of current-day North Korean life, it is still people's primary love and refuge.

A Thought-Controlled Society

Childhood may be the only happy time in North Korea before the reality of life in a thought-controlled, totalitarian society sinks in. The KWP's control over every aspect of a person's life asserts itself in gradual steps, starting with membership in the Young Pioneer Corps, then the Kim Il Sung Socialist Youth League (see Glossary), and finally, for those who pass the test, the Korean Workers' Party (see Mass Organizations, ch. 4).

The one day that seems to stand out as the most exciting day of childhood is the day a boy or girl becomes a Young Pioneer between the ages of nine and 11. It marks the only gala celebration of a child's life up to that point, because birthdays are not celebrated in any special way. Children receive the Young Pioneer red scarves and buttons at a ceremony held at school and attended by their families, usually on a national holiday such as Kim Il Sung's birthday (April 15), Army Day (April 25), or National Day (September 9). Each new Young Pioneer receives presents from the family, such as a new pen, notebook, or school bag. These were the only gift-wrapped presents that one North Korean defector ever remembered receiving.

There are about 3 million Young Pioneers in North Korea. They can be seen everywhere in P'yŏngyang and other cities marching two by two in orderly fashion, usually singing, with the yellow epaulets on their bright blue uniforms and red scarves tied around their necks. They receive two hours of ideological training every day and give a full day of volunteer labor on Saturdays. These commitments are nothing compared to later demands on their time, when they become members of the Kim Il Sung Socialist Youth League between the ages of 14 and 16.

The political pressures of the adult world begin to engulf teenagers when they are 14 to 16 years old. If any one event can be singled out as marking the end of childhood, it is entry into the Kim Il Sung Socialist Youth League, which brings tremendous new pressures to conform, endless new requirements for work, study, self-criticism, dedication, and service to the state. The symbolism involved in giving up one's bright red Young Pioneer scarf in exchange for the much more somber league button seems to capture the mood exactly.

Entrance to the league is by examination, but it is not difficult, and almost everyone eventually passes it by the time he or she is 16 years old. There is no family celebration when a child joins the league, unlike entry into the Young Pioneer Corps. There is simply a meeting at school attended by the students and their teachers but not their families. Not knowing the changes that are in store for them, the new league members have no real sense of the significance of the event. Only when they look back, defectors say, can they appreciate entry into the league as the watershed in life that it really is.

Having by then completed primary school and moved on to middle school, most North Koreans have had a chance to observe the workings of *sŏngbun* in society. They have gained some insight into their own standing in the rigidly class-conscious society. At this point, some begin a lifetime of adjustment to the unhappy fact of having been born with bad *sŏngbun* and thereby deprived of any chance of great success in life, while others begin to relax in the comfortable feeling of having been lucky enough to be born with good *sŏngbun*.

Volunteer Labor

Everyone in North Korea older than 16 years of age is required to perform volunteer labor for the state. One of the criteria for KWP membership is the amount of volunteer labor one has done as a member of the Kim Il Sung Socialist Youth League. There is always pressure—throughout life—to do more than is required.

The USS Pueblo, *now a tourist attraction on the Taedong River in P'yŏngyang*
Courtesy Chosŏn *(P'yŏngyang), July 2005, 12*

Visitors to P'yŏngyang in the 1970s used to comment on the amazing construction activity late at night. They described huge construction sites of several city blocks in size, swarming with thousands of workers, poorly dressed, laboring for long hours into the night, the whole scene illuminated by a series of light bulbs strung up above. They understandably, but incorrectly, assumed that these were regular construction workers on the night shift, their shabby clothes and wan appearance suggesting their poor standard of living. In fact, as defectors later revealed, these were middle-school and college students, unused to hard labor and wearing their oldest clothes, performing their stint of volunteer labor. Apparently, there was a certain excitement about this kind of nighttime construction project in P'yŏngyang. Students enjoyed seeing friends whom they had not met for awhile. There was a kind of camaraderie and esprit de corps. Girls and boys were both there, so there was something of a party atmosphere. Students got extra credit for night volunteer labor, which improved the chances of their being accepted into the party. The work was not strenuous and required no special skills.

Certain projects are known to have been constructed by student rather than adult volunteers, who generally are recruited for larger projects. For instance, students, bused in for construction work during school vacations, built a new highway between Kaesŏng and Sinŭiju (see Special Economic Zones, ch. 3). It is more usual for student volunteer laborers to do most of the road repairs or excavation for new roads in North Korea, as distinct from road construction or more technically complex work. Students played a major role in the construction of three national monuments dedicated to Kim Il Sung on his seventieth birthday on April 15, 1982, and were reported to have been "inspired" by the thought of donating their labor to these projects.

Kim Il Sung Socialist Youth League officials are responsible for organizing student volunteer labor. They are told the number of laborers needed for each project, and they see to it that all students in their jurisdiction are assigned on an equitable basis.

Most volunteer labor is not as much fun as student projects in P'yŏngyang. People quickly tire of it, and after many years people become jaded about it. One defector described the volunteer labor he performed as a student in P'yŏngyang. He helped move heavy equipment on the roads, polished stone floors in newly constructed buildings, cleaned up after renovations, helped with the construction of a swimming pool, and helped farmers transplant rice in the spring and then harvest it in the late summer.

Almost all North Korean students in upper-middle school, high school, and college, as well as many adults, including members of military units, help with the spring planting and fall harvests. Schools are essentially closed during these periods, as are many offices and factories. People seem to dislike work on the farms most of all. Volunteer laborers camp out on the front porch of farmers' homes in crowded conditions. They generally receive inadequate food, certainly less than they are used to getting, and farmers find it difficult to put up with the people living temporarily in and around their homes. Sometimes the tension escalates into skirmishes.

Students are required to give 30 to 40 days of volunteer labor during the spring rice transplanting season, 15 to 20 days during the harvest, and an unspecified number of days during the monsoon season to repair flood damage. Additionally, they must perform other kinds of volunteer labor during their summer vacation, during winter break in December, and on school afternoons, including Saturday. This can easily add up to more than 150 days a year. In crises, such as droughts or floods, which were commonplace during North Korea's difficult years in the mid-1990s, students are mobilized for indefinite periods, putting in more than the average 150 days of work per year. Young men, who normally participate in a 60-day military training program during the summer, are exempt from volunteer labor at that time, but female students do volunteer labor during their summer break. All this adds to an incredible amount of volunteer labor per student per year. None of it is paid for, of course, so it is probably not accurately reflected in state statistics on national income.

According to defectors, most students probably would not object to volunteer labor if they did not have to do so much of it, especially so much rice transplanting. They all say there is too much work, and it takes too much time from studying. But they seem to accept volunteer labor as part of life. They only resent being asked to give so much and the unending pressure to give more. While the work itself may not be so bad, the pressure to do more is "unrelenting."

Political Study Sessions

In addition to obligatory volunteer labor, North Korean students and adults must participate in political study sessions three or four times a week and self-criticism meetings once a week. Study sessions are separate from academic studies, although the latter also include a strong ideological content. Generally, study sessions focus on contemporary issues and events. They may be devoted to the latest editorial in the party newspaper, *Nodong Shinmun* (Workers' Daily), the party line on the current economic situation, new directives from Kim Jong Il, or distilled current events in South Korea and other countries. There is continual study of Kim Il Sung's life and teachings, much of it repeating what students are taught in school. By the time they have graduated from college, most students have read all of Kim's works and have taken detailed notes on them.

Self-Criticism Meetings

Some of the most difficult moments of a person's life in North Korea are spent in self-criticism meetings, which begin with joining the Kim Il Sung Socialist Youth League and continue until life's end. In the 1960s, these meetings were held monthly, but in the early 1970s Kim Jong Il is reported to have advised his father, based on his own experience as a student, to make these meetings weekly instead of monthly and of shorter duration and to sanction criticism of less serious offenses, such as smoking and staying up too late, so as to lessen the pressure that built up between monthly meetings. Apparently, the pressure is somewhat less under the new system, although people dread these meetings.

Each school and work unit sets aside a particular afternoon or evening every week for criticism meetings, which consist of both self-criticism and criticism of others. According to a reliable source who endured many such sessions, it is a "terrifying thing to stand up in front of others and be criticized" and almost as upsetting to be under constant pressure to criticize others. People are encouraged to keep a notebook and write down all the things that they and their friends and neighbors have done wrong during the week. They use these notes as talking points in the criticism sessions.

There is a knack to surviving these sessions with minimum danger and minimum psychological stress. The knack is to join forces with friends and agree ahead of time on whom to criticize that day and for what. That person is not surprised, then, by the criticism of friends and is prepared to respond. The individual also learns the safer things to criticize and how to turn the discussion quickly to Kim's teachings on that subject. For instance, in criticizing oneself or others for staying up late, it is important to explain that such behavior not only makes one lazy and sleepy the next day but is suggestive of a bourgeois attitude. Then the wrongdoer can go on to cite Kim's warning against other kinds of bourgeois behavior, deflecting the focus of the criticism from his or her own transgression to a broader discussion of bourgeois behavior. The trick is in making oneself and others seem guilty but not dangerously so and, in the process, to score points by citing Kim Il Sung constantly.

According to Kim Jong Il's directives, everyone is supposed to speak at each meeting, either in self-criticism or in criticism of others, but this does not always happen owing to lack of time. The pressure mounts for anyone left out to speak at the next meeting. Sometimes, self-criticism sessions can get very tense, especially if political subjects are discussed. One student remembered a friend who never again spoke to another student who criticized him at length for skipping a political class.

By all accounts, criticism meetings are among the most dreaded moments of the week. As a way of blocking out the fear, one student said he never really listened during the meetings. His mind was always on other things. "Nothing [he] heard would have changed [his] mind about anyone anyway," knowing it all to be so fake.

So long as these sessions focus on basically unimportant behavior, they are not in themselves threatening. What is important to the regime is the behavior that people are persuaded to avoid for fear of being discovered and criticized. In this sense, criticism meetings are a very effective instrument of control. What keeps North Koreans in line is the knowledge that they are always being watched and reported on by their friends and neighbors, as well as security personnel. Criticism sessions establish that Orwellian climate of constant watchfulness in conditioning North Koreans, even as young students, to notice their fellow students and report on their behavior.

According to those who have lived in the system for years, criticism meetings have the effect of encouraging some of the worst human traits: a disregard for others' feelings, a willingness to use others to further one's own career, disloyalty, lying, moral superiority, and a super-critical attitude toward others. Remembering that these sessions begin when a student is only 14 to 16 years old, one can appreciate that young people are subjected to social and political pressures far beyond their capacity to handle. The maturity that is called for in walking the thin line between overzealous criticism of others, with the risk of losing friends, and a lackadaisical attitude, with the threat of party censure, is beyond the skill of most people of this age. Small wonder that childhood in North Korea ends abruptly with league membership and consequent exposure to the deadly business of self-criticism sessions.

The Elite Life in P'yŏngyang

The inequality of life under the *sŏngbun* system could not be more dramatically illustrated than in Kim Il Sung's building a "dream city" for the privileged elite that is off-limits to the rest of the population. In no other country is there such a striking difference between living in one city and living anyplace else in the entire country.

P'yŏngyang was reduced to rubble during the Korean War. Since then it has been rebuilt according to a design personally approved by Kim Il Sung. The streets, laid out in a north–south, east–west grid, give a well-ordered appearance, and its public buildings, which are on a grand scale, make it a monumental city. The elegant decor of its public buildings features terraced landscaping, illuminated fountains and statues, marble floors, high sculptured ceilings, mosaic wall decorations, plush red carpeting and oriental rugs, and exquisite imported crystal chandeliers.

North Korea's showcase capital of P'yŏngyang is not only atypical of the rest of the county but atypical of East Asia in general. The natural beauty of its parks and rivers, the grandeur of its public buildings and its wide, tree-lined avenues—all sparkling clean—and the careful control of the chosen few living there, creates an impression of a spacious, uncrowded Asian city. P'yŏngyang has been described by foreign visitors as one of the most beautiful cities they have ever seen. In winter, with snow on the ground, they have noted an eerie, frozen beauty somewhat suggestive of a Siberian city with its Russian-style architecture relieved by more modern buildings of graceful Korean design. In the spring and summer, one's impression is of flowers, willow trees, parkland, and rivers. Despite all this natural beauty, it strikes most foreigners as silent, remote, and unlike the vibrancy and liveliness of most other Asian cities. Its grandeur and attractiveness are not accompanied by what one would most expect to find in the capital of a country: a large population going about its business in a spontaneous, unprogrammed way. In P'yŏngyang everything is planned, never spontaneous. Its chosen population consists of the super-privileged—few in number and privileged beyond the ordinary North Korean's wildest imagination—who enjoy the "good life" by North Korean standards but the worst life, in world opinion, in terms of basic human rights.

A priority of Kim's in designing his dream city was to limit the size of its population. According to defectors, everyone wants to live in P'yŏngyang. There would be a mass movement of people into the city, were it not for the tight controls, with guards at every entry and registration required of all residents. To maintain its orderly, uncluttered appearance, bicycles and trucks are forbidden in major sections. There are no privately owned vehicles, so the only automobiles are those belonging to the government for official use. People travel by bus, trolley, or subway (see Transportation, ch. 3). The mere existence of a subway in P'yŏngyang, much less one with elaborate tile mosaics and crystal chandeliers, seems surreal in a country where most people walk to and from work and only the fortunate are bused to their factories.

In most of North Korea, men and women go to bathhouses of relatively primitive design two or three times a month. In P'yŏngyang, the privileged go to the Health and Recreation Center, open seven days a week, featuring a showcase gym, huge indoor swimming pool, and elaborate sauna facilities. They have the most modern hospital facilities, unheard of anywhere else in North Korea. The P'yŏngyang Maternity Hospital has a closed-circuit television system that allows visitors to talk with patients and see newborn babies in the nursery. A showcase nursery school, which caters to the sons and daughters of Ministry of Foreign Affairs officials, has a heated swimming pool, a fancy merry-go-round, an electric train, and a host of expensive tricycles. None of the other 60,000 childcare and kindergarten facilities in the country are equipped in such a way. Some 10,000 privileged children, ages eight to 16, go to the P'yŏngyang Children's Palace, a huge complex of four buildings containing more than 500 rooms, with an assembly hall seating 1,200. The Children's Palace offers courses in music, dance, martial arts, science, mechanics, gymnastics, painting, and sculpture, as well as an assortment of sports activities. One Westerner observed that the three grand pianos in one room would have been "unavailable to any student in his country without a master's degree in pianoforte." Most foreign visitors are genuinely impressed with the technical proficiency of the students studying ballet and violin. In the evening, these youngsters

Propaganda poster showing representatives of the army, industry, women, and intellectuals. In the background is the national seal of the Democratic People's Republic of Korea. The caption reads: "Let us sacrifice for our fatherland as a citizen armed with strong consciousness."
Courtesy Chosŏn Yaesul *(P'yŏngyang), January 2003, 47*

공민적자각을안고조국을위해헌신해

put on musical shows for foreign visitors, such as the one U.S. Secretary of State Madeleine Albright attended in 2000. A permanent staff of 500 full-time teachers and 1,000 part-time teachers direct the activities at the Children's Palace.

North Korea's concept of an after-school center for extracurricular activities was modeled on an expanded version of the Swiss experience. Kim Il Sung was especially proud of the Children's Palace. He used to visit it three or four times a year. He was there for the opening of the first elevator installed in a North Korean building.

The North Koreans instituted a novel system for ensuring that the privileged always enjoy the most modern conveniences. People are constantly moved in and out of apartments in P'yŏngyang as newer ones are built. Because apartment buildings are occupied by people working in the same office—in P'yŏngyang most likely a government ministry—they can be moved as a group. There is no disruption of social ties, as one's neighbors move on together into a new, higher-standard apartment building.

For North Koreans who have seen P'yŏngyang rebuilt from the ashes of the Korean War, there is genuine pride in the glory of the city. Kim Il Sung himself took great personal pride in P'yŏngyang. He considered it his "own creation," his "personal child." He was well aware of the importance of morale in a war-torn country, and he is reported to have designed it "to enhance the ego and morale of the whole nation." He loved the city and once said he would never risk its destruction. It is truly a dream city, in the sense that more than 88 percent of North Korea's population can only dream of living in this city of 2.9 million. Only the very apex of North Korean society enjoys its incomparable amenities.

The Privileged Life Beyond Money

In an effort to create the impression of a classless society, the North Korean government likes to cite statistics on income to support its contention of great equality. However, money is not a good measure of privilege in North Korea, nor are the rationing system or any of the established rules and regulations. The system of privilege operates outside the established system of wages and rations and the normal distribution of goods and services.

Salary levels are particularly deceptive. The highest paid cabinet ministers, who earn around 250 wŏn (for value of the wŏn—see Glossary) per month, and professors at Kim Il Sung University and top artists and musicians, who earn around 200 wŏn a month, are paid only three to four times the wage of the average North Korean factory worker, who earns 60 to 90 wŏn per month. However, cabinet ministers and other high-ranking officials receive many extra benefits. They are entitled to free high-quality cigarettes, woolen clothes, and leather shoes. Ordinary citizens would not have access to special shops where these and other items, such as beef, pork, wine, liquor, candy, eggs, and anchovies, can be purchased at discount prices. There are different shops for different levels of the hierarchy so that people are not aware of what is available to others.

On important national occasions, high-level officials are given special gifts, such as imported color televisions, fountain pens, and wristwatches. They go to private showings of Western movies and have access to Western magazines and books, banned for ordinary North Koreans. They live in exclusive apartment buildings with elevators (instead of long walk-up stairways on the outside of the building) and have a living room, separate dining room, kitchen, bathroom, and two to four bedrooms. Their apartments are furnished with a color television, refrigerator, sewing machine, electric fan, and, in some cases, air conditioning, all of which are beyond the hope of the average citizen. Such officials are driven to work in chauffeured limousines.

The elite have other special services at their disposal, including prestigious medical facilities that dispense rare and expensive medicines, all free of charge. Most North Koreans would not even be aware of the existence of these medical clinics. There are special clubs for the elite that include bowling alleys and tennis courts, tennis being a game that most North Koreans have never seen. Among the luxurious government-owned retreats tucked away from public view, there are resorts on the beach at Wŏnsan and hillside villas in the mountains along the east coast that are sometimes used by visiting foreign dignitaries but otherwise are reserved for top party and government leaders.

Unlike his father, who spent the first half of his life as a guerrilla fighter in harsh conditions and who seemed to retain a taste for the simpler life, Kim Jong Il has been raised amidst privilege, given the best available education, finest clothes, good food, luxury automobiles, lavish vacation homes with swimming pools, tennis, land for horseback riding, and Western movies, of which he is a connoisseur. In P'yŏngyang he presumably lives in the large presidential mansion that was built for his father in the late 1970s. The house is reported to be a three-story building with a five-story presidential hall and a separate three-story conference and museum building. The complex has a moat on two sides and formal gardens and lawns, is set back from the street, cordoned off from normal traffic, and obscured from public view. No foreigner is known to have been taken there.

The average North Korean has no idea how Kim and his coterie live. The rarified lifestyle and hidden wealth are known only to the privileged few. The system has promoted an elitism that is the very antithesis of the communist notion of egalitarianism.

There is one area in which the elite have no special privilege: political freedom. As a person rises through the ranks to the top leadership, more, rather than less, is expected in terms of political obeisance to the Kim cult. As the individual has more to lose in a fall from power, he or she is naturally disinclined to jeopardize a career by a less than fulsome show of fidelity. Thus, one finds the most exaggerated worship of the cult at the upper levels of the government. The ambassador in an embassy is likely to be the most fanatical observer of the cult. Such fidelity may not be his true feeling, but it is the price of survival. He is likely to set the example in terms of long hours of studying Kim's teachings and participation in criticism sessions. Ministry of Foreign Affairs personnel are routinely brought home for a month's political reindoctrination every two years. Their privileged status brings them no respite from constant political surveillance. No one escapes that.

Daily Life

Most North Koreans have no means of acquiring the prerogatives of privilege. They might have access to a television, refrigerator, and sewing machine in communal rooms in their factories or cooperative farms. A lucky few might have a wristwatch or a bicycle that was won as a result of an economic competition within their factory or office. Whatever their income, they are unable to buy more than their allotment of basic foodstuffs, such as rice, corn, and sugar, all of which are rationed. And, in contrast to the privileged, who get their allotment of food grains in rice, ordinary citizens get a mixture of rice and other grains.

Certain benefits come without charge. Typical housing for the ordinary North Korean family is provided free of charge by the work unit. It consists of a living-dining room, one bedroom, a kitchen, and shared toilet facilities, regardless of the size of the family. Education and medical care also are free, but there is a significant difference between the medical and educational services provided for the privileged and nonprivileged. Access to automobiles and vacation retreats and exemption from volunteer labor are out of the question for the majority. Finally, and most importantly, the intangibles in life are not a matter of free choice. Ordinary citizens have no choice where they live, what job they do, where they can travel, or what they might be willing to give up to send their children to college.

Wages are a particularly misleading measure of equality in North Korea, appearing to indicate that the elite live only twice as well as ordinary North Korean working people and about three or four times as well as the lowest-paid unskilled workers. There is a salary range for each category of wage earners depending on the size and location of a factory, the nature of a person's job within the factory, and the seniority of an individual worker. A work-team rating system further adjusts wages on the basis of performance. Workers can be rewarded or penalized for such things as the care they take of equipment, the quality of their work, their initiative in solving production problems, and their safety record. The wage structure is basically modeled after that of the Soviet Union with a few adjustments.

Wages have no bearing on food consumption, basic work and school clothes, and other essential consumer goods that are dispersed through the government distribution system. Nor do they determine the level and kind of education and medical care, which are provided free of charge by the work or school unit in keeping with the *sŏngbun* system. Salaries can be thought of as something of a cross between wages as known in most of the world and children's allowances, which are given for extra expenditures above and beyond basic housing, food, clothing, education, and medical care provided by parents. North Koreans can spend their wages on extra food, clothing, cigarettes, haircuts, cosmetics, entertainment (dinner at a restaurant or the movies), or occasionally the purchase of a major item such as a wristwatch or bicycle, but only with permission from the work unit.

The limited role of money in the economy is reflected in the distortion between wages and prices, especially the price of nonessential goods that the regime wants to limit. A nylon sweater and two pairs of nylon stockings, considered nonessential luxury items, are priced at the average North Korean's monthly salary. The average daily wage of 2.5 wŏn would not cover the cost of one kilogram of peanuts, one meter of nylon cloth, one pair of nylon socks, or a pair of nylon stockings. It could buy one meter of cotton cloth, a toothbrush and toothpaste, one private bath in a bathhouse and a cake of soap, a haircut and styling, or a set of table tennis paddles and balls. There is simply no way that an average family could ever hope to save enough to buy a refrigerator (selling for 300 to 400 wŏn) or a black-and-white television (300 to 700 wŏn).

Until the late 1990s, one of the distinguishing features of the North Korean economy was the uniformity of prices of goods throughout the country, the similarity of goods and services available in urban and rural areas, and the provision of similar shopping facilities in different areas, in keeping with Kim Il Sung's intention to provide a basic equality in the system, with allowances for the people at the top but with enforced uniformity for all others. Kim used to boast that "any item sold in a North Korean 'daily necessity' store could be bought in the most remote area at the same price as in any other place." Since the famine of the mid-1990s, the emergence (with the regime's blessing) of local free markets outside the government's public distribution system has brought some disparity in prices throughout the country determined by economic forces of supply and demand in different locales. However, the regime continued to assert control over the distribution of more goods, especially food, as agricultural production had somewhat improved.

Neighborhoods

In building his new socialist society after the war, Kim was influenced by the Swedish experience of self-sufficient urban neighborhoods. For every block of living quarters for 5,000 to 6,000 inhabitants (administered as a unit called a *dong*), he created the same array of shops, typically on the first floor of a high-rise apartment building, including a food store supplying rice, vegetables, fish, and other foodstuffs and a barbershop, beauty parlor, tailor, public bathhouse, shoe-repair shop, fuel-supply depot, branch post office, medical clinic, children's nursery school, and library, all of which are run by the *dong* administrative committee. In rural areas, where there are fewer inhabitants, the same group of stores is provided for each county, the population of which would also be about 5,000 to 6,000 people. Wherever one travels in North Korea, including P'yŏngyang, one sees this same grouping of stores that Kim considered essential to everyday living.

The residents of each urban *dong* or each rural county (*gun* or *kun*) are expected, indeed forced, to shop in their neighborhood stores. They are registered to shop there and no place else. They cannot redeem their rice rations elsewhere. Each store can track the purchases of its registered customers; there is no need for coupons. If a family is going out to dinner at a restaurant, the neighborhood store can authorize the restaurant's purchase of so many grams of rice and deduct that amount from the family's running account.

Kim's neighborhood concept contributes to the overwhelming sense of uniformity about the country. Just as every place has the same prefabricated dining halls at factories, schools, and military installations, one sees the same group of stores, often in the same layout. The people are all exposed to essentially the same shopping experience, although in the larger cities there also are bookstores, photographic studios, flower shops, music stores, optical shops, sports equipment stores, and even pet stores for those who can afford them.

Consumer Goods and Services

In organizing North Korean society on a self-sufficient neighborhood concept, Kim avoided some of the commuting problems encountered by Soviet consumers who used to complain of having to walk long distances to shop. The difficulty associated with shopping in North Korea is occasioned by the fact that everyone shops at the same times: on the way home from work or during the midday break. There are no other times to shop because almost everyone is at work or attending school. Visitors to North Korea all attest to the emptiness of stores during the day except during these rush hours. North Koreans also must shop every day. Without refrigeration, most people have no means of keeping food fresh, especially in summer.

The regime has controlled the consumption of consumer goods and services through the rationing of basic foodstuffs, the direct distribution of essential work and school clothes, and tight control over the distribution of all other goods (including extra clothing and additional foods, basic necessities such as haircuts and bathing services, and nonessential items such as wristwatches and bicycles) through a system of artificially low wages and artificially high prices. While

Newly built traditional-style rural houses, Chagang Provin
Courtesy Kŭmsukangsan *(P'yŏngyang), June 2000, 4*

the price of basic necessities such as haircuts, public baths, subwa
fares, school supplies, and home fuel (wood and coal) is relativel
low, luxury items such as wool, finished clothing, electrical appli
ances, and imported items are priced exorbitantly, well above the
reach of most workers.

Diet

The system has effectively limited food consumption and in the
process had a significant impact on the birthrate. Most people simply
cannot afford to have more than two children, even with both parents
working. The average number of children per family, according to
2007 estimates, is two, low for an Asian country.

Kim envisaged the consumption of food based on the energy
required to do a job rather than the prestige of the job. Thus, a person's allotment of food grains does not necessarily parallel his or her
wages. Miners and ocean fishermen and others doing heavy work,
including the military, are allotted more grain than government and
party officials engaged in less strenuous physical activities. However, the privileged among the latter receive their grain allowance in
rice rather than a combination of food grains and are paid higher
wages, enabling them to buy more food and other consumer goods,
shop at special stores with discounted prices for luxury items not
available elsewhere, and receive a plethora of nonmonetary benefits,
including better housing, better medical care, and higher education.

The kind of rice—polished or unpolished—a North Korean is allotted under this system also is very important. North Koreans have a definite preference for rice over corn, barley, or wheat. Only high government and party officials enjoy polished rice. A cabinet minister who receives 700 grams of grain in the form of polished rice is considered much more favored than a blast-furnace operator who receives 900 grams of grain per day as 50 percent unpolished rice, 40 percent corn, and 10 percent wheat flour. Rations for children are considered generous compared to rations for adults. Thus, a family consisting of adults only is generally less well off in terms of. rationed food. It is a common occurrence for childless households to be short of grain well before the end of the month.

North Korean families receive grain rations only for members of the immediate family. When they have visiting guests or relatives or a wedding or funeral, they must ask their guests to bring their own rice rations.

The basic diet for most North Koreans is rice and vegetables, three times a day, with fruit occasionally (when in season), chicken two or three times a month, and red meat five or six times a year. Heavy on carbohydrates, low in fats, proteins, vitamins, and minerals, it is not a balanced or varied diet. According to defectors, the monotony of the same meal, three times a day, for long periods is a major source of dissatisfaction. Moreover, chronic malnutrition is a serious problem, as 27 percent of the population lives at or below the absolute poverty level.

After enjoying a steady improvement in their diet from the late 1950s through the 1970s, North Korean consumers must have been disappointed with the lack of progress in the 1980s through the mid-1990s. A dramatic improvement in food supplies in the late 1970s had engendered high hopes for continued progress. Instead, hopes were dashed by an actual decline in rice allotments, both in rural and urban areas, continued shortages of fresh fruits, meats (except poultry), fish, kimchi, cooking oils, cigarettes, and liquor. According to defectors, the decline in rice allotments was a major source of dissatisfaction. However, the worst was yet to come.

A Society in Crisis

North Korea's economy received a severe jolt with the collapse of the Soviet Union in 1991 and the cut-off of Soviet exports of oil and food at "friendship" (subsidized) prices. This shock led to the closing of factories and coal mines and resulted in power shortages. Then there was a decrease in Chinese exports of food, fertilizer, oil, and coking coal because of China's economic reforms. North Korea's agricultural production began to decline just as food imports also were

declining. Because of its inhospitable environment for crop production, the country had developed an agriculture that was highly dependent on a range of industrial inputs, particularly chemical fertilizers, insecticides, and electrically powered irrigation systems.

The government's public distribution system was beginning to fail as early as 1991; by 1994 it had totally collapsed in some localities (see Reform of the Public Distribution System, ch. 3). These problems were temporarily overshadowed in July 1994 by the unexpected death of Kim Il Sung, which left an exhausted population virtually paralyzed in a state of deep mourning. Then the country was hit by devastating floods, droughts, and famine in the mid-1990s (see Causes of the Famine; Effects of the Famine, ch. 3).

The famine took its greatest toll on such vulnerable groups as children and the elderly. Older people reportedly were choosing not to eat so that others in their family might survive. The entire faculty of one school, except for two professors, was reported to have perished. Nineteen percent of one urban area reportedly died. The regime's harsh response to the crisis was to perform triage in cities in the north and east and to let the general population fend for itself. Proportionally high numbers of people died there. Starving North Koreans were told to stay inside when foreign humanitarian workers were in town so that the outside world would not know the extent of the disaster.

A major change in North Korean society can be traced to the tragic events of the mid-1990s. People, already worn out and weakened, became seriously demoralized, traumatized by having to decide which children to feed over others, and depressed over so many deaths in a family and in the country at large. Regime propaganda was replaced by a new brutality over the population associated in the people's minds with the ascent to power in 1994 of Kim Jong Il. The government distribution system continued to collapse as farmers' markets, operating on their own, diverted food from official channels in establishing the first glimmers of an unregulated commercial system. Out of necessity, households were forced to secure a larger share of their food from the new outlets, either farmers' markets or general markets in the cities or through informal barter exchanges. As the market has come to supply a greater and greater share of total consumption, a new divide has appeared in the society. On one side are those who are able to augment their wages with foreign exchange (in areas close to the border with China, on the east coast where foreign seafarers call, and in P'yŏngyang where the elite have contact with foreigners). On the other side are those who live on shrinking local currency wages with no access to foreign exchange or other income-earning opportunities. The latter, spending about 30 percent of their income on government-distributed food and another 30 percent on nonfood essentials, have only about 30 percent of their budgets to cover up to 50 percent or more of their caloric needs. Surveys suggest that these households spend up to 80 percent of their income on food. Some have managed to survive only by selling their possessions or establishing a sideline business, such as making and selling sweatshirts or selling homegrown vegetables.

The rise of a free market outside the centrally planned economy and the breakdown in the government food distribution system created a new economic competition in the population that did not exist when the government had tight control over the dispersal of all goods. It lessened the people's dependence on the regime, increased opportunities for individual initiative, and lessened the cult-like hold on the people's thinking that all good things come from Kim. It seems all but inevitable that the trauma and dislocations since the mid-1990s have increased dissatisfaction with the regime, whether admitted or not.

In the short space of seven years (1991–97), the country experienced more destabilizing change in its economy, political system, and society than since the Korean War. It was the worst economic decline in the twentieth century of a country not experiencing war, a decline that altered the nature of society and brought a response from the government that has included a new element of fear and indifference from a previously less draconian totalitarian regime.

As the famine intensified, thousands of people left home in search of food. Some took the much riskier step of fleeing across the border into China. The flood of refugees into China created a serious problem for the North Korean government in its relations with China, which has long tried to limit the influx of illegal North Koreans into Northeast China. Beijing periodically has cracked down with arrests and the forced repatriation of some 200,000 to 300,000 of the North Korean refugees who had sought refuge in China since the mid-1990s. Faced with the loss of control over starving people wandering away from home in search of food, the North Korean government responded by establishing a network of ad hoc prison-labor camps, detention centers characterized by extreme deprivation and torture, in which those caught fleeing to or returning from China were incarcerated for periods of up to six months (see Punishment and the Penal System, ch. 5).

A Militarized Society

North Korea is the world's most militarized society. For more than 50 years, the regime has allocated between 25 and 33 percent of its gross national product (GNP—see Glossary) to the military, supporting the 1.2 million-strong armed forces and reserve and paramilitary forces of 7.7 million (see Organization and Equipment of the Armed Forces, ch. 5). For most men and some women, military service follows middle school as a matter of course. Of the physically fit, only the privileged few (Kim Jong Il being one of the elite group who went from middle school to Kim Il Sung University without ever serving in the military) and those at the other extreme—with very bad *sŏngbun*—are exempt from military service. Most young men are anxious to join the military, if only to avoid the stigma that is attached to those who do not. For most, it offers the promise of a better future. At a minimum, it improves the chances of getting a better job after discharge. A sailor trained as a radio operator, for example, later might be assigned as the radio operator on a civilian fishing boat. Although one's career is essentially determined by one's *sŏngbun*, a young man's performance in the military service can alter the direction of his career within certain prescribed limits.

In a country that has traditionally placed people in precise categories or rankings within the society, the military ranks high in North Korea. Parents are proud to have their sons in the army, and for soldiers there is the psychic boost of being a member of a privileged group. Practically every family has at least one member on active duty, in the reserves, or retired from the military. There is a close association between the population and the defense establishment because of the military's constant assistance to the civilian population in nonmilitary ways, such as road construction, industrial construction, civil engineering projects, and rice planting and harvesting (see Reserve Forces, ch. 5). A major drawback of military service is the long separation of sons from their families. Most young men do not see their parents during their entire enlistment. Most are not granted leave, even in times of family crisis, such as the death of a parent. This prolonged absence is a major source of discontent in the military ranks and a major sorrow for parents.

From a sociological viewpoint, the importance of the military's extensive interaction with the civilian economy, especially in farming activities, is its reinforcement of the sameness of life. Service in the military is not an escape from an otherwise inevitable round of rural drudgery. For some who grew up in cities, it is an introduction—more than they might want—to life on a collective farm. Military service offers no escape from political study, either. If anything, soldiers are subjected to more intensive political indoctrination than civilians. They attend classes at least three days a week and self-criticism sessions at least once a week. Political meetings held to launch major campaigns have been known to last 24 hours and to degrade unit readiness as a result of sleep deprivation. Foreigners have noted how tired North Korean troops appear.

In years of economic collapse, the government distributed international food aid mainly to the military and the elite class in P'yŏngyang. Thus, the political and military elite have had a variety of channels for acquiring food not available to the general population. These include the "first draw" on the domestic harvest, access to grains and other foods sold on the domestic market through privileged access to foreign exchange, and direct access to imports from China and South Korea and other international food aid that the government distributes through what is left of the centralized food distribution system. Compared to the rest of society, which was left to fend for itself at the height of the famine, the military has fared well in terrible times.

Family Life

With most able-bodied young men in the military, except for the elite few in college, it is not surprising that foreigners inevitably remark on the conspicuous absence of young men in the workplace. Farmers are either women or old men. Most of the workers at factories, especially textile factories, also are women. According to North Korean statistics, women account for more than 50 percent of the total workforce but probably as much as 90 percent of the civilian labor force between the ages of 16 and 30. This statistic represents nothing less than a social revolution in an Asian country where fewer than 5 percent of industrial workers were women in traditional, precommunist times. The role of women changed dramatically and quickly in the early 1950s from the traditional role of full-time housewife and mother to full-time worker, in addition to wife and mother.

Another major change has been the increase in women's education. Women may well account for almost two-thirds of college students. Graduates of teachers' colleges and medical schools are almost all women; most men of the same age are in the military. The reliance on women in the workplace is a necessity in a nation with 20 percent of its male population and almost all its young men between the ages of ages 17 to 30 serving in the military.

Although they compete favorably with men at the low and middle levels, few women have risen to top management positions in fields other than teaching and medicine (except for women athletes and artists). Women dominate the KWP in terms of overall membership and offices held at lower levels but are poorly represented at higher levels. For instance, women hold the majority of party committee jobs at the factory and neighborhood levels but hold a far lower proportion of party jobs at the city and county levels and even fewer posts at the provincial and national levels. The same is true of women in government. Whereas they are very active at lower levels, such as on election committees, women hold relatively few higher-level government posts.

In traditional times, women married in their late teens and early twenties; often their bridegrooms were even younger. Today laws prohibit marriage of women younger than 27 and men younger than 30. Were it not for these laws, which are strictly enforced, there would be a large age differential between husbands and wives as a result of young men's long service in the military.

Kim Il Sung held fast to traditional ideas of courtship and marriage. Arranged marriages are still very much accepted in North Korea and apparently preferred. As in traditional times, young men and women have little or no dating or courtship experience prior to marriage. Western notions of courtship and marriage now accepted in South Korea, China, and other Asian nations would be viewed by most North Koreans as a corruption of traditional values rather than a release from outmoded strictures.

It is not arranged marriages or the limitations on premarital social life that are so much hated as the laws against early marriage. Most young women have finished middle school and started to work by the time they are 16; they have to wait another 11 years before they can marry. Young men are a decade older by the time they have finished military service. The enforcement of late marriages has had the effect of controlling the birthrate, whether or not that was the major reason for the state's ban on early marriages.

In the changed social times of today, males and females study in coeducational schools at all levels (including college and Kim Il Sung University) and work together in factories and offices and on the farms. There are inevitable pressures on young people thrown together in everyday life but prohibited from marrying until they are in their late twenties. There is little information about how young people cope with these pressures. According to defectors, it is not a subject that North Koreans discuss even with their closest friends. It would seem that they simply accept traditional values reinforced by the regime's need for a large military.

Foreigners who have visited both North Korea and China are invariably struck by the contrast between the familiar scene in China of young couples strolling together in parks and the absence of any such sight in North Korea. Occasionally, pairs of young women or young men can be seen walking alone but never a male-female couple. Usually, young people are seen in groups of three or more. They do not get closer to each other than an arm's length. The most they would do is sit down for a few moments to talk confidentially. Not even married couples walk arm in arm; there are no public displays of affection. Unmarried men and women would never dare to hold hands in public.

At school, young men and women have friendships, even romantic friendships, but sexual relations are taboo. Both the man and the woman would be risking the standing of their family as well as their own future and career. Special friendships are acknowledged in the exchange of notes or love letters, but private meetings are rare. Illicit sex is a serious offense, and strict punishment is meted out. It is grounds for dismissal from school, expulsion from political organizations, and sometimes discharge from the military. If a woman becomes pregnant out of wedlock, an abortion can be performed up to five months. Illegitimate children are very rare. When such a baby is born, it falls under the care of the state. The mother must surrender the child to the authorities, who are given full responsibility in deciding what is best for the child. This is in keeping with the state's attitude toward the custody of children in divorce cases, where again the authorities give little weight to parental rights compared to their view of the best interests of the children.

In short, there is simply no place for young couples seeking private moments together, except possibly at the movies. This situation explains why some people still go to the movies despite the tedious nature of the regime-scripted stories. There are no bars, dance halls, discos, or coffeehouses. What is left for those who establish romantic friendships at school are a few shared private moments together after class, after criticism sessions, or during volunteer labor stints. Even a walk together in the park or in the countryside is accompanied by risk and requires great care. Students are constantly on their guard, knowing full well that their behavior with members of the opposite sex is a prime topic for self-criticism sessions. Social behavior in this and other areas is self-regulated through the control mechanism of endless self-criticism sessions.

Whatever secret friendships they may make, young people know that eventually they will marry someone with a similar background selected by their parents and approved by the KWP. The tradition of arranged marriages has served the regime's purposes well for various reasons, but the overwhelming criterion has always been *sŏngbun*. The system tends to preserve the purity of the privileged class, keeping it free of less desirable elements. Those with bad *sŏngbun* have no choice but to marry others of the same background.

Women tilling the soil, January 2006
Courtesy Kathi Zellweger, Caritas–Hong Kong

Whereas in precommunist days, a go-between oversaw the negotiations between the two families, today the party acts as the go-between. Personal records, kept by the KWP secretary of each factory, collective farm, or government agency, provide the necessary information to match couples of similar background. Permission from the party is absolutely required. Because the husband's or wife's place of work has to provide accommodations, a couple cannot live together without the party's approval.

People can ask for the party's permission to marry, or they can leave the choice of a marriage partner to the KWP entirely. Interestingly, the better a person's *sŏngbun*, the more likely he or she is to rely on the party. It is easier to accept the party's verdict if one is thereby assured of a good career. At the lower end of the social spectrum, collective-farm workers, miners, and unskilled factory workers, whose careers are not likely to be significantly affected by their choice of a spouse, seem to play a greater role in the selection of their marriage partners. The regime is mindful of this natural selection process in assigning young men, newly discharged from the military, to collective farms and factories where there are extra single women. Apparently, some are temporarily assigned to textile factories, where most of the workers are women, where they can meet single women. Later, after they have married, they are transferred to other jobs.

The society is still characterized by the traditional tendency of families to remain in the same general area where their ancestors lived for generations. Marriages between people from different geographical areas are discouraged. Marriages between urban males and rural females are particularly discouraged as a means of limiting migration into the cities. Children of collective farmers have little chance of moving out of the countryside into the cities, unless they truly excel in school and are given the rare opportunity of a higher education, with the possibility of a job in the city.

The state's downplaying of the wedding ceremony has been one of the most obvious social changes in North Korea, considering the elaborate weddings that traditionally involved costly ceremonies, feasts, and gift exchanges between the two families. The regime has outlawed all such costly, showy weddings, primarily for economic reasons but perhaps also because of the tradition of simple weddings that Kim Il Sung and his anti-Japanese guerrillas established. Typically, the ceremony is held at home, with a small reception afterward at home or at a restaurant. Most weddings are held on Sundays or holidays because those are the only times that people are not working. The wedding ceremony itself is rather perfunctory. The bride and groom simply bow to a picture of Kim, in a communist update of the traditional bow to the bride's and groom's parents. Then they kiss each other briefly, a North Korean couple's only public kiss. The presiding official—a work-unit or party functionary—gives a congratulatory speech. There is no exchange of wedding rings or other jewelry. The bride keeps her maiden name. Children take their father's name.

Although simple by traditional standards, wedding receptions are nonetheless joyous occasions for North Koreans, offering, as they do, one of the few opportunities to indulge in eating, drinking, and singing. Only for a wedding can North Koreans buy special quantities of wine, rice cookies, and cakes. The major constraint on the number of guests is the amount of food and liquor that can be provided. Usually relatives living nearby and a few close friends of the bride and groom, including their supervisors, will be invited. A couple is authorized a skirt and jacket for the bride, a new suit for the groom, and a set of bedclothes. A special touch at weddings is the taking of pictures. This is probably the only occasion when ordinary North Koreans are photographed, but many families are not able to afford the services of a photographer.

Honeymoons are out of the question. A newlywed couple typically takes three or four days off from work on paid vacation. They may not be able to live together for several months, perhaps even for a year or more. They must wait to be assigned housing by the husband's place of work, although they might live at one or the other's parents' home in the interim.

Defectors have reported many unhappy marriages in North Korea. Whether this is because they were arranged marriages or not, most marriages reflect the stress and strain of a life where both spouses leave home early in the morning, return home late at night, eat supper, and go to bed. They have very little time together and almost no time for leisurely activities. There is minimal prospect of divorce and almost no chance for extramarital romance. Adulterous relationships are dangerous. If discovered, they result in job demotion and expulsion from the party. Only the elite are thought to be immune from the party's swift and inexorable punishment, and even they must be careful. According to one defector: "Everyone works together and knows where everyone else should be. People are missed at once if they do not go home after work. Besides, the working hours are so long that there is no time or energy left over."

The stability of the family is reinforced by attitudes toward divorce. As in traditional times, marriage in North Korea is still viewed as an alliance between families, suggesting something much more permanent than the union of two people. Marriage as an institution has been idealized by the regime, and divorce is criticized. Divorce is another area in which the regime's attitude has reinforced traditional values. In actual practice, it is very difficult to get a divorce. For one thing, it is difficult to get permission to travel in order to institute legal proceedings; divorce application fees are high; and one has to get the party's approval to seek a divorce. Divorce is harmful to one's career, so most people in high positions are deterred from seeking a divorce. At a minimum, it would ruin the chances for advancement; more likely, it would result in a demotion. The fear of losing one's children is another serious deterrent to divorce. For all these reasons, divorce is a rare occurrence.

Women continue to work after they marry as a matter of course. Almost all able-bodied women work until retirement at age 60. Under the banner of full equality between the sexes, the regime has forced a totally new lifestyle on North Korean women, who have had absolutely no choice in the matter. Social equality with men has meant only a more difficult life for women, with many hours devoted to hard work on the job and additional hours devoted to political study and volunteer labor, plus all the traditional responsibilities of home and children.

Women may be the most dissatisfied people in the society. Their major complaints are reported to be the lack of help at home, too little time with their children, and too much time in political study. There are also feelings of job discrimination in the assignment of women to the more menial jobs after a limited education. Women are not spared from heavy work, either. Almost half of the stevedores observed at the port of Namp'o appear to be women; other women have worked as rock drillers and workers in fish-processing plants in temperatures well below freezing. The long years that men have to spend in the military have forced women into these physically demanding and dangerous jobs.

Women, as well as men, are enormously overworked. For women, the day begins earlier and ends later than it does for men. In rural areas and urban areas without indoor plumbing, working wives and mothers rise early to fetch water from a centralized location. They, like men, must be at work by 8:00 AM. Morning exercise music blares over loudspeakers, and participation in morning exercise drills, although voluntary, is encouraged. Young children are dropped off at nurseries or kindergartens on the way to work. All across North Korea, from 8:00 to 9:00 in the morning workers are in political study meetings under the direction of a party official. This is the time set aside for study of the day's editorial in *Nodong Shinmun* and for new party and government policies and decisions to be relayed to the people. Toward the end of the hour, office directors and plant managers lead a discussion of work plans for the day. Work starts at 9:00 AM and continues until 1:00 PM, with a short break for exercises. After a long midday rest period, during which many people take a nap, work continues until around 8:00 in the evening, after which study sessions and self-criticism meetings are conducted until 10:00 PM. On the way home, mothers pick up their children at the nurseries and then stop at the central kitchen in their neighborhood or on their collective farm to pick up cooked rice for dinner. Older children are at home waiting, usually sleeping or doing their homework or housework. There is an unchanging regularity about people's lives, six days a week, 52 weeks a year.

Children

The time North Koreans spend with their families may be limited, but that time is treasured and engenders feelings that are intense. From all available evidence, parents dote on their children no less than parents anywhere else in the world. In fact, if anything, they seem to live for their children, perhaps because their own lives offer little but hope for a better future for their children. Parents make sacrifices gladly, saving as much as they can all during their lives to secure the best for their children.

Just as in traditional times, North Koreans grow up today with a strong sense of loyalty to both their parents and the state. Children are taught to love and respect their parents in the traditional Asian way. The regime does nothing to distort those natural family feelings. Its concern has been to incorporate such feelings into a broader love for Kim Il Sung and the state.

Kim is portrayed in official regime propaganda not only as a fatherly figure but also as a model son. A 1980 article entitled "Kim Il Sung Termed Model for Revering Elders" tells how he warmed his mother's cold hands with his own breath after she returned from work each day in the winter and gave up the pleasure of playing on a swing because it tore his pants, which his mother then had to mend. "When his parents or elders called him," said the article, "he arose from his spot at once no matter how much fun he had been having, answered 'yes' and then ran to them, bowed his head and waited for what they were going to say." According to Kim himself, "Communists love their parents, wives, children, and their fellow comrades, respect the elderly, live frugal lives and always maintain a humble mien." Kim Jong Il is also described as a filial son. When he was five years old, a propagandist wrote, he insisted on personally guarding his father from evil imperialists with a little wooden rifle.

Love of children has become a national dogma, following the example set by Kim Il Sung, who easily surpassed even the most consummate Western politicians in his seemingly endless joy in kissing babies and hugging young children. He visited state nurseries constantly. He referred to the children of North Korea as the "kings and queens" of the country, the "hope of the future." He seemed genuinely to delight in young children. It was part of his personality and appeal, and it captured the North Korean spirit and attitude perfectly.

Children in North Korea are showered with material things, such as toys and games, to the limit of their parents' and the state's ability to provide them. An example of this is the fancy equipment—playground equipment, sports equipment, and musical instruments—on which state nurseries spend an inordinate amount of money.

North Korean children attend nursery school from the age of four months, if not earlier. There are day nurseries in every village, large cooperative farm, or major workshop, where the children go home every evening with their parents. There are three-day nurseries at the county level, where the children go home on Wednesday evening and again on Saturday through Sunday. And there are weekly boarding nurseries in P'yŏngyang and other big cities, where the children either go home on weekends or live permanently while their parents are serving abroad. The equipment, routine, and teaching at nursery schools are supposedly standardized, although this is doubtful in practice. All nurseries provide the same comprehensive care, including medical checkups by physicians or nurses and regular haircuts and shampoos by barbers. Thus, parents are freed from many of the routine child-care chores that would otherwise keep a mother from work.

Children are taught discipline and love for the state and their parents from the earliest age. They are taught that Kim is the source of everything good and that they should love, honor, and obey him. They are taught respect for their elders, which is expressed in the traditional custom of children bowing to their parents, teachers, and others in authority. Informed observers of societies in both China and North Korea have noted that authority relationships between children and adults in North Korea are, if anything, even more structured than in China. The good manners and discipline learned at an early age tend to become reflex action that North Korean defectors actually find difficult to abandon later, in adjusting to life in another country. Classroom discipline is very tight, and the role of the teacher is supreme. Spanking children, as a form of discipline by teachers, is forbidden. Violations of school discipline, such as not paying attention in class or leaving the school grounds, are quickly addressed. First, the school notifies the parents. If the student does not quickly improve, his or her ration is cut. At this point, the *sŏngbun* of both the student and the parents has slipped several notches.

Despite their disciplined behavior learned early on, there is a lively, high-spirited, self-confident attitude in North Korean children that foreigners immediately notice. It is possible that this is partly the result of the regime's constant reiteration of Kim Il Sung's *chuch'e* philosophy, basically a mind-over-matter view of the world in which all things are possible if people work hard enough to achieve them, in which slogans such as "We have nothing to envy in the world," do have a positive, reassuring effect.

North Korean children spend relatively few hours at home with their families; however, children are with other children at a younger age and for longer periods of time than in most contemporary societies. Presumably, they are more used to a group environment than the average American child of the same age. They are taught a variety of skills at a very early age—singing, dancing, athletics, and instrumental music—which may rank as one of the regime's major social accomplishments. Foreigners are often amazed at the musical and gymnastic abilities of young North Korean children who perform in these areas with great poise, self-confidence, and maturity. The "happy smiling faces" of children seem to be in stark contrast to the "grim, unsmiling expression" on the face of North Korean adults

Chuch'e Tower, built in 1982 on the bank of the Taedong River, commemorates Kim Il Sung's seventieth birthday; the design is attributed to Kim Jong Il.
Courtesy Kathi Zellweger, Caritas–Hong Kong

with whom foreign visitors come in contact. Compared to later life, childhood is a happy time.

Leisure Activities

With their days filled with work or school, volunteer labor, political study, and self-criticism meetings, North Koreans have precious little time to spend by themselves, with their friends, or at home with family. Essentially, they have Saturday evenings and Sundays free. The regime, which advocates that people ought to "do away with the slightest indolence and relaxation in life and work and live with revolutionary morale," provides little in the way of recreational facilities, except for movie theaters, city parks, some amusement centers, and sports events. Public restaurants are generally beyond a family's budget, and there are no coffeehouses, bars, or cabarets. Young people might have ice skates or simple fishing equipment. Otherwise, their only recreational equipment is likely to be a soccer ball, basketball, volleyball, or table tennis paddles. Table tennis is played on concrete tables permanently installed throughout North Korea in public places such as school playgrounds and city parks.

113

North Koreans are sports minded, almost to the point of obsession. Students are required to participate in after-school sports as an extension of their normal school day. Most schools offer soccer, basketball, volleyball, handball, table tennis, boxing, gymnastics, and track. Kim Jong Il is reported to enjoy tennis and horseback riding, both sports unavailable to the general population.

There is great interest in the national competition among North Korea's professional sports teams, especially the men's soccer teams. Often, the games are televised. Popular interest in spectator sports is one of the main escapes from the political pressures of life.

Movies are inexpensive but are not popular because all are North Korean–made films with a predictable propaganda theme. A typical story line involves a Korean family split apart by the Korean War, some family members in the North having a bright and happy existence and those living in the South having tormented lives. At the end, the family is always reunited at the glorious day of reunification, and the movie ends with homage to Kim Il Sung. People quickly tire of the story line and go to see only those movies that feature their favorite movie stars.

The circus is a popular recreation. A resident circus in P'yŏngyang performs year-round, featuring acrobatic acts and magic tricks. Visiting foreigners are uniformly impressed with the skills of the performers. Students in other parts of the country are bused to P'yŏngyang to see the circus, as well as museums and other national institutions. Field trips to P'yŏngyang are part of every North Korean's education.

An amusement of young people the world over—pets—are not a part of North Korean lifestyle. Dogs and cats are thought of not as pets but as food. They are not kept inside as house pets and are not allowed in cities, including P'yŏngyang. The only pets in cities are birds and aquarium fish, both of which can be bought at local pet stores. They are quite popular but expensive. Only the privileged can afford to buy birds, usually canaries.

The major recreation at home and at school seems to be card playing, traditionally a favorite pastime. There are no organized dances or concerts for students, and they appear to spend little time reading for pleasure. Outside of Kim Il Sung's collected works, school textbooks, and official propaganda, no other books are available. Virtually no works of Western origin have been printed in the country, and few appear to have been smuggled into the country until recently. The only news of the outside world getting into North Korea are the occasional books smuggled in from China and illicit radio broadcasts received by the few radios brought in from China. No literary underground has developed as it did in the Soviet Union, and there are no well-known underground dissident writers. The inadequate lighting in homes and schools effectively rules out reading at night.

Reports of North Koreans huddled around radios smuggled in from China listening to British Broadcasting Corporation and Voice of America broadcasts offer the first hint of news of the outside world reaching North Korean citizens. Videos of taboo Western movies, which also have been smuggled in from China, apparently have reached a limited number of people who put themselves at great risk in watching them. These first glimmers of an underground secret society represent the first sign of a crack—a very small one indeed—in the regime's hitherto successful block of all outside news. Although North Korea launched its first e-mail service in 2001, Internet access is severely restricted.

Religion

Article 68 of the constitution grants freedom of religious belief and guarantees the right to construct buildings for religious use and religious ceremonies (see The Constitutional Framework, ch. 4). Although it may nominally provide for freedom of religious belief, in practice the government not only prohibits organized religious activity but also persecutes religious believers. Many observers agree that the official religion is the cult of Kim. The cult provides a religious fervor in an atheist state that in reality outlaws all religious beliefs and practices. Semireligious aspects of the cult include the making of Kim Il Sung's birthplace into a shrine for worshiping Kim. The religious mystique of his life includes an association with Mount Paektu, the "holy mountain of revolution," where Kim Il Sung lived in hiding during the war years and where his son Kim Jong Il is supposed to have been born, according to legend (not true), a mountain that has always been revered as the mystical place of origin of the Korean people. In North Korean embassies abroad, in most factories and homes, and in many schools, there are little rooms set aside as chapels for worshiping Kim. Kim Il Sung's picture hangs beside lighted candles. Most North Koreans begin and end their day with a bow to Kim's portrait. These semireligious devotions to a national leader who has assumed the status of a demigod constitute the official and only "religion" allowed in North Korea.

In the early 1900s, P'yŏngyang was the center of a very active Protestant missionary effort in Korea. Kim Il Sung's parents and grandfather were Christians who went to church regularly when they lived in P'yŏngyang and later when they moved to Manchuria. However, the missionaries' efforts are not visible now. There are no openly professed Christians in North Korea today—such an admission could be reason for imprisonment—and Christian mission centers have long since disappeared. Officials claim that U.S. bombs destroyed every single Christian church during the Korean War. Old customs based on both Eastern and Western religious beliefs persist, such as dressing the dead in new clothing and placing them in coffins for burial. However, religious believers, such as the families of people who defected to South Korea after the war and the old elite class, are regarded as members of the "disloyal" class, "enemies of the state" who can be imprisoned for that reason alone. Churches are regarded as symbols of imperialist oppression. Defectors report that even in the privacy of the family, North Koreans are afraid to profess a belief in God.

A 1992 defector, a North Korean table tennis champion who, at age 18, was the youngest political prisoner at the prison camp where he was imprisoned for walking across a frozen river into China on the spur of the moment "out of curiosity" after skiing down Mount Paektu at a ski resort used by the sons and daughters of high officials, was emphatic on the subject:

> When Billy Graham visited North Korea, he said Christianity is reviving. I'll tell you the real story of religious life in North Korea. There's absolutely no religion in North Korea. I saw so many people in camp who came in because of religious belief. Even secretly praying is enough to get you sent to camp. Probably everyone in North Korea who is a religious believer is sent to a camp. I want to write a letter to Billy Graham: 'If you really want to know religion in North Korea, go to a prison camp.' When Billy Graham went to a church service, he should have asked people in the congregation to recite Bible verses.

The people who attended the staged religious services for Billy Graham and other visiting dignitaries are presumed to have been acting out their roles as devout worshipers. They do not attend church regularly, only when the regime has foreign dignitaries to impress.

Only those born before 1950 would have any recollection of the old religious beliefs and practices. As Lee Sang-tae, a member of the Central Committee of the General League of Writers, explained, when asked if the use of gigantic choirs in *Song of Paradise* and other North Korean "revolutionary" musical extravaganzas traced back to church music brought in by Western missionaries: "Absolutely not. We have had no such influence from the missionaries. We developed our songs based on our traditional heritage. Before liberation, we had religions—Buddhism, Christianity—but after liberation the influence of these disappeared." Lee spoke for the new generation, Kim Jong Il's generation, to whom the religious beliefs of their parents have clearly not been passed on. Therein lies a significant difference between Kim Il Sung and Kim Jong Il. Whereas Kim the elder could remember attending church and even playing the organ at church services and would have had a clear memory of his parents' and grandparents' religious devotions, Kim Jong Il has no such heritage. He knew his father as a man who had by then renounced Christian doctrine, who claimed that he was "not affected by religion" despite his youthful connections with the church, and who founded an atheist state with his self-worship substituted for God.

A December 1980 editorial in *Nodong Shinmun* explicitly elevated the cult to a national religion, inviting foreigners to join. In a direct challenge to the Christian faith, which reportedly has some 14,000 adherents, and a brazen attempt to replace the father/son of the Christian trinity with the Kim father/son deity, the editorial proclaimed: "People of the world, if you are looking for miracles, come to Korea! Christians, do not go to Jerusalem. Come rather to Korea. Do not believe in God. Believe in the great man."

Former Buddhist temples, which apparently survived the war because of their remote location in mountainous areas, are considered cultural relics rather than active places of worship and have been taken over by the state and converted to secular use. Those at Mount Kŭmgang and Mount Mohyang, for example, are considered national treasures and have been preserved and restored. The latter features an academy for Buddhist studies. Some 10,000 practicing Buddhists reportedly exist in North Korea. Two churches, the Protestant Pongsu Church and Catholic Changchung Cathedral, were opened in P'yŏngyang in 1988, just in time for the World Festival of Youth and Students the following year and obviously to provide the illusion of freedom of religion to foreigners attending the festival. At the Pongsu Church on a Sunday during the festival, worshipers sang "Jesus Loves Me" in Korean. According to Bradley K. Martin, an American journalist and author of *Under the Loving Care of the Fatherly Leader: North Korea and the Kim Dynasty*, who was there, "many of them appeared to know (the hymn) by heart." Martin noted that a pastor prayed "in the name of Jesus Christ" for the success of the festival, preached on a political theme—the need for removal of nuclear weapons from the peninsula, and prayed for Korean reunification. Martin also reported that church members and clergy were not KWP members and that they removed their Kim Il Sung badges while in church. He was told that Protestants who did not attend the Pongsu Church worshipped at home but that it was rare, in either instance, to see anyone under the age of 40.

Another American correspondent in P'yŏngyang to attend the youth festival visited the newly opened Catholic church and noticed churchgoers depositing their Kim Il Sung badges in a bowl as they entered. The priest, as it turned out, drove a Mercedes and made more money than the highest-ranking party member the journalist had been allowed to meet, a sure sign that he was acting the part of a priest for the benefit of the foreign visitors. When the journalist asked his young North Korean interpreter "Who is more important to you, Kim Il Sung or God?" the interpreter is reported to have looked thoroughly confused for the first time in the interview. "Who's God?" he asked. Again, all of this, including the churchgoers' apparent familiarity with the hymns, could have been staged.

As others have concluded, this attempt by the regime to show a tolerant attitude toward Christianity at the youth festival was intended to improve P'yŏngyang's standing in the West at a time when Kim Il Sung was trying to drive a wedge between Seoul and Washington. In March–April 1992, American evangelist Billy Graham was invited to North Korea for the same reason and also attended services at the Protestant Pongsu Church. Kim Il Sung appears to have backed away from the direct challenge to established religions exemplified in the 1980 *Nodong Shinmun* editorial. After Kim's death in 1994, foreigners have noticed no activity at the church on many subsequent visits. Kim Il Sung may have been personally impressed with Mr. Graham and may have built the two Christian churches in P'yŏngyang to impress Western visitors, but, interestingly, Kim Jong Il has not made a similar pretense of religious services in P'yŏngyang since he took power two years after the Graham visit. He has accorded the Graham family VIP treatment on their subsequent visits to North Korea but no open show of fake religious services. When Billy Graham's son Franklin visited in 2000, he was not allowed to preach.

In view of Kim Jong Il's lack of pretense in recent years about the absence of religious observances in North Korea, the announcement in July 2006 that California's megachurch pastor the Reverend Rick Warren, author of the book *The Purpose-Driven Life*, which is popular in South Korea, had accepted an invitation to preach in North Korea in a 15,000-seat stadium at an outdoor evangelistic crusade in March 2007, the first such event in the officially atheist state in 60 years, came as quite a surprise to most observers of North Korea. The visit was to mark the 100th anniversary of the 1907 P'yŏngyang Revival, one of the most important events in the spread of Christianity to Korea. The event was being arranged by a group of South Korean businessmen, not North Korean officials, but the latter evidently agreed so as to give the appearance of religious freedom and tolerance after the worldwide condemnation North Korea has received for its July 4, 2006, launch of seven missiles capable of bearing nuclear weapons. Kim Jong Il's surprising reversal in allowing a Potemkin-like evangelistic crusade, after 10 years' open disregard of the world's criticism of his country's lack of religious freedom, suggests a desperate need to counter world opprobrium. A future visit by Billy and Franklin Graham also was under discussion with North Korean officials in August 2006.

As Hwang Jang-yop, the former chief ideologue who articulated North Korea's *chuch'e* philosophy and is the highest-level North Korean official to have defected, has said, the churches in P'yŏngyang "are fake churches built for show," and the monks living in the Buddhist temples "are of course fake monks." Genuine believers in North Korea cannot profess their faith, said Hwang, "only fake believers are allowed to do so."

A woman defector from North Korea revealed her secret life as a Christian before she fled in 1999. Her parents were Christian, and she carried on the family tradition. She said that religious believers "have been captured and gunned to death, and their families sent to jails for political criminals.... Believers are forced to go underground because of the harsh oppression. Nobody could freely talk about religion during the 1960s and 1970s." However, the defector found that despite the suppression, religious beliefs were hard to eradicate, and underground church members stayed in contact through meetings. People who owned short-wave radios listened to South Korean Christian broadcasts and then shared what they had heard with their coreligionists. Meetings took place at friends' homes where illegal "home services" were held.

In so many ways, but especially in religious beliefs and practices, have North and South Korea diverged since the Korean War. It is only one, but a most important, difference between the two societies that will loom large in the eventual reunification of Korea. The official religion in North Korea as it is practiced today—the cult of Kim Il Sung—would seemingly be incompatible with any recognized religious belief in the world today.

As an apparent sign of opening to Russia, construction of a Russian Orthodox church began in P'yŏngyang in 2003, following a visit to the Russian Far East by Kim Jong Il in 2002, and it was consecrated in August 2006. The North Korean government paid for construction of the church, and the Russian Orthodox Church provided the icons, sacred vessels, and bells. A Russian-trained North Korean priest was put in charge.

An indigenous monotheistic religion—Ch'ŏndogyo (Heavenly Way)—an outgrowth of the nineteenth-century Tonghak Movement (see Glossary), also perseveres. Ch'ŏndogyo stresses the equality and unity of man with the universe and was traditionally popular among the rural population. Its teachings draw from Buddhism, Confucianism, Daoism, and Catholicism. Ch'ŏndogyo has around 2.7 million adherents who have a KWP-controlled political voice via the Chongu (Friends) Party.

Education

The North Korean leadership takes great pride in its free education system. When the communists came to power in 1946, illiteracy was widespread, and fewer than 20 percent of all Koreans had gone beyond elementary school. Now 99 percent of the population is literate. To accomplish this end, the country dispensed with complex Chinese characters in favor of sole reliance on the indigenous, simple, and phonetically precise *chosŏn'gul* (Korean script; known in South Korea as hangul) writing system. Against its advantages in being a relatively easy language with a nationalistic appeal, reliance on *chosŏn'gul* has had the disadvantage of further isolating North Korea from other countries of East Asia where knowledge of Chinese characters remains the "linguistic glue" binding China, South Korea, and Japan together. Ignorance of Chinese characters has been a major drawback for North Korea in its efforts to expand trade and other foreign contacts and an embarrassment in terms of its academic and scholarly standards.

Having lost most of the intellectuals and skilled technicians living in the North in the mass exodus to the South after the Korean War, the regime felt a great sense of urgency to develop a new class of skilled technicians to rebuild the country. By 1956 it had established a program of universal compulsory primary education of six years, including kindergarten, that was extended to the junior-middle school level by 1958, providing students with a total of seven years of free education. Emphasis also was placed on adult education in an effort to make the whole population literate through a night program for farmers that operated during the winter months. A major expansion of technical schools also was undertaken, with specialized courses in mining, engineering, mechanics, communications, energy, fishing, medicine, law, music, and art. North Korea's only four-year university, Kim Il Sung University in P'yŏngyang, was established in 1946.

The shortage of teachers and funds delayed the regime's more ambitious goal of establishing a free, compulsory nine-year educa-

tion system until 1967. It was the first such program in East Asia, both China and Japan then having only six-year compulsory systems with tuition partially free. The current 11-year compulsory, free education program, involving two years of kindergarten, four years of primary school, and five years of middle school, was established in the mid-1970s. According to North Korean official statistics for 2000, there were 1.5 million children in 27,017 nursery schools, 748,416 children in 14,167 kindergartens, 1.6 million students in 4,886 four-year primary schools, and 2.1 million students in 4,772 middle schools. Nearly 1.9 million students attended more than 300 colleges and two-year universities. In 2005 there were an estimated 2.5 million students in primary schools, another 2.5 million students in middle school, and about 1 million students in high school. Yet another source cites a total of 8 million enrolled in education, from nursery school through elementary and middle school, high school, college, and university, including correspondence courses and educational courses for workers at their job sites (so-called factory colleges). It is impossible to confirm these statistics that the regime releases, but they give some idea of the emphasis on education, although one must make allowance for the significant amount of volunteer labor that students above the age of 11, and particularly above the age of 14, give to economic projects throughout the year, especially at rice planting and harvesting time and all during the summer. The country's elaborate, state-financed system of nurseries and "children's palaces" for prekindergarten children is not included in the 11-year compulsory education program.

Primary Education

Beginning in primary school, the education system is intended, in Kim's own words, to train North Koreans to "serve the existing social system." Even in primary school, children commit passages of Kim's speeches to memory and recite them at the front of the class, at other times sitting in perfect silence and upright attention. As one can imagine, there are reportedly few behavior problems. One teacher explained: "We are educating them in communist morality. We are educating them in a unitary idea—thinking in the same way and acting in the same way."

There are typically one primary school in each village and one middle school in each district made up of two or three villages. Normally, a middle school in a city accommodates about 1,000 students and a rural middle school about 500 or 600 students. Defectors estimate the size of an average class to be about 30 students. Because of limited classroom facilities, many schools operate in two shifts, with an afternoon overlap accommodating non-classroom activities such as physical education, militia training, and study hall.

Middle School and Beyond

Boys and girls receive essentially the same education in coeducational institutions through middle school. On completion of the 11-year compulsory program, which ends around the age of 15 or 16, most young women go to work, either on farms or in local factories, and most males begin their obligatory military service. Approximately 30 percent of all male students, usually the sons of high-ranking government and military officials, are exempted from military service to continue their education through high school and college or, possibly, university. Kim Jong Il, for instance, never served in the army but went straight from middle school to high school to Kim Il Sung University. After completing their military duty, about 5 percent of former military draftees enter a one-year preparatory (high school) course for college or university. High schools are "specialized" schools, as are colleges, which may be engineering, industrial, agricultural, medical, foreign languages, music, fine arts, drama, athletic, teacher-training, or KWP colleges. Admission to college or university (all of which are two-year universities except for the four-year Kim Il Sung University) is somewhat easier after service in the military than directly from middle school. The military decides who will go on to college and who will be assigned to manual labor.

Beyond middle school, North Korea has devoted its major efforts toward increasing the supply of technically and scientifically proficient personnel by expanding the enrollment at and resources of technological colleges, vocational schools (usually two-year schools divided into agricultural and mechanical programs), and factory colleges, and by sending selected groups of students abroad, primarily to Russia and Eastern Europe, for scientific and technical education. Kim Jong Il appears to have been the driving force in the new program to send North Korean students abroad for training. In April 1998, he spoke favorably of Deng Xiaoping's "great feat in sending 2,000 or so students abroad annually" from China and expressed his hope that North Korea could emulate China on this point.

There has been an improvement in mass education at the lower grades and impressive training of technicians for the workforce since the late twentieth century. However, Western technicians who have supervised the construction and early production processes of plants imported from the West have despaired of North Korean engineering incompetence, disregard for safety procedures, careless maintenance and repair procedures, and stubborn refusal to accept advice.

Higher Education

The absence of true higher education and an educated, intellectual class is the most serious deficiency of the system. Sixty years after its founding, Kim Il Sung University remains the sole civilian four-year university. Its graduates, numbering about 3,000 a year out of a total student body of 12,000, who constitute the educational elite of the country, represent less than 0.01 percent of the population. The university, like every other educational institution and perhaps more than others, subordinates education to unrelenting political indoctrination. Students in the social sciences spend almost 50 percent of their time in ideological study. Students in the science departments devote about 20 percent of their time to Kim study. Most of the books in the university's library are various editions of Kim's collected works, bound in leather. A separate catalog, which takes up one room, indexes all of his speeches. As students become more educated and advance to higher levels in school, and at Kim Il Sung University, they actually have to spend more time studying Kim's teachings and expend more energy in public observance of the Kim cult. In a system that puts a premium on political loyalty, the bright and ambitious cultivate their political skills and worry less about academic proficiency.

From all reports, there is dissatisfaction with the limited opportunities for higher education. Many students who want to go on to high school or college and are qualified to do so are barred, either because of *sŏngbun* or because of the limited number of schools of higher learning. Only about 30 or 40 percent of middle-school graduates go directly to high school, and another 5 percent attend high school after completing military service; fewer than 10 percent of high school graduates go on to college or university.

Imbalances in the curriculum constitute another serious deficiency. The study of science predominates, while the social sciences are all but neglected, except for the study of Marxism–Leninism and the communist revolution in Korea. According to one former student, more than three out of four classrooms at Kim Il Sung University consist of laboratories for the study of biology, chemistry, geology, and related subjects. Foreign visitors have been singularly unimpressed with the laboratories at the university, the best that North Korea has to offer.

There are indications that Kim Jong Il realizes the dire need for economists and financial experts as North Korea struggles to recover from its economic collapse in the late 1990s, expand trade with other countries, and promote foreign investment in North Korea, at least to the extent that it can do so without allowing unwanted foreign influences to seep into the country. The dilemma for the regime is the difficulty in learning economics without exposure to the benefits of a free-market system.

Outside of science, music, drama, and certain technical skills, the education system is unimpressive, most notably in the social sciences and foreign-language departments. Because of the limited number of trained linguists, North Korea has been unable to host several international conferences at the same time or even some large ones at any given time. An international table tennis meet held in P'yŏngyang in 1979 dramatized the acute need for translators in many different languages. Shortly thereafter, the School of Foreign Languages broke away from Kim Il Sung University to become a separate institution. Around that same time, Kim Il Sung made the study of English compulsory in upper-level middle schools. Prior to that, students in middle school were required to study Russian; after 1978, both English and Russian were mandatory. At the same time, in a crash program to train English-speaking technicians and party and government officials, North Koreans were sent to special language-training programs in Japan, Guyana, Yugoslavia, and Iraq.

North Korea's kidnapping of foreign nationals to teach their languages to its diplomatic corps and kidnapping of foreign actors and actresses to spearhead its movie industry between 1977 and 1983 are now well known. Kim Jong Il's hand can be seen in these criminal acts, which may have accomplished his immediate purpose as minister of culture in jump-starting a nonexistent foreign-language program but at the cost, some years later, of a disastrous setback in international relations with the countries involved. The nation's relations with Japan, in particular, have been affected significantly by North Korea's surprising admission in 2003 that it did in fact kidnap Japanese citizens off the beach in Japan, as Japan had long claimed and North Korea had adamantly denied, for the purpose of teaching Japanese to its foreign diplomats.

The basic problem that affects the quality of a North Korean's education is the conflict between reality and the state's insistence on its own brand of the "truth." The quality of North Korean education can never be any better, or any closer to the truth, than the official party line. North Koreans are taught, for instance, and have no reason to question such basic untruths as: Russia, not the United States or Britain, was primarily responsible for the defeat of Japan and Germany in World War II. A good idea of the level of studies can be observed from the caliber of what is called original research. There are only 10 to 15 journals in the fields of chemistry, physics, geography, other physical sciences, linguistics, history, and archaeology that could be considered remotely scholarly, and Western scholars have found no original ideas or research techniques of any real merit. None of these journals are available in translation outside of North Korea. There has been some good archaeological work and some research on Korean dialects, but there are no North Korean scholars with international standing in any field. Science may be the only area in which a North Korean can get a fairly good education with a relatively small component of ideological indoctrination. Some of the rising economic stars have been trained in the sciences, bespeaking both the superiority of a scientific education and the absence of an economics program.

In short, the regime has educated a whole generation of North Koreans in Kim Il Sung's image, more sophisticated than he in the technical and scientific areas but essentially practical-minded people interested in solving immediate issues at hand. The current generation of North Koreans has had little in the way of intellectually challenging experience, and the members of the older generation who might have retained some of the earmarks of a traditional education have passed from the scene. The loss of a highly educated elite, like the loss of traditional religious beliefs, has long-term implications for North Korea's eventual reentry onto the world scene after more than 60 years of political, social, and cultural isolation. Corrections to the education system would require years to show results.

Health Care

To the extent the state can make it available, medical care is provided free of charge. In assuming full responsibility for the health of its people, the regime has given priority to preventive medicine, and physical exercise is seen as the first line of defense against illness. Children and adults are expected to participate in physical exercise during work breaks and school recesses. They also are encouraged to take part in recreational sports, such as running, gymnastics, volleyball, ice skating, and traditional Korean games. Mass gymnastic displays, involving tens of thousands of uniformed participants, are a regular feature of major holidays and visits of important foreigners to P'yŏngyang.

The government has instituted nationwide regular medical checkups. It is this feature of North Korea's health program, plus the practice of cleanliness, that most impresses foreigners. Checkups are provided on a routine basis at every school, factory, cooperative farm, office, and military unit. People are given a complete annual checkup and in addition are required to have monthly checkups for the treatment of minor conditions, such as colds. In some places, physicians go to schools and factories; otherwise people visit local clinics. In either case, because health care is organized around people's place of work or school, members of the same family do not see the same physician. There is no choice of physician. Individuals are required to follow the orders of their assigned physician and cannot refuse treatment. There is continuity in medical records; a person's lifetime "health card" is automatically forwarded to the new health clinic if he or she moves.

The regime has been very aggressive in attacking epidemic diseases, including typhus, smallpox, cholera, and encephalitis, by instituting a nationwide inoculation program, which, however, suffers from a chronic shortage of serums. Physicians oversee the routine spraying of public places such as trains, buses, restaurants, and hotels with DDT and other insecticides. Foreigners report such spraying of trains after every stop.

The prevalence of tuberculosis is generally blamed on malnutrition and hard work. At one time, it was the leading cause of death in North Korea. In 2005 it ranked farther down on the list behind cancer, heart disease, strokes, and digestive and respiratory ailments. However, during the late 1990s, when famine claimed the lives of 1 million or more North Koreans, the immune systems of the vulnerable, mainly the elderly and the young, weakened as caloric intake fell, and many people succumbed to diseases such as tuberculosis before actually starving to death. As of 2005, no cases of human immunodeficiency virus/

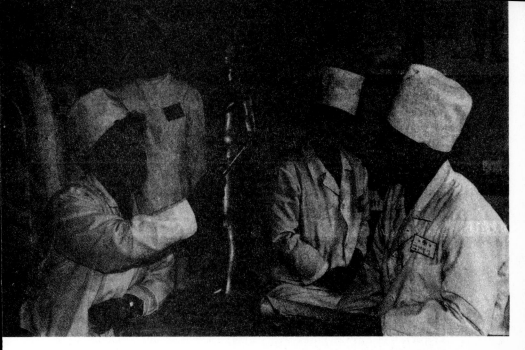

Research staff of the Acupuncture and Moxibustion Division, Koryŏ Institute of Medical Science, P'yŏngyang
Courtesy Chosŏn *(P'yŏngyang), June 2004, 22*

acquired immune deficiency syndrome (HIV/AIDS) had been officially reported.

As one of its first priorities after the war, the regime sought to train more physicians at long-established medical colleges in P'yŏngyang, Hamhŭng, Ch'ŏngjin, and Sariwŏn, plus newly established medical junior colleges located in each province. In terms of the number of physicians and hospitals per capita, North Korea ranks high in the world today, although it is unclear just how well trained these physicians are. In the past, North Korea reportedly had one doctor for every 700 inhabitants and one hospital bed for every 350 inhabitants. Health expenditures in 2001 represented 2.5 percent of gross domestic product (GDP—see Glossary). Despite these expenditures, the country is thought to be some 15 to 20 years behind in medical research.

Medicine is not a prestigious profession in North Korea. Medical doctors, lawyers, professors, and other intellectuals of prerevolutionary days were denounced as enemies of the state and relegated to the lower classes. Many young men choose not to go to medical school; more than 75 percent of North Korea's physicians are women. There are no nursing colleges; women with a high-school education or less serve as nurses.

There is a significant variation in the quality of medical care throughout the country. Central hospitals in P'yŏngyang, such as the

Red Cross Hospital and the P'yŏngyang Medical College Hospital, have the most modern equipment and hundreds of cancer and heart disease specialists. City and provincial hospitals, such as the P'yŏngyang Hospital and Haeju Hospital, are reserved for seriously ill patients. There also are county and ward hospitals, factory hospitals for factories with 7,000 or more employees, and rural health centers. On a smaller scale, clinics that have no beds and essentially give first-aid treatment are run by nurses or midwives, not trained medical doctors.

All eye surgery reportedly is done in the central hospitals in P'yŏngyang. Foreign visitors who have observed the modern operating rooms and equipment in these hospitals see not only the best, but, in some cases, the only facilities for certain kinds of operations or cancer treatment. Cataract surgery is not available to the average North Korean, a situation that may confine him or her to life without reading after a certain age. The P'yŏngyang Maternity Hospital, another showcase hospital, has become a regular stop on the VIP tour of P'yŏngyang since its opening in late 1980.

The epitome in medical care is provided to top party and government officials at the Government Hospital in P'yŏngyang (also known as the Ponghwa Clinic). Dr. Ch'oe Ung-sam, the first director of the clinic and Kim Il Sung's longtime chief personal physician, graduated from a Japanese medical school and later served as dean of Ch'ŏngjin Medical College. In addition to the clinic, he operated a special medical service providing 24-hour medical care for both Kim Il Sung and Kim Jong Il, plus special services for cabinet ministers and top KWP officials. Unlike other hospitals, the Ponghwa Clinic has central heating and, in each patient's room, air conditioning, a sofa, two armchairs, and a coffee table. Its elite patients look out over a floral, terraced courtyard. Most North Koreans are not aware of the existence of the Ponghwa Clinic, but anyone going near it would notice the government cars parked in front. Foreign visitors are not taken to the Ponghwa Clinic, despite North Korean interest in showing off the nation's other premier facilities.

Except for a few pediatric hospitals, tuberculosis sanatoriums, and the central hospitals in P'yŏngyang, most hospitals are general hospitals. A typical one would have about 100 to 150 beds, with most rooms accommodating from 10 to 15 patients each. The majority of the patients are there for surgery; the most common operations are for appendicitis, tonsillitis, boils, and abscesses. Only the most modern hospitals have beds with mattresses; most others have wooden-board beds; patients bring their own bedding. Visitors are not allowed in patients' rooms. The rules isolating hospital patients from other people are strictly enforced throughout the country. Patients are not allowed to leave their rooms, and they are not allowed to smoke. While they are in the hospital, they must submit their food ration card and eat only meals provided by the hospital. Even by North Korean standards, the food is poor. Going to the hospital is not a comfortable experience.

North Koreans' major complaints about medical care are the shortage and extremely high cost of medicines, especially antibiotics, which are in great demand. Pharmaceutical imports from Japan, Russia, and China are reserved for the elite. Antibiotics available to the general public are produced domestically. Control over scarce supplies is exerted by physicians who are authorized to prescribe only those medicines that are available, in amounts that can be filled. Most modern drugs are not sold on the open market; foreign visitors always note the absence of pharmacies selling medicines. Only traditional medicines produced domestically are available at special drugstores. Black-market sale of medicines has long been pervasive.

The regime has claimed a dramatic improvement in the health and longevity of its population. According to North Korean statistics, the average life expectancy was a little more than 38 years in the 1936–40 period; in 2007 life expectancy was estimated at 69.2 years for men and 74.8 years for women. Other projections are much lower for both men and women. Life expectancy is not expected to improve as the first decade of the twenty-first century proceeds.

Prior to the famine of the mid-1990s with its horrific death toll, North Koreans reportedly were pleased with the advances made in medicine, especially in the fight against traditional epidemic diseases and the improvement in surgical care. Free medical care has been considered one of the regime's most impressive accomplishments. However, the people know nothing about the advances made in other countries. They know only what the state has told them, and they have been told—and apparently believe—that medical care in South Korea and the West is a luxury that only the rich can afford. They must be much more cynical now, however, after watching a million or more of their loved ones die in one of the great famines of the twentieth century. Estimates of the death toll vary from the government's quasi-official figure of 220,000 to the estimate of 3.5 million by the South Korean nongovernmental organization Good Friends. Typical of a famine, most deaths were due to disease, not starvation. The mingling of drinking water with sewage in the flooding in 1996 led to gastrointestinal diseases, which led to dehydration, especially in children. With their immune systems already weakened as a result of poor nutrition, they were vulnerable to a number of illnesses.

There also have been serious long-term health effects of the famine, some irreversible, which will erase many of the medical advances of past years. According to a 2004 UN survey, there has been serious stunting (low height for age) and wasting (low weight for height) of children under six, as a result of chronic malnutrition. The rate of stunting was found to be 37 percent; 23 percent were underweight (weight for age); and 7 percent showed signs of wasting. Not surprisingly, given the regime's handling of scarce food supplies, the survey revealed considerable regional variation. The stunting rate in P'yŏngyang was found to be half that in cities of the north and east that are geographically removed from rural areas, cities where the government was unable or unwilling to transport scarce foodstuffs. According to a 2004 UN Food and Agriculture Organization report, North Korea's population is one of the most undernourished in the world, in the company of the very poorest nations such as Sierra Leone, Ethiopia, and Haiti. Despite the flow of international aid since the mid-1990s, there has been no significant improvement in nutritional levels since 1995.

With the loss of at least 5 percent of its population during the famine in the mid-1990s, and a lower birthrate and higher mortality rate since then, North Korea has seen a drop in its population and a deterioration in the health of the people that would normally be seen only in wartime. Estimates in 2007 indicate a birthrate of nearly 15.0 births per 1,000 population, a death rate of just over 7.2 deaths per 1,000, and an infant mortality rate of 22.5 per 1,000 live births. The total fertility rate for 2007 has been estimated at two children per woman.

The long-term health effects of a famine that ranks as one of the worst of the twentieth century, coupled with chronic food shortages that continue into a second decade and promise only more malnourished North Korean children, will plague North Korea for years to come. Its hopes for steady growth in its population, to compete with South Korea's much larger population, have been soundly dashed. Meanwhile, the smaller, sicker population that remains after so many deaths will likely need greater expenditures on health—and more food for better nutrition—than the regime can afford without continued international aid or a drop in military expenditures.

*   *   *

Much of this chapter is based on the author's 1999 book, *Kim Il-song's North Korea*. The book is a declassified Central Intelligence Agency study originally prepared in the early 1980s and based on all the sources available to the U.S. Government at that time, including interviews with North Korean defectors, foreign diplomats either stationed in P'yŏngyang or traveling to North Korea, East European technicians working at North Korean industrial sites, and other visitors to the country.

Bradley K. Martin's *Under the Loving Care of the Fatherly Leader: North Korea and the Kim Dynasty* is the best source of information on the society published since 2003. Other excellent studies that provide a more specific focus on a particular feature of North Korean society are David R. Hawk's report *The Hidden Gulag: Exposing North Korea's Prison Camps*; Stephan Haggard and Marcus Noland's *Hunger and Human Rights: The Politics of Famine in North Korea*; and *The Great North Korean Famine: Famine, Politics, and Foreign Policy* by Andrew S. Natsios.

Since the famine of the mid-1990s and the flood of North Korean refugees into China seeking to escape the deteriorating food conditions and the tightening totalitarian controls, defector reports have provided a better and better understanding of North Korean society. These defector reports have been featured in newspaper and magazine articles, as well as academic journals and conferences. Several early twenty-first-century videos of a public execution in North Korea of people who have helped the refugees along the Chinese border have provided new sources of up-to-date, irrefutable information.

Foreign visitors to North Korea, all carefully screened by the regime beforehand, continue to write feature articles about their visits to P'yŏngyang. They are usually not allowed to travel outside P'yŏngyang, however, the one exception to this having been the international humanitarian aid officials who have been allowed in many areas but not, for instance, in the northeast provinces. (For further information and complete citations, see Bibliography.)

Chapter 3. The Economy

The lead statuary of the Monument for Socialism, Revolution, and Construction of Socialism, Mansudae Square, P'yŏngyang, completed in April 1972. The handle on the torch is inscribed "chuch'e," while the book says "Selected Works of Kim Il Sung."
Courtesy Pulmyŏl ŭi t'ap *(Tower of Immortality), P'yŏngyang: Munye Ch'ulpansa, 1985, 63*

THE ECONOMY of the Democratic People's Republic of Korea (DPRK), or North Korea, has undergone tremendous changes since the 1990s began. Compared to its neighbors—the Republic of Korea (South Korea), China, Russia, and Japan—North Korea is by far the poorest and most backward country in Northeast Asia. The stresses that North Korea's economy underwent in the 1990s under the leadership of Kim Jong Il led many observers to expect that it would soon implode. That the North Korean regime has survived far longer than most expected and continues to function, and even reform its economy, is an intriguing puzzle. However, although North Korea has survived, its economy is in shambles and has contracted steeply. By the late 1990s, these pressures finally had forced the North Korean leadership to begin undertaking economic reforms, essentially abandoning the Soviet-style centrally planned—or command—economy to which it had clung since the late 1940s under the leadership of Kim Il Sung. Whether those reforms can have their intended effect is a question that will only be answered in the future.

North Korea has been—and remains—one of the most closed societies in the world. Reliable information about the state and condition of its economy, as well as information about its economic organization, is exceedingly scarce. North Korea has made comparatively substantial strides toward openness since the 1990s, especially after the June 2000 summit between South Korea's president Kim Dae Jung and Korean Workers' Party (KWP) general secretary Kim Jong Il, that increasingly deepened interactions between the two Koreas. This greater openness has led to better information than was previously available, although the quality and quantity of information about basic economic functions, such as gross domestic product (GDP—see Glossary), growth rates, and industrial production, remain superficial and suspect at best.

Economic Development, 1940s–90s

The Economy after World War II

North Korea has been one of the most closed, autarkic, and centralized economies in the world since the late 1940s. Although this situation began to change in the early twenty-first century, the economy remains one of the most obscure and recondite. For decades, the economy was organized around the doctrine of *chuch'e* (see Glossary). Although in reality North Korea was heavily dependent on aid and technology transfers from the Soviet Union and China, the attempt to be virtually autarkic was a main aspect of its economy until the late 1990s.

At the end of the era of Japanese colonization of the Korean Peninsula (1910–45), North Korea inherited the basic infrastructure of a modern economy and achieved considerable success because of the ability of the communist regime to marshal underused resources and idle labor and to impose a low rate of consumption. The Japanese had developed extensive heavy industry, particularly in the metallurgy and chemical industries, hydroelectric power, and mining in the northern half of Korea, where they introduced modern mining methods. The southern half of the peninsula produced most of the rice and the majority of textiles. The hydroelectric and chemical plants were said to be second to none in Asia at that time in terms of both their scale and technology. The same applied to the railroad and communication networks.

There were, however, serious defects in the industrial structures and their location. The Korean economy, geared primarily to benefit the Japanese homeland, was made dependent on Japan. Heavy industry was limited to the production of mainly raw materials, semifinished goods, and war supplies, which were then shipped to Japan for final processing, consumption, or deployment. Japan did not allow Korea to develop a machine-tool industry. Most industrial sectors were strategically located on the eastern or western coasts near ports so as to connect them efficiently with Japan. Railroad networks ran mainly along the north–south axis, facilitating Japan's access to the Asian mainland. Because the Japanese held almost all key government positions and owned and controlled the industrial and financial enterprises, only a few Koreans acquired the basic skills essential for modernization. Moreover, the Japanese left behind an agrarian structure—land tenure system, size of land holdings and farm operations, and pattern of land use and farm income—that needed much reform.

The sudden termination of the Japanese occupation at the end of World War II, in August 1945, and the subsequent partition of the nation brought economic chaos (see National Division in the 1940s, ch. 1). Severance of the complementary "agricultural" South from the "industrial" North and from Japan meant that North Korea's traditional market for raw materials and semifinished goods as well as its sources of food and manufactured goods were cut off. Furthermore, the withdrawal of the entrepreneurial and engineering skills supplied mainly by Japanese personnel affected the economic base. Thus, the task facing the communist regime in the North was to develop a viable economy, which it reoriented mainly toward other communist-run nations, while at the same time rectifying the "malformation" in the colonial industrial structure. The problem was further compounded by the devastation of the industrial base during the Korean War (see The Korean War, 1950–53, ch. 1). North Korea's economic development did not begin in earnest until after the Korean War.

North Korea's Development Strategy

During what North Korea called its "peaceful construction" period before the Korean War, the fundamental task of the economy was to overtake the level of output and efficiency attained toward the end of the Japanese occupation. This effort included restructuring and developing a viable economy oriented toward the communist-bloc nations and beginning the process of socializing the economy. Nationalization of key industrial enterprises and land reform, both of which were carried out in 1946, laid the groundwork for two successive one-year plans in 1947 and 1948, respectively, and for the Two-Year Plan (1949–50). During this period, a piece-rate wage system and an independent accounting system began to be applied, and the commercial network increasingly came under state and cooperative ownership.

The basic goal of the Three-Year Postwar Reconstruction Plan (1954–56) was to reconstruct an economy devastated by the Korean War. The plan stressed more than merely regaining the prewar output levels. China, the Soviet Union, and East European countries provided reconstruction assistance. The highest priority was developing heavy industry, but an earnest effort to collectivize farming also began. At the end of 1957, output of most industrial commodities, except for a few items, such as chemical fertilizers, carbides, and sulfuric acid, where the recovery took longer, had returned to 1949 levels.

Having basically completed the task of reconstruction, the state planned to lay a solid foundation for industrialization while completing the socialization process and solving the basic problems of food and shelter during the Five-Year Plan (1957–61). The socialization process was completed by 1958 in all sectors of the economy, and the Ch'ŏllima Work Team Movement (see Glossary) was introduced. Although growth rates reportedly were high, there were serious imbalances among different economic sectors. Because rewards went to individuals and enterprises that met production quotas, frantic efforts to fulfill plan targets in competition with other enterprises and industries caused efforts to be disproportionate between various enterprises, between industry and agriculture, and between light and heavy industries. Because resources were limited and the transportation system suffered bottlenecks, supplies went primarily to politically well-connected enterprises or those whose managers complained the loudest. An enterprise or industry that performed better than others often did so at the expense of others.

Until 1960 North Korea's economy grew faster than that in the South. During the reconstruction period after the Korean War, there were opportunities for extensive economic growth. This general pattern of initially high growth resulting in a strong rate of capital formation was mirrored in the other Soviet-style economies. Toward the end of the 1950s, as reconstruction work was completed and idle capacity began to diminish, the economy had to shift from the extensive to the intensive stage, where the simple discipline of marshaling underused resources became less effective. In the new stage, inefficiency arising from emerging bottlenecks led to diminishing returns. Further growth could be attained only by increasing efficiency and technological progress (see The Economy, ch. 1).

Beginning in the early 1960s, a series of pervasive and serious bottlenecks began to impede development. Blockages generally were created by the lack of arable land, skilled labor, energy, and transportation and by deficiencies in the extraction industries. Moreover, both land and marine transportation lacked modern equipment and infrastructure. The inability of the energy and mining sectors, as well as of the transportation network, to supply power and raw materials as rapidly as the manufacturing plants could absorb them began to slow industrial growth. The Five-Year Plan targets were mostly completed by 1959, and the year 1960 was officially categorized as a "buffer year" before the next plan started in 1961.

The First Seven-Year Plan (1961–67) built on the groundwork of the previous plans but changed the focus of industrialization. Heavy industry, with the machine-tool industry as its linchpin, gained continuing priority. During the plan, however, and because of the withdrawal of Soviet aid during the Sino–Soviet dispute, the economy experienced widespread slowdowns and reverses for the first time, in sharp contrast to the rapid and uninterrupted growth during the previous plans. Poor performance forced the regime to extend the plan for three additional years, to 1970. During the last part of the de facto 10-year plan, emphasis shifted to pursuing parallel development of the economy and of defense capabilities.

The Six-Year Plan (1971–76) followed immediately after the previous plan, but in the aftermath of the poor performance of the previous plan, growth targets of the Six-Year Plan were scaled down substantially. Because some of the proposed targets in the First Seven-Year Plan had not been attained even by 1970, the Six-Year Plan did not deviate much from its predecessor in basic goals. The Six-Year Plan placed more emphasis on technological advance, self-sufficiency in industrial raw materials, improving product quality, correcting imbalances among different sectors, and developing the power and extractive industries; the last of these had been deemed largely responsible for slowdowns during the First Seven-Year Plan. The plan called for attaining a self-sufficiency rate of 60 to 70 percent in all industrial sectors by substituting domestic raw materials wherever possible and by organizing and renovating technical processes to make such substitution feasible. Improving transport capacity became one of the urgent tasks in accelerating economic development—understandably because it was one of the major bottlenecks threatening the Six-Year Plan.

By the end of August 1975, North Korea claimed to have fulfilled the Six-Year Plan 16 months ahead of schedule. Under the circumstances, it was expected that the next plan would start without delay in 1976, a year early. However, it was not until nearly 30 months later that the plan was unveiled; 1976 and 1977 became "buffer" years.

The inability of the planners to formulate and institute economic plans continuously reveals as much about the inefficacy of planning itself as about the extent of the economic difficulties and administrative disruptions facing North Korea. Targets for successive plans, for example, had to be based on the accomplishments of preceding plans. If these targets were underfulfilled, all targets of the next plan had to be reformulated and adjusted.

The basic thrust of the Second Seven-Year Plan (1978–84) was to achieve the three-pronged goals of self-reliance, modernization, and "scientification." Although the emphasis on self-reliance was not new, it had not previously been the explicit focus of an economic plan. During the 1970s, North Korea was not nearly as closed off to the international community as it became during and after the 1980s. Although trade accounted for a relatively small proportion of the country's total economy during the Cold War, North Korea still traded with other countries. And, while most of the trade was conducted with China and the Soviet Union, a surprisingly large proportion of trade occurred outside the communist bloc. For example, during the 1970s, about 10 percent of North Korea's trade was with Japan, and more than 15 percent was with nations belonging to the Organisation for Economic Co-Operation and Development (OECD—see Glossary).

This new emphasis on self-reliance might have been a reaction to the mounting foreign debt originating from large-scale imports of

Western machinery and equipment in the mid-1970s. Through modernization North Korea hoped to increase mechanization and automation in all sectors of the economy through the process of scientification, the adoption of up-to-date production and management techniques. The specific objectives of the economic plan were: to strengthen the fuel, energy, and resource bases of industry through priority development of the energy and extractive industries; to modernize industry; to substitute domestic resources for certain imported raw materials; to expand freight-carrying capacity; and to accelerate a technical revolution in agriculture.

All indications are that the Second Seven-Year Plan was not successful. North Korea generally downplayed the accomplishments of the plan, and no other plan received less official fanfare. It was officially claimed that the economy had grown at an annual rate of 8.8 percent during the plan, somewhat below the planned rate of 9.6 percent. The reliability of this aggregate measure, however, is highly questionable. By official admission, the targets of only six commodities were attained (cereals and grains among them). After the plan concluded, there was no new economic plan for two years, an indication of both the plan's failure and the severity of the economic and planning problems confronting the economy in the mid-1980s.

The main targets of the Third Seven-Year Plan (1987–93) were to achieve the "Ten Long-Range Major Goals of the 1980s for the Construction of the Socialist Economy." These goals included the three previous policy goals of self-reliance, modernization, and scientification. Furthermore, the plan gave more attention to developing foreign trade and joint ventures. Because of the collapse of the socialist bloc in the late 1980s, the plan never had a serious chance of succeeding, and in 1993 North Korea admitted it was not successful. On December 8, 1993, Premier Kang Song-san said that, "Due to the collapse of socialist countries and the socialist market, our country's economic cooperation and trade have faced setbacks. This has brought serious damage to our economic construction, and therefore our Third Seven-Year Plan has had a hard time achieving its goals." After 1993, North Korea did not promulgate plans.

The end of the Cold War (1945–89) severely shook North Korea. During the Cold War, North Korea had been able to rely on extensive Soviet and Chinese military, technological, and economic aid. This aid had been large in absolute terms, and, more importantly, had provided North Korea access to more advanced technology than it could otherwise have obtained on its own. Beginning in 1989, the North Korean economy underwent a series of shock waves. The limits to a centrally planned economy had already begun to be reached during

A streetcar in downtown P'yŏngyang, June 2006
Courtesy Overseas Pan-Korean Center, Washington, DC

the 1980s, and to compound these problems, the Soviet Union and China abandoned North Korea and stopped providing aid and materials at "friendship prices." Both the Soviet Union and China also normalized relations with South Korea. From US$260 million in aid to the North in 1980, by 1987 North Korea was actually running a deficit with the Soviet Union, and by 1990 all aid from Moscow had ceased. In 1992 China also decided to make North Korea pay market prices for goods previously sold at friendship prices, thus further aggravating North Korea's problems. As a result, North Korean imports of oil and grain from China dropped dramatically in the early 1990s. For example, while North Korea had imported 1.5 million tons of coal from China in 1988, by 1996 that amount had dropped precipitously, to only 100,000 tons.

The severe problems inherent in a centrally planned economy had fully manifested themselves by the mid-1980s, and the economy had started its decline even before the Soviet Union and China abandoned aid to the North. By 1990 North Korea's economy had begun to contract, experiencing negative GDP growth rates from 1990 to 1998. Only in 1999 did that growth actually turn positive for the first time in a decade. By 2003, South Korea's Ministry of Unification estimated gross national product (GNP—see Glossary) per capita in North Korea at US$762, and a total GNP of US$17 billion, while industrial capacity was half what it had been in 1989.

Economic Infrastructure Since the Early 1990s

Comparisons with South Korea

Although North Korea recovered more quickly from the Korean War than the South, by the mid-1960s, South Korea had begun its economic development, and its economy was growing rapidly. By the 1980s, South Korea had caught and surpassed the North in both absolute GDP and per capita income. North Korea recovered rapidly from the war of 1950–53, in large measure as a result of extensive aid from the Soviet Union and China. At its peak in 1960, North Korea's absolute GNP was almost 80 percent that of South Korea's. However, as the South began its development under President Park Chung-hee in the 1960s, the North rapidly fell behind. Within a decade, North Korea's economy was half the absolute size of South Korea's, and by 1990 it was only 10 percent of the South's. By 2003, most estimates put the South's economy at 33 times larger than the North's. The South has a population roughly twice that of the North, and although per capita incomes were roughly similar until around 1975, the South's continued economic dynamism meant that by 1990 South Korean per capita income was roughly US$6,000, while that in the North was about US$1,000. By 2003, the per capita income gap between the two countries had again expanded dramatically. North Korea's GNP per capita was then roughly US$762, while that in the South was 10 times more, at US$17,800.

Organization

North Korea historically was organized on lines similar to other centrally planned economies. Property rights belonged largely to the state, resources were allocated through plans and not through markets, and prices and money were not the central features of the economy. Up until 1998, the state constitution recognized two general economic categories: state-owned enterprises and worker cooperatives (see The Constitutional Framework, ch. 4). From the late 1940s to the late 1980s, North Korea had one of the most complete socialist economies in the world.

The KWP is the supreme power in North Korea, and it has full control over the government and state organs. The constitutional revisions of September 1998 retained the stipulations that the "Democratic People's Republic of Korea shall conduct all activities under the leadership of the Workers' Party." No decision can be made without the approval of the party, and the party retains full control over economic enterprises, factories, and the cooperative farms.

The system of party control over the economy was formalized in the Taean Work System (see Glossary), which Kim Il Sung announced on a visit he made to the Taean County Electrical Appliance Plant in December 1961. The Taean Work System continued for 41 years. Under this system, factory party committees' collective leadership oversaw production activities, and these factory party committees were under the direct control of the provincial KWP chapters. The factory party committee was responsible not only for business and technical aspects of the factory, but also for political and moral aspects. The secretary of the factory, a member of the provincial party chapter, presided over the factory party committee, organized production and management goals, and was responsible for ensuring that policy and political directives were followed in the factory. This role gave the secretary tremendous control, despite the appearance of a consensual decision-making organization, and some party chiefs abused their power by making unilateral decisions without regard to the managers of the factory. North Korea abandoned the Taean Work System in July 2002 and introduced a new economic management system (see Legal and Administrative Reforms, this ch.).

Forced collectivization of the North Korean agricultural system occurred between 1945 and 1958. More than 1 million farm households were turned into collectivized farms, with a smaller number of designated "state farms." North Korea achieved this change without massive loss of life or disruption, and this relatively successful collectivization stands in contrast to the Chinese and Soviet experiences, where forced collectivization led to mass famine and loss of life in the millions. By the late 1990s, there were approximately 3,000 cooperatives, 300 state farms, and 240 other farms. During the 1950s, Kim Il Sung announced in a series of speeches the basic framework of collectivization for agricultural development and self-sufficiency in North Korea. These speeches included four basic principles: mechanization, chemicalization, irrigation, and electrification. This framework came to be known as the Ch'ŏngsan-ni Method (see Glossary) of agriculture, taking its name from a small agricultural collective near P'yŏngyang, where, in 1960, Kim had spent time talking with farmers and reportedly providing "on-the-spot guidance." The KWP Central Committee formally adopted the four principles and the Ch'ŏngsan-ni Method on February 25, 1964. As with the Taean Work System, the Ch'ŏngsan-ni Method largely ceased to function by the early 2000s.

The Ch'ŏngsan-ni Method was essentially unchanged until the constitutional revisions of September 1998 formally permitted private ownership of assets, as well as instituting the Cabinet of Ministers,

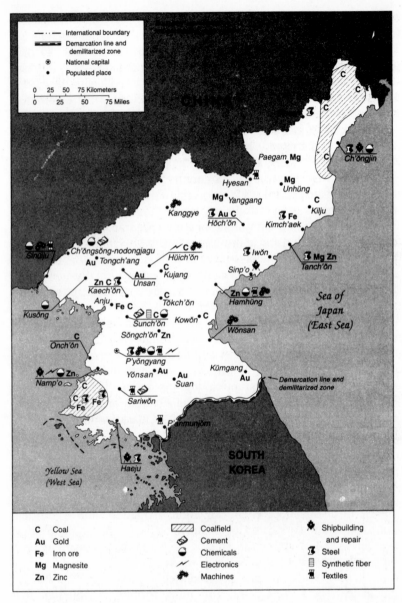

Source: Based on information from Korean Resources Corporation, "Korea Mineral Information Service," Seoul, 2005, http://kores.net/; and John C. Wu, "The Mineral Industry of North Korea" in United States Geological Survey, *Mineral Year Book*, 3, Area Reports: International, Washington, DC, 2005, http://minerals.usgs.gov/minerals/pubs/country/2005/knmyb05.pdf.

Figure 6. Selected Industrial and Mining Activity, 2005

composed mainly of the heads of ministries (see The Executive, ch. 4). Concurrently, the government administrative reform of September 1998 aimed to cut expenditures and increase efficiency through greater centralization of functionally related bureaucracies at the center, and through delegation of responsibilities to local units. These actions had the result of decreasing central control over local administrative authorities.

Most notably, North Korea's industrial structure profile is one of a relatively industrialized country. In 2003 agriculture made up only 27.2 percent of the economy, mining 7.8 percent, manufacturing 18.5 percent, and services 32.8 percent. This is the profile of a country that has managed to begin moving beyond abject poverty.

North Korea's growth rates have varied significantly by industry. Although growth was slow from 2001 to 2003, there was expansion across all major sectors. Mining and power generation showed the most growth (3.2 percent and 4.2 percent, respectively), but services, manufacturing, and agriculture also all reveal positive growth. Following the 1990 drop-off in oil imports and the floods and famine of the mid- to late 1990s, although the overall economy contracted by almost 25 percent, trade volume has increased. Agricultural output has rebounded from a low in 1997, but production of most industrial and mining goods remains reduced. mostly as a result of the lack of energy and demand.

Natural Resources

North Korea's major natural resources include coal, copper, fluorspar, gold, graphite, iron ore, lead, magnesite, pyrites, salt, tungsten, and zinc (see fig. 6). The country also has uranium ore deposits, which often have been cited in the international crisis over North Korea's nuclear weapons program that may include a uranium enrichment program in addition to its known plutonium reprocessing program (see The United States, ch. 4).

Some 22.4 percent—about 27,000 square kilometers—of North Korea's land is arable. Of this area, about 8 percent is in permanent crops. Because of adverse weather conditions, agriculture is heavily dependent on insecticides, chemical fertilizers, and electrically driven irrigation systems. The latter require energy resources that North Korea desperately lacks since the cut-off of Russian oil imports in the early 1990s and shortages of hydroelectric power since the prolonged drought in the mid-1990s. For all these reasons, the North never has been and is not likely ever to be self-sufficient in food (see Agriculture, the Famine of 1995–98, and Economic Changes; Foreign Economic Relations, this ch.).

Energy and Power Generation

A major problem for the North Korean economy lies in its energy sector. A stable energy supply is fundamental to a sustainable economy, and North Korea's outdated and crumbling energy grid is a drag on the entire economy. Energy shortages began in 1990 when the Soviet Union and China severely reduced their fuel exports to North Korea. The reduction in imports resulted in part from continued Western economic sanctions against the North and in part from North Korea's inability to pay for energy imports with hard currency.

Much of the energy infrastructure is outdated, poorly maintained, and based on obsolete technology. Because the power grid is so old and dilapidated, even if supply constraints were eased by increased imports, the actual transmission of energy, especially electricity, would remain problematic. Outdated distribution facilities and inefficient management also lead to a major loss of power during transmission itself. The system has been driven to collapse because of the lack of investment in the energy infrastructure, and because North Korea faces limitations on both the technology and the capital needed to improve energy efficiency, rehabilitate its transmission grid, and develop reliable power plants. According to South Korea's Ministry of Unification, 70 percent of North Korea's power facilities have either been abandoned or are in urgent need of repair.

Since 1990 North Korea's energy use has declined, marked mainly by a drastic drop in oil imports. For example, North Korea's crude oil imports in 2002 were 23 percent of those of 1990, and there has been no rise in refining capacity since 1975.

The decline in oil imports has had a negative impact since the early 1990s. North Korea's total volume of power-generation capacity in 1998 was 7.1 million kilowatts, and by 2003 it had only risen to 7.7 million kilowatts. Whereas in 1990 North Korea produced 27.7 billion kilowatt-hours of electricity, in 2002 it produced only 19 billion kilowatt-hours, or 6 percent of South Korea's production. Night-time satellite photography showing electric light usage reveals North Korea, except for P'yŏngyang, as a "black hole" in Northeast Asia.

A light-water nuclear-reactor project in Kŭmho, on the eastern coast in South Hamgyŏng Province, opened in December 1997 as a cooperative undertaking between North Korea and the Korean Peninsula Energy Development Organization (KEDO), a multilateral consortium composed initially of representatives from the European Union (EU), Japan, South Korea, and the United States. Kŭmho was a relative success story until work stopped on the reactors in 2004 as a result of tension between North Korea and the United States over suspected North Korean infringements of the 1994 Agreed Framework (see Glossary; The United States, ch. 4). This project was not intended for widespread economic use but was designed to allow workers from Japan, South Korea, and the United States into the building site. Because foreign workers actually lived at the site, North Korean and foreign officials had to reach a number of agreements covering such issues as currency exchange, mail and communications exchange, and travel and housing.

Although the North is attempting to develop renewable sources of energy, such as hydroelectric power and wind power, these sources still do not meet primary-energy demand. Hydroelectric power constituted 17 percent of North Korea's energy use in 2002, but coal remained the mainstay of energy production, accounting for 70 percent of primary-energy use. Until major renovations in the energy sector can be implemented, the entire North Korean economy will remain severely impeded. Because North Korea lacks the technology and the capital with which to upgrade transmission and generation facilities, the task of renovation will be a long process, if it occurs at all.

Transportation

Railroad, highway, air, and water transportation all are used in North Korea. Railroads are the most important mode of transportation, linking all major cities and accounting for about 86 percent of freight and about 80 percent of passenger traffic. Roads, on the other hand, support only 12 percent of the freight-transporting capacity, and rivers and the sea, only 2 percent. Transportation by air, other than for military purposes within North Korea, is negligible (see fig. 7; fig. 8).

Railroads and Rapid Transit

In 2002 North Korea had 5,214 kilometers of railroads, some 167 percent of the South's total. Even though the North has more kilometers of railroads than the South, 80 percent of these railroads are electrified, and thus operations frequently are suspended because of a lack of power in the grid. It is believed that North Korea has about 300 electric and numerous diesel locomotives. About 35 million passenger journeys occur each year. The great majority of North Korea's freight is carried by rail in the interior, amounting to about 38.5 million tons annually.

Two major railroad lines run north–south in the interior, and one each along the east and west coasts. Two east–west lines connect Wŏnsan and P'yŏngyang by a central and a southerly route, and a

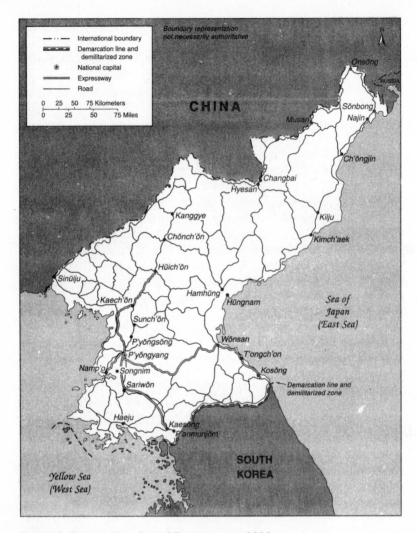

Figure 7. Primary Roads and Expressways, 2005

part of a third link line constructed in the 1980s connects provinces in the mountainous far north near the border with China. The railroad system is linked with the railroads of China and Russia, although gauge inconsistencies necessitate some dual gauging with Russia. As North Korea and South Korea continue to reconnect rail lines between the two countries, there has also been a need to strengthen the carrying capacity of the northern railroads, which have deteriorated as a result of the lack of infrastructure maintenance since the 1980s.

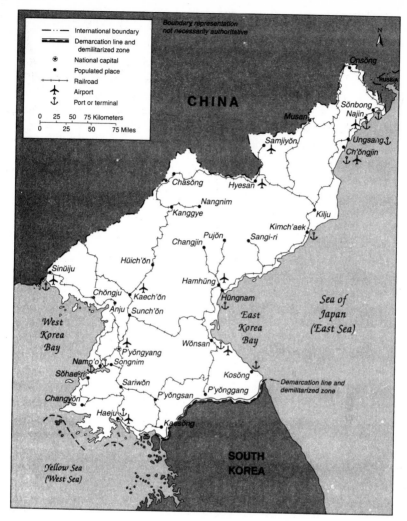

Figure 8. Primary Railroads, Ports, and Airports, 2006

A subway system opened in P'yŏngyang in 1973 with one line; another line was added in 1978. The system has an estimated 22.5 kilometers of track and 17 stations.

Roads

North Korea's road network was estimated at 31,200 kilometers in 1999. Of this total, only 1,997 kilometers were paved, of which only 682 kilometers were multilane highways. By 2005 expressways linked P'yŏngyang with Hŭich'ŏn to the north, with Wŏnsan to the east, Namp'o to the west, and Kaesŏng to the south near the western section of the Demilitarized Zone (DMZ—see Glossary). Wŏnsan, on the east coast, is linked by expressway to Kosŏng near the eastern section of the DMZ. However, 29,203 kilometers (93.6 percent of the 1999 total) of North Korea's roads had gravel, crushed stone, or dirt surfaces, and maintenance on many roads was poor. Most of the paved roads are less than two lanes wide.

Maritime Capabilities

North Korea has a harbor loading capacity of 35.5 million tons, 7 percent of the capacity of South Korea. The major port facilities—all ice free—are at Namp'o and Haeju on the west coast and Najin (often referred to in the media as Rajin), Ch'ŏngjin, Hŭngnam, and Wŏnsan on the east coast. United Nations (UN) statistics for 2002 report that North Korea had ships totaling 870,000 gross registered tons. In 2006 the merchant fleet itself was composed of 232 ships of 1,000 gross registered tons or more. These ships included, by type, the following: 176 cargo carriers, 14 bulk carriers, four container ships, three live-stock carriers, five dual-purpose passenger/cargo ships, 17 petroleum tankers, three refrigerated-cargo ships, eight roll-on/roll-off ships, one chemical tanker, and one vehicle carrier ship.

Civil Aviation

In 2003 North Korea had an estimated 78 usable airports, 35 of which had permanent-surface runways and 43, unpaved runways. North Korea's Sunan International Airport is located 20 kilometers northeast of P'yŏngyang and offers about 20 flights per week on North Korean, Chinese, and Russian carriers. Other major airports are located at Ch'ŏngjin, Hamhŭng, Najin, and Wŏnsan. There are also 19 heliports. The state-run airline, which uses a fleet of 15 Soviet-made planes, is Air Koryo. It provides domestic service to three airports and foreign service to eight cities in China, Thailand, Germany, and Russia. North Korean aircraft seldom are used for transporting cargo. In 2001, according to UN statistics, only 5 tons per kilometer were carried by air, as compared with South Korea's 11,503 tons per kilometer.

Forestry and Fishing

Because of oil shortages, most forestry products are used for fuel, with only small amounts of timber (roundwood) going for construction and manufacturing. In 2002, according to an estimate by the Food and Agriculture Organization (FAO) of the UN, North Korea produced 7.1 million meters of roundwood. Fishing provides an important supplement to the diet and for export. The catch in 2001 totaled 200,000 tons of wild-caught freshwater and saltwater fish, shellfish, and mollusks and about 63,700 tons produced using aquaculture.

Telecommunications and the Internet

North Korea's telecommunications and Internet networks run largely on obsolete Soviet- and Chinese-made equipment dating from the 1950s and 1960s. The sector is deprived of any new government financing and is faced with unreliable electricity supply and severe deficits in modern equipment, spare parts, elementary components, and raw materials. As a result, the networks are highly unreliable and inefficient, cost-insensitive, labor extensive, and subject to frequent breakdowns.

Despite these problems, one-third of North Korean villagers have access to prepaid cell phones and other telephones that allow them to make long-distance calls both domestically and internationally at some personal risk. North Korea also has several dozen modern telecommunications facilities and academic research institutes with sophisticated telecommunications equipment, allowing them access to and use of modern telecommunications technologies, including wireless radio and telephone, satellite communications, and the Internet. Only a few privileged North Koreans have such access, and public Internet use is restricted by the state.

The North Korean Ministry of Posts and Telecommunications, working with the International Telecommunication Union and the United Nations Development Programme (UNDP), has laid fiber-optic cable lines throughout North Korea. By 2000 a nationwide communication network using fiber-optic cables had been set up, and by 2003 some 938,000 telephones were in use. The P'yŏngyang Informatics Center has begun developing software, focusing on the commercial markets. The center's products include a secure fax program that is being marketed through a Japanese company. According to political scientist Alexandre Mansurov, several North Korean computer institutes are equipped with between 200 and 300 Acer Pentium IV desktop computers hooked up to multiple Sun Microsystem servers running Microsoft Windows platforms with programs such as Microsoft Office, Adobe Photoshop, and other word-processing and desktop-publishing software. In May 2002, the first public Internet café opened in P'yŏngyang, equipped with six personal computers and charging US$3 per hour (roughly one-sixth the monthly salary of an average worker). By 2005 there were six or seven Internet cafés in P'yŏngyang, one equipped with 100 computers. The

North Korean government operates five official Web sites in Japan and one in China, and its diplomats around the world communicate with P'yŏngyang through e-mail. North Korea is said to have developed extensive "intranets," including the Kwangmyong-net reportedly used by more than 2 million subscribers, and the Hoon-net, used mainly by foreigners.

Chinese telecommunication companies are aggressively expanding their reach into North Korea. In 2003 Chinese cell-phone companies started building relay stations along the North Korean border, and as many as 20,000 North Koreans have access to Chinese cell phones, despite government attempts to ban their use. High-ranking Korean People's Army (KPA) and KWP cadres do have access to Global Standard for Mobile (GSM) communications-based mobile phones in P'yŏngyang. Foreign government delegations visiting P'yŏngyang, especially from the South, use satellite phones for communication with their respective capitals. The first GSM cellular telephone network for 5,000 subscribers was established in the Najin–Sŏnbong area in early 2002, and a mobile-telephone network for foreign subscribers was launched in P'yŏngyang at the end of 2002.

Government Budget

The Ministry of Finance controls all aspects of the government's budget. The state budget is a major government instrument in carrying out the country's economic goals. Expenditures represented about 75 percent of GNP in the mid-1980s—the allocation of which reflected the priorities assigned to different economic sectors. Taxes were abolished in 1974 as "remnants of an antiquated society." This action, however, did not have any significant effect on state revenue because the overwhelming proportion of government funds—an average of 98.1 percent during 1961–70—was from turnover (sales) taxes, deductions from profits paid by state enterprises, and various user fees on machinery and equipment, irrigation facilities, television sets, and water.

In order to provide a certain degree of local autonomy as well as to lessen the financial burden of the central government, a "local budget system" was introduced in 1973. Under this system, provincial authorities are responsible for the operating costs of institutions and enterprises not under direct central government control, such as schools, hospitals, shops, and local consumer-goods production. In return, they are expected to organize as many profitable ventures as possible and to turn over profits to the central government.

Around November each year, the state budget for the following fiscal year (see Glossary) is drafted, subject to revision around

March. Typically, total revenues exceed expenditures by a small margin, with the surplus carried over to the following year. According to these broad statistics, North Korea's central government expenditures for 2002 were US$10 billion, or 58 percent of total GDP. The largest share of the budget, nearly US$4.2 billion (41.6 percent), was devoted to the national economy, while US$1.4 billion, or 14.4 percent, went to the military. A total of 38.8 percent of the government budget was devoted to "People's Policy," which included public welfare, science, health, and education. Defense spending as a share of total expenditures traditionally has constituted a major part of the government budget (see Defense Industry, ch. 5).

The Ministry of Finance also controls government finance, including banks. North Korea nationalized banks in August 1946 and, on December 6, 1947, established the Central Bank of the Democratic People's Republic of Korea. The Foreign Trade Bank of the Democratic People's Republic of Korea was founded in 1959 to conduct international business for the Central Bank. Since 1987, there have been a number of joint-venture banks and also four insurance companies.

The Central Bank issues currency, regulates the money supply, sets official foreign-exchange rates, deals with the purchase and sale of gold and foreign exchange, and handles foreign loans. The Foreign Trade Bank, under the supervision of the Central Bank, handles transactions and letters of credit related to foreign trade and controls the foreign-exchange payments of foreign-trade organizations and other enterprises. The Kŭmgang Bank is a specialized bank that handles transactions of foreign-trade organizations dealing with exports and imports of machinery, metals, mineral products, and chemical products. The Daesong Bank handles transactions of the Daesong Trading Company and other trading organizations.

Agriculture, the Famine of 1995–98, and Economic Changes

Collapse in the 1990s

The agricultural system in North Korea essentially collapsed in the 1990s, with severe economic and social repercussions throughout the country. Under the best weather conditions, the climate in North Korea allows only one growing season, from June to October, and some experts estimate that even in normal times, North Korea would have a 12 percent shortfall in the grain production required to feed its people. Before the division of the peninsula, the northern half imported food from the more-fertile South. With the division of the peninsula, North Korea attempted to be self-sufficient in food production, a largely unattainable goal. That North Korea is unable to attain self-sufficiency in agriculture is not surprising—most centrally planned economies have inherent limitations because of the structure of land ownership and use, as well as the collectivized nature of the organization and management of agricultural production. In the case of North Korea, the Ch'ŏngsan-ni Method emphasized mass mobilization and political conditioning, to the detriment of efficient agricultural practices.

During the 1995–97 period, North Korea experienced a series of ecological shocks—drought and flooding—that devastated the already weakened agricultural sector and resulted in a nationwide famine. It is highly unusual for an industrialized country with a relatively advanced standard of living to experience famine. Famine and floods since the mid-1990s have devastated the agricultural sector, and reports of starvation and undernourishment are commonplace. Indeed, some scholars have estimated that from a peak around 1989, North Korea's agricultural production contracted by up to 50 percent.

When North Korea collectivized agriculture and centralized decision making in the 1950s, with the goal of food self-sufficiency, it achieved large quantitative increases in output. These increases were mainly the result of even-larger quantitative increases in inputs, such as fertilizers, and clearing land not normally suitable for agriculture. Between 1961 and 1988, grain production expanded by 2.8 percent per year.

However, while these increases in fertilizer use, irrigation, and electrification explain the past success of North Korean agriculture, they also explain the subsequent decline in the 1990s. Pursuit of food self-sufficiency led to a heavy reliance on chemicals and fertilizer. Overuse of the arable land led to acidification and erosion of the soil. Marginally productive areas increasingly were converted to farmland, and this practice led to flooding as the topsoil eroded and deforestation occurred (see The Physical Environment, ch. 2). According to UN agronomists, the soil deposition into the river system raised river bottoms to such a degree that the rivers are no longer capable of absorbing the water from heavy rains or spring thaw. The annual flooding that occurs thus has become increasingly severe. Furthermore, fertilizer use dropped dramatically in the 1990s as the North lost the ability to import fertilizers at friendship prices from China and the former Soviet Union. For example, although North Korea had used 319 kilograms of nitrogenous fertilizers per hectare in 1990, that amount had dropped to 35 kilograms per hectare by 1996.

As a result of these problems, by the early 1990s the agricultural system was even less able to produce enough grains and other foodstuffs to feed the population. For example, in 1992 grain demand

Red Cross food aid at Haeju Port, South Hwanghae Province, January 2005
Courtesy Ministry of Unification, Seoul

exceeded supply by more than 1 million tons. Initially, North Korea drew down stockpiles and attempted other short-term measures, such as exhorting the citizens to eat only two meals a day. However, even before the ecological disruptions of the mid-1990s, the system had begun to collapse.

Causes of the Famine

The famine in the mid-1990s was a result of both systemic and proximate causes. By the early 1990s, there was clear evidence of a severe decline across the entire North Korean economy. Having lost the Soviet Union and China as major subsidy providers, the economy began to falter. In particular, the loss of agricultural subsidies and fertilizer and energy imports from the Soviet Union and China had an immediate impact on agricultural output.

The failure of collective farming was also a factor in the collapse of agricultural production. The main systemic problem in collectivized farming—as in all centralized economies—is the disparity between effort and reward. In North Korea, farmers were paid on the basis of points for workdays, as well as political loyalty to the state. However, monitoring effort is difficult in dispersed agricultural settings, and often workers physically would be in the fields but make no serious effort at work. As long as the system was able to receive large amounts of inputs in the form of cheap fertilizer and capital equipment from its socialist allies, output could generally increase, even though the productivity of the individual workers was not improving and, in fact, probably decreasing. When the inputs began to decline in the early 1990s, the system was unable to adjust accordingly.

The proximate cause of the famine itself began with massive summer floods in 1995 that destroyed that year's harvest. Floods in July and August that year inundated 400,000 hectares of arable land, displaced 500,000 people, and reduced grain production by 1.9 million tons, which was about 30 percent of the annual grain supply. Severe flooding continued in 1996 and was followed abruptly in 1997 by a severe drought. In 1997 North Korea's Central News Agency reported that large reservoirs were 10 to 20 percent below normal, and almost 620 smaller reservoirs were close to empty. Prolonged drought and light snowfall in the winter of 1997–98 led to another grain shortfall of 1.9 million tons. A chronic shortage of energy resources further compounded the situation.

Effects of the Famine

North Korea underwent a severe economic, environmental, and demographic crisis in the mid-1990s. However, the extent of that crisis is still unknown, because outside observers have not had good access to the most-affected areas in North Korea. In particular, there is considerable scholarly dispute over the actual number of deaths that occurred as a result of the famine. A bipartisan team of U.S. congressional staff members visited North Korea in August 1998 and concluded that famine-related deaths amounted to 300,000 to 800,000 annually. The famine was so severe that North Korea was forced to ask for international aid, for the first time allowing officials of the United Nations Children's Fund (UNICEF) and the FAO World Food Programme into every province in North Korea.

Post-Famine Situation

North Korea had its best harvest in a decade in 2004. Even so, the harvest was not enough to feed its people. A report by the FAO World Food Programme projected domestic cereals availability in 2004–5 at 4.24 million tons, a 2.4 percent increase from the previous year. The 2004 rice paddy harvest was estimated at 2.4 million tons, while corn output was unchanged at 1.7 million tons. The forecast need for the year 2004–5 was estimated at 5.1 million tons, leaving a gap of 900,000 tons.

After the devastating famine of the mid-1990s, the agricultural sector began to stabilize in the early twenty-first century. Realistically, however, North Korea will never be able to attain food self-sufficiency. Indeed, even South Korea has never been in that position. Under the best of conditions, self-sufficiency in agriculture is impossible for North Korea, and the current conditions are far from ideal. Although the agricultural sector has been partially privatized, the overuse of fertilizer and subsequent deforestation of arable land have ruined much of the potentially arable land for a generation to come. Furthermore, lacking a fully free market and access to capital and technology, the system has not come anywhere near efficiency, and there is little potential for reform in the near future.

Economic Reforms

By the 1980s, the inherent limitations of North Korea's centrally planned economy had begun to be reached, as demonstrated by the failure of the Second Seven-Year Plan (1978–84). Compounding this situation, the end of the Cold War and the loss of support from China and the Soviet Union in close succession, as well as the famine of the mid-1990s, combined to devastate the North Korean economy. In response, North Korea cautiously began to move toward what it called *economic adjustments* (the term *reform* would have suggested there had been something wrong with the state's economic system, but the leadership allowed that *adjustments* could be made). Although North Korea initially made mostly empty pronouncements about economic reform, more dramatic changes occurred in 2002.

On July 1, 2002, North Korea significantly adjusted the public distribution system that had been a major element of the centrally planned economy. North Korea adopted monetized economic transactions and changed the incentives for labor and companies. The nation also adopted a number of policies and strategies designed to increase foreign investment and trade. However, although the reforms were centrally planned and administered, they were not comprehensive. As a result, a multilayered and partly decentralized economy emerged, where prices were allowed to float and private ownership and markets were permitted, but the state still owned most of the major enterprises and still controlled workers in many other ways. The government promulgated new laws that covered central planning, agriculture, mineral resources, and industrial sectors. Concurrently, there were new laws on stock, joint-stock companies, joint ventures with foreign firms, and a number of other decrees that opened the economy to more foreign participation. Administrative and managerial responsibilities were delegated from KWP officials to industrial and commercial managers. Assets in oil refining, mining, manufacturing, textiles, and food processing became subject to corporate ownership.

The changes of 2002 were categorically different from those announced earlier. In July 2003, the former U.S. ambassador to South Korea, James Laney, and Jason Shaplen, a former adviser to KEDO, noted that, "In the two months prior to the October 2002 HEU [highly enriched uranium] revelation, North Korea had, with remarkable speed, undertaken an important series of positive initiatives that seemed the polar opposite of its posturing on the nuclear issue … [representing] the most promising signs of change on the peninsula in decades."

These reforms affected the entire society, whereas previous reform efforts were partial, segmented, and largely restricted to peripheral sectors of the economy. The earlier reform efforts extended only to areas easily controlled by the regime, such as foreign direct investment or special economic zones that could be cordoned off from North Korean society at large. The implication of wider reforms was that the regime was taking a much larger step—and having a greater impact on society—than before. It also meant that the regime was making a bigger gamble, because the effects of the changes would be difficult to control. Although the partial reform efforts of 2002 may be too limited to bring about economic recovery, the effect on society is increasingly irreversible. Yet with much control remaining within the government, economic reform is still partial. North Korea is no longer a centrally planned economy, but the new institutions for "market socialism" are either nascent or nonexistent.

There is considerable skepticism among foreign analysts as to whether these changes are genuine or simply a minimalist attempt by the regime to "muddle through." There is also skepticism as to whether any reform measures can actually make a difference in North Korea's economy. Some experts have argued that only complete and thorough political and economic change can generate sustainable economy activity. Others see more potential for success in the set of "China-style" reforms that North Korea has begun. Although the ultimate assessment of the reforms will only occur in the future, it is possible to conclude that they are significant, and categorically different from the adjustments of the past. At the same time, because these developments are continuing to occur in the mid-2000s, a comprehensive description of the reforms is also difficult, because government institutions, laws, and policies are changing rapidly.

Farmers at work in the rice paddy; the sign exhorts them to work "All together to the rice-planting battle!"
Courtesy Korea Today *(P'yŏngyang), May 1996, 11*

Reform of the Public Distribution System

The most significant of the July 2002 central government set of economic reforms was the introduction of a pricing system whereby the market sets most prices. Except for crops, rationing was abolished, and goods are now traded using currency. Although prices continue to be administered, "by fiat, state prices are brought in line with prices observed in the markets." In addition, workers were given a one-time salary raise, with salaries increasing 10 to 40 times, depending on occupation, and prices surged 40 to 80 times. Workers previously had been paid regardless of performance. Under the new system, however, they earn according to how much they work, and those who do not work are not eligible for some services provided by the government.

Rationing under the old public distribution system had largely collapsed in the mid-1990s as the economy went through severe shocks. The main feature of the system was food rationing, which applied to almost two-thirds of the citizenry. Industrial workers received the major portion of public distributions; state-farm and collective-farm workers received smaller distributions from the system, making up the difference from their own agricultural production. Although originally designed to provide each citizen with sufficient food rations, as the economy and in particular agricultural production contracted, the rations were reduced initially from 600 to 800 grams per day, depending on the type of labor involved, to 400 or 450 grams per day by late 1999. Many people could not afford to buy enough extra food.

In response to the breakdown of the public distribution system, small-scale markets began sprouting up all over North Korea. Although in 2000 the private sector was estimated to constitute less than 4 percent of the entire economy, the expansion of private markets was rapid. Experts suggest that the private markets generated as much as 25 percent of the food supply in 2004. Farmers' markets, long grudgingly accepted, became much more important to the entire economy. Thus, many of the acts undertaken by the central government in 2002 were actually merely an official sanction of events and changes that were already underway.

At the same time, the government decentralized much of the economic decision-making authority to local representatives. Measures included cutting government subsidies, allowing farmers' markets to operate, and transferring managerial decisions for industry and agriculture from the party and the central government (through factory party committees) into the hands of local production units. In theory, enterprises were required to cover their own costs, managers were forced to meet hard budget constraints, and evaluation of workers was no longer based on the number of days they showed up, but rather on productivity and profit. To what extent this reform has been realized in practice is not clear, although there were reports in 2004 and 2005 that the system was beginning to function as expected. State-owned enterprises were allowed to trade part of their production and materials in a new "socialist goods trading market," to export their products themselves, and to earn the capital necessary for their operation to function. State-owned enterprises also were allowed to restructure their operations as they saw fit. Farmers were given the right to make decisions on how to cultivate their land, with the government retaining ownership of the land.

In order to participate in the private sector, households began to keep foreign currency. In 2000 the Bank of Korea in Seoul estimated that North Korean households held approximately US$964 million in total foreign currency, with the average household holding the equivalent of US$186. This practice not only put the North Korean households firmly in the marketplace but also took money away from private savings accounts denominated in wŏn (for value of the wŏn—see Glossary), thus affecting the central government's ability to direct lending and projects. Of the foreign currency, more than 60 percent was in U.S. dollars, with the remainder in Chinese renminbi or Japanese yen. North Koreans' need for foreign currency initially was largely a result of the breakdown of rationing that occurred after 1995, which forced citizens to move into the black market in search of food and other goods. Black-market operators refused to take North Korean wŏn and demanded hard currency.

Information about the pace and extent of the market reforms is sketchy, because North Korea has not opened its economy to full international participation or scrutiny. However, anecdotal evidence abounds that notable change has taken place. A microbrewery opened in P'yŏngyang's Yanggakdo Hotel in 2002, 11 restaurants selling goat delicacies had opened in P'yŏngyang by 2004, and the capital has a "food street" lined with restaurants that cater to the well-off and to foreigners. Visitors to P'yŏngyang in 2004 reported that more than 35 distinct markets were in operation, the best known being the Tongil Market in the downtown area. These market operations are not privately owned—usually they are run by a work unit—but they are profit generating, according to Nicholas Bonner of Koryo Tours, a company that specializes in travel tours to North Korea. Estimates suggest that there might be as many as 400 markets throughout in the country.

It seems increasingly clear that the centrally planned economy had to be abandoned—that the decision was less one of choice than of necessity. *Chosun Ilbo* reported from Seoul on December 9, 2002, that the North Korean regime was forced to lift a ban on private businesses because "popular disaffection was about to explode." Former World Bank economist Bradley Babson notes that "small family businesses of 3–5 workers are expanding with official recognition, producing a variety of hand-made products for sale in local markets."

Since July 2002, North Korea has continued to modify the wage and price structures. In March 2003, the government allowed merchants to sell not only farm products but also manufactured goods and other commodities and permitted manufacturers to sell directly to the market. On November 23, 2003, the regime charged industrial conglomerates with responsibility for investments in their own facilities. In the past, all facility investments had been made by the state. This change means that manufacturers are now responsible for replacing their own facilities.

In 2004 the central government reduced the minimum wage paid to employees of foreign companies from US$80 or US$90 per month to US$38 per month. Vice Minister of Foreign Trade Kim Yong-sun said that "We have recently drastically reduced the minimum wage to 30 Euros [US$38] ... in the past, we only allowed foreign companies entry into specialized economic zones, but now we will allow them to set up in other places around the North. If [a company] wishes to participate in the development of the mineral industry in the North, we can grant rights, and the same goes for establishing a bank. We are taking a series of steps to lessen investment restrictions in each industry."

Although the enterprises remain under the control of the state, and although salaries in many sectors are still dictated by the government, it is clear that the introduction of limited supply and demand has generated an increase in market activity in North Korea.

Banking and Finance

The financial system of North Korea remained almost entirely state controlled in 2002; however, the government began to implement change in this sector, as well. In the past, some foreign banks had been allowed to form businesses in North Korea. For example, in 1995 the Dutch bank ING signed a joint-venture agreement with the North Korean Foreign Insurance Company, establishing an investment bank in North Korea that was 70 percent owned by ING. This was the first Western bank in North Korea, although ING later pulled out. In the wake of the 2002 reforms, Daesong Bank of North Korea announced a relationship with Sberbank of Russia in November 2004, designed to increase the ease with which customers of both banks could transfer foreign currency and make payments. Additionally, in July 2004 North Korea began, with an Australian firm, a joint venture called Korea Maranatha Enterprise Development Limited. The venture was owned equally by North Korea's Ministry of Finance and the Maranatha Trust of Australia, with the goal of lending small amounts of money to North Korean enterprises in a bid to develop the country's small and medium-sized businesses. Officials of Korea Maranatha described the operation as a pilot program, said that the entity began operations with two clients, and hoped to increase its operations if the venture proved successful.

Beginning in February 2002, North Korea also devalued the wŏn relative to the dollar. During the 1990s, North Korea had maintained an obviously overvalued rate of 2.15 wŏn to the U.S. dollar. In February 2003, the black-market rate went from 200 wŏn per dollar to 400 wŏn per dollar, and by November 2003 the wŏn was exchanging at 1,000 wŏn per dollar. In September 2004, the official exchange rate was 160 wŏn to the euro (the currency adopted by North Korea in December 2002 for foreign-exchange transactions). However, the black-market exchange rate was 10 times that amount (see Assessment of the Economic Reforms, this ch.).

Another aspect of the new financial changes was the issue of public bonds to North Korea's citizens. In 2003 the North Korean government floated bonds for the first time since the start of the Korean War in 1950. On March 26, 2003, the minister of finance announced

The P'yŏngyang Silk Mill, P'yŏngyang
Courtesy Korea Today *(P'yŏngyang), January 1997, 6*

that P'yŏngyang would borrow money from the public by issuing bonds. The bonds, floated on May 1, 2003, had a maturity date of April 30, 2013, in denominations of 500, 1,000, and 5,000 wŏn. The bonds carried no interest rate and were redeemable in installments starting in December 2008, but if their holders drew lucky numbers in lotteries to be held once every six months, they would receive an unspecified "prize."

Some observers believe that the bond program is a positive step as a fiscal policy improvement measure that brings North Korea further into the modern world. Others believe it will only add to the burdens of workers and laborers and was designed by the government to increase its budget by using surplus money that currently resides in the hands of citizens.

Although there has been some reform in the financial sector in the first years of the century, on the whole the financial system remains tightly controlled. The government has made little effort to establish a viable financial capital market, and, as of 2007, there were no independent financial institutions and no appreciable bond market other than the unusual system P'yŏngyang had set up.

Legal and Administrative Reforms

In addition to changes to the centrally planned economy itself, the government changed a number of laws and amended the constitution to provide a legal framework for domestic economic reform and to increase foreign trade and investment. A major element of those legal changes were the constitutional revisions of September 1998, which formally permitted private ownership of assets, provided a more clearly delineated basis for foreign investment and trade, and established the Cabinet of Ministers, composed mainly of the heads of economic ministries. Concurrently, the administrative reform of September 1998 aimed to reduce government expenditures and increase government efficiency through greater consolidation of functionally related bureaucracies at the center, and through delegation of responsibilities to local units. This reform had the result of decreasing central control over local administrative authorities.

Although there has been foreign investment in North Korea since the 1970s, a relatively major effort to open the North to the international economy has occurred only since the mid-1990s. There were 11 constitutional amendments relating to foreign investment in 1998 alone. In 1999 the government amended joint-production and joint-venture laws to allow for projects outside the Najin–Sŏnbong International Trade Zone. Until that time, 100 percent foreign-owned investment enterprises were allowed to set up businesses only in the Najin–Sŏnbong zone. The government continues to establish the legal foundations that permit and regulate international investment. The Processing Trade Law, Lock Gate Law, and Copyright Law came into effect in April 2001 to expand the scope of foreign trade. These measures regulate which sectors are open to foreign investment and in which sectors foreign firms may own 100 percent of the capital, with protection from nationalization and guarantees of the right to lease and use land for up to 50 years and of tax and tariff preferences.

As part of the July 1, 2002, reforms, the KWP formally abandoned the Taean Work System and introduced a new economic-management system. The new system turned over to the manager responsibility for running a factory and reduced the political and economic role of the factory party secretary. It tasked the manager with running the factory on a self-accounting system and changed the wage system. In the new system, salaries for workers were raised, and merit pay was introduced to reward those who work harder or more efficiently. However, the factory party committee is still the formal leadership of the factory, and the party secretary retains the chairmanship of the committee, which continues to provide the secretary with the opportunity to wield power in the factory. Thus, although nominally the power of the KWP was reduced and the actual manager's power was increased, it is not clear how dramatic this shift is in practice.

North Korea set up the External Economic Legal Advice Office in June 1999 in order to settle legal issues with regard to international investment and trade relations. In August 2004, the North also allowed the establishment of the country's first private law firm, as part of its efforts to attract international investors. Hay, Kalb Associates, a British-owned firm, opened a joint-venture company employing a dozen local lawyers with offices on Kim Il Sung Square on August 15, 2004.

In a revision of its criminal law on April 29, 2004, North Korea changed and strengthened legal measures to protect private property while stiffening penalties for antistate crimes. The revision, the fifth since 1950, reflects P'yŏngyang's ambition to achieve two goals at the same time: safeguarding its regime and boosting its impoverished economy. The law introduced lengthy new provisions regarding the principle of legality and classified in detail previously obscure provisions regarding private ownership. The number of articles dealing with economic crimes increased from 18 to 74. These articles cover such issues as provisions punishing foreign investors for tax evasion, infringement of trademark rights, illegal commercial transactions, and violation of import and export orders.

In December 2004, North Korea announced a real estate law that gave individuals some rights to sell their houses at will in the first half of 2005. Because the number of illegal house trades among individuals increased after the "economic adjustment policy" in July 2002, regulating the trade gave the government some control over such activities.

Many of the legal and administrative changes since 1998 were designed to clarify and further strengthen the rights and responsibilities of foreign firms in North Korea. Other changes covered the organization and control of domestic economic activity. Because so many of the laws have been enacted relatively recently, it is unclear how they will operate in practice and how vigorously the government will enforce and implement them.

Special Economic Zones

A major element of North Korea's reform was the development of special economic zones. These zones vary in their particulars, but all were established with special tax and tariff incentives for foreigners, with the aim of attracting investment and foreign exchange, spurring employment, and boosting the local development of improved technologies and infrastructure through greater interaction with foreign firms. North Korea has established four such zones. The first of these areas was the Najin–Sŏnbong International Trade Zone, established in 1991 and located in territory carved out of the northeast

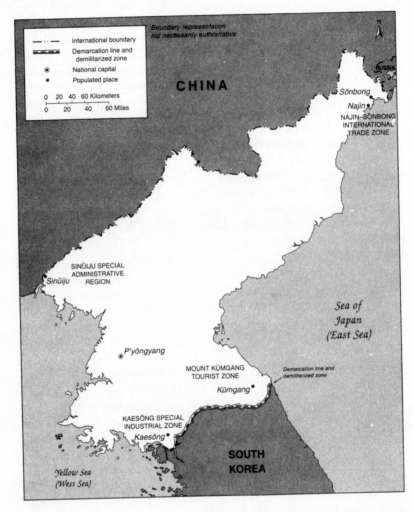

Figure 9. Special Economic Zones, 2006

province of North Hamgyŏng, near the border with Russia. By the early twenty-first century, three more regions had been added: the Sinŭiju Special Administrative Region, in North P'yŏngan Province, along the border with China on the Yellow Sea (or, as Koreans prefer, the West Sea) was established in 2001; the Mount Kŭmgang Tourist Zone, in Kangwŏn Province, in the southeast coastal area along the DMZ, was established in 1998; and the Kaesŏng Special Industrial Zone, in the city of Kaesŏng (formerly Kaesŏng Province), within sight of the DMZ near P'anmunjŏm, was established in 2002 (see fig. 9).

Like most other policies undertaken by the North Korean regime, the zones show slow and halting progress. The Najin–Sŏnbong zone has had a mixed history: by the end of 1999, total foreign investment was estimated at US$125 million, almost half of which came from the Emperor Group of Hong Kong for its construction of a hotel and casino. However, with help from the United Nations Development Programme (UNDP), in late 1998 North Korea opened its own business school in the zone, the Najin Business Institute, along with a business information center.

In January 2001, the government announced the establishment of a large special economic zone in the city of Sinŭiju, located on the Amnok River (known as the Yalu in China) border with China and intended to encompass 128 square kilometers. As planned, the Sinŭiju region would allow foreign currencies to be used and was designed to take advantage of the restored railroad link between North Korea and South Korea. Sinŭiju reportedly was given 50 years of independent authority in almost all political and economic aspects, including legislation, administration, and judicial power. P'yŏngyang claimed that it would not interfere except to handle diplomacy and national defense issues. Sinŭiju was even to be given the right to issue visas independently. A Chinese businessman, Yang Bin, originally was put in charge of the zone, although Yang's legal complications with the Chinese government over unrelated business activities in China sidetracked his appointment. Sinŭiju has made little progress, in large part as a result of difficulties over its administration and leadership. However, it is important to note that it was the Chinese who held up progress, not North Korean mismanagement.

Since its opening in 1998, the Mount Kŭmgang Tourism Zone has shown more success. In accordance with an agreement signed between the Hyundai Group in South Korea and the North Korean government, the Mount Kŭmgang zone allows South Korean cruise-ship passengers to take tours of Mount Kŭmgang, one of Korea's most famous and beautiful mountains. Hyundai Asan started the three-day packages to Mount Kŭmgang in 1998 using a sea route, and an overland route has been available since September 2003. On July 3, 2004, a one-day trip to the mountain became possible as the two Koreas agreed to extend the hours during which visitors may pass through the DMZ. The total number of visitors to the Mount Kŭmgang zone reached 800,000 by the start of 2005.

A fourth zone, in Kaesŏng, a historical capital of Korea, was established in 2002 and began operations in 2004; it has been more successful. The Kaesŏng Special Industrial Zone is mainly a North Korean–South Korean joint venture (see Kaesŏng Industrial Venture, this ch.).

Mount Kŭmgang Tourist Zone, 2006
Courtesy Munhwasarangbang Company, Seoul

Top-Down Reform Measures

In assessing the reforms, an important point to be made about North Korea's economic policy is that the reform measures were centrally planned and top-down, and thus the measures enjoyed the support of the highest political levels in North Korea. For example, Kim Jong Il himself was quoted as saying, "Things are not what they used to be in the 1960s. So no one should follow the way people used to do things in the past.... We should make constant efforts to renew the landscape and replace the one which was formed in the past, to meet the requirements of a new era." This reform initiative was a gamble for Kim because it also meant that he risked being personally connected to its failure.

An article in the semi-official English-language *People's Korea* in 2002 reflected this attitude. It said, "these measures, effective July 1, are intended to comprehensively improve the people's living standard based on the new economic policy mapped out by General Secretary Kim Jong Il to build an economically powerful nation." The article continued, "the recent series of economic measures came in line with General Secretary Kim Jong Il's new economic policy, whose essence is that the basic method of socialist economic management is to gain maximum profits while adhering to socialist principles."

In addition, the regime emphasized that the reforms were a gradual and long-term process, writing that: "it was in the year 2000 that this new economic policy of Kim Jong Il began to be put into practice in earnest on a national scale. It contained the strengthening of the cabinet's role as the headquarters of the national economy, the transfer of authority of economic planning to each leading economic organ at all levels, the rational reorganization of factories and enterprises and the improvement of their management; and the differentiation and specialization of production." Choe Hong-kyu, a bureau director in the State Planning Commission, was quoted in *People's Korea* as saying: "Kim Jong Il stresses that all the outworn and dogmatic 'Soviet-type' patterns and customs should be renounced in the fields of economic planning, financing, and labor management ... he also points to the fact that foreign trade should be conducted in accordance with the mechanism and principles of capitalism."

These official pronouncements by the leadership echoed the increasingly open admission that society was changing in response to the economic difficulties that North Korea was experiencing. On August 1, 2002, Supreme People's Assembly president Kim Yong-nam said: "We are directing our whole efforts to restructure our economic base to be in line with the information technology revolution ... we are reforming the economic system on the principle of profitability."

There is further evidence of the explicit consent of the top leadership. The 2003 New Year's Day editorials in *Nodong Shinmun* (Workers' Daily) cited "new measures for economic management," and noted that "it is urgent to improve economic management and rapidly develop science and technology: we should manage and operate the economy in such a way as to ensure the largest profitability while firmly adhering to socialist principles." Minister of Finance Mun Il-bong gave a speech on March 26, 2003, saying that "in all institutions and enterprises a system of calculation based on money will have to be correctly installed, production and financial accounting systems be strengthened, production and management activities be carried out thoroughly by calculating the actual profits." Thus, the government has attempted to retain control of the system, while at the same time recognizing the need to make changes in its economic practices.

Assessment of the Economic Reforms

Since the formal abrogation of the centrally planned economy in July 2002, most anecdotal reports indicate that the markets—after experiencing an initial and significant surge in prices—have continued to function relatively normally. There was no widespread chaos, farmers' markets moved to fill the void in supplies caused by rationing, and the population appeared to have adjusted to the changing circumstances. The economic reforms tested the government's ability to deal with inflation, troubled enterprises, and the urban poor created by the monetization of the economy. Low supply and low output have led to massive increases in prices and further devaluation of the wŏn.

The FAO's World Food Programme estimated that the price of rice and corn rationed through the public distribution system remained low and stable, 44 wŏn and 24 wŏn per kilogram, respectively. Yet prices at the private markets were much higher. The nominal price of rice increased 550 percent, and perhaps even more. In November 2004, the price of rice was 600 wŏn per kilogram, almost 30 percent of a typical monthly wage. Corn was 320 wŏn per kilogram. In the months following the introduction of price reforms, there was rapid inflation.

By comparison, in 1979 China's initial price reforms drove up the price of rice by 25 percent. In North Korea, prices have gone up by at least 600 percent, and the wŏn has depreciated from the official exchange rate of 150 wŏn to US$1 in 2002 to at least 1,000 wŏn, with some estimating the black-market values at between 2,500 and 3,000 wŏn to the dollar in 2006. The reforms probably enabled Kim Jong Il to gain some measure of control of the economy by hurting those black marketeers who held large amounts of wŏn before the currency devaluation, because the value of their wŏn holdings plummeted with the devaluation against the dollar. However, fixed-income workers also were badly affected by the rise in prices. In addition, many workers were laid off by companies forced to cut costs. Finally, fragmentary evidence suggests that even those sectors of the labor force favored with the largest wage hikes (6,000 wŏn) were discontented. Defectors crossing into China complained that the promise of higher wages had not been kept, with workers receiving only an additional 800 wŏn and then nothing extra after October 2003. This failure may have created a new class of urban poor that could be difficult to control in the future, although there is only limited evidence of any unrest.

The regime has made major changes in the way in which the economy functions. Undoubtedly these changes have been designed by Kim Jong Il and the ruling regime to retain control while dealing with the undeniable economic problems in the country. However, the changes have created confusion and perhaps even chaos. While there is considerable disagreement among observers as to what the actual motivations of the regime are, and also skepticism as to whether the reforms can work, the point remains that the changes affect the entire society and are thus politically consequential.

The evidence points to the conclusion that North Korea's economic reforms are cautious and tentative, not wholesale. They also are clumsy. Inflation is rampant, but production has not been freed to respond accordingly. A North Korean opening up will not foster the kind of immediate wholesale rhetorical and practical changes that the United States apparently expects. Examining the reforms, economist Marcus Noland wrote in 2003: "It is not at all clear that the current leadership is willing to countenance the erosion of state control that would accompany the degree of marketization necessary to revitalize the economy."

Indeed, it is unclear whether any reform measures can actually make much of a difference in North Korea's economy. Nevertheless, these reforms are significant, and, more importantly, they will be extremely difficult to reverse. It is one thing to declare a special economic zone in the northeastern region of Najin–Sŏnbong and far more significant to affect the daily lives of every citizen by introducing market reforms. Willingly or unwillingly, the Kim Jong Il regime has started down a path that is difficult to reverse and also holds the potential to spark real change in North Korea.

Foreign Economic Relations

In addition to domestic economic reforms that began in 2002, North Korea has become increasingly open to a foreign presence. The legal and constitutional changes that the regime has made since 1998 provide a more clearly delineated framework for foreign trade and investment in North Korea. By 2005 overall levels of trade had surpassed those of 1991 (when trade was US$2.5 billion), as the upward trend continued from a nadir in 1998 (when trade decreased to US$1.4 billion). Total foreign trade for 2005 was around US$4 billion, or around 10 percent of GDP.

The regime also began to take small and tentative steps aimed at exposing North Korean bureaucrats to how market capitalism functions in practice. Because government bureaucrats have been trained entirely in a system of central planning, they lack the basic knowledge about how markets function and how to operate in such an environment. Beginning in 2001, former military officers were assigned as directors of factories and enterprises, in an apparent attempt to transform them from military elites into economic elites. There is skepticism on this point, with some observers seeing this action as an attempt by the military to increase its control over the economy. Even if this assumption were true, however, the result is that the military itself is becoming more involved in the daily functioning of economic matters.

Political scientist Park Kyung-ae notes that nongovernmental contacts between North Korea and various foreign nations increased significantly in the late 1990s. For example, two North Korean medical and energy delegations visited the United States in 1999, and other visits to the United States in 1998 included economic delegations that focused on poultry, academic exchanges, and energy. In 2001 more than 480 North Koreans visited Australia, China, Italy, and Sweden for training programs in finance, trade, and accounting. Other groups of officials have studied in Canada, Mexico, the Philippines, Singapore, and Thailand. By far, the most delegations have traveled to China, although industrial management training also has occurred in India and Malaysia. In Europe, North Koreans have studied medical techniques in Switzerland, and agricultural and cultural groups have visited Austria, Denmark, Hungary, Italy, the Netherlands, Sweden, and the United Kingdom.

In the wake of the agricultural and economic troubles of the 1990s, North Korea also has depended heavily on foreign aid. From 1995 to 2000, North Korea received more than US$2 billion in aid from other nations and international organizations. The bulk of this aid was from South Korea and covered projects such as the Mount

Kŭmgang zone, the 1994 Agreed Framework, and food and medical aid for famine victims.

Despite political troubles with the North, the United States also has been a major donor to North Korea for humanitarian reasons. Between 1995 and 2003, the United States contributed US$615 million in food aid and US$5 million in medical assistance. The U.S. contribution to KEDO amounted to more than US$400 million before all work on the KEDO project was stopped in 2004.

Although North Korea remains a very closed and isolated country, there has been considerable opening in foreign economic policy since the late 1990s. Mostly because of economic stagnation earlier in the decade, the North also has been far more open to international aid donors. As a result of this opening, foreign firms had achieved more penetration into North Korea in the early twenty-first century than at any time since the Korean War.

North–South Relations

Sunshine Policy and New Economic Development

South Korea is clearly the country that has most vigorously pursued attempts to engage North Korea economically. In 1998 South Korean president Kim Dae Jung developed the Sunshine Policy, whereby South Korea abandoned its long-standing policy of hostility to the North and instead began to follow a path designed to engage the North through economic and cultural contacts. The change in strategy has proved popular in the South. Roh Moo Hyun won the 2002 presidential election by a resounding 49 percent to 40 percent over competitor Lee Hoi Chang, based largely on Roh's campaign promise to continue the Sunshine Policy.

Following the shift to the Sunshine Policy, South Korea rapidly increased its contacts with the North: North–South merchandise trade increased 50 percent from 2001 to 2002, to US$641.7 million. The following year, trade between North Korea and South Korea rose 13 percent, to US$724.2 million.

South Korean conglomerates rapidly expanded their activities in the North with the official approval of both South Korean and North Korean governments. In 2002 permission was granted to 39 South Korean firms to establish cooperative partnership arrangements with North Korea. In 2005 Samsung successfully negotiated with the North Korean government to place its logo in P'yŏngyang and had begun exporting consumer electronics from its electronic industrial complex of more than 1.6 million square meters in factories in the North. LG Corporation has been manufacturing televisions in North

The port of Namp'o, South P'yŏngan Province
Courtesy Korea Today *(P'yŏngyang), January 1997, 6*

Korea since 1996. By 2004, there were more than 1,000 South Koreans living and working in North Korea, and the port of Namp'o had 180 South Korean companies.

By the end of 2004, more than 400 South Korean companies had set up offices in Yanji, a city in the Yanbian Korean Autonomous Prefecture in China's Jilin Province, close to its border with North Korea. These firms have invested a total of US$161.8 million, the greatest amount of all the foreign investors. Indications are that the South Korean investments will keep growing. Of these companies, about 40 already have moved into North Korea's Sŏnbong and Najin development districts, establishing food, cigarette, and garment factories. The garment factories alone were employing 20,000 North Koreans in 2005. In addition, many other companies are pursuing joint ventures in transportation, wood processing, cultivation of marine products, agricultural development, restaurants, trade, and tourism.

Cooperation also increased rapidly between the two Korean governments in the early 2000s. In November 2004, the Korea Resources Corporation, a quasigovernmental organization in South Korea, announced that it would open a liaison office in North Korea. Park Yang-soo, president of the corporation, said that in order "to cooperate on economic development between South Korea and North Korea, our state-run corporation plans to set up a liaison office or branch office for raw materials in P'yŏngyang next year." South Korea had never had a liaison office in the North, and at the time of Park's announcement, South Korea and North Korea technically were still at war. The goal of the liaison office is to exploit mineral deposits in the North, beginning with an annual goal of exporting 10,000 to12,000 tons of graphite to the South. As of late 2007, the opening of the office was on hold.

More than 200,000 South Koreans visited North Korea in 2003–4. The number of South Korean visitors to the North, excluding South Korean tourists to the Mount Kŭmgang resort, has experiènced yearly increases of 20 percent since 2000.

Another governmental project was the plan to reconnect the Kyŏngŭi Railroad—a connection between North Korea and South Korea through the DMZ, which had been severed since the Korean War. This railroad will connect the entire Korean Peninsula to Chinese and Russian railroad networks that, in turn, connect to cities in China and European Russia. The economic and political implications of the railroad reconnection are potentially fairly large, because it would allow shipment of goods from Japan and South Korea to Europe via North Korea. It also could be a conduit for further trade and investment in the region. The Korea Transport Institute estimates that earnings could be significant within three years of completion of the railroad, perhaps up to US$149 million in fees annually.

The Kyŏngŭi Railroad also is significant in political terms. Even during the 2002 United States–North Korea standoff, North Korea and South Korea continued to work toward reconnecting the Kyŏngŭi Railroad. The railroad has required clearing a section of the DMZ of land mines. In order to actually clear the DMZ, military meetings were required, and the fact that both militaries were able to agree is a significant step in the reduction of tension on the peninsula. Work on the line continued throughout the crisis of 2002. The land mines were cleared by December 2002, and the laying of railroad track was completed. Construction work was completed in 2006.

Kaesŏng Industrial Venture

The major venture between North and South is the establishment of a special economic zone and industrial district just north of the DMZ in the ancient capital city of Kaesŏng. Planned to use South Korean capital and North Korean labor, the zone includes a railroad and a highway that connect North and South through the DMZ. Hyundai Asan of South Korea and the Asia–Pacific Peace Committee of the North struck a deal in August 2000 to develop an industrial

Workers sorting and weighing new prescription drugs at a
Sariwŏn pharmaceutical factory, North Hwanghae Province
Courtesy Chosŏn *(P'yŏngyang), December 2005, 32*

park. The Land Corporation, a South Korean state-invested corporation, contracted with the North for a 50-year lease of the area, and the
North provided South Korean businesses favorable tax rates and cur-
rency-exchange conditions in return. The two Koreas broke ground
on the first phase of development on June 30, 2003, a ceremony to
mark the inauguration of the Kaesŏng Special Industrial Zone Management Committee and start the construction of enterprises to operate in the zone was held in Kaesŏng in October 2004, and the entire
park was expected to be completed by 2007. When finished, the park
will cover 66 square kilometers and might eventually employ
100,000 North Koreans and 150,000 South Koreans. The potential
value of products produced in Kaesŏng could reach US$21 billion per
year, according to the Federation of Korean Industries.

On December 1, 2004, the highway through the DMZ to Kaesŏng
was officially opened. After completion of the 4.2 kilometer-long
highway crossing the Demarcation Line (see Glossary) that divides
the DMZ up to the Tongil Tower and connecting the two Koreas, the
road officially opened as the Main East Sea Road. The railroad connecting Kaesŏng to the South was also completed in June 2003, nine
months after beginning work clearing land mines in the DMZ. In
December 2004, the North and the South also reached an agreement
on the supply of electric power to the Kaesŏng Special Industrial
Zone, according to the Korea Electric Power Corporation. Under the

agreement, the South began transferring electric power to the North in January 2005, marking the first time electricity has been transferred across the DMZ since the Korean War broke out in 1950. The South Korean government said it would seek provisions in future free-trade talks that will permit preferential duties for products from the Kaesŏng zone so that they will be treated as if they had been produced in the South.

North Korean-made iron kitchen pots began to appear in department stores in Seoul in December 2004, as the first products of an inter-Korean joint economic project to become available in the South. The South Korean manufacturing company, LivingArt, is one of 15 companies from South Korea that have begun to produce in Kaesŏng's pilot area of nearly 100,000 square meters. Such was the excitement in South Korea that the first set of 1,000 pots sold out in the first day. Woori Bank, South Korea's second-largest lender, opened a branch in Kaesŏng in December 2004.

The Economy in Transition

North Korea's economy is in transition. The old, centrally planned economy has essentially been abandoned, but a full embrace of market capitalism has not yet occurred. Some 15 years after the fall of the Soviet Union, North Korea continues to survive, stumbling along with an economy that is barely functional. The North has endured far longer than most observers expected, and although it is tempting to predict that the regime—and the economy—will collapse in the near future, prudence cautions against any predictions about prospects. Market signals are beginning to pervade the economy, and more information from the outside world is beginning to penetrate the country. Ultimately, this development will have a transformative effect in North Korea. How soon this transformation will occur is far less certain.

*   *   *

The economy of North Korea is in tremendous flux, and new sources of information are constantly appearing. The South Korean Ministry of Unification has an excellent English-language Web site (http://www.unikorea.go.kr/en/), and both the Korean and English sites have detailed and comprehensive information that is consistently the most up-to-date available. The Nautilus Institute of Berkeley, California, has an informative Web site (http://www.nautilus.org/) that includes briefings, policy papers, and data on all aspects of North

Korea, including extensive discussion of the economic reforms. South Korea's Naewoe Press publishes a monthly review of North Korea called *Vantage Point* that incorporates the best English- and Korean-language information available. The Economist Intelligence Unit offers reliable economic data on North Korea through its quarterly *Country Report: North Korea.*

The Korea Central News Agency (KCNA) of the DPRK has a Web site that contains its current and past news releases (http://www.kcna.co.jp/). Among other North Korean sources that consistently contain economic topics are *Chosŏn chungang yŏn'gam* (Korean Central Yearbook), an annual with sections on the economy and other related topics; *Kŭlloja* (The Worker), a monthly journal of the KWP Central Committee; *Nodong Shinmun* (Workers' Daily), the KWP's daily newspaper; and *Foreign Trade of the Democratic People's Republic of Korea* and *Korea Today*, monthly English-language periodicals.

Other South Korean research institutes that have extensive scholarly publications on North Korea are the Korea Institute of National Unification (www.kinu.or.kr), the Sejong Institute (www.sejong.org), and the Institute of Foreign Affairs and National Security (www.ifans.go.kr). The most useful Japanese source is *Kita Chōsen no keizai to bōeki no tenbō* (North Korean Economic and Trade Prospects), an annual published by the Japan External Trade Organization (JETRO) that contains up-to-date surveys of the economy and statistical data on trade. Another informative Japanese source is the monthly periodical *Kita Chōsen kenkyū* (Studies on North Korea).

Other valuable sources in English are the January–February issue of *Asian Survey*, which carries the annual survey on North Korea; the United Nations' *International Trade Statistics Yearbook*; the International Monetary Fund's *Direction of Trade Statistics Yearbook*; and the U.S. Open Source Center (formerly the Foreign Broadcast Information Service) translations of North Korean broadcasts available via the U.S. National Technical Information Service's World News Connection (http://wnc.fedworld.gov/). (For further information and complete citations, see Bibliography.)

Three strong arms—from top: the farmer, the party intellectual, and the worker—grasping the pole of the Korean Workers' Party flag with the three-part symbol of the hammer, writing brush, and sickle. The caption at the bottom reads: "Party's leadership means our life"; the inscription at top reads: "Victory if protected, death if abandoned."
Courtesy Chosŏn Yaesul *(P'yŏngyang), January 1996, 66*

THE DEMOCRATIC PEOPLE'S REPUBLIC OF KOREA (DPRK), or North Korea, was founded on September 9, 1948. Its claim to sovereignty was facilitated by the World War II Allied powers' defeat of imperial Japan in 1945, ending Japan's 35-year occupation of the Korean Peninsula, and was the direct result of failed attempts at trusteeship models and later of failed United Nations (UN)–administered elections in 1948 to unify the two occupation zones. The North was under the sway of the Soviet Union while the South was under U.S. control. UN-administered elections—impeded by the Soviets in the North—were held only in the South on May 10, 1948, leading to the establishment in August of that year of the Republic of Korea (South Korea).

North Korea is one of modern history's few truly Orwellian and nepotistic systems. The first leader of North Korea, Kim Il Sung, was born in 1912. He served as an officer in the Soviet army and was an anti-Japanese guerrilla fighter in Manchuria in the 1930s, before returning to North Korea in September 1945, whereupon Soviet authorities anointed him as leader. Kim had taken a position of power in 1946, soon holding absolute, solipsistic control as general secretary of the North's communist Korean Workers' Party (KWP) and president of the state until July 8, 1994, when his sudden death led to the ascension of his son Kim Jong Il as the next leader. Born on February 16, 1941 (although, since 1982 his official birth date has been February 16, 1942, to match it symbolically with Kim Il Sung's birthday, which was April 15, 1912), and groomed since the early 1970s as the heir apparent, Kim Jong Il was given positions of increasing importance in the KWP hierarchy throughout the 1980s. At the KWP's Sixth Party Congress in October 1980, Kim Jong Il's succession was consolidated with his phased assumption of control over the civil administration, followed by his designation as supreme commander of the Korean People's Army (KPA) in December 1991. His assumption of rule was formalized in September 1998, presumably after the official period of mourning for Kim Il Sung had ended. Kim Jong Il rules the country as supreme commander of the military and as chairman of the National Defense Commission. The formal position of president remains held posthumously by his father.

The cult of personality and the nepotism of the Kim family constitute unique features of North Korean politics. In the past, for example, Kim Il Sung's wife, Kim Song-ae, was a member of the KWP Central Committee, a member of the Standing Committee of the

Supreme People's Assembly, a deputy to the assembly, and chairwoman of the Korean Democratic Women's Union Central Committee. Kim Il Sung's daughter, Kim Kyong-hui, was a member of the KWP Central Committee and deputy to the Supreme People's Assembly, and his son-in-law, Chang Song-taek, was premier, alternate member of the KWP Central Committee, and deputy to the Supreme People's Assembly. Kang Song-san, Kim Il Sung's cousin by marriage, was premier and a member of the KWP Central Committee and its Political Bureau, deputy to the Supreme People's Assembly, and member of the state Central People's Committee. Ho Tam, who died in 1991, was Kim Il Sung's brother-in-law, a member of the KWP Central Committee and Political Bureau, chairman of the Supreme People's Assembly Foreign Affairs Committee, deputy to the Supreme People's Assembly, and chairman of the Committee for the Peaceful Reunification of the Fatherland. In 2005 Kim Jong Il appeared to be grooming one of his sons, Kim Jong Chul, to succeed him. His eldest son, Kim Jong Nam, was another possibility for succession, but he appeared to have lost standing in the family hierarchy as a result of his arrest and detainment at Japan's Narita International Airport in 2001 while traveling on a forged passport.

Although the Korean Communist Party dated from the 1920s, North Korea claims that the KWP was founded by Kim Il Sung in 1945. Since that time, despite the existence of other small political organizations, North Korea has been under the one-party rule of the KWP (see Mass Organizations, this ch.). Throughout Kim Il Sung's reign, the party remained the most politically significant entity; its preeminence in all spheres of society placed it beyond the reach of dissent or disagreement. Party membership is composed of the "advanced fighters" among North Korea's working people: workers, peasants, and working intellectuals who are said to struggle devotedly for the success of the socialist and communist cause. The KWP claims a membership of 3 million. The ruling elite considers KWP members the major mobilizing and developmental cadres, or *kanbu* (see Glossary). In principle, every worker, peasant, soldier, and revolutionary element can join the party.

What distinguishes Kim Jong Il's rule from his father's has been the relative decline in influence of the KWP and the rise of the military as the predominant organ of government and society. "Military-first" (*sŏngun*) politics is reflected not only in the leadership positions held formally by Kim Jong Il (chairman of the National Defense Commission) but also in the relative elimination of many major KWP functions (for example, plenary meetings). The most powerful government institution under Kim Il Sung was the Political Bureau of the KWP Central Committee. The National Defense Com-

The national flag has three horizontal bands of blue (top), red (triple width), and blue; the red band is edged in white; on the hoist side of the red band is a white disk with a red five-pointed star. The official seal shows a large hydraulic power plant under Mount Paektu and the light of a five-pointed red star with ears of rice forming an oval frame bound with a red ribbon inscribed: "Democratic People's Republic of Korea."
Courtesy Korea Today *(P'yŏngyang), August 1994, front cover*

mission has effectively displaced the Political Bureau as the predominant decision-making authority. The privileging of the military undeniably is related to Kim Jong Il's moves to consolidate both power and legitimacy in the shadow of his father's military credentials and uncontested rule.

The political system is guided by the concept of *chuch'e* (see Glossary)—"national self-reliance" in all activities. The essence of *chuch'e* is to apply creatively the general principles of Marxism and Leninism in the North Korean way. As historian Dae-Sook Suh has noted, *chuch'e* is "not the philosophical exposition of an abstract idea; rather, it is firmly rooted in the North Korean people and Kim Il Sung." In April 1992, North Korea promulgated an amended state constitution that deleted Marxism and Leninism as principal national ideas and instead emphasized *chuch'e*. Reinforcing this trend, constitutional amendments in 1998 recognized the concept of private ownership for the first time and granted some autonomy to technocrats and local light industry from central party control. The regime, moreover, now admits flaws in the socialist-style economy as the source of the problems rather than blaming its economic woes on outside forces, as it traditionally has done. A *Nodong Shinmun* (Workers' Daily) editorial on November 21, 2001, thus declared: "... the socialist economic management method is still immature and not perfect .... If we stick to this hackneyed and outdated method, which is not applicable to the realities of today, then we will be unable to develop our economy." Wide-ranging economic reforms announced in July 2002 represented further steps away from the Marxist and socialist models (see Prospects: The Significance of Reform, this ch.). But in spite of these changes, the regime clings firmly to the *chuch'e* ideology.

This apparent contradiction, in large part, is because the ideology is inextricably intertwined with the glorification, bordering on deification, of Kim Il Sung and Kim Jong Il's authority and cult of personality. Kim and his father used the ideology, party, military, and government to consolidate power. The two Kims have been addressed by many honorary titles, including "great leader (father)," "dear leader (son)," and *suryŏng* (see Glossary), which can be taken to mean the son of the nation, national hero, liberator, and fatherly leader. According to the party, there can be no greater honor or duty than being loyal to one or the other of the two Kims "absolutely and unconditionally." Executive power is not checked by any constitutional provision. The government structures' principal purpose is to ensure strict popular compliance with the policies of Kim Jong Il; such compliance implants an appearance of institutional imprimatur on Kim's highly personalized and absolute rule. Although the internal workings of North Korean politics are extremely opaque, politics as a function of competition for power by aspiring groups and promotion of the interests of special groups appears to be less germane to the North Korean setting.

The most significant twenty-first-century political event in North Korea relates to the July 2002 market-liberalization reforms (see Economic Reforms, ch. 3). These are generally associated with four measures: basic monetization of the economy and the legalization of makeshift markets; currency depreciation; transplanting managerial decisions for industry and agriculture from the central government (factory party committees) into the hands of local production units; and pressing forward with special administrative and industrial zones to induce foreign investment. These measures represent both the North's best attempt at serious reform and its most dangerous gamble in terms of regime resiliency. If major change is the objective, the reforms are the clearest expression of P'yŏngyang's genuine intentions to move away from a command-style economy to one that might enable the regime to reach some modicum of economic stability, which, in turn, could mean that the North is serious about trading away its nuclear threat for the aid necessary to push forward with these reforms. If the liberalization is a gamble, the North may be pursuing the reforms despite its nuclear ambitions, with the hope that it can achieve both goals (that is, hard currency inflows and retention of some nuclear capabilities). The reality may lie between these two. But there is no denying that these reforms also make the regime more vulnerable to basic supply and demand and price pressures in a way never encountered before in North Korea.

Relationships Among the Government, Party, and Military

From the founding of the DPRK in 1948 through the early 1990s, the KWP held a commanding position vis-à-vis the government. A definitive shift toward "military-first," or *sŏngun*, politics took place with the 1994 death of Kim Il Sung and the succession to power of Kim Jong Il. The significance of this shift meant the promotion of the military as the central organ of government at the expense of the KWP.

Also, from 1948 to the early 1990s, government organs were regarded as executors of the general line and policies of the KWP. Government was expected to implement the policies and directives of the party by mobilizing the masses. All government officials or functionaries were exhorted to behave as servants of the people, rather than as overbearing "bureaucrats." The persistence in party literature of admonitions against formalism strongly suggests that authoritarian bureaucratic behavior remains a major source of concern to the party leadership. This concern may explain in part the party's intensified efforts, beginning in the early 1970s, to wage an ideological struggle against the bureaucratic work style of officials. The general trend was toward tightened party control and supervision of all organs of administrative and economic policy implementation.

In January 1990, Kim Jong Il introduced the slogan "to serve the people" and directed party functionaries to mingle with the people and to work devotedly as their faithful servants. Kim stated that the collapse of socialism in some countries was a stern lesson to North Korea and was related to failures in party building and party activity. He stressed the importance of reinforcing the party's ideological unity and cohesion and elucidated tasks that would strengthen education in the principle of *chuch'e*, revolutionary traditional education, and socialist and patriotic education.

The KWP continues to be the formulator of national purpose, priorities, and administrative hierarchy. It is the central coordinator of administrative and economic activities at the national and local levels. Through its own organizational channels, which permeate all government and economic agencies, the party continues to oversee administrative operations and enforce state discipline. Without exception, key government positions are filled by party loyalists, most of whom are trained in the North Korean system, which emphasizes ideology and practical expertise.

The shift to "military-first" politics is generally associated with Kim Jong Il's formal assumption of the National Defense Commission chairmanship after the death of Kim Il Sung in July 1994. In a 1991 plenary session of the KWP Sixth Party Congress, Kim Il Sung made his son the supreme commander of the KPA. A few months later, the elder Kim named the younger Kim marshal (*wŏnsu*) of the DPRK, effectively putting operational control of the military under his son. Kim Il Sung held the National Defense Commission chairmanship until April 1993, when he turned this position over to his son, who assumed full duties only upon the death of his father.

The National Defense Commission constitutionally is the highest institution within the military establishment only, but in practice, under Kim Jong Il, the National Defense Commission has become the dominant decision-making body of the state (see fig. 10). Many believe this shift is the manifestation of the younger Kim's consolidation of power and legitimacy after the death of his father. Kim

Jong Il possessed none of the credentials of his father, either in the party or in the military. The younger Kim thus sought to co-opt the military by elevating its position within North Korea relative to the party as the primary means of legitimizing his own rule. There is speculation that Minister of People's Armed Forces O Chin-u, a confidant of Kim Il Sung, was a key figure in assuring the military's obedience and acceptance of Kim Jong Il, despite the young Kim's lack of any military credentials such as his father had possessed. The only other possible leadership candidate, Premier Kim Il (no relation), had been removed from his post in 1976.

Military-first politics was formalized in about 1995. It was at this time that the concept was introduced as "a revolutionary idea of attaching great importance to the army" and "politics emphasizing the perfect unity and the single-hearted unity of the Party, Army and people, and the role of the army as the vanguards." Phrases such as "the *sŏngun* revolutionary idea," "*sŏngun* revolutionary leadership," and "*sŏngun* politics" also have been employed since 1998. The basic concept of *sŏngun* is to rely on the military as the primary leg of the "revolution," economic reconstruction, and North Korean–style socialism. Implicit in this principle is the prioritization of the military's needs as a key component of the state's national objectives.

One of the justifications for military-first politics is achievement of the national objective of *kangsong taeguk* (rich nation and strong army), a concept introduced in 1999 by Kim Jong Il. As such, an inseparable link between North Korean patriotism and support for Kim's grip on the military has been established, explaining why the majority of Kim's public appearances have been with the KPA.

The National Defense Commission's rise as the hegemonic institution within the North Korean government began in April 1992, when a constitutional revision separated the National Defense Commission's chairmanship from the presidency, establishing the commission as an independent body. The 1992 state constitutional revisions also ended long-held practices in which the president was supreme commander of the armed forces and chairman of the National Defense Commission, shifting power instead to the Supreme People's Assembly and the National Defense Commission. The key significance of these revisions is that the president (a position that only two years later would be held posthumously by Kim Il Sung) was made the nominal head of state, but with the power to appoint the National Defense Commission chairman. The first session of the 10-term Supreme People's Assembly on September 5, 1998, reinforced the National Defense Commission's grip by empowering it with authority over all military affairs and defense projects. The National Defense Commission, although

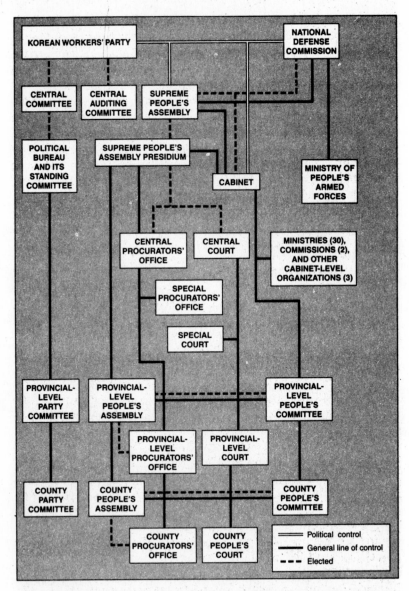

Source: Based on information from Republic of Korea, Ministry of Unification, Information
Center on North Korea, "Power Structure of North Korea," 2006, http://unibook.
unikorea.go.kr/dataroom/images/table_d_01.gif; and U.S. Central Intelligence
Agency, "North Korea," *Chiefs of State and Cabinet Members of Foreign Governments*, June 28, 2006, https://www.cia.gov/cia/publications/chiefs/chiefs94.html.

Figure 10. Party, State, and Government Power, 2006

nominally under the Supreme People's Assembly, essentially constitutes the highest executive body, headed by its chairman, Kim Jong Il. The primary military organ in the KWP is the Military Affairs Department, also run by Kim Jong Il through his position as party general secretary (see National Defense Organizations, ch. 5).

In 2007 the National Defense Commission consisted of a chairman (Kim Jong Il); first vice chairman (Cho Myŏng-nok); two vice chairmen (Kim Yŏng-chun and Yi Yong-mu); and three members (Kim Il-ch'ŏl, Chŏn Pyŏng-ho, and Kim Yang-gŏn), each with five-year terms. The National Defense Commission has the power to direct all activities of the armed forces and national defense projects, establish and disband central defense institutions, appoint and dismiss senior military officers, confer military titles and grant titles for top commanders, and declare a state of war and issue mobilization orders in an emergency.

The Korean Workers' Party

The Korean Workers' Party (KWP), according to the preamble of the party constitution, is the "vanguard organization of the working class," and the "highest type of revolutionary body among all organizations of the working masses." The National Party Congress is the supreme party organ and approves reports of other party organs, adopts basic party policies and tactics, and elects members to the KWP Central Committee and the Central Auditing Committee. The elections, however, are perfunctory because the members of these bodies are actually chosen by Kim Jong Il and his few trusted colleagues. When the National Party Congress is not in session, the Central Committee acts as the official agent of the party. The Central Committee is supposed to meet at least once every six months and has the responsibility of electing the party general secretary (Kim Jong Il), members of the Political Bureau, and its Standing Committee (or Presidium, the highest operational party organization). The Central Committee also elects members of the KWP Secretariat (which implements administrative decisions, personnel management, and other important party matters) and members of the Central Military Commission (which formulates the party's military policies, action plans, and defense industry development. The commission's last known chairman was Kim Il Sung; it should not be confused with the similarly named Military Affairs Department. The Central Committee additionally elects the members of the Central Inspection Committee, which maintains party discipline, reviews petitions and appeals from provincial and directly governed city party organizations, and investigates members violating party policies or at odds with the top leadership. A party congress is supposed to be convened every five years, but as of 2007, one had not been held since the Sixth Party Congress in 1980. Party congresses are attended by delegates elected by the members of provincial-level party assemblies at the ratio of one delegate for every 1,000 party members.

Until his death in July 1994, Kim Il Sung held all key party positions, including being KWP general secretary, member of the Standing Committee of the Political Bureau, and chairman of the Central Military Commission. Kim Jong Il was not appointed general secretary until October 8, 1997. Although technically open to mass membership, access to the KWP is denied to those without a "reliable" class background. The KWP operates as the core of the North Korean polity, with more than 3 million members. The party carries the identity of a class-based and individual-leadership organization. The KWP has two alliance parties, the Korean Social Democratic Party and the Chongu (Friends) Party, supportive of the Ch'ŏndogyo religion (see Religion, ch. 2). Kim Jong Il has formally led the KWP since 1997, although informally the party has been under his control since 1994. Kim Jong Il's accession was followed by a round of purges in the KWP, in which some of his father's old followers were removed from office.

The Sixth Party Congress, convened October 10–14, 1980, was attended by 3,220 party delegates (3,062 full members and 158 alternate members) and 177 foreign delegates from 118 countries. Attendance significantly increased from the approximately 1,800 delegates who attended the Fifth Party Congress in November 1970. The 1980 congress was convened by the KWP Central Committee to review, discuss, and endorse reports by the Central Committee, the Central Auditing Committee, and other central organs covering the activities of these bodies since the previous congress 10 years earlier. The Sixth Party Congress also elected a new Central Committee.

In his report to the congress, Kim Il Sung outlined a set of goals and policies for the 1980s. He proposed the establishment of a Democratic Confederal Republic of Koryŏ as a reasonable way to achieve the independent and peaceful reunification of the country. He also clarified a new 10-point policy for the unified state and stressed that North Korea and South Korea should recognize and tolerate each other's ideas and social systems, that the unified central government should be represented by P'yŏngyang and Seoul on an equal footing, and that both sides should exercise regional autonomy with equal rights and duties. Specifically, the unified government should respect the social systems and the wishes of administrative organizations and of every party, every group, and every sector of people in the North and the South, and the central government should prevent one side from imposing its will on the other.

Kim Il Sung also emphasized the Three Revolutions (see Glossary), which are aimed at hastening the process of political and ideological transformation based on *chuch'e* ideology, improving the material and technical standards of the economy, and developing socialist national culture. According to Kim, these revolutions were the responsibility of the Three Revolutions Team Movement (see Glossary)—"a new method of guiding the revolution," which combined political and ideological guidance with scientific and technical guidance. This approach enabled superior authorities to help the lower levels and rouse masses of the working people to accelerate the Three Revolutions. The teams performed their guidance work by sending their members to factories, enterprises, and cooperative farms. Their members are party cadres, including those from the KWP Central Committee, reliable officials of the government, persons from economic and mass organizations, scientists and technicians, and young intellectuals. Kim Il Sung left no question that the Three Revolutions Team Movement had succeeded the Ch'ŏllima Movement (see Glossary) and would remain the principal vehicle through which the party pursued its political and economic objectives in the 1980s.

The linkage between party and economic work also was addressed by Kim Il Sung. In acknowledging the urgent task of economic construction, he stated that party work should be geared toward efficient economic construction and that success in party work should be measured by success in economic construction. Accordingly, party organizations were told to "push forward economic work actively, give prominence to economic officials, and help them well." Party officials also were advised to watch out for signs of independence on the part of technocrats. The membership and organization of the KWP are specified in the party rules.

There are two kinds of party members: regular and probationary. Membership is open to those 18 years of age and older but is granted only to those who have demonstrated their qualifications; applications are submitted to a cell along with a proper endorsement from two party members with at least two years in good standing. An application is acted on by the plenary session of a cell; an affirmative decision is subject to ratification by a county-level party committee. After approving an application, a one-year probationary period is mandatory, but it may be waived under certain unspecified "special circumstances," allowing the candidate to become a full member. Recruitment is under the direction of the Organization and Guidance Department and its local branches.

The Constitutional Framework

The state constitutions of North Korea have been patterned after those of other communist states. The constitutional framework delineates a highly centralized governmental system and the relationship between the people and the state. The constitution was adopted in 1948, completely revised in December 1972, revised again in April 1992, and then amended and supplemented in September 1998. Innovations of the 1972 constitution included the establishment of the positions of president and vice presidents and a supercabinet called the Central People's Committee.

The revised 1998 state constitution has 166 articles (15 fewer than the 1992 constitution) in seven chapters. As with the 1992 revision, the 1998 constitution continues to uphold *chuch'e* at the expense of Marxism–Leninism and includes articles encouraging joint ventures within special economic zones, guaranteeing the "legal rights and interests of foreigners," and establishing a framework for expanded ties with capitalist countries. The 1992 revision had provided a legal framework for the 1991 appointment of Kim Jong Il as supreme commander of the armed forces by removing the military from the command of the president and by placing the military under the control of the National Defense Commission, of which he is chairman. The 1998 constitution confirms this power.

The 18 articles of chapter 1 of the 1998 constitution deal with politics. Article 1 defines North Korea as an independent socialist state representing the interests of all the Korean people. Article 15 states that the DPRK defends the democratic, national rights of Koreans overseas and their rights as recognized under international law. Sovereignty emanates from four expressly mentioned social groups: "workers, peasants, working intellectuals, and all other working people." State organs are organized and operate on the principle of democratic centralism. Article 9 declares that "the complete victory of socialism in the northern half of Korea" will be accomplished through the execution of the three revolutions of ideology, technology, and culture, while struggling to realize unification of the fatherland by following the principles of independence, peaceful unification, and grand national unity. In the 1972 constitution, socialism was to have been accomplished by driving out foreign forces on a countrywide scale and by reunifying the nation peacefully on a democratic basis. Other articles in this chapter of the 1998 constitution refer to the main party line, the Ch'ŏngsan-ni Method (see Glossary) and spirit, and the Three Revolutions Team Movement. The constitution states that foreign policy and foreign activities are based on the principles of independence, peace, and solidarity. Diplomatic, political, economic, and cultural relations are to be established with all friendly countries based on the principles of complete equality, independence, mutual respect, noninterference in each other's internal affairs, and mutual benefit.

Economic affairs were codified in chapter 2. The constitution declares that the means of production are owned by state and social cooperative organizations. Article 22 reiterates that natural resources, railroads, airports, transportation, communication organs, major factories, enterprises, ports, and banks are state owned. Article 24 defines personal property as that "meeting the simple and individuals aims of the citizen." Benefits derived from supplementary pursuits, such as the small garden plots of collectivized farmers, are considered personal property; such benefits were protected by the state as private property and are guaranteed by law as a right of inheritance. According to article 33, the planned, national economy is directed and managed through the now largely abandoned Taean Work System (see Glossary; Organization, ch. 3).

Culture, education, and public health are covered in chapter 3. Article 45 stipulates that the state develop a mandatory 11-year education system, including two years of compulsory preschool education (see Education, ch. 2). Article 47 says that education is provided at no cost and that the state grants allowances to students enrolled in universities and colleges. Article 56 notes that medical service is universal and free (see Health Care, ch. 2). (Medical care and the right to education are also covered in articles 72 and 73 in chapter 5.) Article 57 places environmental protection measures before production; this emphasis is in line with recent attention given to preserving the natural environment and creating a hygienic living and working environment by preventing environmental pollution.

Chapter 4, consisting of only four articles, covers national defense. Emphasis is given to the mission of the armed forces, a self-reliant defense, and unity between the military forces and the people.

Chapter 5 extensively details the fundamental rights and duties of citizens. Citizens over the age of 17 may exercise the right to vote and be elected to office regardless of gender, race, occupation, length of residency, property status, education, party affiliation, political views, or religion. Citizens serving in the armed forces may vote and be elected; insane persons and those deprived by court decisions of the right to vote are disenfranchised. According to article 67, citizens have freedom of speech, press, assembly, demonstration, and association. Citizens also have the right to work, and article 70 stipulates that they work according to their ability and be remunerated according to the quantity and quality of work performed. Article 71 provides for a system of working hours, holidays, paid leave, sanatoriums, and rest homes funded by the state, as well as for cultural facilities. Article 77 accords women equal social status and rights with men. Women are granted maternity leave and shortened working hours if they have large families. Marriage and the family are protected by the state, according to the next article.

Chapter 6, on the structure of the state, has 75 articles in seven sections. The chapter covers the Supreme People's Assembly, the National Defense Commission, the Central People's Committee, the State Administration Council, local people's assemblies, local people's committees, the Central Procurators' Office, and the Central Court.

Chapter 7 covers the national emblem, flag, and capital. It describes the first two items, designates P'yŏngyang as the national capital, and identifies the national anthem as the "Patriotic Song." In a change from the 1972 constitution, the 1992 and 1998 revisions mandated that "the sacred mountain of the revolution"—Mount Paektu—be added to the national emblem. It stands above the previously existing symbols: a hydroelectric power plant, the beaming light of a five-pointed red star, ovally framed ears of rice bound with a red band, and the inscription Chosŏn Minjujuŭi Inmin Konghwaguk (Democratic People's Republic of Korea).

With the 1998 constitution, the post of state president, the Central People's Committee, and the Supreme People's Assembly Standing Committee were abolished, giving most of the power shared by these institutions to the Supreme People's Assembly Presidium. The constitution's preamble states that Kim Il Sung is the "eternal president" of North Korea and stipulates that the constitution itself "shall be called Kim Il Sung's Constitution." Under these revisions, the president of the Supreme People's Assembly Presidium became the de jure head of state, representing North Korea in external affairs, and head of the supreme sovereign institution. Article 100 notes that the National Defense Commission is the "highest military leading organ of state power and an organ for general control over national defense." Although article 105 states that the commission is "accountable to the Supreme People's Assembly," with Kim Jong Il as chairman, the commission holds the de facto supreme power of state.

The Structure of Government

The Legislature

According to article 87 of the 1998 constitution, the Supreme People's Assembly is "the highest organ of state power." However, it is not influential and does not initiate legislation independently of other party and state organs. Invariably, the legislative process is set in motion by executive bodies according to the predetermined policies of the party leadership. The Supreme People's Assembly is not known

Supreme People's Assembly, P'yŏngyang
Courtesy Tracy Woodward
Hall inside the Supreme People's Assembly
Courtesy Tracy Woodward

ever to have criticized, modified, or rejected a bill or a measure placed before it, or to have proposed an alternative bill or measure.

The constitution provides for the Supreme People's Assembly to be elected every five years by universal suffrage. Article 88 indicates that legislative power is exercised by the Supreme People's Assembly and its Presidium when the full Supreme People's Assembly is not in session. Earlier the Standing Committee of the Supreme People's Assembly exercised this power, but in 1998 it was abolished and replaced with the Presidium. Elections to the Eleventh Supreme People's Assembly were held in August 2003, with 687 deputies elected. The KWP approves a single list of candidates who stand for election without opposition. Deputies usually meet once a year in regular sessions in March or April, but since 1985 they also have met occasionally in extraordinary sessions in November or December.

The president of the Presidium of the Supreme People's Assembly represents North Korea in relations with foreign countries. Assembly sessions are convened by the Presidium, whose president since 1998 has been Kim Yong-nam, a former vice premier and former minister of foreign affairs. There are also two vice presidents, two honorary vice presidents, a secretary general, and 12 members of the Presidium. Until April 1994, the Supreme People's Assembly convened nearly every year, but after Kim Il Sung's death in July 1994, it did not convene until the tenth term was held in September 2000. Supreme People's Assembly Presidium members are elected by the deputies, as are the Supreme People's Assembly president and vice presidents. The Supreme People's Assembly has three committees: bills, budget, and qualifications screening. Before the September 1998 constitutional amendments, the Supreme People's Assembly also had foreign affairs and reunification-policy deliberation committees.

Article 91 states that the Supreme People's Assembly has the authority to adopt, amend, and supplement the constitution and departmental laws; establish the basic principles of domestic and foreign policies; and approve major departmental laws adopted by the Supreme People's Assembly Presidium in the intervals between the sessions of the Supreme People's Assembly. It also may elect or transfer the chairman and other members (on recommendation of the chairman) of the National Defense Commission; elect or remove the president of the Supreme People's Assembly Presidium; elect or transfer the premier and vice premiers and members of the cabinet; appoint or remove the procurator general; elect or transfer the chief justice; and elect or transfer its own top officials. The Supreme People's Assembly is empowered to examine and approve the state plan for the development of the national economy and a report on its fulfillment;

examine and approve a report on the state budget and on its implementation; receive a report on the work of the cabinet and national institutions and adopt measures, if necessary; and decide whether to ratify or abrogate treaties. Assembly decisions are made by a simple majority and signified by a show of hands. Deputies, each representing a constituency of approximately 30,000 persons, are guaranteed inviolability and immunity from arrest. Between assembly sessions, the Presidium acts for the Supreme People's Assembly.

The Executive

President and Vice Presidents

Prior to Kim Il Sung's death in July 1994, the president was the head of state and the head of government in his capacity as chairman of the Central People's Committee. The constitution stated that two vice presidents were to "assist" the president, but it did not elaborate on a mode of succession. Following Kim's death and the constitutional amendments of 1998, Kim Jong Il as National Defense Commission chairman assumed presidential responsibilities but not the title. The preface to the constitution as amended in 1998 reads: "The DPRK and the entire Korean people will uphold the great leader Comrade Kim Il Sung as the eternal President of the Republic." Thus, Kim Il Sung posthumously occupies the presidency; the positions of vice president remain unfilled. The titles of president and vice president in North Korea now refer only to the president and vice presidents of the Supreme People's Assembly.

Presidential powers were stated only in generalities. The chief executive convened and guided the State Administration Council as occasion demanded. Under the 1972 constitution, he was also the supreme commander of the armed forces and chairman of the National Defense Commission, although Kim Il Sung appointed his son to the former position in December 1991 and to the latter position in April 1993 (see National Command Authorities, ch. 5). The president's prior assent was required for all laws, decrees, decisions, and directives, and his edicts commanded the force of law more authoritatively than any other legislation. The president promulgated the laws and ordinances of the Supreme People's Assembly; the decisions of the Standing Committee of the Supreme People's Assembly (abolished in 1998); and the laws, ordinances, and decisions of the Central People's Committee. The president also granted pardons, ratified or abrogated treaties, and received foreign envoys or requested their recall. No one served in top government posts without the president's recommendation. Even the judiciary and the prosecutors were accountable to Kim Il Sung. In accordance with article 91 of the 1998 constitution, these presidential functions now reside with the Supreme People's Assembly.

It was not until 1997 that the younger Kim officially took over the leadership of the KWP. The following year, the presidency was reserved for the revered deceased leader. Kim Jong Il consolidated his power in the positions left to him. The 1998 constitution declares that the chairman of the National Defense Commission "holds the highest post of the state."

Cabinet

Between 1972 and 1998, the highest administrative arm of the government was the State Administration Council. Before then, the cabinet had been the highest level of the executive branch, but the 1972 constitution changed its name and function. The council was directed by the president and the Central People's Committee and was composed of the premier, vice premiers, ministers, commission chairmen, and other cabinet-level members of the central agencies.

The 1998 constitution changed the State Administration Council into a cabinet and upgraded its status and power. The cabinet is the supreme administrative and executive organ and a general state management organ. Previously the State Administration Council had been subject to the control of the president and the Central People's Committee. Since 1998 the cabinet has had the authority to formulate measures for the implementation of national policies; enact, amend, or supplement regulations pertaining to national administration; establish or abolish key administrative economic organs and industrial establishments and formulate plans to improve national management organizations; and implement inspection and controlling activities to maintain order in national management. The cabinet has exclusive responsibility for all economic administrative projects.

Under the 1998 constitution, the premier represents the government (article 120) and functions independently. In 2007 the cabinet was headed by Premier Kim Yong-il. Under him were three vice premiers, 30 ministers, two cabinet-level commission chairmen, the president of the Academy of Sciences, the president of the Central Bank, the director of the Central Statistics Bureau, and a chief secretary of the cabinet. Besides the 30 civilian ministries that are part of the cabinet, there is a thirty-first ministry—the Ministry of People's Armed Forces—that is not subordinate to the cabinet but reports instead to the National Defense Commission.

The Judiciary

In the North Korean judicial process, both adjudicative and prosecuting bodies function as powerful weapons for the proletarian dictatorship. The constitution states that the Central Court, courts at the provincial or special-city level, the people's courts, and special courts administer justice. The Central Court, the highest court of appeal, stands at the apex of the court system. The president of the Central Court since September 1998 has been Kim P'yŏng-ryul. In the case of the one special city (Namp'o) directly under central authority, provincial or municipal courts serve as the courts of first instance for civil and criminal cases at the intermediate level. At the lowest level are the people's courts, established in ordinary cities, counties, and urban districts. Special courts exist for the armed forces and for railroad workers. The military special courts have jurisdiction over all crimes committed by members of the armed forces or the personnel of the Ministry of People's Security. The railroad courts have jurisdiction over criminal cases involving rail and water transport workers. In addition, the Korean Maritime Arbitration Committee adjudicates maritime legal affairs.

In theory, the corresponding local people's assemblies elect judges and people's assessors, or lay judges. In practice, however, the KWP generally appoints judges, who do not require legal education or practical legal experience for their roles. In addition to administering justice based on criminal and civil codes, the courts are in charge of political indoctrination through "re-education." The issue of punishment is not expressly stated in the constitution or the criminal code.

The collective interests of the workers, peasants, soldiers, and working intellectuals are protected by a parallel hierarchy of organs controlled at the top by the Central Procurators' Office (accountable to the Supreme People's Assembly Presidium when the full Supreme People's Assembly is in recess). This office acts as the state's procurator and checks on the activities of all public organs and citizens to ensure their compliance with the law and their "active struggle against all lawbreakers." Its authority extends to the courts, the decisions of which (including those of the Central Court) are subject to routine scrutiny. A judgment of the Central Court may be appealed to the plenary session of the Central Court, of which the state's chief procurator is a statutory member.

The chief prosecutor, known as the procurator general, is appointed by and accountable in theory, although not in fact, to the Supreme People's Assembly. There are one procurator general and three deputy procurator generals.

Local Government

There are three levels of local government: provinces (*do*) and provincial-level municipalities (*chikalsi*, or *jikhalsi*); a special city (*t'ŭkpyŏlsi*), ordinary cities (*si* or *shi*), urban districts (*kuyŏk*), and rural counties (*gun*, or *kun*); and traditional villages (*ri*, or *ni*). Cities are subdivided into wards (*gu*), and some cities and wards are subdivided into neighborhoods (*dong*), the lowest level of urban government to have its own office and staff. Towns and townships (*myŏn*) have not functioned as administrative units in North Korea since the Korean War (1950–53), but they still exist in South Korea. At the village level, administrative and economic matters are the responsibility of the chairman of the cooperative farm management committee in each village.

North Korea has nine provinces: Chagang, North Hamgyŏng, South Hamgyŏng, North Hwanghae, South Hwanghae, Kangwŏn, North P'yŏngan, South P'yŏngan, and Yanggang. There also are two provincial-level municipalities—P'yŏngyang and Najin–Sŏnbong—and one special city, Namp'o. Kaesŏng, which was once a *chikalsi*, had its territory incorporated into South Hwanghae Province in 2003. Additionally, there are 17 ordinary cities under provincial authority; 36 urban districts; more than 200 counties; and some 4,000 villages. Among these divisions, the counties serve as the intermediate administrative link between provincial authorities and the grass-roots-level village organizations. Local organs at the county level provide other forms of guidance to such basic units as neighborhoods (*dong*) and workers' districts (*nodongja-ku*).

Three types of local organs elect local officials to carry out centrally planned policies and programs. These organs are local KWP committees, local people's assemblies, and local administrative committees, with functions such as administrative and urban and rural economic guidance committees. These committees are local extensions of higher bodies at the national level, namely, the KWP, the Supreme People's Assembly, and the cabinet.

The local people's assemblies, established at all administrative levels, perform the same symbolic functions as the Supreme People's Assembly. They provide a façade of popular support and involvement and serve as a vehicle through which loyal and meritorious local inhabitants are given visible recognition as deputies to the assemblies. The assemblies meet once or twice a year, for only a few days at each session. Their duties are to approve the plan for local economic development and the local budget; to elect the officers of other local bodies, including the judges and people's assessors of the courts within their jurisdictions; and to review the decisions and directives issued by local organs at their corresponding and lower levels. The local people's assemblies have no standing committees. Between regular sessions, their duties are performed by the local people's committees, whose members are elected by assemblies at corresponding levels and are responsible both to the assemblies and to the local people's committees at higher levels.

The officers and members of the people's committees are influential locally as party functionaries and as senior administrative cadres. These committees can convene the people's assemblies; prepare for the election of deputies to the local assemblies; implement the decisions of the assemblies at the corresponding level and those of the people's committees at higher levels; and control and supervise the work of administrative bodies, enterprises, and social and cooperative organizations in their respective jurisdictions.

The day-to-day affairs of local communities are handled by the local administrative committees. The chairman, vice chairmen, secretary, and members of these bodies are elected by the local people's committees at the corresponding levels.

Political Ideology

The Role of *Chuch'e*

Chuch'e ideology is the basic cornerstone of party construction, party works, and government operations. *Chuch'e* is sanctified as the essence of what has been officially called Kim Il Sung Chuui (Kimilsungism) since April 1974. *Chuch'e* is also claimed as "the present-day Marxism–Leninism." North Korean leaders advocate *chuch'e* ideology as the only correct guiding ideology in their revolutionary movement.

Chuch'e also is referred to as "the unitary ideology" or as "the monolithic ideology of the Party." It is inseparable from and, for all intents and purposes, synonymous with Kim Il Sung's leadership and was said to have been "created" or "fathered" by the great leader as an original "encyclopedic thought which provides a complete answer to any question that arises in the struggle for national liberation and class emancipation, in the building of socialism and communism." *Chuch'e* is viewed as the embodiment of revealed truth attesting to the wisdom of Kim's leadership as exemplified in countless speeches and "on-the-spot guidance."

Chuch'e was proclaimed in December 1955, when Kim emphasized the critical need for a Korea-centered revolution rather than one designed to benefit, in his words, "another country." *Chuch'e* is designed to inspire national pride and identity and to mold national consciousness into a potentially powerful focus for internal solidarity centered on Kim and the KWP.

According to Kim, *chuch'e* means "the independent stance of rejecting dependence on others and of using one's own powers, believing in one's own strength and displaying the revolutionary spirit of self-reliance." *Chuch'e* is an ideology geared to North Korea's contemporary goals—an independent foreign policy, a self-sufficient economy, and a self-reliant defense posture. Kim Il Sung's enunciation of *chuch'e* in 1955 was aimed at developing a monolithic and effective system of authority under his exclusive leadership. The invocation of *chuch'e* was a psychological tool with which to stigmatize the foreign-oriented dissenters and remove them from the center of power. Targeted for elimination were groups of pro-Soviet and pro-Chinese dissenters who opposed Kim.

The Origins of *Chuch'e*

There are three major schools of thought regarding the origins of the *chuch'e* ideology: the instrumental, traditional political culture, and individual original perspectives. The instrumental viewpoint emphasizes both domestic and foreign political factors as the root of the *chuch'e* ideology. Some believe that Kim's unstable hold on power during and immediately following the Korean War caused him to deploy ideological purges in order to consolidate his political position, using the *chuch'e* principle of national solidarity as a domestic instrument to forge his personality cult.

The second perspective on *chuch'e*'s origin takes a longer view and focuses on the influence of traditional political culture in Korea, seeing *chuch'e* as a reflection of a centuries-old tradition of independence from foreign powers. Geographically central to the strategic interests of powerful neighbors, Korea has long been a pawn in great power rivalries, with perhaps more recorded foreign invasions than any other territory in history.

The third explanation for the origin of the *chuch'e* ideology is the North Koreans' broadly accepted view that it is a prime example of their late supreme leader's brilliance and originality. This perspective insists that *chuch'e* was the intellectual result of Kim Il Sung's highly exaggerated and romanticized personal experience as a guerrilla fighting Japanese imperialism in the 1930s.

Chuch'e did not become a prominent ideology overnight. During the first 10 years of North Korea's existence, Marxism–Leninism was accepted unquestioningly as the only source of doctrinal authority. Nationalism was toned down in deference to the country's connections to the Soviet Union and China. In the mid-1950s, however, *chuch'e*

Monument in P'yŏngyang to the founder of the nation. The inscription reads "Comrade Kim Il Sung is our eternal sun."
Courtesy Korea Today *(P'yŏngyang), April 1995, 2*

was presented as a "creative" application of Marxism–Leninism. In his attempt to establish an interrelationship between Marxism–Leninism and *chuch'e*, Kim contended that although Marxism–Leninism was valid as the fundamental law of revolution, it needed an authoritative interpreter to define a new set of practical ideological guidelines appropriate to the revolutionary environment in North Korea.

Application of *Chuch'e* in the North Korean State

Kim Il Sung's practical ideology was given a test of relevance from the outset. In the late 1950s, he was able to mobilize internal support when he purged pro-Soviet and pro-Chinese dissenters from party ranks. During the first half of the 1960s, Kim faced an even more formidable challenge when he had to endure a series of tense situations that had potentially adverse implications for North Korea's economic development and national security. Among these were a sharp decrease in aid from the Soviet Union and China; discord between the Soviet Union and China and its disquieting implications for North Korea's confrontation with the United States and South Korea; P'yŏngyang's disagreements with Moscow and apprehensions about the reliability of the Soviet Union as an ally; and the rise of an authoritarian regime in Seoul under General Park Chunghee, in power 1961–79.

These developments emphasized self-reliance—the need to rely on domestic resources, heighten vigilance against possible external challenges, and strengthen domestic political solidarity. Sacrifice, austerity, unity, and patriotism became dominant themes in the party's efforts to instill in the people the importance of *chuch'e* and collective discipline. By the mid-1960s, however, North Korea could afford to relax somewhat; its strained relations with the Soviet Union had eased, as reflected, in part, by Moscow's decision to rush economic and military assistance to P'yŏngyang.

Beginning in 1965, *chuch'e* was presented as the essence of Kim Il Sung's leadership and of party lines and policies for every conceivable revolutionary situation. Kim's past leadership record was put forward as the "guide and compass" for the present and future and as a source of strength sufficient to propel the faithful through any adversity. Nonetheless, the linkage of *chuch'e* to Marxism–Leninism remained a creed of the party. The April 1972 issue of *Kulloja* (The Worker) still referred to the KWP as "a Marxist–Leninist Party"; the journal pointed out that "the only valid policy for Korean communists is Marxism–Leninism" and called for "its creative application to our realities."

Since 1974, however, it has become increasingly evident that the emphasis is on the glorification of *chuch'e* as "the only scientific revolutionary thought representing our era of *chuch'e* and communist future and the most effective revolutionary theoretical structure that leads to the future of communist society along the surest shortcut." This new emphasis was based on the contention that a different historical era, with its unique sociopolitical circumstances, requires an appropriately unique revolutionary ideology. Accordingly, Marxism and Leninism were valid doctrines in their own times but had outlived their usefulness in the era of *chuch'e*, which prophesies the downfall of imperialism and the worldwide victory of socialism and communism.

As the years have passed, references to Marxism–Leninism in party literature have steadily decreased. By 1980 the terms "Marxism" and "Leninism" had all but disappeared from the pages of *Kulloja*. An unsigned article in the March 1980 *Kulloja* proclaimed, "within the Party none but the leader Kim Il Sung's revolutionary thought, the *chuch'e* ideology, prevails and there is no room for any hodgepodge thought contrary to it." The report Kim Il Sung presented to the Sixth Party Congress in October 1980 did not contain a single reference to Marxism–Leninism, in marked contrast to his report to the Fifth Party Congress in November 1970. In the 1980 report, Kim declared: "the whole party is rallied rock-firm around its Central Committee and knit together in ideology and purpose on the basis of the *chuch'e* idea. The Party has no room for any other idea than the *chuch'e* idea, and no force can ever break its unity and cohesion based on this idea."

Chuch'e is instrumental in providing a consistent and unifying framework for commitment and action in the North Korean political arena. It offers an underpinning for the party's incessant demand for spartan austerity, sacrifice, discipline, and dedication. Since the mid-1970s, however, it appears that *chuch'e* has become glorified as an end in itself. In his annual New Year's message on January 1, 1992, Kim Il Sung emphasized the invincibility of *chuch'e* ideology: "I take great pride in and highly appreciate the fact that our people have overcome the ordeals of history and displayed to the full the heroic mettle of the revolutionary people and the indomitable spirit of *chuch'e* Korea, firmly united behind the party.... No difficulty is insurmountable nor is any fortress impregnable for us when our party leads the people with the ever-victorious *chuch'e*-oriented strategy and tactics and when all the people turn out as one under the party's leadership."

After Kim Il Sung's death, Kim Jong Il continued to use *chuch'e* ideology to consolidate his tight control of his regime. It became legally embodied in the 1998 constitution, and throughout the 1990s and early 2000s Kim Jong Il espoused *chuch'e* ideology in various publications, emphasizing "*chuch'e* realism," as a uniquely creative method in North Korean socialist realism, quite different from the existing "socialistic realism." Such writings presumably were an attempt to explain the necessity of North Korea's pursuit of socialist ideals, despite the crumbling of the Soviet Union and the Eastern bloc states.

More recently, a new interpretation of the "self-reliant revival" has seen greater emphasis since the declaration of the "New Thinking Initiative" in 2001, which was an attempt at economic rehabilitation. In the past, "self-reliant revival" was widely understood as a phrase used to describe the spirit of the struggle necessary to produce on one's own things that were lacking or in short supply, or to resolve problems, no matter what, even if that meant resorting to old and antiquated methods. However, Kim Jong Il declared that "self-reliant revival is not possible apart from science and technology," while talking with party officials in December 2000. And a February 28, 2001, *Nodong Shinmun* article claimed that "building a self-reliant national economy does not mean building an economy with the doors closed," reminding readers that the country had departed from a closed economy. The article signaled that North Korea is pursuing the construction of a strong and prosperous nation, and the concept of self-reliant revival is changing with the time and circumstances.

Such changes may be a reflection of Kim Jong Il's decision to pursue self-reliant revival as long as it is economically beneficial, although it is unclear whether a commensurate relaxation of economic and political control will necessarily result.

Party Leadership and Elite Recruitment

Composition

The party congress, the highest KWP organ, meets infrequently. The most recently held congress was the Sixth Party Congress of October 1980. The official agent of the party congress is the Central Committee. In 2005 the Central Committee had 329 members: 180 full members and 149 alternate members. Nearly 40 percent of these members—131 individuals—are first-term members. The technocrats—economists, managers, and technicians—predominate among the membership. The Central Committee is supposed to hold a plenum, or plenary session, at least once every six months to discuss major issues. However, the Central Committee has not convened since Kim Il Sung's death in 1994. The plenum also elects the general secretary, members of the Political Bureau (called the Political Committee until October 1980), and its Standing Committee, or Presidium, established in October 1980.

Influence and prestige within the party power structure are directly associated with the rank order in which the members of the Central Committee are listed. Key posts in party, government, and economic organs are assigned; higher-ranking Central Committee members also are found in the armed forces, educational and cultural institutions, and other social and mass organizations. Many leaders concurrently hold multiple positions within the party, the government, and the military.

The Political Bureau has 14 members. Several central organizations are subordinate to the Political Bureau Standing Committee (of which the only known member is Kim Jong Il). One of the most important executive organs is the Secretariat of the Central Committee, led by General Secretary Kim Jong Il and eight other secretaries. Each secretary is in charge of one or more departmental party functions. Other key bodies include the Central Military Commission headed by Kim Jong Il; the Central Auditing Committee, the fiscal watchdog of the party; and the Central Inspection Committee, which enforces party discipline and acts as a trial and appeals board for disciplinary cases.

The various departments of the Secretariat of the Central Committee depend for implementation of party policies and directives on

*Kim Il Sung (left) with Kim Jong Il during the Sixth Korean Workers' Party
Congress, P'yŏngyang, October 1980
Courtesy* Chosŏn *(P'yŏngyang), September 2000, 6*

the party committees in the provincial- and county-level administrative divisions and in organizations where there are more than 100 party members—for example, major enterprises, factories, government offices, military units, and schools. In the countryside, village party committees are formed with a minimum of 50 party members. The basic party units are cells to which all party members belong and through which they participate in party organizational activities. Attendance at cell meetings and party study sessions, held at least once a week, is mandatory.

Party Members

The KWP claimed a membership of more than 3 million persons as of 1988, a significant increase from the 2 million members announced in 1976. Later information on party membership strength has not been forthcoming from North Korea. This increase may have been a result of the active mobilization drive for the Three Revolutions Team Movement. The KWP has three constituencies: industrial workers, peasants, and intellectuals, that is, office workers. Since 1948 industrial workers have constituted the largest percentage of party members, followed by peasants and intellectuals. Beginning in the 1970s, when North Korea's population reached the 50 percent urban mark, the composition of the groups belonging to the party changed. More people working in state-owned enterprises became party members, and the number of members working in agricultural cooperatives decreased.

Party Cadres

The recruitment and training of party cadres (*kanbu*) has long been the primary concern of party leadership. Party cadres are those officials placed in key positions in party organizations, ranging from the Political Bureau to the village party committees; in government agencies; in economic enterprises; in military and internal security units; in educational institutions; and in mass organizations. The duties of cadres are to educate and lead party and nonparty members of society and to ensure that party policies and directives are carried out faithfully. The party penetrates all aspects of life. Associations and guidance committees exist at all levels of society, with a local party cadre serving as a key member of each committee.

Some cadres are concerned principally with ideological matters, whereas others need to be both ideologically prepared and able to give guidance to the technical or managerial activities of the state. Regardless of specialization, all party cadres must devote two hours a day to the study of *chuch'e* ideology and Kim Il Sung's policies and instruction. The party has a number of schools for cadre training. At the national level, the most prestigious school is the Kim Il Sung Higher Party School in P'yŏngyang, administered directly by the Central Committee and attended by high-level party officials. Below the national level, there are communist colleges in each province for the education of county-level cadres. Village-level cadres are sent to county training schools.

The rules governing cadre selection have undergone subtle changes in emphasis. Through the early 1970s, "good class origin," individual ability, and ideological posture were given more or less equal consideration in the appointment of cadres. Since the mid-1970s, however, the doctrinally ordained "class principle" has been downgraded on the assumption that the actual social or class status of people should not be judged on the basis of their past family backgrounds but on their "present class preparation and mental attitudes." The party increasingly stresses individual merit and "absolute" loyalty as the criteria for acceptance into the elite status of cadre. Merit and competence have come to mean "a knowledge of the economy and technology." Such knowledge is considered crucial because, as Kim Il Sung stressed in July 1974, "Party organizational work should be intimately linked to economic work and intra-party work should be conducted to ensure success in socialist construction and backup economic work."

An equally important, if not more important, criterion for cadre selection is political loyalty, inasmuch as not all cadres of correct class origin or all highly competent cadres are expected to pass the rigorous tests of party life. These tests entail absolute loyalty to Kim Il Sung and Kim Jong Il and the party, thorough familiarity with *chuch'e* ideology, refusal to temporize in the face of adversity, and a readiness to respond to the party's call under any conditions and at all times.

Although information on the composition of cadre membership is limited, the number of cadres of non-worker and non-peasant origin has increased steadily. These cadres generally are classified as "working intellectuals" engaged in occupations ranging from party and government activities to educational, technical, and artistic pursuits. Another notable trend is the infusion of younger and better-educated cadres into the party ranks. An accent on youth and innovation was very much in evidence after 1973 when Kim Jong Il assumed the leading role in the Three Revolutions Team Movement.

The Ruling Elite

Persons with at least one major position in leading party, government, and military organs are considered the ruling elite. This group includes all political leaders who are, at a given time, directly involved in the preparation of major policy decisions and who participate in the inner circle of policy making. The ruling elite includes Political Bureau members and secretaries of the KWP, Central People's Committee members, members of the State Administration Council, and members of the Central Military Commission and the National Defense Commission. Because overlapping membership is common in public office, top-ranking officeholders number less than 100. In any event, those having the most influential voice in policy formulation are members of the Political Bureau Standing Committee.

Top leaders share a number of common social characteristics. There is no clear evidence of regional underrepresentation. Nonetheless, many Hamgyŏng natives are included in the inner circle.

Leadership Succession

Beginning in the fall of 1975, North Koreans used the term *party center* to refer to Kim Jong Il. However, for a few years after its initial introduction the term appeared only infrequently, because Kim Il Sung's efforts to promote his son met some resistance. Kim Il Sung purged many of his son's opponents, however, and neither Kim faced any active opposition thereafter.

Kim Il Sung took the rank of grand marshal (*taewŏnsu*) on April 13, 1992, and on April 20, 1992, Kim Jong Il, as supreme commander of the armed forces, gained the rank of marshal (*wŏnsu*). Kim Il Sung was the president and chairman of the National Defense Commission, with command and control of the armed forces, until Kim Jong Il assumed the latter position in April 1993.

There were many scenarios for leadership succession. Some of the prospects derived from a common postulation that arrangements after the death of Kim Il Sung would take at least a few years to clarify because of the decades-long preparation of a succession plan. South Korean scholar Yang Sung-chul labeled this "positive skepticism" and called short-term failure, such as a coup d'état or a revolution, "negative skepticism." "Negative skepticism" was not to be dismissed, however, because of Kim Jong Il's weaknesses—his lack of charisma, poor international recognition, and unknown governing skills—as well as the sagging domestic economy and external factors, such as inter-Korean, North Korea–Japan, and North Korea–United States relations (see Foreign Policy, this ch.).

Kim Jong Il's appointment as commander of the Korean People's Army suggested that the succession issue had finally been solved because the military was once considered his weak point; he already had full control of the state and the economic administration. Kim Jong Il also manages political affairs and KWP commercial operations as a primary authority and handles symbolic roles, such as meeting with foreign leaders and appearing at national celebrations.

In addition, Kim Jong Il plays a prominent role in the KWP propaganda machine—mass media, literature, and art. Many literary works and performance works—including films, operas, and plays—have been produced under the "revolutionary tradition" of the KWP and Kim's guidance. Kim uses popular culture to broaden his public image and gain popular support (see Leisure Activities, ch. 2; Japan, this ch.).

Kim Jong Il tried to expedite economic growth and productivity using the Three Revolutions Team Movement, which was designed to inspire the broad masses into actively participating in the Three Revolutions. At the Fifth Party Congress, Kim Il Sung emphasized the necessity of pressing ahead more vigorously with the Three Revolutions so as to consolidate the socialist system. In response, Kim Jong Il developed the follow-up slogan, "Let us meet the requirements of the *chuch'e* in ideology, technology and culture." Most units forged ahead with "ideological education" to teach the party members and other workers to become revolutionaries of the *chuch'e* idea. In many spheres of the national economy, productivity also is expected to increase as a result of the technology emphasis of

The Tower of Immortality in P'yŏngyang; the inscription reads "The Great Leader Comrade Kim Il Sung Is with Us Forever." Courtesy Korea Today (P'yŏngyang), December 1997, 31

the campaigns. In addition, the "cultural revolution" addresses promoting literacy and cultural identity.

Chuch'e, instrumental in providing a consistent and unifying framework for commitment and action in the political arena, offers a foundation for the party's incessant demand for spartan austerity, sacrifice, discipline, and dedication. It has not yet been determined, however, whether *chuch'e* is an asset or a liability for Kim. Nonetheless, Kim is likely to continue to emphasize *chuch'e* as the only satisfactory answer to all challenging questions in North Korea, particularly because he attributes the collapse of communism in the Soviet Union and East European countries to their lack of *chuch'e* ideology.

Graduates of the first class of the Man'gyŏngdae Revolutionary Institute, established in 1947, support Kim Jong Il's power base. Many of these graduates occupy key positions in government and the military. For example, O Guk-nyol and General Paek Hak-nim—the latter, the former minister of people's security—are members of the Central Military Commission, the KWP Central Committee, and the Supreme People's Assembly; Kim Hwan, a former minister of chemical industry and vice premier, is a member of both the KWP Central Committee and the Supreme People's Assembly; and Kim Yong-sun, an alternate member of the Political Bureau, is the director of the International Affairs Department, KWP Central Committee.

Kim Jong Nam, the eldest of Kim Jong Il's children, appeared likely to be the chosen successor until 2001, when he was arrested in Narita International Airport in Japan for traveling on a forged passport from the Dominican Republic. It is now believed that Kim Jong Chul, Kim's second son, will be the heir. Kim Jong Chul holds a position at the KWP Central Committee Leadership Division, just as Kim Jong Il did when he was trained to succeed his father.

In May 2005, reports of dissident activities against the regime began to trickle out of the country, including video images purported to be of defaced Kim Jong Il portraits. Other rumors indicated that official Kim Jong Il portraits were being removed from public buildings. It is unclear whether these reports were authentic and whether the incidents were isolated or widespread, but shortly thereafter, public executions of traitors also were reported.

Mass Organizations

All mass organizations are guided and controlled by the KWP. A number of political and social organizations appear concerned with the promotion of special-interest groups but actually serve as auxiliaries to the party. Many of these organizations were founded in the early years of the KWP to serve as vehicles for the party's efforts to penetrate a broader cross section of the population.

Mass organizations have another important function: to create the impression that there are noncommunist social, political, cultural, and professional groups that can work with their South Korean counterparts toward national reunification. Most of these organizations were established to develop a unified strategy in dealing with the ruling establishment of South Korea and other foreign countries and organizations. As of 2006, these included the Korean Social Democratic Party, Chongu Party, Socialist Working Youth League, Committee for the Peaceful Reunification of the Fatherland, Korean Democratic Women's Union, Korean National Peace Committee, Korean Students Committee, General Federation of Trade Unions, and many others. The Committee for the Peaceful Reunification of the Fatherland has been actively involved in the two Koreas' reconciliation talks since the early 1990s.

Among auxiliary organizations, one frequently covered in the media is the Kim Il Sung Socialist Youth League. Directly subordinate to the party Central Committee, it is the only mass organization expressly mentioned in the KWP constitution. The league is the party's most important ideological and organizational training ground, with branches and cells wherever there are regular party organizations. Youth league cells exist in the army, factories, cooperative farms, schools, cultural institutions, and government agencies. The organization is hailed as a "militant reserve" of the party; its members are described as heirs to the revolution, reliable reserves, and active assistants of the party. Young people between the ages of 14 and 26 are eligible to join the league regardless of other organizational affiliations, provided they meet requirements similar to those for party membership. The junior version of the youth league is the Young Pioneer Corps, open to children between the ages of nine and about 15. The P'yŏngyang Children's Palace is maintained by league members for the extracurricular activities of Young Pioneer Corps members.

The principal vehicle for P'yŏngyang's united front strategy in dealing with South Korea and foreign counterparts is the Democratic Front for the Reunification of the Fatherland, popularly known as the Fatherland Front. The Fatherland Front actually is an umbrella for various other organizations and thus ostensibly is a nonpolitical, nongovernmental organization. Choch'ongryŏn (see Glossary), the General Association of Korean Residents in Japan, is one of the best known of the foreign auxiliary organizations. Its mission is to enlist the allegiance of the more than 600,000 Korean residents in Japan. At least one-third of these residents, who also are courted assiduously by Seoul, are considered supporters of P'yŏngyang. The remaining two-thirds of the members are either South Korean loyalists or neutral. Those who are friendly toward North Korea are regarded by P'yŏngyang as its citizens and are educated at Korean schools in Japan that are financially subsidized by North Korea. These Koreans are expected to work for the North Korean cause either in Japan or as returnees to North Korea.

The activities of these mass organizations occasionally are reported in the news; however, it is usually difficult to ascertain what they actually do. Organizations such as the Korean Social Democratic Party and the Chongu Party disclose only the officially published names of their leaders and do not report anything about their membership or activities.

The Media

Article 67 of the 1998 constitution states that North Korean citizens are guaranteed freedom of speech, press, assembly, demonstration, and association. Of course, such activities are permitted only in support of government and KWP objectives. Kim Jong Il has even written a handbook for aspiring journalists, entitled *The Great Teacher of Journalists*. It provides guidelines on portraying the leadership in the most favorable way. Other articles of the constitution require citizens to follow the socialist norms of life; for example, a collective spirit takes precedence over individual political or civil liberties.

Domestic media censorship is strictly enforced, and deviation from the official government line is not tolerated. The regime prohibits listening to foreign media broadcasts, and violators reportedly are subject to severe punishment. Senior party cadres, however, have good access to the foreign media. No external media are allowed free access to North Korea, but an agreement to share in Japan's telecommunications satellites was reached in September 1990.

Newspapers, broadcasting, and other mass media are major vehicles for information dissemination and political propaganda. Although most households have radios and some have television sets, neither radios nor televisions can be tuned to anything other than official programming. Only some 10 percent of the radios and 30 percent of the televisions are in private households (see Telecommunications and the Internet, ch. 3). Government control extends to artistic and academic circles, and visitors report that the primary function of movies, books, and the performing arts is to contribute to the cult of personality surrounding Kim Il Sung.

The media are government controlled. As of 2006, there were four main television stations, approximately 17 AM stations, 14 FM stations, 14 domestic shortwave stations, and a powerful international shortwave station. The latter broadcasts in English, French, German, Russian, Spanish, and several Asian languages. Korean Central Broadcasting Station and P'yŏngyang Broadcasting Station (Radio P'yŏngyang) are the central radio stations; there are also several local stations and stations for overseas broadcasts. "One marginally positive development in the past couple of years," according to a 2003 International Press Institute report, "was the decision by the government to scrap radio broadcastings aimed at blaming South Korea for almost everything."

A number of newspapers are published. *Nodong Shinmun*, the news organ of the party Central Committee, has a circulation of approximately 1.5 million. *Kulloja*, the theoretical organ of the party Central Committee, claims a circulation of about 300,000 readers. *Minju Chosŏn* (Democratic Korea) is the government newspaper, and *Nodong Chŏngnyŏn* (Working Youth) is the newspaper of the Socialist Working Youth League. There also are specialized newspapers for teachers, the army, and railway workers.

The Korean Central News Agency (Chosŏn Chungyang Tŏngsinsa —KCNA) is the primary agency for gathering and disseminating news. KCNA publishes the daily paper *Chosŏn Chungyang T'ongsin* (Korean Central News), *Sajin T'ongsin* (Photographic News), and *Chosŏn*

The Unification of the Fatherland Three-Constitutions Memorial; the inscription at top, with the unified Korean Peninsula, reads "Three Constitutions."
Courtesy Chosŏn *(P'yŏngyang), March 2002, 15*

Chungyang Yŏnbo (Korean Central Yearbook). KCNA issues daily press releases in English, French, Spanish, and Russian; newscasts in these and other languages are beamed overseas. The Foreign Languages Press Group issues the monthly magazines *Korea Today* and *Korea Pictorial*, the quarterly *Foreign Trade of the Democratic People's Republic of Korea*, and the weekly newspaper the *P'yŏngyang Times* published in English, French, and Spanish. All of these latter publications are available on the Internet from an official North Korean Web site.

Despite all of these media, information from the outside world is not freely available, nor is information from North Korea available without censorship. Very few ordinary people in North Korea have access to the Internet. Although in the early twenty-first century more foreign journalists have been allowed into the country than in earlier years, movement within North Korea is restricted, and what is allowed is closely monitored.

Foreign Policy

North Korea's foreign relations are shaped by a mixture of historical, nationalistic, ideological, and pragmatic considerations. The territorial division of the peninsula looms large in the political thinking of North Korean leaders and is a driving force in their management of internal and external affairs. Over the centuries, unequal relations, foreign depredation, dependence on foreigners for assorted favors, and the emulation of foreign cultures and institutions are less the exception than the rule in Korea's perceptions of the outside world. These patterns give rise to the widely shared assumption among Koreans that their capacity to control their national destiny is limited by geopolitical constraints.

Inter-Korean Affairs

The reunification of the two Koreas is seen as a difficult goal by both the North and South. Although P'yŏngyang and Seoul agreed in principle in 1972 that unification should be achieved peacefully and without foreign interference, they continued to differ substantially on the practical methods of attaining reunification; this area of disagreement has not narrowed in subsequent years. Inter-Korean dialogue in North Korea is the responsibility of the State Security Department (see State Security Department, ch. 5).

North Korea's goal of unification remains constant, but tactics have changed depending on the perception of opportunities and limitations implicit in shifting domestic and external currents and events. From the beginning, North Korea has insisted that an inter-Korean political formula should be based on parity or equality, rather than population. Because South Korea has more than twice the population of North Korea, a supreme Korean council set up according to a one-person, one-vote formula would give South Korea a commanding position. Another constant is P'yŏngyang's insistence that the Korean question be settled as an internal Korean affair without foreign interference.

P'yŏngyang's position that unification should be achieved by peaceful means was belied by circumstances surrounding the outbreak of the Korean War in 1950 and by subsequent infiltrations, the digging of invasion tunnels under the Demilitarized Zone (DMZ—see Glossary), and other incidents. North Korea's contention that the conflict was started by South Korea and the United States failed to impress South Korea's population and has been proven false by Soviet archives. The war, in effect, reinforced the obvious ideological and systemic incompatibilities that were in place at the time of the division of the peninsula in 1945. At the 1954 Geneva Conference, North Korea proposed the formation of an all-Korean commission to achieve unification and a single, elected legislature; the withdrawal of all foreign troops from the Korean Peninsula; and the formal declaration by outside powers of the need for peaceful development and unification in Korea. P'yŏngyang also proposed that the armies of both countries

Kim Dae Jung, president of South Korea, meets Kim Jong Il, P'yŏngyang, June 2000. Courtesy Chosŏn *(P'yŏngyang), August 2000, 1*

be reduced to 100,000 persons each within a year, that neither side enter into any military alliance, and that measures be taken to facilitate economic and cultural exchanges. The sincerity of these proposals is at best debatable, but the positions taken by North Korea in the early Cold War years clearly reflected confidence and competitiveness with South Korea in military, economic, and political terms.

Inter-Korean affairs became more complex in 1970 and 1971, in part because of the U.S. decision to withdraw some of its troops from South Korea and because of moves by the United States and China to improve their relations. In August 1971, amid signs of a thaw in the Cold War and an uncertain international environment, the Red Cross societies of Seoul and P'yŏngyang agreed to open talks aimed at the eventual reunion of dispersed families. These high-level talks—between Kim Il Sung's brother and the chief of the South Korean Central Intelligence Agency—were held alternately in the two capitals and paralleled behind-the-scenes contacts to initiate political negotiations, reportedly at South Korea's suggestion. The talks continued to make progress and resulted in a joint communiqué issued on July 4, 1972, in which the two countries agreed to abide by three principles of unification: to work toward reunifying the coun-try independently and without foreign interference; to transcend dif-ferences in ideology and political systems; and to unify the peninsula peacefully without the use of armed force.

Despite the various committees set up by the 1972 communiqué, it quickly became obvious to both sides that they had fundamentally divergent approaches. North Korea's position "front-loaded" all significant concessions from the South, including the withdrawal of all foreign troops from South Korea, while the South sought to build transparency and trust first through confidence-building measures and "low politics" cooperation.

At the Sixth Party Congress in October 1980, Kim Il Sung proposed the establishment of the Democratic Confederal Republic of Koryŏ, which would be based on a single unified state, leaving the two systems intact and federating the two governments. The Supreme National Assembly, with an equal number of representatives from North and South and an appropriate number of representatives of overseas Koreans, would be formed with a confederal standing committee to "guide the regional governments of the North and the South and to administer all the affairs of the confederal state." The regional governments of the North and South would have independent policies—within limits—consistent with the fundamental interests and demands of the whole nation and would strive to narrow their differences in all areas. But South Korea rejected the confederation as a propaganda ploy.

No significant dialogue occurred between the two countries until the middle of 1984, when South Korea suffered a devastating flood. North Korea proposed to send relief goods to flood victims in South Korea, and the offer was accepted. This occasion provided the momentum for both sides to resume their suspended dialogue. In 1985 the two countries exchanged performing arts groups, and 92 members of separated families met. In January 1986, however, North Korea once again suddenly cut off all talks with South Korea, blaming "Team Spirit," the annual U.S.–South Korean joint military exercise.

In 1988 the South Korean government of Roh Tae-woo pursued a new "northern diplomacy" or Nordpolitik (see Glossary) aimed at North Korea's allies. Ostensibly, it was an initiative to prevent ideology from trumping national interest as Seoul sought to broaden relations in the region, but the strategy's true payoff was its ability to woo both China and the Soviet Union into diplomatic relations, thereby constituting the ultimate diplomatic coup over the North. South Korea's efforts in conjunction with the North's economic difficulties compelled a basic change in P'yŏngyang's strategy toward Seoul.

Five rounds of meetings were held alternately in Seoul and P'yŏngyang before the Agreement on Reconciliation, Nonaggression, Exchanges, and Cooperation between the South and the North was signed on December 13, 1991. The accord reaffirmed the 1972 principles of peaceful unification, issued a joint declaration of non-aggression, and instituted a variety of other confidence-building measures (for example, advance warning of troop movements and exercises and the installation of a telephone hot line between top military commanders). Several joint inter-Korean subcommittees were established to work out the specifics for implementing the general terms of the accord on economic cooperation, travel and communication, cultural exchanges, political affairs, and military affairs. Separate from the prime minister-level dialogue, yet closely associated with it, were talks held between the two Red Cross organizations about reunification of families.

The two Koreas also stated in a parallel agreement that their peninsula should be "free of nuclear weapons." The ensuing Joint Declaration on the Denuclearization of the Korean Peninsula, which was signed on January 20, 1992, and took force on February 19, 1992, called for the establishment of a Joint Nuclear Control Commission to negotiate a credible and effective bilateral nuclear inspection regime. Although negotiations produced substantive progress on the drafting of detailed accords to achieve ratification of the 1991 Agreement on Reconciliation, Nonaggression, Exchanges, and Cooperation, nothing was implemented.

The next major watershed in inter-Korean relations revolved around the Sunshine Policy of the South Korean government under Kim Dae Jung. Various events led to the formation of this policy. Kim Dae Jung entered office in 1998 at the height of South Korea's financial crisis, and after a period of time in which the lessons of German unification had seeped into all of South Korean society. The focus of national attention on extricating South Korea from its economic crisis, in combination with the liberal ideologies long held by the new president, allowed Kim to put forward a new view of inter-Korean relations with relatively little opposition. Kim called for an open-ended engagement of North Korea in which unreciprocated cooperation was acceptable, and indeed expected. The Sunshine Policy encouraged all countries to engage with the North, in a departure from the position of his predecessor, South Korean president Kim Young-sam, who desired all engagement with the North to be routed through Seoul. This new approach facilitated the North's normalization of diplomatic relations with a number of European countries, including the United Kingdom and other European Union nations. By seeking to create a modicum of trust and transparency through Seoul's one-sided generosity, the Sunshine Policy constituted an entirely different stance from the decades of zero-sum diplomatic contention between North and South. The policy also resulted in the establishment of a joint-venture scenic sport and tourism project, at Mount Kŭmgang, in the North near the DMZ, as well as the reconnection of railroad lines between the two Koreas.

The Sunshine Policy's culmination was the historic June 2000 summit in which Kim Dae Jung went to North Korea to meet with Kim Jong Il. The joint communiqué from the meeting reaffirmed the principles of peaceful unification and proposed more family reunions. But the most long-lasting impact of the summit was the image of the two leaders embracing, broadcast throughout South Korea. A cathartic moment for many Koreans, this event had the effect of changing South Korean popular views of the North, virtually overnight. Images of a demonized North Korean leader were replaced by an infatuation with him. Views of a North Korean "threat" were lost on much of the younger generation of South Koreans, despite the absence of any amelioration of the military situation on the ground (see Doctrine, Strategy, and Tactics, ch. 5).

In spite of later revelations that the South Korean government made unofficial cash payments to facilitate the June 2000 summit, the Sunshine Policy continued to gain popularity among the younger generation in the South and in the government of Roh Moo Hyun (president of South Korea, 2003–8), although it was renamed the Peace and Prosperity Policy. A wave of demonstrations, which accompanied the electoral victory of Roh in 2002, have led some to believe that the younger generation (that is, under age 50) in South Korea has aligned itself more with the fate of North Korea than with the country's traditional ally, the United States. While not denying that South Koreans are in the midst of a new reconciliation mood with the North in the aftermath of the Sunshine Policy, this mood is subject to several constraints.

First is the sober realization that the U.S. military presence is still critical to South Korean security. Demonstrations protesting that presence died down significantly after Washington initiated plans to reduce its troops on the peninsula as part of a larger realignment of forces in Asia. Second, changes in North Korea's nuclear posture could result in changes in the public perception. If part of the generosity toward the North stemmed from an inner confidence in Seoul that South Korea holds decisive superiority across all national indicators of power, the 2006 nuclear test by the North altered those visions. Third, it remains unclear whether any of the impact of the Sunshine Policy has reached deep into North Korea. Should these engagement efforts reveal no change in North Korean preferences over the long term, South Korean supporters of the policy might be discouraged.

China and the Soviet Union/Russia

North Korea owes its survival as a separate political entity to China and the Soviet Union. Both countries provided critical military assistance—personnel and matériel—during the Korean War. From then until the early 1990s, China and the Soviet Union both were North Korea's most important markets and its major suppliers of oil and other basic necessities. Similarly, China and the Soviet Union were reliable pillars of diplomatic support.

Moscow and Beijing's normalization of diplomatic relations with South Korea in 1990 and 1992, respectively, presaged a sea change in North Korea's foreign policy. Despite the professed *chuch'e* ideology, Soviet and Chinese patronage to the North constituted mainstays of the economy. When both Cold War patrons terminated this support on normalization of relations with Seoul, the North's economy began to register negative growth rates for much of the rest of the decade (see Collapse in the 1990s, ch. 3). Famine conditions in the mid-1990s were also partially a consequence of the North's loss of aid from its patrons. P'yŏngyang's relations with the Soviet Union and then Russia were permanently damaged. Moscow's abrupt shedding of the North as Russia sought to gain access to US$3 billion in loans from the wealthier South Korea (as part of its 1990 diplomatic normalization with Seoul) greatly offended Kim Il Sung. China sought a less draconian break with the North, emphasizing the need for strong relations with both Koreas.

Close North Korea–China ties continue, but Beijing strives to maintain a balance in its relationship with the two Koreas, a far cry from its previous four decades of dealing solely with P'yŏngyang. China welcomed the 1992 Joint Declaration on the Denuclearization of the Korean Peninsula, making clear its preference for a non-nuclear Korea. Beijing also urged P'yŏngyang to cooperate with the International Atomic Energy Agency (IAEA—see Glossary). Beijing clearly views its economic interest on the peninsula as being linked with the South; China has surpassed the United States as South Korea's largest trading partner. Yet, for strategic and historical reasons, China maintains its policy of keeping the North Korean regime afloat.

Since 2003, talks among six nations (North Korea, South Korea, China, Japan, Russia, and the United States)—the so-called Six-Party Talks—have offered a forum that enabled China to play a larger diplomatic role on the Korean Peninsula. Hosting the talks in Beijing and taking on the self-proclaimed label of "honest broker," China sought to score diplomatic points in the region and enhance its influence. In the end, however, the equation for Beijing remains a peculiar but compelling one. It seeks a nonnuclear North Korea as well as an economically reformed state, but China continues to provide energy and food assistance to the North even in the absence of progress on denuclearization or reform because of the potential costs of regime collapse.

The Soviet Union stunned North Korea in September 1990 when it established diplomatic relations with South Korea. Since then and the subsequent collapse of the Soviet Union in August 1991, North Korea has worked to build a relationship with Russia's new political leaders. North Korea's efforts to recapture some of the previous closeness and economic benefits of its relationship with the former Soviet Union are seriously hampered, however, by Russia's preoccupation with its own political and economic woes. Trade between the two nations has dropped dramatically since 1990, as North Korea cannot compete with the quality of goods South Korea can offer. Whereas in the past the Soviet Union had readily extended credit to North Korea, Russia has demanded hard currency for North Korea's purchases. Russia also has signaled North Korea that it intends to revise a 1961 defense treaty between North Korea and the Soviet Union. The revision most likely will mean that Russia will not be obligated to assist North Korea militarily except in the event that North Korea is invaded.

In large part as a result of changes in its historical relationships with China and the Soviet Union, North Korea faces a foreign policy paradox. Although it arguably has more diplomatic relations with Western countries than ever before, as a result of the Sunshine Policy, P'yŏngyang is at the same time more diplomatically, politically, and economically isolated. The end of both China's and the Soviet Union's Cold War patronage has much to do with this new situation. The future direction of North Korea–China relations will be a critical indicator of the viability of the North Korean regime. If Beijing continues to view the costs of "muddling through"—a phrase coined by Marcus Noland, a noted economist, and now widely used—North Korea's economic hardship as better than the costs of collapse, then the regime may be capable of subsisting in its current state. If, however, the status quo results in a nuclear North Korea, then the costs to Beijing of "muddling through" may grow sufficiently high to warrant change of the regime itself.

Japan

Until the late 1980s, North Korea's post–World War II policy toward Japan was mainly aimed at minimizing cooperation between Japan and South Korea and at deterring Japan's rearmament while

Kim Jong Il shaking hands with China's President Hu Jintao, Beijing,
April 2004
Courtesy Chosŏn *(P'yŏngyang), June 2004, 1*
Russia's President Vladimir V. Putin holds talks with Kim Jong Il,
P'yŏngyang, July 19–20, 2000.
Courtesy Chosŏn *(P'yŏngyang), September 2000, 4*

striving for closer diplomatic and commercial ties with Japan. Crucial to this position was the fostering within Japan of support for North Korea, especially among the Japanese who supported their nation's communist and socialist parties and the ethnic Korean residents of Japan. Over the years, however, North Korea did much to discredit itself in the eyes of many potential supporters in Japan. The cases of missing Japanese citizens attributed to North Korean kidnappings went unresolved. And Japanese citizens who had accompanied their spouses to North Korea had endured severe hardships and were prevented from communicating with relatives and friends in Japan. Japan watched with dismay as, in April 1970, North Korea gave safe haven to elements of the Japanese Red Army, a terrorist group. North Korea's inability and refusal to pay its debts to Japanese traders also reinforced popular Japanese disdain for North Korea.

Coincidental with the changing patterns in its relations with China and Russia, North Korea has moved to improve its strained relations with Japan. P'yŏngyang's primary motives appear to be a quest for relief from diplomatic and economic isolation, which has also caused serious shortages of food, energy, and hard currency. Normalization of relations with Japan also raises the possibility of North Korea's gaining monetary compensation for the period of Japan's colonial occupation (1910–45), a precedent set when Japan normalized relations with South Korea.

The first round of diplomatic normalization talks was held in 1991 but quickly broke down over the question of compensation. North Korea demanded compensation for damages incurred during colonial rule as well as for "sufferings and losses" in the period after World War II. Later rounds of normalization talks in the late 1990s and early 2000s were stymied by mutual rigidity: the North Koreans demanded colonial reparations and refused to discuss Tokyo's concerns over P'yŏngyang's deployment of short-range ballistic missiles threatening Japan. Tokyo set as preconditions for progress North Korea's provision of information regarding nationals abducted from Japan by North Korean agents in the 1970s and a satisfactory resolution to the nuclear weapons issue.

With talks stalled, an apparent breakthrough materialized in September 2002 when Prime Minister Koizumi Junichiro agreed to visit North Korea for a one-day summit with Kim Jong Il. Building on the momentum created by the inter-Korean June 2000 summit, there were high hopes of a major improvement in relations. Kim Jong Il's admission at this summit that North Korea had indeed kidnapped Japanese nationals, however, resulted in a groundswell of popular anger in Japan. The public backlash at the news that some of these abductees had died without explanation was so severe that Tokyo pressed harder for additional information on the circumstance of their deaths as a precondition for talks. Bilateral relations were further complicated over this issue when Tokyo refused to return the abductees and relatives after they had been granted permission to visit Japan. A second summit between Kim Jong Il and Koizumi in May 2004 did not fully resolve this major impediment to normalizing relations.

Security tensions between P'yŏngyang and Tokyo augmented the political problems over abductees during the same period. In August 1998, the North staged a ballistic missile test over Japan that heightened concerns immeasurably. This event marked the start of a significant augmentation of Japanese security capabilities. In response to the ballistic missile test, Japan launched its first intelligence-gathering satellites. During the period 2000–4, moreover, several incidents at sea involving North Korean ships and Japan's Maritime Self-Defense

Force vessels occurred, with the Japanese shooting at and sinking a North Korean vessel. Also, in response to the North Korean threat, in 2003–4 Japan undertook a set of legislative reforms that enhanced Tokyo's capacity to participate in a multilateral proliferation-security initiative as well as to impose bilateral sanctions against North Korea, even without a United Nations (UN) Security Council resolution. As of 2006, Japan had not exercised these capabilities. A militarily proactive Japan will be perhaps the most long-lasting legacy of North Korea's threat.

The United States

North Korea's relationship with the United States since 1945 has been marked by almost continuous confrontation and mistrust. North Korea views the United States as the strongest imperialist force in the world, the successor to Japanese imperialism, and a malevolent hegemon in a unipolar world in the post–Cold War period. U.S. concerns about North Korea as an international outlaw derive from P'yŏngyang's activities in nuclear proliferation and weapons development, sales of weapons technology, illicit narcotics and counterfeit currency trafficking, human rights violations, and the conventional military threat to Washington's allies in the region.

The uneasy armistice that halted the intense fighting of the Korean War on July 27, 1953, occasionally has been broken. Perpetuating the mutual distrust was North Korea's 1968 seizure of the intelligence-gathering ship USS *Pueblo*, the downing of a U.S. reconnaissance plane in 1969, and the 1976 killing of two U.S. army officers at the P'anmunjŏm Joint Security Area in the middle of the DMZ. North Korea's assassination in 1983 of several South Korean cabinet officials educated in the United States and the terrorist bombing of a Baghdad–Seoul South Korean airliner in midair off the coast of Burma in 1987 likewise have reinforced U.S. perceptions of North Korea as unworthy of having diplomatic or economic ties with the United States.

In 1988 the United States launched its own modest diplomatic initiative to reduce P'yŏngyang's isolation and to encourage its opening to the outside world. Consequently, the U.S. government began facilitating cultural, scholarly, journalistic, athletic, and other exchanges with North Korea. After a hesitant start, by the early 1990s almost monthly exchanges were occurring in these areas between the two nations, a halting but significant movement away from total estrangement.

The United States supported the simultaneous admission of both Koreas into the UN in September 1991. That same month, President George H.W. Bush announced the withdrawal of all U.S. tactical nuclear weapons worldwide. In January 1992, after North Korea had publicly committed itself to the signing of a nuclear safeguards agreement with the IAEA and to permitting IAEA inspections of its primary nuclear facility at Yŏngbyŏn, about 50 kilometers north of P'yŏngyang, President Bush and South Korean president Roh Tae-woo cancelled the 1992 joint annual "Team Spirit" military exercise.

In February 1992, the U.S. Department of State's undersecretary for political affairs, Arnold Kantor, met with his North Korean counterpart, the director of the KWP Central Committee's International Affairs Department, Kim Yong-sun, in New York City. At this meeting, the United States set forth the steps it wanted North Korea to take prior to normalization of relations. North Korea had to facilitate progress in the North–South dialogue; end its export of missile and related technology; renounce terrorism; cooperate in determining the fate of all U.S. Korean War unaccounted-for military personnel; demonstrate increasing respect for human rights; and conclude a credible and effective North–South nuclear inspection regime designed to complement inspections conducted by the IAEA. Once a credible and effective bilateral North–South inspection regime had been implemented, the U.S. Government would initiate a policy-level dialogue with North Korea to formulate specifics for resolving other outstanding U.S. concerns. The culmination of this diplomacy was the June 1993 North Korea–United States joint statement in which the two sides expressed their hope for relations to be based on the principles of respect for each other's sovereignty and noninterference in each other's internal affairs.

The 1993–94 nuclear crisis with North Korea brought to an end this short-lived thaw in relations. North Korea's refusal to cease and disclose nuclear activities at its facilities in Yŏngbyŏn, in defiance of IAEA directives and agreements, became the center of a crisis very close to war in June 1994. Last-minute diplomacy by former President Jimmy Carter, just as the United States was considering plans to reinforce its military presence in the region, enabled North Korea–United States bilateral negotiations that led to the October 1994 Agreed Framework for the denuclearization of North Korea. Negotiated by North Korea's Kang Sok-ju and U.S. ambassador Robert Gallucci, this agreement required P'yŏngyang to freeze, put under international monitoring, and ultimately dismantle its nuclear activities at Yŏngbyŏn. In exchange for these actions, the United States, Japan, and South Korea were to form the Korean Peninsula Energy Development Organization consortium to provide two light-water reactors. The United States also agreed to provide interim energy supplies in the form of heavy fuel oil to the North for the duration of the project.

On October 11, 2000, the first vice chairman of the National Defense Commission, Vice Marshal Cho Myŏng-nok, met with President William J. Clinton at the White House, Washington, DC. Courtesy Audio-Visual Division, William J. Clinton Presidential Library, Little Rock, Arkansas

Given the degree of mutual mistrust, this agreement was iterated in stages such that each side could demonstrate cooperation at each step of the implementation process. Over the longer term, the Agreed Framework held out the hope of further improvements in relations between North Korea and its neighbors across a range of issues including missiles, conventional military threats, political normalization, economic aid, and other key issues.

Concerns about whether the 1994 agreement was being implemented in good faith began almost immediately after its consummation. Because of pressure from the U.S. Congress, Washington fell behind in the delivery of interim fuel-oil shipments, although, until the termination of these shipments in December 2002, the United States fulfilled every shipment. For its part, North Korea went against the spirit of the agreement by engaging in provocative acts against South Korea and Japan, testing ballistic missiles, and pursuing other weapons activities suspected to be in violation of the agreement.

The Agreed Framework appeared on the brink of collapse over suspected nuclear weapons activities at Kumchangri, about 90 kilometers north of P'yŏngyang, in North P'yŏngan Province, in 1998. After a protracted negotiation process, inspections of Kumchangri turned up nothing, but mistrust was very high, and skepticism about

North Korean intentions to comply with the 1994 agreement were palpable in Washington. A policy review conducted by former Secretary of Defense William J. Perry in 1999 laid out two paths along which U.S.–North Korean relations could proceed. The first was continued implementation of the Agreed Framework as a springboard for cooperation on other issues of concern such as ballistic missiles. The other path would involve alternative, more coercive actions. A flurry of diplomatic activity subsequent to the Perry policy review led to the visit of North Korean envoy Cho Myŏng-nok to the United States in October 2000 and a joint statement of no hostile intent. U.S. Secretary of State Madeleine Albright reciprocated with an unprecedented October 2000 visit to P'yŏngyang and meetings with Kim Jong Il. Discussions about a visit by President Clinton and a potential agreement on missiles took place but were never concluded.

In October 2002, the George W. Bush administration stated that North Korea was in violation of the 1994 agreement with a clandestine second nuclear weapons program, using highly enriched uranium technology. North Korea asserted that it was entitled to such weapons if the United States maintained its hostile policy and then proceeded in the winter of 2002 to break out of the 1994 agreement, unsealing buildings, disabling monitoring cameras, and expelling IAEA inspectors from the Yŏngbyŏn facility. A new forum for discussion was established—the Six-Party Talks—hosted by China, which sought to persuade North Korea to give up its nuclear weapons in a complete, verifiable, and irreversible manner. At these talks, the United States laid out proposals for nuclear disarmament by offering energy assistance from some of the six parties in return for a North Korean commitment to verifiable nuclear dismantlement.

Prospects: The Significance of Reform

The most significant twenty-first-century political development in North Korea relates to the July 2002 market-liberalization reforms, generally associated with four measures. The first was a basic monetization of the economy. The government abolished the coupon-based public distribution system for food rations and relaxed price controls, thereby allowing supply and demand to determine prices. In order to meet the rise in prices, the government also hiked wage levels, which had been almost uniform across sectors. For some sectors, the rise was as much as fortyfold and for other "special" wage sectors (government officials, soldiers, miners, and farmers) as much as sixtyfold. Small-scale markets have sprouted up all over North Korea, and the public ration system has broken down (see Reform of the Public Distribution System, ch. 3).

The second reform measure was adopted in August 2002, when the government abandoned the artificially high value of the North Korean wŏn (for value of the wŏn, see Glossary), adjusting the currency exchange rate from 2.15 wŏn per US$1 to 150 wŏn per US$1. This measure was aimed at inducing foreign investment and providing export incentives for domestic firms. The "unofficial" value of the currency has depreciated much further since the reforms.

A third reform measure was the government's decentralization of economic decisions. Measures entailed cutting government subsidies, allowing farmers' markets to operate, and devolving managerial decisions for industry and agriculture from the central government (via factory party committees) into the hands of local production units. Enterprises now have to cover their own costs. Managers have to meet hard budget constraints. Workers are not evaluated based on the number of days they show up to work, but on productivity and profit. Farmers are now allowed to plant small private plots of land in addition to those plots designated for state production.

The fourth reform measure was the government's pursuit of special administrative districts and industrial zones in order to induce foreign investment. The Sinŭiju Special Administrative Region, in North P'yŏngan Province on the Yellow Sea (or West Sea, as it is called in North Korea) is an open economic zone for foreign businesses designed to exist completely outside North Korea's regular legal strictures. The Kaesŏng Special Industrial Zone is another project designed in particular to attract small and medium-sized South Korean businesses, and the Mount Kŭmgang Tourist Zone operated by Hyundai provides hard currency to the North from tourism. All three projects sought to avoid the mistakes and failures of the Najin–Sŏnbong International Trade Zone, in the northeast near Russia, created by the North in 1991, although these later projects are still hampered by the lack of adequate infrastructure, among other problems (see Special Economic Zones, ch. 3).

The July 2002 reforms were unarguably a significant development. They represented the first attempt in the regime's history at large-scale economic change. In addition, while P'yŏngyang's propaganda continued to maintain anticapitalist rhetoric and spurned market economic principles, unlike the cases of China and Vietnam, the regime admitted flaws in the socialist-style economy. The significance of these reforms, however, does not make them successful. The obstacles to successful reform are numerous.

First, it is unclear whether the July 2002 measures represent the equivalent of North Korea's religious "conversion" to capitalism. Neither the language nor the nature of these initial reforms appears to have the same conviction as those seen in China or Vietnam.

Moreover, many of the reforms arguably may constitute coping mechanisms to deal with immediate problems rather than a wholesale, prescient shift in economic ideology. For example, North Korea authorized monetization of the economy and permitted farmers' markets to buy and sell goods largely because the public distribution system had broken down. Similarly, local managers were given more leeway, not because the central government trusted their entrepreneurial capabilities, but because plunging outputs and high absentee rates for workers who went searching for food rather than reporting to work required some drastic measures.

When the reform package initially was announced in 2002, the government was reluctant to call these measures "reforms," instead referring to an "economic adjustment policy" that would "solidify the nation's socialist principles and planned economic system." Such statements contradict earlier pronouncements by P'yŏngyang about the difficulties of socialism, raising questions about whether an ideological and systemic conversion has yet occurred. Economist Hong Ink-pyo has observed that "market freedom is not the goal" and that the North Korean authorities intend to normalize the planned economy by enhancing efficiency and productivity in industry, and to restore the official economic sector so as to absorb or contract the private economic sector.

The economic reforms will test the government's ability to deal with the triple problems of inflation, economic losers, and the urban poor created by the monetization of the economy. Low supply and low output have led to massive increases in prices and further devaluation of the wŏn. By comparison, in 1979 China's initial price reforms drove up the price of rice by 25 percent; in North Korea, the price has gone up by at least 600 percent, and the wŏn depreciated from 150 wŏn (to US$1) in 2002 to 900 wŏn to the dollar in 2003, with some estimating the black-market values at 3,000 wŏn to the dollar in 2005. The North Korean currency has fallen dramatically against China's renminbi as well, depreciating from 30 wŏn to the renminbi in August 2002 to 120 wŏn in 2003, to more than 130 wŏn in 2004. Despite wage hikes averaging 15 to 20 times the 2002 level, these increased wages, if they are truly paid, still cannot keep pace with the skyrocketing retail prices, estimated at more than 27 times the growth in wage rates.

Although companies in 2006 were allowed greater flexibility in production, the basic absence of any capital inputs allows flexibility in name only. The designated "winners" as a result of these reforms would probably include farmers. They are now allowed to produce food for sale on the open market, after meeting state production quotas.

They benefit from the inflated prices as a result of increased demand. The state also attempted to introduce new seeds and fertilizers to increase crop yields.

Even in a best-case scenario of increased agricultural output stimulated by the reforms, however, the agricultural sector represents a fraction of the economy. The North Korean economy, since the days of the Japanese occupation, has been largely an industrial economy with some 70 percent of the population residing in cities. And there is no internal capacity to increase agricultural output because of the decrepit infrastructure, lack of capital inputs and limited arable land, creating many losers across society. The reforms enabled Kim Jong Il to gain some control of the economy by hurting those black marketers who held large amounts of wŏn before the currency devaluation. Fixed-income workers were badly hit by the combination of price hikes and weakening of the North Korean currency. In addition, many workers were laid off by companies forced to cut costs. Finally, there is fragmentary evidence that even those sectors of the labor force favored by the wage hikes were discontented. Urban factory workers fell into a wage-productivity trap where they initially were given two months' salary of 3,000 wŏn—which was not enough to support a family of four for one month—but nothing beyond that. In order to gain wages, the workers needed to produce, but in 2004 factories in North Korea operated at less than 30 percent capacity. Even among those sectors given the highest wage increases (6,000 wŏn) there was widespread discontent. Refugees crossing the border into China complained that the promise of higher wages had not been kept, with workers receiving only 800 wŏn and then nothing after October 2003. There is the possibility that "money illusion" is wearing off in North Korea, giving way to a new class of urban poor, potentially numbering in the millions, that could be difficult to control.

The ultimate success of the reforms rests on the North's capacity to secure international food supplies until the changes start to increase agricultural output domestically; secure loans to finance shortages in cash-flow for managerial enterprises; and obtain technical training in accounting, fiscal policy, finance and other requisite skills. A report on a U.S. Senate trip to North Korea in 2004 described the basic dilemma: in order for the reforms to succeed, the North must overcome chronic shortages of electricity, food, timber, coal, capital, technology, and trained personnel. Or as a Hongkong and Shanghai Banking Corporation (HSBC) report published in February 2003 explained, the absence of such inputs impedes any chance of sustained economic growth, and without such growth there is no way to produce the needed inputs. The

North's ability to secure this magnitude of assistance depends on a satisfactory resolution of the nuclear crisis. But P'yŏngyang continues to demand these economic inputs from the United States and others as a condition of addressing the world's political concerns about its nuclear programs.

*   *   *

Sources on North Korea vary considerably in reliability and balance, so they should be used with care, particularly in the case of information emanating from North Korea. Information from South Korea also has a political bias. Major articles in *Nodong Shinmun* (Workers' Daily), *Kulloja* (The Worker), and other Korean-language publications are available in U.S. Open Source Center (formerly the Foreign Broadcast Information Service) translations of North Korean broadcasts via the U.S. National Technical Information Service's World News Connection (http://wnc.fedworld.gov/).

For in-depth coverage of North Korea, one of the most comprehensive sources is *Pukhan Chosŏn* (North Korean Handbook), in Korean, prepared by South Korea's Kuktong Munje Yŏn'guso (Institute for East Asian Studies). *Pukhan* (North Korea), the monthly organ of Pukhan Yŏn'guso, the Research Institute on North Korea in Seoul; and *Kita Chōsen Kenkyo* (Studies on North Korea), a Japanese-language monthly of the Kokusai Kankei Kyodo Kenkyo-jo (Joint Research Institute on International Relations) in Tokyo are also useful. *Vantage Point*, an English-language monthly periodical issued by Naewoe Press in Seoul, and *East Asian Review*, an English-language quarterly published by the Institute for East Asian Studies in Seoul, provide in-depth studies of North Korean social, economic, and political developments.

Other sources include the annual survey articles on North Korea in *Asian Survey* and the *Europa World Year Book*. Various portal sites at the Library of Congress offer access to selected official and nongovernmental Web sites. These include North Korean resources listed in Portals to the World (http://www.loc.gov/rr/international/asian/northkorea/northkorea.html) and on the Law Library's Nations of the World (http://www.loc.gov/law/guide/northkorea.html). North Korean official Web sites include the Democratic People's Republic of Korea (http://www.korea.dpr.com/) and Naenara Korea Computer Center in the DPRKorea (http://www.kcckp.net/en/). (For further information and complete citations, see Bibliography.)

Bas-relief on P'yŏngyang's Arch of Triumph showing members of the various branches of the Korean People's Army celebrating the liberation of their country
Courtesy Pulmyŏl ŭi t'ap *(Tower of Immortality), P'yŏngyang: Munye Ch'ulpansa, 1985, 283*

AS THE WORLD'S MOST MILITARIZED STATE in proportion to population, the Democratic People's Republic of Korea (DPRK), or North Korea, fields a massive combat force that ranks fourth in the world in size behind the armed forces of China, the United States, and India. North Korea's major forward deployment of armed forces near the demilitarized zone (DMZ—see Glossary) that divides the Korean Peninsula puts it in a confrontational relationship with the Republic of Korea (South Korea) and the United States, as one of the final legacies of the Cold War.

The division of Korea originated as a consequence of a territorial partition that was imposed by the United States and the former Soviet Union to facilitate the surrender of Japanese forces at the end of World War II (1939–45; see National Division in the 1940s, ch. 1). Agreeing to divide the Korean Peninsula into dual occupation zones at the thirty-eighth parallel, the former Soviet Union occupied the North and the United States the South in what was intended as a temporary division. Instead, antithetical political systems and opposing armed forces were established in the two areas; all subsequent efforts to reunify the two states have failed.

Military Heritage

The origins of North Korea's modern armed forces, which were founded on February 8, 1948, as the Korean People's Army (KPA or Chosŏn Inmin'gun), can be traced through three forging factors: its Kapsan (see Glossary) partisan lineage (1932–45), Soviet occupation (1945–48), and Chinese communist associations (1932–50). These three factors, perhaps more than any others, have contributed uniquely to the formation of the KPA leadership, force structure, doctrine, and tactics.

During the 1930s and 1940s, many Koreans and Chinese joined guerrilla units to oppose Japan's annexation of Korea (1910) and Manchuria (1931). According to North Korean historiography, Kim Il Sung (1912–94) organized his Anti-Japanese Guerrilla Army (or Han il Yugyŏtae) on April 25, 1932; it was later renamed the Korean People's Revolutionary Army (KPRA or Chosŏn Inmin Hyŏngmyŏnggun). In 1936 the KPRA joined with the Chinese Communist Party's newly formed Northeast Anti-Japanese United Army, which fought as a coherent unit until its defeat in battle by the Japanese Imperial Army in 1941. Remnants of the defeated northeast army, including Kim Il Sung and many fellow Koreans, escaped to the Soviet Far East, where they joined the Soviet Eighty-eighth Special Brigade. Many of these Korean exiles (the Kapsan faction) were given leadership positions within the brigade, including Kim Il Sung, who commanded the First Battalion.

At the end of World War II, Koreans repatriated from the Soviet Union were either Kapsan faction members (Kim Il Sung loyalists) or long-term Soviet-Korean residents; the former group would eventually be elevated to positions of government and military authority. There were factional power struggles among the various Korean troops. The pro-Chinese Yan'an faction had its origins in the Korean nationalist movement in China. Kim Mu-chŏng (1904–51), a veteran of the Chinese Communist Party's Long March (1934–35), established the Korean Volunteer Army (KVA or Chosŏn Ŭiyonggun) in Yan'an with Chinese communist backing. Under Chinese communist protection, the Yan'an faction trained several thousand soldiers and political cadres and was a political and military force to be reckoned with when it attempted to return to Korea in 1945.

From August 1945 until December 1948, the Soviet Red Army (later the Soviet Civil Administration) occupied Korea north of the thirty-eighth parallel, where it exercised broad control over administration, including national security. During the Soviet occupation, the North Korean government was fully organized and included the Ministry of Defense and the KPA. In 1948 the KPA had 60,000 personnel assigned to four infantry divisions and a tank battalion that was equipped with Soviet weapons systems and trained and organized according to Soviet doctrine and tactics, which were adapted to accommodate North Korea's infantry-centric force structure. Another 40,000 personnel were organized into a border constabulary that was subordinate to the Ministry of Internal Affairs.

In the 18 months between the Soviet withdrawal and the Korean War (1950–53), the KPA rapidly grew to 160,000 personnel organized into 10 infantry divisions, a tank division, an air division, and a motorcycle regiment; the extra 40,000 personnel formed the border constabulary. This rapid expansion was not only facilitated by the steady influx of Soviet matériel and the domestic conscription of an additional 40,000 personnel but also greatly augmented by the transfer of perhaps as many as 60,000 ethnic Korean soldiers from Chinese communist forces to the KPA in 1949 and 1950.

National Command Authorities

National command authority in North Korea is consolidated in one person—Kim Jong Il (officially born in 1942). This solidification of absolute authority was a carefully arranged process that was initiated by Kim's father, the late President Kim Il Sung, and occurred through several successive appointments (or elections) to various positions, including vice chairman of the National Defense Commission in May 1990, supreme commander of the KPA in December 1991, marshal in April 1992, and chairman of the National Defense Commission in April 1993. More than three years after Kim Il Sung's death, in October 1997, the Korean Workers' Party (KWP) elected Kim Jong Il as its general secretary, and both the KWP Central Committee and the Central Military Commission elected him chairman of the party's Central Military Commission.

In accordance with the 1998 revised state constitution, the National Defense Commission is the highest military leadership body of state power and the organ of overall administration of national defense. Constitutionally, the National Defense Commission is accountable to the Supreme People's Assembly (see The Legislature, ch. 4). However, in fact, if not in law, the National Defense Commission chairman, Kim Jong Il, holds the highest position responsible for North Korea's political, economic, and military resources (see The Constitutional Framework; Relationships Among the Government, Party, and Military, ch. 4).

National Defense Organizations

The KWP Central Military Commission and the state National Defense Commission, both bodies chaired by Kim Jong Il, hold coordinating authority over the armed forces (see fig. 11). The Central Military Commission of the KWP Central Committee (also headed by General Secretary Kim Jong Il) provides broad political and policy guidance, while the National Defense Commission exercises command and administrative control over the armed forces.

Central Military Commission

The party Central Military Commission is subordinate to the party Central Committee and, as enumerated in article 27 of the KWP constitution, serves as the party's leading body on all military matters, including establishing policies, plans, and defense acquisition priorities (see The Korean Workers' Party, ch. 4). The Central Military Commission, and by extension the party Central Committee, coordinates its work through the party Secretariat's military, munitions industry, operations, civil defense, and organization and guidance departments and the party Political Bureau's chain of command, which extends through the General Political Bureau of level of all military units.

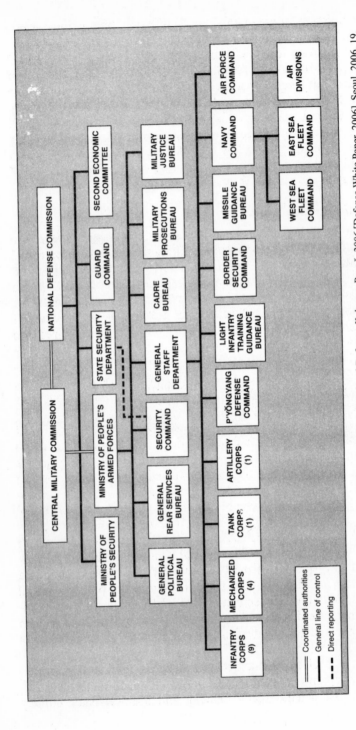

Source: Based on information from Republic of Korea, Ministry of National Defense, *Kukpang Paesŏ, 2006* [Defense White Paper, 2006], Seoul, 2006, 19.

Figure 11. Simplified National Military Command Structure, 2006

The members of the party Central Military Commission concurrently hold key defense and military positions. In 2007 these members and positions included Kim Il-ch'ŏl, minister of people's armed forces; Cho Myŏng-nok, director of the General Political Bureau of the Ministry of People's Armed Forces; Kim Yŏng-chun, chief of the General Staff Department; Yi Ha-il, director of the KWP Military Affairs Department; Kim Ik-hyŏn, director of the party Civil Defense Department; Pak Ki-sŏ, commander of the P'yŏngyang Defense Command; Kim Ch'ŏl-man, former chairman of the Second Economic Committee; Yi Yong-ch'ŏl, first vice director of the KWP Organization and Guidance Department; and others.

National Defense Commission

In the 1998 constitution, clauses related to national defense are arranged in two chapters. Those specifying the roles and missions of the armed forces are in chapter 4, National Defense, articles 58 through 61. Clauses stipulating the powers of the National Defense Commission are located in chapter 6, State Organs, section 2: The National Defense Commission, articles 100 through 105. Section 2 empowers the National Defense Commission chairman to direct and command the armed forces and to guide overall national defense affairs. This section also establishes the National Defense Commission as the highest military leadership body of state power and the organ of overall administration of national defense. It also defines its organization and specifies its duties and authorities.

Article 101 specifies that the National Defense Commission shall consist of a chairman, a first vice chairman, one or more other vice chairmen, and other members. This body is elected by the Supreme People's Assembly and serves a five-year term, which can be extended if an election is not held because of "unavoidable circumstances." The National Defense Commission includes Marshal Kim Jong Il, chairman; Vice Marshal Cho Myŏng-nok, first vice chairman and director of the General Political Bureau; Vice Marshal Yi Yong-mu, vice chairman; Vice Marshal Kim Yŏng-chun, vice chairman and former chief of the General Staff Department; and three members: Vice Marshal Kim Il-ch'ŏl, minister of people's armed forces; Chŏn Pyŏng-ho, secretary of the KWP; General Hyŏn Ch'ŏl-hae, former vice director of the General Political Bureau; and Kim Yang-gŏn, councilor and director of the KWP's International Affairs Department.

Article 103 gives the National Defense Commission the constitutional power to direct the armed forces; establish and abolish state institutions in the defense sector; appoint and dismiss senior military officers; enact and confer military titles on senior officers; and mobilize for emergencies and declare war. Constitutionally, the Supreme People's Assembly is charged with oversight of the National Defense Commission per articles 105 and 110; however, in practice the National Defense Commission is not accountable to any regulatory body. Subordinate to the National Defense Commission are the Ministry of People's Security, State Security Department, Guard Command, and Ministry of People's Armed Forces (see Internal Security, this ch.).

Ministry of People's Armed Forces

The Ministry of People's Armed Forces coordinates administrative defense activities and represents the military externally. Since September 1998, the ministry has been led by Vice Marshal Kim Il-ch'ŏl. Although a ministry, it is not subordinate to the cabinet but answers directly to Kim Jong Il in his role as chairman of the National Defense Commission. Within the ministry, the General Staff Department, General Political Bureau, and Security Command form a ruling triumvirate that operates in a construct of checks and balances.

The General Staff Department is led by Chief of the General Staff General Kim Kyuk-sik, who exercises unitary command authority—operational responsibility over the KPA ground, air, naval, special operations, and reserve forces. Subordinate to the General Staff Department are more than 20 bureaus and an elaborate organization of military schools, academies, and universities. Akin to other nations' Joint Chiefs of Staff, the General Staff Department is directly responsible for all military strategy, planning, operations, and training. These duties specifically fall under the purview of the General Staff Department Operations Bureau and are carried out by its 10 military departments. The First Department is in charge of administrative affairs, while the Second Department develops operations plans. The Third Department supervises the forward infantry corps (I, II, IV, and V Corps), and the Fourth Department supervises all other infantry corps. The Fifth Department oversees the Light Infantry Training Guidance Bureau, the Sixth Department supervises the Air Force Command, and the Seventh Department supervises the Navy Command. The Eighth Department plans operations for subordinate units of other General Staff Department bureaus, the Ninth Department conducts corps-level training exercises, and the Tenth Department (or Information Department) supervises the North Korean members of the Military Armistice Commission.

The General Political Bureau is the regime's political apparatus for controlling the KPA, and it is led by the eminently powerful

A bemedaled Korean People's Army on parade in P'yŏngyang during the celebration of the ninetieth birthday of Kim Il Sung, also the seventieth anniversary of the establishment of the Korean Workers' Party, April 25, 2005
Courtesy Chosŏn *(P'yŏngyang), June 2002, front cover*

director general Vice Marshal Cho Myŏng-nok (second in the national hierarchy behind Kim Jong Il). As the KPA's political guidance system, it permeates every organization of the KPA down through company levels. Operating under the supervision of the party Central Committee, the General Political Bureau is responsible for propaganda, educational, and cultural activities. Moreover, based on delegation of authority from the National Defense Commission, the bureau also authorizes the movement of military units. Inserting political officers into unit movements is a precautionary measure against unauthorized, possibly regime-threatening movement of units by commanders.

The Security Command is an intramilitary surveillance agency that is responsible for internal affairs and for exposing corrupt and disloyal elements within the KPA. Commanded by a military officer, Colonel General Kim Wŏn-hong, and organized under the Ministry of People's Armed Forces, the command is directly accountable to the State Security Department. Similar to the General Political Bureau, the Security Command also operates a separate but parallel chain of command that extends down to the battalion level. Battalion-level security command officers clandestinely employ six or seven informants per company to report politically disloyal elements. Those who are accused often are apprehended, interrogated (routinely tortured for a confession), tried by military court, and sentenced, as deemed appropriate. The Security Command not only conducts surveillance of the military chain of command but also observes and reports on the actions of the political officers.

Other bureaus of the General Staff Department include the General Rear Services Bureau, which controls KPA logistical support activities, and the Cadre Bureau, which oversees officer personnel matters, including promotions, awards, and records. The Military Justice Bureau establishes military judicial policy and supervises the lower military courts, and the Military Prosecutions Bureau prosecutes cases that appear before the Military Justice Bureau and oversees the activities of subordinate prosecution elements.

National Security Policy Formulation

The KWP Central Military Commission and the state National Defense Commission hold coordinating authority over the armed forces. Together (and both under the chairmanship of Kim Jong Il), they represent North Korea's core national security policy-making component.

North Korea's national security structure has a four-tiered military operational component. In this structure, orders originate from the national coordinated authorities and are passed through the minister of People's Armed Forces to the chief of the General Political Bureau and then to the chief of the General Staff Department. However, as head of state, party, and defense and in his role as KPA supreme commander, Kim Jong Il can abbreviate this process by issuing operational orders directly to the chief of the General Staff Department, a two-tiered process. During wartime operation, a supreme command headquarters would be activated to prosecute the war, thereby normalizing this two-tiered process.

Kim Jong Il's control of the military is further strengthened by his appointments of loyalists to state, party, and military positions. Among his closest military advisers are Vice Marshal Cho Myŏng-nok, director of the General Political Bureau; Vice Marshal Kim Yŏng-chun, former chief of the General Staff Department; Vice Marshal Kim Il-ch'ŏl, minster of people's armed forces; General Hyŏn Ch'ŏl-hae, former vice director of the General Political Bureau; General Pak Chae-kyŏng, vice director of Propaganda Department of the General Political Bureau; General Kim Myŏng-kuk, director of the Operations Bureau of the General Staff Department; and Colonel General Kim Wŏn-hong, chief of the Security Command.

Elements of the administrative-logistical component of the national security structure include the Second Economic Committee, which is directly subordinate to the National Defense Commission and controls the defense industry under the guidance of the party Munitions Industry Department; in 2007 the chief of the latter was Chŏn Pyŏng-ho (see Defense Industry, this ch.). The General Staff Department and the General Rear Services Bureau of the Ministry of People's Armed Forces prepare military budgets under the guidance of the Political Bureau and Central Military Commission. Proposed budgets are approved by the Central Military Commission and passed into law by the essentially rubber-stamp legislature, the Supreme People's Assembly.

Organization and Equipment of the Armed Forces

General Staff Department

North Korea has enormous armed forces, numbering more than 1.2 million personnel on active duty and an additional 7.7 million personnel in paramilitary and reserve forces (see Reserve Forces, this ch.). The KPA is a unitary or joint force that is led operationally by the General Staff Department.

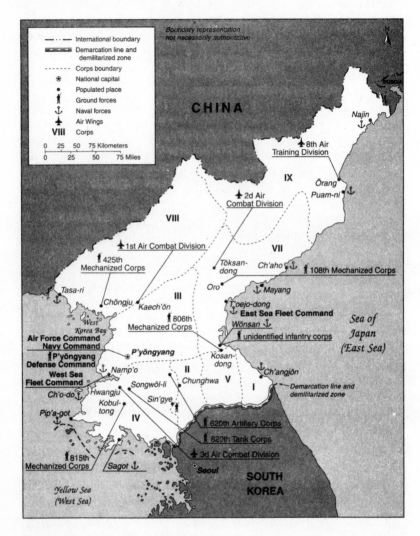

Figure 12. Deployment of Ground and Naval Forces and Air Wings, 2006

In early 2007, General Kim Kyuk-sik became chief of the General Staff Department, replacing Vice Marshal Kim Yŏng-chun, who became vice chairman of the National Defense Commission. The department is staffed with members from all of its components and is responsible for manning, training, equipping, administering, and supporting the KPA and planning, organizing, and employing the KPA to accomplish its missions. Subordinate to the General Staff Department are military commands, bureaus, and institutions that perform command and administrative functions, provide warfighting capabilities, and coordinate deployment of the armed forces. Broadly defined, the military commands—ground, air, naval, and special operations forces—are collectively termed the KPA.

Army

North Korea has amassed the world's third largest ground forces—with 1 million personnel—and the world's largest artillery force—with 13,500 pieces. Seventy percent of the ground forces are permanently deployed south of P'yŏngyang and Wŏnsan and within about 80 kilometers of the DMZ. The ground forces' size, organization, disposition, and combat readiness provide North Korea with options for either offensive operations to attempt to reunify the peninsula forcibly or defensive operations against perceived threats.

The ground forces are organized into 19 major commands that are deployed in echelon by mission and include nine infantry corps, four mechanized corps, a tank corps, an artillery corps, P'yŏngyang Defense Command, Border Security Command, the Missile Guidance Bureau, and the Light Infantry Training Guidance Bureau. Major combat formations include some 80 infantry divisions (including training divisions), 30 artillery brigades, 25 special warfare brigades, 20 mechanized brigades, 10 tank brigades, and seven tank regiments.

The forward echelon is organized with four infantry corps deployed abreast (from west to east: IV Corps, II Corps, V Corps, and I Corps) along the DMZ (see fig. 12). The 620th Artillery Corps also is deployed forward and operates from hardened artillery sites. Some 250 long-range artillery systems (240-millimeter multiple rocket launchers and 170-millimeter self-propelled howitzers) are within striking range of Seoul from their current positions. Also located south of the P'yŏngyang–Wŏnsan line are, from west to east, the 815th Mechanized Corps within the IV Corps boundary (in the vicinity of Kobul-tong); the 820th Tank Corps also within the IV Corps boundary (near Songwŏl-li); and the 806th Mechanized Corps within the V Corps boundary (in the vicinity of Kosan-dong).

Two geographically postured infantry corps are organized in the central echelon. They are III Corps in the west and VII Corps in the east; in addition, there is an unidentified infantry corps located within the VII Corps boundary, and the P'yŏngyang Defense Command is based at the national capital. Organized in the rear echelon are two strategically postured infantry corps: VIII Corps in the west and IX (formerly VI) Corps in the east; the 425th Mechanized Corps is located in the VIII Corps boundary (in the vicinity of Chŏngju), and the 108th Mechanized Corps is within the VII Corps boundary (near Oro).

Since 2000 the Missile Guidance Bureau (possibly renamed the Artillery Guidance Bureau) was organized or reorganized to unify command and control of North Korean theater missile units, which are deployed operationally to several locations. The Light Infantry Training Guidance Bureau is a special operations forces (SOF) command that directly controls assigned forces and might control other strategic SOF, specifically, the air and naval sniper brigades.

The major army weapons systems and equipment include tanks, armored personnel carriers, artillery, antiaircraft artillery, and bridging assets. The army has some 3,700 tanks that are categorized as either light or medium armaments. Light tanks include the PT–76, T–62, and T–63 light amphibious tank; medium tanks include T–54, T–55, T–59, and T–62 models. The tanks are organized into medium and light tank companies (10 tanks each), battalions (three tank companies), brigades (four medium and one light tank battalions), and the tank corps (five tank brigades).

The armored vehicle inventory has about 2,100 armored personnel carriers, including the wheeled BTR series, Type M–1973, and a lesser quantity of the track-mounted BMP. Ground forces use armored personnel carriers for multiple roles that include maneuver, reconnaissance, and command and control. Typically, mechanized infantry units organize this equipment into mortar and mechanized infantry companies (often 10 vehicles each), mechanized battalions (three mechanized infantry companies and one mortar company), mechanized brigades (one mechanized infantry battalion and four motorized infantry battalions), and mechanized corps (five mechanized infantry brigades).

With more than 13,500 artillery pieces, the world's largest artillery force includes free-rocket-over-ground (FROG) artillery systems, 107-millimeter to 240-millimeter multiple rocket launchers, and 100-millimeter to 170-millimeter howitzers. Artillery formations are organized by type and assigned to regiments, divisions, and corps: regiment assignments include an 18-gun 122-millimeter howitzer battalion and a nine-launcher 107-millimeter or 140-millimeter multiple rocket launcher battery; division assignments include two 12-gun 152-millimeter howitzer battalions, one 18-gun 122-millimeter howitzer battalion, and one 12-launcher 122-millimeter multiple rocket launcher battalion; and corps assignments include six 18-gun 170-millimeter howitzer battalions and six 18-launcher 240-millimeter multiple rocket launcher battalions. To support maneuver operations, artillery is task-organized into regimental, division, and corps artillery groups, which are routinely augmented with additional artillery units that are attached from higher echelons.

The army has amassed more than 15,600 antiaircraft artillery pieces for theater missile-defense and counterair operations. Strategically employed and integrated to defend critical geopolitical assets, surface-to-air (SA) missile systems include several fixed and semifixed SA–2, SA–3, and SA–5 medium and medium-to-high-altitude missile systems. Short-range air-defense systems are deployed at the corps, division, and regimental levels and include an organized selection of 14.5-millimeter, 37-millimeter, and 57-millimeter antiaircraft artillery pieces. Short-range, man-portable SA–7B launchers also contribute to localized air defense and are employed down to battalion level.

Although the army conducts training exercises at all levels of command, most training occurs at the regimental level or below, and mainly at company and platoon levels. Exercises involving units that consume scarce resources, such as fuel, oil, and lubricants, occur infrequently, inhibiting the readiness of exploitation forces, which may cause integration difficulties during division and corps operations.

On March 7, 2006, the commander of the United Nations Command, Republic of Korea–United States Combined Forces Command, and U.S. Forces Korea, General Burwell B. Bell, testified before the U.S. Senate Armed Services Committee concerning North Korea's military posture. General Bell assessed that despite aging equipment and simplistic methods, North Korean conventional military forces pose a continuing threat because of their sheer size and forward positions.

Special Operations Forces

The KPA has a mixture of conventional and unconventional warfare units. North Korea's special operations forces (SOF) are the world's largest and have the highest military funding priority. Estimates of strength range from 87,000 to 92,000 and 100,000 to 120,000 personnel, depending on whether or not both strategic (the lower numbers) and tactical forces (the higher numbers) are counted. The uncertainty over the number of forces is derived mainly from the varying definitions of what actually constitutes KPA special operations forces, which include light infantry, airborne, sniper, and reconnaissance forces. Organized into 25 brigades and nine separate battalions, the special operations forces are believed to be the best trained and to have the highest morale of all North Korean ground forces. SOF operations are categorized by the supported echelon: strategic, operational, and tactical. Strategic SOF are employed in reconnaissance, sniper, and agent operations and support national or Ministry of People's Armed Forces objectives. Operational SOF support corps operations, and tactical SOF support forward-division operations.

The Ministry of People's Armed Forces controls strategic SOF through four commands, the Reconnaissance Bureau, Light Infantry Training Guidance Bureau, Air Force Command, and Navy Command. The Reconnaissance Bureau is subordinate to the Ministry of People's Armed Forces, is responsible for the collection of strategic and tactical intelligence, and directly controls one sniper brigade and five reconnaissance battalions. The bureau also exercises operational control over agents engaged in collecting military intelligence and in the training and dispatch of unconventional warfare teams. The Light Infantry Training Guidance Bureau is a subordinate command of the General Staff Department and directly controls four light infantry brigades, three airborne brigades, and a sniper brigade.

The Air Force Command has two sniper brigades of 3,500 personnel each and up to 300 An–2 biplanes that are used mainly for infiltrating SOF assets into South Korea's rear areas. Because of the ability of the An–2 to fly at low speeds and at very low altitudes, this otherwise antiquated aircraft provides the KPA with a fairly reliable means of infiltration. The Navy Command has two seaborne sniper brigades with a combined force of about 7,000 personnel that are capable of being infiltrated rapidly along South Korea's coast. Of the navy's 260 landing craft, more than 50 percent are of the landing craft air-cushion variety, well suited to traversing large mud flats, seasonal frozen coastal waters, and areas of great tidal variance.

Operational and tactical SOF units are organized at corps and division levels, respectively. At the operational level, each of the four forward infantry corps has a reconnaissance battalion, light infantry brigade, and sniper brigade; each of the four mechanized corps has a light infantry brigade. (Rear area infantry corps are organized as light infantry brigades, but because of their geographical separation from the front line, these units are not considered as SOF.) At the tactical level, each of the 20 or so forward infantry divisions has an assigned light infantry battalion.

Reconnaissance battalions are employed in rear areas—strategic and operational—to collect intelligence and information on high-value targets. Battalions are organized with a headquarters, signal platoon, recruit-training company, training company, and four reconnaissance companies of fewer than 100 troops each. Reconnaissance companies are organized with four platoons each, including four five-man teams (basic operating units) that are lightly armed with rifles and sidearms.

The KPA in a river-crossing exercise at an undisclosed location
Courtesy Chosŏn *(P'yŏngyang), July 2003, 17*

Light infantry units are employed at the strategic, operational, and tactical levels; they operate in battalions or companies to conduct raids on command and control centers and artillery positions and to secure choke points along axes of advance. Light infantry brigades are robust organizations with a headquarters, signal company, equipment company, transportation company, and six light infantry battalions. Light infantry battalions have a recruit-training company, signal company, air defense platoon, and six light infantry companies. Light infantry companies have two light infantry platoons, each with a three-tube, 60-millimeter mortar platoon and four light infantry squads.

Sniper brigades generally operate in teams to conduct raids, demolition, and reconnaissance and to collect intelligence. Sniper brigades are organized less robustly than light-infantry sniper brigades and have a headquarters, signal company, and six sniper battalions; each battalion has a signal platoon and five sniper companies, and each company has a three-tube mortar squad and three sniper platoons.

KPA special operations forces were developed to meet three basic requirements: to breach the flankless fixed defense of South Korea; to create a second front in the enemy rear area, disrupting in-depth reinforcements and logistical support during a conflict; and to conduct battlefield and strategic reconnaissance. Missions to counter opposing forces and to conduct internal security were added over time.

Strategic missions require deep insertions either in advance of hostilities or in the initial stages by naval or air platforms. Based on available insertion platforms, North Korea has a strategic lift capability of about 21,000 SOF personnel, which includes about 15,000 personnel by sea and another 6,000 personnel by air. The majority of SOF elements infiltrate over land to execute operational and tactical missions.

Air Force

In 2007 Colonel General O Kŭm-ch'ŏl headed the Korean People's Air Force Command, which has roots dating back to 1946. The Air Force Command has adapted Soviet and Chinese doctrines and tactics to accommodate internal requirements and resources. Its primary mission is air defense; secondary missions include tactical air support to the ground and naval forces, transportation and logistical support, and SOF insertion.

The air force is organized around four air divisions, three air combat divisions, and one air training division, with a total of 110,000 personnel, including 7,000 special operations troops. The First Air Combat Division is headquartered at Kaech'ŏn, South P'yŏngan Province, and operates in the northwest. The Second Air Combat Division is headquartered at Tŏksan-dong, near Hamhŭng, South Hamgyŏng Province, and operates in the east. The Third Air Combat Division is headquartered at Hwangju, North Hwanghae Province, and operates in the south. The Eighth Air Training Division (a unit designation that is speculative) is headquartered at Ŏrang, North Hamgyŏng Province, and operates in the northeast. Additional forces include a helicopter brigade, and support units include the Fifth and Sixth transport brigades. About 40 percent of air force fighters are forward deployed. The Air Force Command itself is headquartered in P'yŏngyang and controls, operates, and maintains all military and civilian aircraft, airfields, and airports throughout North Korea.

Significantly smaller than the ground forces, the air force has about 110,000 airmen and is equipped with an aging fleet of more than 1,600 aircraft that includes about 780 fighters, 80 bombers, 300 helicopters, 300 An–2 biplanes, and more than 100 support craft. About 70 percent of the fixed-wing aircraft are first- and second-generation Soviet-made fighters and bombers, including MiG–15, –17, –19, and –21 fighters and Il–28 fighter-bombers. The air force also has many third- and fourth-generation Soviet-made aircraft such as MiG–23 and MiG–29 fighters and Su–25 ground attack aircraft.

Among its rotor-wing fleet are a significant number of Mi–2s, Mi–4s, Mi–8s, Mi–17s, and Hughes–500 multirole helicopters.

The air force operates 20 strategic air bases and about another 70 operational bases and reserve and emergency runways nationwide. The majority of tactical aircraft are concentrated at air bases around P'yŏngyang and in the southern provinces. P'yŏngyang can place almost all its military aircraft in hardened—mostly underground—shelters. In the early 1990s, North Korea activated four forward air bases near the DMZ, which increased its initial southward reach and conversely decreased warning and reaction times for Seoul.

The air force operates two main flight schools, Kim Ch'aek Air Force Academy in Ch'ŏngjin and Kyŏngsŏng Flight Officer School in Kyŏngsŏng, both of which are located in North Hamgyŏng Province. Both institutions are four-year commissioning programs that provide students with about 70 hours of flight training on propeller-driven Yak–18 or CJ–6 aircraft. Graduating second lieutenants attend 22 months of advanced flight training, where they receive about 100 hours of flight instruction on either MiG–15 or MiG–17 fighters. After flight school, new pilots are assigned to an operational unit, where they receive another two years of training before they are rated as combat pilots. As with other types of military training, fuel shortages have required the air force to increase flight-simulator training time while sharply curtailing actual flying time to little more than 10 hours a year per pilot, a factor contributing to decreasing operational readiness.

Navy

In 2007 Admiral Kim Yun-sim commanded the Korean People's Navy Command. Headquartered since 1946 in P'yŏngyang, the navy is subordinate to the Ministry of People's Armed Forces. With fewer personnel than a single forward-infantry corps, the 60,000-person "brown-water" navy is primarily a coastal defense force. The North Korean navy does not have naval air or marine components.

The navy has 12 squadrons of around 1,000 vessels organized into two fleets, the West (or Yellow) Sea Fleet and the East Sea Fleet, and 19 naval bases. The fleets do not exchange vessels, and their areas of operations and missions determine their organizational structure; mutual support is difficult at best. The West Sea Fleet is headquartered at Namp'o and has major bases at Pip'a-got and Sagot and smaller bases at Tasa-ri and Ch'o-do. The East Sea Fleet has its headquarters at T'oejo-dong, with major bases at Najin and Wŏnsan and lesser bases at Puam-ni, Ch'aho, Mayang Island, and Ch'angjŏn near the DMZ. Additionally, there are many smaller bases along both coasts.

The smallest of the three services, the navy is equipped with a mismatched fleet of more than 430 surface combatants, nearly 90 submarines, 230 support vessels, and 260 landing craft. About 150 of these vessels are not under navy control but instead are assigned to the Ministry of People's Armed Forces Coastal Security Bureau. Equipped with corvettes, guided-missile patrol boats, torpedo boats, and fire-support boats, the navy maintains about 60 percent of the surface combatants forward of the P'yŏngyang–Wŏnsan line. Of these relatively small ships, the guided-missile patrol boats, which are equipped with either two or four tubes of Styx antiship missiles each, pose a credible threat against ships of much larger size.

North Korea's submarine force is the world's largest, including about 60 submarines of the 1,800-ton Romeo and 300-ton Sango classes and as many as 10 Yugo-class submersibles. The Romeo- and Sango-class submarines are capable of blocking sea-lanes, attacking surface vessels, emplacing mines, and infiltrating SOF. The Yugo-class submersibles are intended for clandestine SOF insertion. Submarines are stationed at Ch'aho, Mayang Island, Namp'o, and Pip'a-got naval bases.

North Korea also has a formidable coastal defense system that includes more than 250 soft and hardened coastal-defense artillery positions and one coastal-defense missile regiment per naval fleet. Coastal-defense artillery systems are equipped mainly with 122-millimeter or 152-millimeter guns; coastal-defense missile regiments are equipped with Silkworm and Seersucker antiship cruise missiles that are either truck- or transporter-erector-launcher-mounted. These coastal-defense positions are located on both coasts and on several islands.

The navy is capable of conducting inshore defensive operations, submarine operations against merchant shipping and unsophisticated naval combatants, offensive and defensive mining operations, and conventional raids. Because of the general imbalance of ship types, the navy has a limited capability to carry out such missions as sea control-or-denial and antisubmarine operations. The primary offensive mission of the navy is to support SOF unit insertions. It also has a limited capability to engage ships and to attack coastal targets.

Reserve Forces

As part of its military policy, North Korea has succeeded in arming much of its population (see Doctrine, Strategy, and Tactics, this ch.). Some 9 million people, or more than one-third of the population,

Women of the Korean People's Navy on parade in Kim Il Sung Square, P'yŏngyang
Courtesy Chosŏn *(P'yŏngyang), October 2003, 11*

KPA solider in training
Courtesy Chosŏn *(P'yŏngyang),*
April 2004, 11

serve with either the active or reserve forces. As many as 7.7 million people between the ages of 14 and 60 are required to serve as reserve forces organized into four broad categories: Red Youth Guard, Reserve Military Training Unit (RMTU), Workers and Peasants Red Guard, and paramilitary units.

For many North Koreans, military service begins by joining the Red Youth Guard, a militia organization that generally resembles a Junior Reserve Officer Training Corps program, during their last years of senior middle school (see A Thought-Controlled Society, ch. 2; Mass Organizations, ch. 4). Membership is available to male and female students who are between 14 and 17 years of age. The Red Youth Guard, with some 940,000 members, is supervised by local military affairs departments, which report up through their respective provincial military affairs departments to the party Central Military Commission. During the school year, the Red Youth Guard receives 450 hours of classroom training and seven days each semester of unit training. The training focus is on pre-induction military familiarization and includes physical training, drill and ceremony, first aid, and weapons familiarization.

The RMTU is North Korea's ready reserve and accounts for approximately 620,000 soldiers assigned to some 37 RMTU infantry divisions. Typically, 17-year-old students who are graduating from senior middle school but not joining the active-duty forces are assigned to a local RMTU. Additionally, service members who complete their active-duty obligation are assigned to an RMTU. Accordingly, males between the ages of 17 and 45 and single females between the ages of 17 and 30 are eligible for RMTU service. Unlike the other reserve forces, the Ministry of People's Armed Forces controls the RMTU, from the General Staff Department through the corps headquarters to their assigned RMTU divisions. Mobilization of RMTUs is controlled by the Logistics Mobilization Bureau of the General Staff Department. These RMTU divisions annually conduct 30 days of mobilization training and 10 days of self-defense training, which prepares them to round out the order of battle of their assigned corps when they serve alongside regular army divisions. Lengthy reserve service obligations mitigate reduced training opportunities while enhancing unit cohesion, producing an adequately capable force that in general is as well equipped as active-duty forces, but with earlier-model equipment.

The Workers and Peasants Red Guard resembles a civil-defense force, and, with as many as 5.7 million personnel, it is North Korea's largest reserve component. Typically, at age 46 men are transferred from their RMTU divisions to a Workers and Peasants Red Guard unit where they continue to serve until discharged at age 60, ending a lifetime of military service that began at age 14 and continued uninterrupted for 46 years. The Workers and Peasants Red Guard is controlled directly by local military affairs departments, which report to their provincial military affairs departments and on up the chain of command to the party Central Military Commission. Operationally organized at the company level by factories, farms, mines, and villages, the Workers and Peasants Red Guard has as its principal mission to provide civil defense in the form of local homeland defense, air defense, and logistic support. As a secondary mission, the Workers and Peasants Red Guard could be mobilized by the party Civil Defense Department to provide troop replacements for RMTU and active-duty forces. The Workers and Peasants Red Guard annually conducts 15 days of mobilization training and 15 days of self-defense training. This force is armed with individual (AK–47 rifles) and crew-served weapons, such as machine guns, mortars, and antiaircraft artillery pieces.

Paramilitary units, which number about 420,000 personnel, maintain a quasimilitary status and wear a military-type uniform. Such organizations include the Ministry of People's Security, Guard Command, College Training Units, and Speed Battle Youth Shock Brigades. The Ministry of People's Security functions as a national police force (see Ministry of People's Security, this ch.). The Guard Command is an independent, corps-sized organization that is responsible for the protection of Kim Jong Il and other senior-level officials (see Guard Command, this ch.). College students are organized into College Training Units and trained for individual replacements, a system by which during combat officers and noncommissioned officers (NCOs) are replaced at the unit level on a one-for-one basis. Speed Battle Youth Shock Brigades, organized in 1975 to "more vigorously prepare the youth to become the reliable successors of the revolution," are youth-level militaristic work-group organizations.

Strategic Weapons

Since the 1970s, North Korea has invested significant resources to increase its indigenous acquisition of ballistic missiles and weapons of mass destruction, which include chemical, biological, and nuclear weapons. These weapons, the development of which has caused considerable international reaction, include ballistic missiles, chemical and biological weapons, and, possibly, nuclear warheads.

Ballistic Missiles

In 1976 North Korea, which had been unable to procure surface-to-surface missiles (SSMs) from China or the Soviet Union, contracted with Egypt for the transfer of several SCUD–B short-range ballistic missiles (SRBMs). These SRBMs were reverse-engineered and facilitated the inauguration of North Korea's indigenous missile-production program. Successfully test-launched in 1984, the reverse-engineered SCUD–B missile was named the Hwasŏng–5 and shortly thereafter placed into full production. Seeking an extended-range capability beyond the Hwasŏng–5's 300-kilometer limit, North Korea further modified this missile to produce the Hwasŏng–6 (or SCUD–C)—a 500-kilometer extended-range SRBM—that in 1990 was test-fired successfully from Musudan-ni launch facility in North Hamgyŏng Province.

Having achieved the ability to strike targets anywhere in South Korea with Hwasŏng missiles, North Korea continued pursuing the ability to target Japan, which culminated on May 23, 1993, in a successful launch of what commonly has been referred to as the Nodong medium-range ballistic missile (MRBM). Whereas the 1993 Nodong missile test flight yielded a range of only 500 kilometers, in April 1998 Pakistan successfully tested a Nodong missile (known in Pakistan as the Ghauri) to a reported distance of 1,500 kilometers; then, in July 1998, Iran conducted a test launch of a Nodong missile (known as Shahab–3) to a distance of 1,000 kilometers. By May 23, 2006, Iran had conducted its tenth test launch of the Shahab–3, an MRBM that has been designed (or modified) to reach ranges up to 2,000 kilometers.

Concurrent with its Nodong missile development, since the 1990s North Korea has been developing an intermediate-range ballistic missile (IRBM), the Taepodong–1, and a long-range, intercontinental ballistic missile (ICBM), the Taepodong–2. The Taepodong–1 has two variants: the shorter range, two-stage system that is purported to be able to deliver a 700- to 1,000-kilogram warhead up to 2,000 kilometers; and the longer range, three-stage, space-launch vehicle (SLV) model which, if configured as a missile, presumably could deliver a light payload up to 5,000 kilometers. In August 1998, North Korea conducted a test launch of a Taepodong–1 SLV, reportedly in an attempt to place its first satellite into orbit. The first two stages apparently separated properly along the flight trajectory, but the third stage malfunctioned, failing to project the satellite into orbit.

In September 1999, only 13 months after the Taepodong–1 test launch, North Korea's Ministry of Foreign Affairs announced a self-imposed ballistic missile moratorium that was reaffirmed in 2001 with a commitment to extend the moratorium until 2003. With the exception of short-range missile launches, including the March 2006 KN–02 (an upgraded Soviet SS–1 (SCUD) SSM with a firing range of 120 kilometers) test launch, the missile launch moratorium remained in force until July 5, 2006, when North Korea shocked much of the world with its first

This Chinese-manufactured MiG–19 fighter was flown by a defector from the Korean People's Air Force to South Korea in 1983. It is now an exhibit at the War Memorial of Korea in Seoul.
Courtesy Robert L. Worden

test launch of a Taepodong–2 missile, which is thought to be based on the Soviet SS submarine-launched ballistic missile. The missile apparently malfunctioned along its trajectory. However, when commander of U.S. Forces Korea General B.B. Bell testified before the U.S. Senate in March 2006, he said that North Korea's continued development of a three-stage variant of the Taepodong missile could be operational within the next decade, providing P'yŏngyang with the capability to target the continental United States directly. Experts have surmised that a two-stage Taepodong–2 could deliver a 700- to 1,000-kilogram warhead to a distance of 10,000 kilometers, and that a three-stage Taepodong–2 could deliver a similar warhead about 15,000 kilometers.

North Korea's ballistic missile inventory includes more than 600 short-range Hwasŏng–5 and Hwasŏng–6 (SCUD) ballistic missiles that can deliver conventional or chemical munitions (and possibly a nuclear warhead) across the Korean Peninsula. North Korea possesses as many as 200 Nodong MRBMs that are capable of targeting Japan with these same payloads. And once made operational, North Korea's two-stage Taepodong–1 MRBM could easily reach Japan, including the island of Okinawa; the two-stage Taepodong–2 IRBM could reach U.S. military forces stationed in Guam, Hawaii, and Alaska; and the three-stage Taepodong–2 ICBM would be unrestrained in its ability to reach targets anywhere in the continental United States. Subordinate to the Missile Guidance Bureau, the KPA ballistic missile forces (either division- or corps-sized) are assumed to be organized as a FROG–7 brigade, a Hwasŏng–5/6 brigade (or regiment), a Nodong brigade (or regiment), and possibly a Taepodong–1/2 battalion.

Chemical and Biological Weapons

The U.S. military assesses that North Korea has a significant inventory of chemicals that could be weaponized on conventional weapons systems (mortars, artillery, rockets, and bombs), missiles; and unconventional delivery platforms. In 2004 South Korea estimated that this chemical stockpile was as large as 2,500 to 5,000 tons of toxicants and included nerve, blister, blood, and vomiting agents. According to the South Korean assessment, North Korea also had the independent ability to cultivate and produce biological weapons, including anthrax, smallpox, and cholera. American military analyst Joseph S. Bermudez Jr. posits that North Korea has 12 chemical agent factories and two chemical weapons factories, at Sakchu and Kanggye, which are responsible for filling, packaging, and shipping chemical munitions to operational units.

Nuclear Weapons

North Korean nuclear-related activities began in 1955, when representatives of the Academy of Sciences participated in an East European conference on the peaceful uses of nuclear energy. In 1956 North Korea signed two agreements with the Soviet Union covering joint nuclear research. Then, in 1959 North Korea signed an intergovernmental atomic energy cooperation agreement—Series 9559 contract—with the Soviet Union, which included Soviet technical assistance and funding to conduct a geological site survey to determine a suitable location for a nuclear reactor; construct a nuclear research facility near Yŏngbyŏn; and train North Korean scientists and specialists and establish a nuclear-related curriculum at Kim Il Sung University (see Education, ch. 2). Chinese and Soviet assistance with training of nuclear scientists and technicians historically has been North Korea's principal source of nuclear expertise, although in 2004 it was revealed that Pakistani nuclear scientist Abdul Qadeer Khan, the "father of the Islamic bomb," had sold nuclear secrets to North Korea for more than 15 years.

The Yŏngbyŏn Nuclear Scientific Research Center, established in 1962, has more than 100 buildings. From 1965 to 1967, Soviet specialists built a two-megawatt thermal research reactor IRT–2000 (IRT is the Russian acronym for *issledovatel'skiy reaktor teplovyy*, or thermal research reactor) for nuclear research—known as Yŏngbyŏn–1—that was later upgraded by North Korean scientists, first to a capacity of five megawatts and then to its current capacity of eight megawatts. Yŏngbyŏn–1 was brought under International Atomic Energy Agency (IAEA—see Glossary) controls in 1974.

During the 1970s and 1980s, North Korea began expanding its nuclear infrastructure. In 1980 the country began construction on an indigenously designed, graphite-moderated, gas-cooled five-megawatt electric reactor, known as Yŏngbyŏn–2, which became operational in 1986. Four years into this project, North Korea attempted a more ambitious endeavor by initiating construction of a 50-megawatt nuclear reactor, called Yŏngbyŏn–3, followed shortly thereafter by construction of a 200-megawatt reactor at T'aech'ŏn; neither of these projects has been completed. In 2006 there reportedly were as many as 22 nuclear-related facilities in North Korea, including nuclear reactors, reprocessing facilities, nuclear fuel plants, research facilities, and uranium mines.

In December 1985, North Korea signed the 1968 Treaty on the Non-Proliferation of Nuclear Weapons (NPT) but delayed signing the IAEA Full-scope Safeguards Agreement until January 30, 1992. Ten days earlier, North Korea and South Korea had signed the Joint Declaration on the Denuclearization of the Korean Peninsula, which pledged that neither country would "test, manufacture, produce, receive, possess, store, deploy or use nuclear weapons" or "possess nuclear reprocessing and uranium enrichment facilities." Moreover, they agreed to reciprocal verification inspections by a Joint Nuclear Control Commission.

During the 1992 inspections at Yŏngbyŏn Nuclear Scientific Research Center, the IAEA discovered that North Korea had diverted reprocessed weapons-grade plutonium from its five-megawatt nuclear reactor. Surprised by this exposure, North Korea expelled the IAEA inspectors and submitted a 90-day resignation from the NPT, which eventually was held in abeyance one day before the resignation took effect. In the months that followed, a potential war between the United States and North Korea was averted when the DPRK signed the October 1994 Agreed Framework, wherein North Korea agreed to freeze and eventually dismantle its plutonium-based nuclear weapons program in exchange for a series of quid pro quo concessions that included normalization of diplomatic and economic relations between the two parties, the transfer to North Korea of two one-gigawatt electric light-water nuclear reactors, and the interim provision to North Korea of 500,000 tons of heavy fuel oil annually.

In October 2002, the United States informed North Korea that it was suspected of operating a clandestine highly enriched uranium (HEU)–based nuclear weapons program. What followed was a series of P'yŏngyang-implemented Agreed Framework reversals that included evicting IAEA inspectors, removing IAEA monitoring equipment, abrogating the NPT, restarting its five-megawatt nuclear reactor, and reprocessing 8,000 nuclear fuel rods. In an effort to denuclearize North Korea, six regional players—the United States, North Korea, China, South Korea, Japan, and Russia—agreed to meet in a series of negotiations termed Six-Party Talks. As of mid-2007, there had been six sessions of Six-Party Talks.

On February 10, 2005, North Korea announced that it was one of the world's nuclear-armed states by issuing a Ministry of Foreign Affairs statement declaring possession of nuclear weapons. Then, within a week of another Foreign Ministry announcement that the state would prove its nuclear capabilities, North Korea conducted what appears to have been a nuclear test, on October 3, 2006. By all indications, this test was a low-yield detonation. Although the veracity of its purported nuclear capacity remains unproven, some experts have surmised that North Korea could have as many as eight to 10 plutonium bombs. These could include one or two weapons from plutonium produced before 1992; four or five weapons from plutonium produced from the 8,000 reprocessed nuclear fuel rods; and three weapons from plutonium that could be produced annually by operating the five-megawatt nuclear reactor that was restarted in January 2003. Additionally, in November 2002 the U.S. Central Intelligence Agency postulated that by mid-decade North Korea could produce at least two HEU bombs annually.

Officer Corps Professional Education and Training

The commissioned officers' military education and training system in North Korea is elaborate and includes numerous schools, academies, colleges, and universities. Among these institutions are officer-candidate schools for each armed service; basic and advanced branch schools for armor, artillery, aviation, rear services, and other branches; mid-career staff colleges; senior war colleges; and specialty schools, such as medical and veterinary service schools.

The majority of officer candidates are selected from noncommissioned officers (NCOs) who display exemplary military qualities and political reliability. Once selected, candidates receive initial branch training and commissioning from service academies and schools. Ground force officer candidates train at branch-specific schools, such as the Combined Artillery Officer School, Armor Officer

An officers' military theory class at the Man'gyŏngdae Revolutionary Institute, P'yŏngyang, 1997
Courtesy Korea Today *(P'yŏngyang), October 1997, 30*

School, and Kang Kŏn General Military Academy (which was established in July 1946 as the Central Security Cadre School, renamed in December 1948 as the First Officer Candidate School, and acquired its current name in October 1950). Air force officer candidates train at either the Kim Ch'aek Air Force Academy or the Kyŏngsŏng Flight Officer School; navy officer candidates train at the Kim Ch'ŏng-suk Naval Academy. Mid-career command and staff training is offered at all the service academies, various branch schools, and the Kim Il Sung Military University. Courses taught at the service academies last six to 12 months, whereas courses that are taught at branch schools tend to be limited to six months.

Two schools are of particular importance: Kim Il Sung Military University and Man'gyŏngdae Revolutionary Institute. Kim Il Sung Military University is the most prestigious military school and offers advanced training to officers of all services. Various degree programs are offered: company and junior field-grade officers can attend a three- to four-year program; senior field-grade and political officers are eligible to attend a one-year program. Founded in October 1948, Man'gyŏngdae Revolutionary Institute is an 11-year military boarding school for children of the party elite. Many graduates of this prestigious institution go on to serve as party members.

Generally, political officer candidates are selected according to merit, party loyalty, and political reliability among KPA General Political Bureau service members. Candidates receive two years of training at the Political Officers School before commissioning and service in the General Political Bureau or as unit-level political officers. Training focuses on politics, economics, party history, *chuch'e* (see Glossary) philosophy, and party loyalty. Advanced training is offered at other institutions, such as Kŭmsŏng Political College and Kim Il Sung Political University (which was established in November 1945 as the P'yŏngyang Institute, renamed in January 1949 as the Second Officer Candidate School, and assumed its current name in February 1972).

Political officers for field-grade positions are routinely selected by the political department at the corps level from party members in the corps headquarters. Supplemental training may include a six-month course at a political college. Candidates for positions at the division or higher level are identified by the Organization Department of the KPA General Political Bureau. They then are screened by the party committee and approved by the party Central Committee's Secretariat before appointment as head of a political department at division or higher level.

Colleges and universities provide most of the training for reserve officers; information available about the training does not differentiate between the officer-selection process and other reserve military training. There may be two separate tracks or a selection process at the end of training.

Enlisted Conscription and Training

North Korea enforces universal conscription for males and selective conscription for females with significant pre-induction and post-service requirements. In April 1993, North Korea enacted the Ten-year Service System, which lengthened universal conscription from an eight- to a 10-year obligation. In October 1996, the Army Service Decree was amended, lengthening (by as much as three years) conscript service obligations to age 30.

Initial draft registration is conducted at age 14, pre-induction physicals are administered at age 16, and graduating senior middle school students typically are drafted at age 17. Eligibility for the draft is based on economic and political factors as well as physical condition. Some young people are able to postpone military service through temporary deferments that are offered for continuing education at high school or college. Technicians, skilled workers, members of special government organizations, and children of the politically influential often are excluded from the draft. Most service personnel are single, as marriage is prohibited in the military until age 30, even for commissioned officers. Women are conscripted selectively at a ratio of about one female to nine males and serve in all three services and branches.

The coordinating national command authorities of the Central Military Commission and National Defense Commission establish annual conscription quotas that are enforced by the provincial, municipal, and county military-mobilization departments. The county departments, in turn, levy conscription requirements on local schools for implementation, and the schools select the most qualified students. After receiving official notification, inductees are assigned to the army, air force, or navy; given a military occupational specialty, such as infantry, communications, or medical; and assigned to a duty unit. The young men or women then go to a service- and branch-specific military training center or training company at regimental or divisional level for basic and occupational specialty training. Initial training varies by type and lasts approximately two months for ground forces and between two and three months for naval and air forces. Additional training is provided on the job at squad, platoon, and company levels.

Training, conducted under constant supervision, essentially emphasizes memorization and repetition but also includes a heavy emphasis on technical skills and vocational training. Lack of a technical base is another reason for the emphasis on repetitive training drills. Nighttime training is extensive, and physical and mental conditioning is stressed. Remedial training for initially substandard performances is not uncommon. Such training methods produce soldiers well versed in the basics even under adverse conditions. The degree to which they are prepared to respond rapidly to changing circumstances is less certain. NCO candidates are selected by merit for advanced military training at NCO schools, which are located at both the corps and the Military Training Bureau of the General Staff Department.

The quality of life of the enlisted soldier is difficult to evaluate. Conditions are harsh; rations are no more than 700 to 850 grams per day, depending on branch and service. Leave and passes are limited and strictly controlled. A two-week leave is allowed, although rarely granted, only once or twice during an entire enlistment. Passes for enlisted personnel are even more rare; neither day nor overnight passes are granted. During tours of duty, day passes are granted for public affairs duties or KWP-related activities. There is conflicting information about the frequency of corporal punishment and the harshness of military justice.

	SOWI	CHUNGWI	SANGWI	TAEWI	SOJWA	CHUNGJWA	SANGJWA	TAEJWA	SOJANG	CHUNG-JANG	SANG-JANG	TAEJANG	CH'ASU	WŎNSU²	TAEWŎNSU²
NORTH KOREAN RANK ARMY[1]	SOWI	CHUNGWI	SANGWI	TAEWI	SOJWA	CHUNGJWA	SANGJWA	TAEJWA	SOJANG	CHUNG-JANG	SANG-JANG	TAEJANG	CH'ASU	WŎNSU²	TAEWŎNSU²
U.S. RANK TITLES	2D LIEUTENANT	1ST LIEUTENANT	CAPTAIN	NO RANK	MAJOR	LIEUTENANT COLONEL	COLONEL	NO RANK	BRIGADIER GENERAL	MAJOR GENERAL	LIEUTENANT GENERAL	GENERAL	NO RANK	GENERAL OF THE ARMY	NO RANK
NORTH KOREAN RANK AIR FORCE[1]	SOWI	CHUNGWI	SANGWI	TAEWI	SOJWA	CHUNGJWA	SANGJWA	TAEJWA	SOJANG	CHUNG-JANG	SANG-JANG	TAEJANG	CH'ASU		
U.S. RANK TITLES	2D LIEUTENANT	1ST LIEUTENANT	CAPTAIN	NO RANK	MAJOR	LIEUTENANT COLONEL	COLONEL	NO RANK	BRIGADIER GENERAL	MAJOR GENERAL	LIEUTENANT GENERAL	GENERAL	GENERAL OF THE AIR FORCE	NO RANK	NO RANK
NORTH KOREAN RANK NAVY[1]	SOWI	CHUNGWI	SANGWI	TAEWI	SOJWA	CHUNGJWA	SANGJWA	TAEJWA	SOJANG	CHUNG-JANG	SANG-JANG	TAEJANG	CH'ASU		
U.S. RANK TITLES	ENSIGN	LIEUTENANT JUNIOR GRADE	LIEUTENANT	NO RANK	LIEUTENANT COMMANDER	COMMANDER	CAPTAIN	NO RANK	REAR ADMIRAL LOWER HALF	REAR ADMIRAL UPPER HALF	VICE ADMIRAL	ADMIRAL	FLEET ADMIRAL	NO RANK	NO RANK

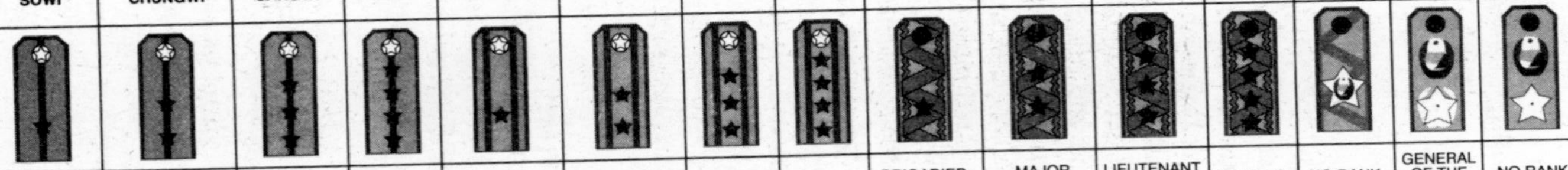

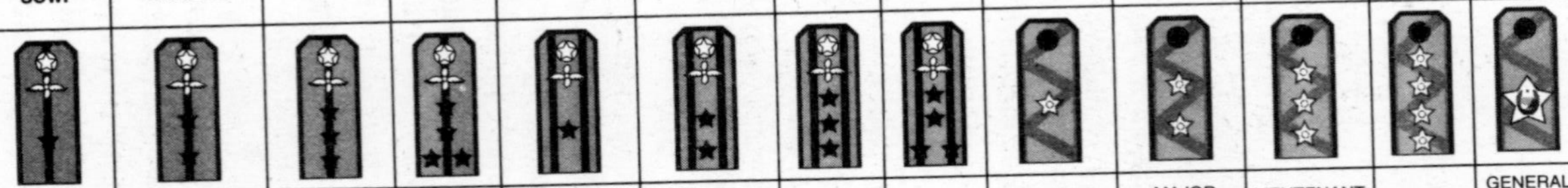

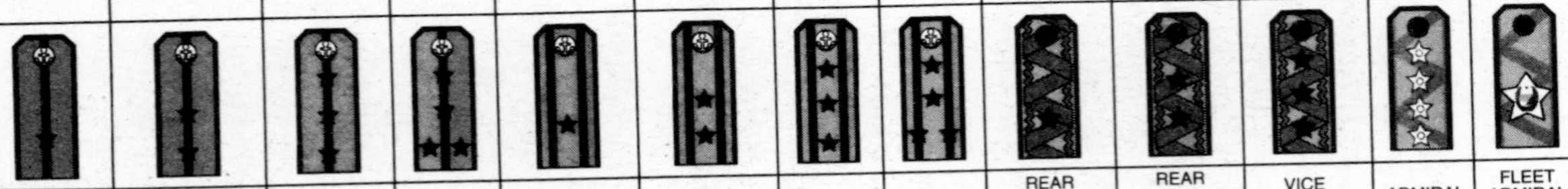

[1] All officer insignia have a gold background, but the color of stripes and borders varies by service: army, red; air force, blue; navy, black. Stars are silver.

[2] Korean ranks translate as marshal and grand marshal, or generalissimo, respectively.

Figure 13. Officer Ranks and Insignia, 2007

A typical daily routine can last from 5:00 AM to 10:00 PM, with at least 10 hours devoted to training and only three hours of unscheduled or rest time, excluding meals. In addition, soldiers perform many duties not related to their basic mission; for example, units are expected to grow crops and to raise livestock or fish to supplement their rations.

Military Ranks

The KPA officer rank structure has 15 grades divided into three categories: commissioned officer (junior and senior), general officer, and marshal. Across services—army, air force, and navy—the KPA title for each rank is the same; however, it translates differently when broadly associated with the U.S. military rank structure (see fig. 13). The North Korean rank names used in this chapter are direct translations from the Korean titles and in some cases differ from the U.S. military rank equivalents in figures 13 and 14. Junior commissioned officer ranks are four-tiered: *sowi* (army and air force junior lieutenant and navy ensign), *chungwi* (army and air force lieutenant and navy junior lieutenant), *sangwi* (army and air force senior lieutenant and navy lieutenant), and *taewi* (army and air force captain and navy senior lieutenant). Senior commissioned officer ranks also are four-tiered: *sojwa* (major/lieutenant commander), *chungjwa* (lieutenant colonel/commander), *sangjwa* (colonel/captain), and *taejwa* (senior colonel/senior captain). General officer ranks are four-tiered: *sojang* (major general/rear admiral), *chungjang* (lieutenant general/vice admiral), *sangjang* (colonel general/admiral), and *taejang* (general/ senior admiral). Marshal ranks are three-tiered: *ch'asu* (vice marshal), *wŏnsu* (marshal), and *taewŏnsu* (grand marshal).

Until December 1991, Kim Il Sung alone held the rank of marshal in his position as supreme commander of the KPA. In December 1991, Kim Jong Il was named supreme commander of the KPA; on April 20, 1992, Kim Il Sung was given the title grand marshal and Kim Jong Il and Minister of People's Armed Forces O Chin-u (1917–95) were named marshal. In an effort to solidify his hold on the military, Kim Jong Il has in turn bestowed the title of marshal and vice marshal on a select group of loyalists. North Korea has two marshals: Kim Jong Il and Yi Ŭl-sŏl, the former commander of the Guard Command who retired in September 2003. Beyond these advancements to marshal and vice marshal, since 1992 Kim Jong Il also has promoted more than 1,200 general officers.

Enlisted promotion historically has been a slow process. In 1998 the junior enlisted rank structure expanded from two categories—*chŏnsa* (private) and *sangdŭngbyŏng* (corporal)—to four (see fig. 14). The

Figure 14. Enlisted Ranks and Insignia, 2007

[1] Army enlisted insignia are gold on a red background. [2] Air Force enlisted insignia are gold on a blue background. [3] Navy enlisted insignia are gold on a black background.

NORTH KOREAN RANK	CHŎNSA	HAGŬP	CHUNGGŬP	SANGGŬP	HASA	CHUNGSA	SANGSA	T'ŬKMUSANGSA
ARMY[1]	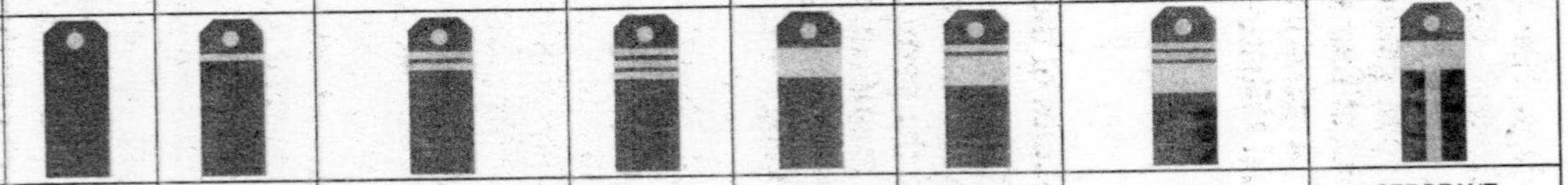							
U.S. RANK TITLE	PRIVATE	PRIVATE 1ST CLASS	CORPORAL/ SPECIALIST	SERGEANT	STAFF SERGEANT	SERGEANT 1ST CLASS	MASTER SERGEANT	SERGEANT MAJOR
NORTH KOREAN RANK	CHŎNSA	HAGŬP	CHUNGGŬP	SANGGŬP	HASA	CHUNGSA	SANGSA	T'ŬKMUSANGSA
AIR FORCE[2]	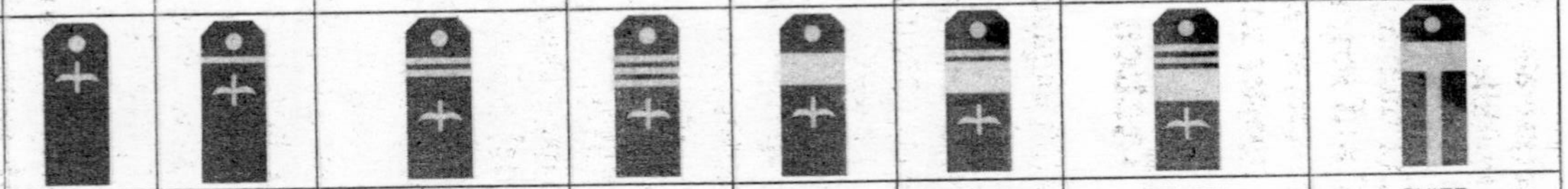		SENIOR AIRMAN / SERGEANT					
U.S. RANK TITLE	AIRMAN	AIRMAN 1ST CLASS	SENIOR AIRMAN	STAFF SERGEANT	TECHNICAL SERGEANT	MASTER SERGEANT	SENIOR MASTER SERGEANT	CHIEF MASTER SERGEANT
NORTH KOREAN RANK	CHŎNSA	HAGŬP	CHUNGGŬP	SANGGŬP	HASA	CHUNGSA	SANGSA	T'ŬKMUSANGSA
NAVY[3]	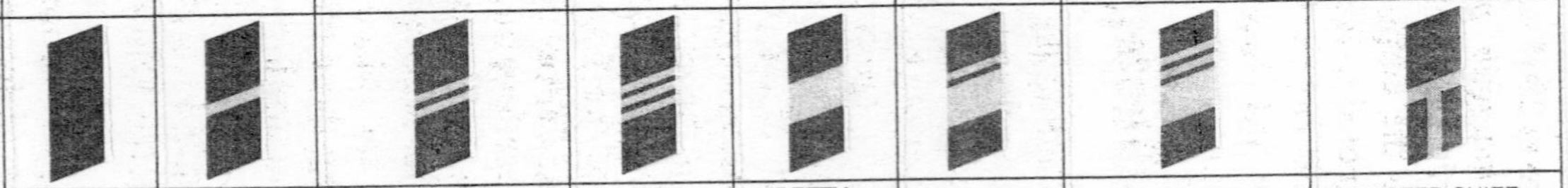							
U.S. RANK TITLE	SEAMAN APPRENTICE	SEAMAN	PETTY OFFICER 3D CLASS	PETTY OFFICER 2D CLASS	PETTY OFFICER 1ST CLASS	CHIEF PETTY OFFICER	SENIOR CHIEF PETTY OFFICER	MASTER CHIEF PETTY OFFICER

rank structure in 2007 was *chŏnsa* (private), *hagŭp pyŏngsa* (junior serviceman), *chunggŭp pyŏngsa* (middle serviceman), and *sanggŭp pyŏngsa* (senior serviceman). Eligible senior servicemen compete for admission to the corps-level NCO training school; upon graduation they are promoted to the grade of staff sergeant, the first of four senior enlisted or NCO ranks. The NCO ranks are *hasa* (staff sergeant), *chungsa* (sergeant first class), *sangsa* (master sergeant), and *t'ŭkmusangsa* (sergeant major).

Doctrine, Strategy, and Tactics

Notwithstanding the inter-Korean engagement policies of the current and former South Korean administrations, North Korea continues to embrace its national objective of communizing the Korean Peninsula, as articulated in the state constitution and the party charter. Specifically, the constitution declares "national reunification as the nation's supreme task," and the KWP constitution states that the "ultimate goal of the party is to spread *chuch'e* ideology and construct a Communist society throughout the world."

To develop the capabilities to realize its national objective, in December 1962 the Fifth Plenum of the Fourth KWP Central Committee adopted the Four-Point Military Guidelines: to arm the people; fortify the nation; create a cadre-based military; and modernize the force. These four military guidelines or defense policy principles are codified in article 60 of the 1998 state constitution.

The KPA has a three-part military strategy: surprise attack; quick, decisive war; and mixed tactics to carry out the national defense policy. Employing these three strategies, the KPA envisions reunifying the Korean Peninsula by initiating hostilities with large-scale asymmetric operations including massive conventional and chemical artillery, missile attacks, and simultaneous insertion of SOF throughout the depths of the battlespace (surprise-attack strategy). Thereafter, first-echelon operational forces (forward corps) would attack through the DMZ, or under it using invasion tunnels, to annihilate opposing forward forces, establish gaps and maneuver corridors to facilitate the rapid passage of second- and third-echelon operational forces (mechanized and armored forces), and complete the annihilation of opposing forces and secure the Korean Peninsula within 30 days (quick, decisive war strategy). To facilitate these aims of surprise attack and quick, decisive war, North Korea plans to fight a closely coordinated two-front war (mixed-tactics strategy). The first front would be fought by conventional forces and the second front by SOF to maximize disruption and destruction of command, control, communications, and intelligence facilities; air and sea ports; logistical bases; and lines of communications.

North Korean military strategy defines KPA doctrine, force structure (manpower and equipment) requirements, and tactics. KPA military doctrine is based on a synthesis of Soviet operational practice and Chinese People's Liberation Army military doctrine adapted to conform to the Korean Peninsula's mountainous terrain and the KPA's emphasis on light infantry as the key force structure. The result of this amalgamation is the KPA's five fundamental principles of war: mass and dispersion, surprise attack, increased maneuverability, cunning and personified tactics (such as initiative, leadership, and deception), and secure secrets (including reconnaissance, counterintelligence, and terrain utilization).

Defense Industry

The defense industry is controlled by the interrelated efforts of the National Defense Commission, the KWP, and the cabinet through a hierarchical association. Annually, the Ministry of People's Armed Forces determines defense requirements and submits them for approval to the National Defense Commission. Thereafter, the National Defense Commission, working with the party Central Military Commission, establishes defense priorities and issues directives, which are disseminated by the cabinet and the Central Military Commission. The cabinet forwards these defense requirements to appropriate agencies for action: as an example, the State Planning Commission uses defense requirements to help inform budget appropriations, which are approved by the Supreme People's Assembly and administered by the Ministry of Finance; other agencies are directed to supply energy and material resources. The Central Military Commission, working through the KWP's Munitions Industry Department, establishes defense industry policies, which are tasked to the Second Economic Committee for implementation.

A subordinate organ of the National Defense Commission, the Second Economic Committee, directs the defense industry with oversight and guidance provided by the party Munitions Industry Department. In 1989 Kim Ch'ŏl-man succeeded Chŏn Pyŏng-ho as chairman of the Second Economic Committee; and then in September 2003, the 85-year-old Kim Ch'ŏl-man was replaced by Paek Se-bong (suspected alias for Kim Jong Chul, second son and possible heir to Kim Jong Il). In his dual capacity as party secretary for munitions and party director for the Munitions Industry Department, Chŏn Pyŏng-ho oversees and guides the work of the Second Economic Committee and thereby the defense industry. Organized into nine bureaus, the Second Economic Committee exercises responsibility for defense industry plans, finances, production, distribution, and foreign military sales.

At the head of the Second Economic Committee is the General Bureau, which is responsible for defense industry plans, budget compilation, and resource procurement and distribution. Defense industry procurement, development, and production are directed by seven machine industry bureaus. The First Machine Industry Bureau oversees small arms, munitions, and general-purpose equipment. The Second Machine Industry Bureau commissions tanks, armored personnel carriers, and trucks. The Third Machine Industry Bureau is responsible for artillery and antiaircraft artillery systems. Missile systems are produced by the Fourth Machine Industry Bureau while the Fifth Machine Industry Bureau is responsible for nuclear, biological, and chemical weapons. The Sixth Machine Industry Bureau manufactures naval vessels, and the Seventh Machine Industry Bureau produces communications equipment and aircraft. The machine industry bureaus supervise defense factories and coordinate internally with the Second Natural Science Institute (formerly the Academy of Defense Sciences) and with corresponding Ministry of People's Armed Forces bureaus and commands. Organized into divisions by specialty, the Second Natural Science Institute directs all defense-industry research and development.

The External Economic Affairs Bureau (also known as Yongaksan Company) is the ninth bureau of the Second Economic Committee and has primary responsibility for foreign military sales and shared responsibility with the machine industry bureaus for defense article procurement. It is suspected that foreign military sales either fund the defense industry or supplement its spending. North Korea's announced defense spending for 2003 was nearly US$1.8 billion or 15.7 percent of the state budget, an increase of US$320 million, from 2002. However, when coupled with profit estimates from the Second Economic Committee's foreign military sales, it is possible that actual 2003 military spending could have reached as much as US$5 billion, or 44.4 percent of the total budget.

North Korea's extensive defense production capability reflects its commitment to self-reliance and its military-first, or *sŏngun,* policy (see Relationships Among the Government, Party, and Military, ch. 4). As it relates to the defense industry, emphasis on the military-first policy has two foci: preferential development of defense articles and accomplishment of announced economic priorities executed in the revolutionary military spirit.

North Korea has an impressive, although technologically dated, military production capacity. From an aggregate of some 180 arms factories, North Korea operates approximately 40 gun factories of varying calibers, 10 armored vehicle factories, 10 naval shipyards, and 50 munitions factories. Many of these factories are constructed underground in strategic rear areas. Additionally, more than 115 nonmilitary factories have a dedicated wartime matériel production mission.

Most of the equipment is of Soviet or Chinese design, but North Korea has modified the original designs to produce both derivatives and indigenously designed versions of armored personnel carriers, self-propelled artillery, tanks, and high-speed landing craft. Ground systems production includes a complete line of crew- and individual-served weapons, tanks, armored vehicles, howitzers, rocket launchers, and missiles. Naval construction includes surface combatants, submarines, landing craft air-cushion vehicles, and a wide range of specialized infiltration craft. Aircraft production includes Mi–2 helicopters, Yak–18 trainers, spare parts, and perhaps coproduction of jet fighters.

Internal Security

Control System

Since its founding in 1948, North Korea has meticulously erected a pervasive system of totalitarian control unique even when compared to the communist systems in the former Soviet Union and Eastern Europe. The North Korean population is rigidly controlled, as individual rights are systematically subordinated to state and party designs. The regime uses education, mass mobilization, persuasion, isolation, coercion, fear, intimidation, and oppression to guarantee political and social conformity. Invasive propaganda and political indoctrination are reinforced by an elaborate internal security apparatus.

The regime's control mechanisms are quite extensive. Security ratings or loyalty groups are established for individuals and influence access to employment, schools, medical facilities, stores, admission to the KWP, and other walks of life. The system in its most elaborate form consists of three loyalty groups: core class (*haeksim kyech'ŭng*), wavering class (*tongyo kyech'ŭng*), and hostile class (*chŏktae kyech'ŭng*), which historically were further divided into 51 categories. Over time, however, the use of subcategories has diminished.

The core class accounts for about 10 to 15 percent of the population and includes KWP members and those with a revolutionary

A North Korean guard post over-looking the Joint Security Area at P'anmunjŏm in the Demilitarized Zone
Courtesy Robert L. Worden

(anti-Japanese) lineage. The wavering class or the basic masses of workers and peasants make up about 40 to 50 percent of the population. The remaining 40 percent of the population includes members of the hostile class—descendants of pro-Japanese collaborators, landowners, relatives of defectors, and prisoners.

There are five main means of social control: residence, travel, employment, clothing and food, and family life. Change of residence is possible only with party approval. Those who move without a permit are not eligible for food rations or housing allotments and are subject to criminal prosecution. Travel is controlled by the Ministry of People's Security, and a travel pass is necessary. Travel on other than official business is limited strictly to attending family functions, and obtaining approval normally is a long and complicated process. The ration system does not apply to individuals while they are traveling, which further curtails movement. Employment is governed by the party; assignments are made on the basis of political reliability and family background. A change in employment is made at the party's convenience.

Punishment and the Penal System

The 1998 state constitution stipulates judicial independence; requires court proceedings to be carried out in accordance with the law; directs court trials to be open to the public (unless otherwise

273

stipulated by law); and guarantees the accused the right of defense (articles 158–60). North Korea's penal code was enacted in 1950 and has since been revised or amended six times, including the Supreme People's Assembly Presidium's most recent revision on April 29, 2004. Despite significant revisions that include replacing strong political and ideological sections with those presenting a more neutral tone, the penal code remains a political tool for safeguarding national sovereignty and the socialist system. The amended 2004 penal code contains an additional 14 areas that elaborate and clarify constituted crimes, which are divisible into two groups of crime: ordinary and political. Of significant note, with this amendment the state adopted the principle of *nullum crimen sine lege* (no crime without a law), which in principle removed power from authorities to criminalize acts not covered by the penal code. The penal code also addresses a wide range of issues from labor laws and workplace safety to torture and capital punishment.

The penal code classifies punishment into four main categories: capital punishment; lifetime confinement to hard labor; termed confinement to hard labor (one to 15 years); correctional labor or "labor-training" (six to 24 months); and a number of less severe punishments, including suspension of electoral rights and confiscation of property. The 2004 penal code reduced the number of antistate crimes punishable by death from five to four: plots to overthrow the state; acts of terrorism; treason, including defection and espionage; and suppression of the people's movement for national liberation. Although the penal code prohibits torture and inhumane treatment, according to reports by South Korea's National Intelligence Service in 2005, and the U.S. Committee for Human Rights in North Korea in 2006, torture is both routine and severe.

On May 6, 2004, the Supreme People's Assembly Presidium also amended the state's criminal procedure law, which was adopted originally in 1950 and amended eight times thereafter. Punishment for criminal behavior is determined by both the type of crime—criminal or political—and the status of the individual. Party influence is pervasive in both criminal and political cases. In criminal cases, the government assigns lawyers for the defense. In political cases, trials often are dispensed with, and the Ministry of People's Security refers such cases directly to the State Security Department for the imposition of punishment.

As specified in the penal code, criminal proceedings are accomplished in six stages: investigation, preliminary examination, indictment, trial, decision, and enforcement. The proceedings begin with an investigation, during which the accused is identified and detained (as necessary), and basic evidence is preserved. Preliminary examination lasts for two months and is the stage where the case against the accused is built. If the prosecutor assesses that there is sufficient evidence to try the accused, then an indictment is submitted before the court holding jurisdiction: people's courts for ordinary crimes not belonging to provincial courts; provincial-level courts for ordinary cases that could result in a death sentence or lifetime imprisonment; military courts for crimes by military members; railroad courts for crimes by railroad employees or rail-related crimes; and the Central Court for appeals (articles 126 and 133 of the criminal procedure law). Lower court trials are divided into two phases: preparation and deliberation phases. Court decisions are determined by a majority ruling of the judge and two people's assessors; enforcement of sentencing immediately follows guilty verdicts.

Whereas the aforementioned criminal proceedings are the prescribed process, practice is another matter, according to the U.S. Department of State's *Country Reports on Human Rights Practices for 2006*. Although North Korea refuses outside observation of its legal system, it is clear that the limited guarantees legally in place often are not well followed. North Korean law limits incarceration during investigation and interrogation to a period of up to two months. The period of incarceration, however, can be extended indefinitely with the approval of the Central Procurators' Office. The approval apparently is given quite freely. It is not uncommon for individuals to be detained for six months or much longer without trial. There has been strong evidence that prisoners are routinely tortured or ill treated during interrogation. Habeas corpus or its equivalent is not recognized in theory or practice. In addition, information about detainees is restricted, and it is often very difficult, if not impossible, for concerned family members to obtain any information about someone being detained.

Criminal procedures are entrusted to four state agencies. The courts, procurators' offices, and the Ministry of People's Security are responsible for public order, and the State Security Department imposes political order (see The Judiciary, ch. 4).

Judicial and Prosecutorial Systems

In accordance with the 1998 constitution, North Korea's judicial and prosecutorial systems are composed of tiered courts and procurators' offices (see The Judiciary, ch. 4). Judicial bodies include the Central Court, military courts, railroad courts, provincial and special-city courts, and county-level people's courts. Appointed prosecutorial officials investigate and prosecute those accused of breaking the law, and such officials serve in the Central Procurators' Office, the Special Procurators' Offices, and lower-level procurators' offices (article 147).

The highest judicial organ, the Central Court, supervises all lower courts and is accountable to the Supreme People's Assembly or to the Supreme People's Assembly Presidium when the former is in recess (articles 161 and 162). The Supreme People's Assembly has the power to appoint or remove the procurator general of the Central Procurators' Office (article 91). The Central Court appoints and recalls judges of the special courts; people's jury assessors are elected by a general meeting of concerned soldiers or employees (article 155). Below the Central Court are the lower courts, whose judges and civilian assessors are elected and recalled by their local people's assemblies (article 134). The constitution does not require legal education as a qualification for being elected as a judge or people's assessor. Over time, however, legal training has received more emphasis, although political reliability remains the prime criterion for holding office.

The Central Procurators' Office parallels the court system and performs three principal duties. The first is to ensure observance of laws by institutions, enterprises, organizations, and citizens. The second is to ensure that decisions and directives of state organs conform to the state constitution, Supreme People's Assembly laws and decisions, National Defense Commission decisions and orders, Supreme People's Assembly Presidium decrees, decisions, and directives, and cabinet decisions. The third is to protect state sovereignty, the social system, and state and social cooperative organizations' property, and to safeguard life, property, and personal rights by instituting and prosecuting legal proceedings against offenders (article 150).

In September 2003, the Supreme People's Assembly reelected Kim Pyŏng-ryul as president of the Central Court. At the same time, Yi Kil-song was appointed as procurator general.

Ministry of People's Security

The Ministry of People's Security (formerly the Ministry of Public Security) is headquartered in P'yŏngyang and since July 2004 General Chu Sang-sŏng, former IV Corps commander, has been the minister. One of the most powerful organizations in North Korea, the ministry has about 130,000 employees and is responsible for overseeing a national police force responsible for maintaining law and order; investigating common criminal cases; conducting preliminary examinations; and managing correctional facilities (excluding political prison camps). The police force also conducts background investigations, the census, and civil registrations; manages government classified documents; protects government and party officials; and patrols government buildings and some government and party construction activities.

Vice ministers direct the affairs of the ministry's 12 bureaus. These are the Security Bureau for law enforcement; the Investigation Bureau for criminal investigation; and the Public Safety Bureau for fire protection, traffic control, public health, and customs. The Registration Bureau issues and maintains citizen identification cards and public records on births, deaths, marriages, residence registration, and passports. The Penal Affairs Bureau is in charge of prisons. The Civil Defense Bureau oversees preparedness for air raids and nuclear, biological, or chemical attacks. The Railroad Security Bureau is responsible for railroad security. There are several engineer bureaus, which are responsible for design and construction: the Sixth Engineer Bureau for subway systems and underground facilities, the Twenty-sixth Engineer Bureau for large-scale public projects, and the Twenty-seventh Engineer Bureau for nuclear-related facilities. The Twenty-eighth Engineer Bureau has responsibility for coal mining, and the Twenty-ninth Engineer Bureau for roads, railroads, and bridges.

Below the ministry level, there are public security offices for each province, special city, municipality, and county. Although dependent on population density, a typical municipality or county with a population of about 120,000 people has a public security office that is staffed with about 350 functionaries, organized into directorates and sections. A public security office of this level generally includes directorates for politics, security, and resident registration. Representative sections are responsible for accounting, communications, firefighting, inspections, investigations, law enforcement, ordnance, and preliminary examinations.

Interior regions of the country have public security suboffices dispersed among a grouping of between two and three villages; however, border and coastal regions maintain suboffices in each village. Typical suboffices have a head of station and a number of security and resident registration officers. Border and coastal suboffices also have security officers from the armed forces' Border Security Command.

State Security Department

In 1973 political security responsibilities were transferred from the Ministry of People's Security to the State Security Department, a subordinate agency of the National Defense Commission that employs more than 30,000 elite agents who ultimately are responsible to Kim Jong Il in his role as director of the State Security Department. Headquartered in P'yŏngyang, the State Security Department carries out a wide range of counterintelligence and internal security functions that normally are associated with secret police, such as the former Soviet KGB. The department has several charges. One is searching for anti-state criminals, a general category that includes those accused of anti-government and dissident activities, economic crimes, and slander of the political leadership. Another charge is conducting foreign and domestic intelligence and counterintelligence operations. Furthermore, the department operates political prison camps and maintains surveillance of overseas North Korean embassy personnel and trade and joint-venture employees.

The State Security Department is organized into 17 bureaus, with functions including communications interception, data analysis, and intelligence. There are bureaus for research, surveillance, preliminary examinations, investigations, interrogations, and political prison camps. The State Security Department's responsibility also includes inter-Korean dialogue and entry and exit management. Moreover, the department covers military industrial security, operational security, and protection. There are bureaus for equipment, finance, supply, and logistics.

Among North Korea's many societal control systems are the political prison camps (euphemistically referred to by the state as *kwalliso-dŭl* or management centers) that are controlled and operated by the Political Prison Camps Bureau. According to South Korea's National Intelligence Service and the U.S. Committee for Human Rights in North Korea, the bureau operates six widely dispersed political prison camps that confine a total of between 150,000 and 200,000 inmates, which may include an individual's family members up to three generations as well as the accused. Some of the political prisons are subdivided into two sections: a maximum control zone for lifetime detentions and a reeducation zone for limited-term detentions. Often operating extrajudicially, the State Security Department apprehends, interrogates, and imprisons the accused (and family members) without the advantage of legal counsel or due process.

The Surveillance Bureau operates a pervasive network of agents and informants from national to village levels. Using a pyramid organizational structure, the State Security Department surveillance agents permeate organizations and communities as each agent surreptitiously employs some 50 quasi-agents who, in turn, each retain about 20 base-level informants. This surveillance process has spawned a national culture of deceit and distrust that intentionally pits one against another for the purpose of subduing the politically ambitious and the general population alike.

KPA troops celebrate the fiftieth anniversary of victory in the Korean War.
Courtesy Chosŏn *(P'yŏngyang), July 2003, 16*

Guard Command

Subordinate to the National Defense Commission, the Guard Command is an independent corps-size organization equipped with artillery, aircraft, tanks, and engineers. Loosely analogous to the U.S. Secret Service, it has primary responsibility for the protection of Kim Jong Il and other senior-level officials. In September 2003, Marshal Yi Ŭl-sŏl, owing to declining health, retired as commander of this elite organization of between 100,000 and 120,000 special agents; the name of his replacement had not been made public in 2007.

Border Security Command and Coastal Security Bureau

Collectively responsible for restricting unauthorized cross-border (land and sea) entries and exits, in the early 1990s the bureaus responsible for border security and coastal security were transferred from the State Security Department to the Ministry of People's Armed Forces. Sometime thereafter, the Border Security Bureau was enlarged to corps level and renamed the Border Security Command. Previously headquartered in Chagang Province, the Border Security Command was relocated to P'yŏngyang in 2002.

Deployed along the northern borders with China and Russia, the Border Security Command is organized as four infantry-type units.

The Tenth Border Security Division (which may be a brigade) is based in North P'yŏngan Province. The Thirty-seventh Border Security Brigade is in Chagang Province, the Forty-fourth Border Security Brigade in Yanggang Province, and the Thirty-second Border Security Brigade in North Hamgyŏng Province. These brigades are deployed west to east from the Yellow Sea to the Sea of Japan (or, as Koreans prefer, the West Sea and East Sea, respectively). Responsible for staffing checkpoints, guarding border crossing points, and conducting patrols, these border security units are estimated to have as many as 40,000 assigned personnel. The command also employs an operational-level reserve force that is organized around an enlarged mechanized brigade and tank brigade, which has a combined force structure of about 20,000 personnel.

The Coastal Security Bureau apparently was disaggregated and its coastal security brigades reassigned to various infantry corps. Collectively, the coastal security forces are equipped with about 150 patrol craft and organized into six coastal border brigades, which are deployed with three brigades on each coast. Deployed on the west coast from north to south are the Eleventh Coastal Security Brigade (North P'yŏngan Province), the Thirteenth Coastal Security Brigade (South P'yŏngan Province), and the Fifteenth Coastal Security Brigade (South Hwanghae Province). On the east coast from south to north are the Twenty-second Coastal Security Brigade (Kangwŏn Province), Seventeenth Coastal Security Brigade (South Hamgyŏng Province), and Nineteenth Coastal Security Brigade (North Hamgyŏng Province). The Coastal Security Bureau is responsible for patrolling the coastlines to prevent illegal entries and exits, maintaining harbor and port security, and policing and protecting the nation's coastal waterways and fishing areas.

National Security Prospects

North Korea's national security is threatened predominantly by issues of internal instability resulting from environmental disasters, famine, poor governance, failed economic policies, and social oppression. The failure or inability of the regime to initiate adequate environmental, political, economic, and social reforms exacerbates an already precarious milieu that perpetuates the continued suffering of North Korea's populace and burdens the international community.

Despite such national security challenges, the regime seems to possess the ability to control internal order and maintains adequate means of self-defense. The massive network of citizen surveillance suppresses overt deviation from acceptable behavior, although there are growing signs that ordinary North Koreans are not putting much effort or commitment into their work. Additionally, beyond retaining an adequate self-defense capability, North Korea's massive armed forces present a credible conventional threat, and its growing strategic weapons arsenal frequently has been used as a tool to influence international politics.

*   *   *

For a survey of North Korea, see Yonhap News Agency's *North Korea Handbook*. The origins of North Korea's armed forces and current military tactics are presented in James M. Minnich's *The North Korean People's Army: Origins and Current Tactics*. The organization of North Korea's armed forces is covered in Joseph S. Bermudez Jr.'s *Shield of the Great Leader: The Armed Forces of North Korea*. North Korea's modern-day origins are reviewed in Dae-Sook Suh's *Kim Il Sung: The North Korean Leader* and in Charles K. Armstrong's *The North Korean Revolution: 1945–1950*. For information on North Korea's judicial system, Kim Soo-Am's *The North Korean Penal Code, Criminal Procedures, and their Actual Application* is useful. For information on North Korea's nuclear-weapons program, the best sources are James Clay Moltz and Alexandre Y. Mansourov's *The North Korea Nuclear Program: Security, Strategy, and New Perspectives from Russia* and James M. Minnich's *The Denuclearization of North Korea: The Agreed Framework and Alternative Options Analyzed*.

The Republic of Korea Ministry of National Defense's annual *Defense White Paper* (published in both Korean and English) is particularly noteworthy. *Asian Survey, Far Eastern Economic Review, Korea and World Affairs*, and *Korean Journal of Defense Analysis* are generally useful and relatively free of bias. South Korean investigative journalism, particularly monthlies such as *Wŏlgan Chosŏn* (Monthly Chosun), produces valuable insights of defectors and travelers to North Korea.

The North Korean media monitoring service of the U.S. Open Source Center (formerly the Foreign Broadcast Information Service) is an excellent source of English-language translations and other materials on many North Korean issues. The service is available from the U.S. National Technical Information Service and accessed through Dialog's *World News Connection* (http://wnc.dialog.com/). (For complete citations and further information, see Bibliography.)

Bibliography

Chapter 1

Armstrong, Charles K. *The North Korean Revolution, 1945–1950.* Ithaca: Cornell University Press, 2003.

Baik, Bong. *Minjok ui t'aeyang Kim Il Sung Changgun* [General Kim Il Sung: The Sun of Our Nation], vols. 1 and 2. P'yŏngyang: Inmin Ch'ulp'ansa, 1968.

Baik, Bong. *Minjok ui t'aeyang Kim Il Sung Changgun* [General Kim Il Sung: The Sun of Our Nation], vol. 3. P'yŏngyang: Inmin Kwahaksa, 1971.

Bradbury, John. "Sino–Soviet Competition in North Korea." *China Quarterly* (London), no. 6 (April–June 1961): 15–28.

Brun, Ellen, and Jacques Hersh. *Socialist Korea: A Case Study in the Strategy of Economic Development.* New York: Monthly Review Press, 1977.

Carrier, Fred J. *North Korean Journey: The Revolution Against Colonialism.* New York: International, 1975.

Choy, Bong Youn. *Korea: A History.* Tokyo: Charles E. Tuttle, 1971.

Conroy, Francis Hilary. *The Japanese Seizure of Korea, 1868–1910: A Study of Realism and Idealism in International Relations.* Philadelphia: University of Pennsylvania Press, 1960.

Cumings, Bruce. "Corporatism in North Korea." *Journal of Korean Studies* 4 (1982–83): 269–94.

Cumings, Bruce. "Ending the Cold War in Korea." *World Policy Journal* 1 (Summer 1984): 769–91.

Cumings, Bruce. "Kim's Korean Communism." *Problems of Communism* 23, no. 2 (March–April 1974): 27–41.

Cumings, Bruce. *Korea's Place in the Sun: A Modern History.* New York: Norton, 2005.

Cumings, Bruce. "North Korea: Security in the Crucible of Great-Power Confrontations." Pages 153–72 in Raju G.C. Thomas, ed., *The Great Power Triangle and Asian Security.* Lexington, Massachusetts: Lexington Books, 1983.

Cumings, Bruce. "The Origins and Development of the Northeast Asian Political Economy: Industrial Sectors, Product Cycles, and Political Consequences." *International Organization* 38 (Winter 1984): 1–40.

Cumings, Bruce. *The Origins of the Korean War.* 2 vols. Princeton: Princeton University Press, 1981–90.

Cumings, Bruce. "Spring Thaw for Korea's Cold War?" *Bulletin of the Atomic Scientists* 48 (April 1992): 14–23.

Cumings, Bruce. "Trilateralism and the New World Order." *World Policy Journal* 8 (Spring 1991): 195–222.

Cumings, Bruce. *The Two Koreas: On the Road to Reunification?* Headline Series, no. 294. New York: Foreign Policy Association, 1991.

Cumings, Bruce, ed. *Child of Conflict: The Korean–American Relationship, 1943–1953.* Seattle: University of Washington Press, 1983.

Day, Rachel. "Happy Anniversary, Dear Leader." *Washington Post,* October 8, 2006: B3.

Democratic People's Republic of Korea. Academy of Science. History Research Institute. *Chosŏn t'ongsa* [General History of Korea]. P'yŏngyang: Kwahagwon Ch'ulp'ansa, 1962.

Eckert, Carter J. *Offspring of Empire: The Koch'ang Kims and the Colonial Origins of Korean Capitalism, 1876–1945.* Seattle: University of Washington Press, 1991.

Eckert, Carter J., Ki-Baik Lee, Young Ick Lew, Michael Robinson, and Edward W. Wagner. *Korea Old and New: A History.* Seoul: Ilchokak for Korea Institute, Harvard University, 1990.

Ethnologue. *Languages of the World: Korean.* http://www.ethnologue.com/show_country.asp? name=KP (accessed July 25, 2005).

Foote, Rosemary. *The Wrong War.* Ithaca: Cornell University Press, 1986.

Grajdanzev, Andrew J. *Modern Korea.* New York: Institute of Pacific Relations, 1944.

Grinker, Roy Andrew. *Korea and Its Futures: Unification and the Unfinished War.* New York: St. Martin's Press, 1998.

Halliday, Jon, and Bruce Cumings. *Korea: The Unknown War.* New York: Pantheon, 1988.

Han, Woo-Keun. *The History of Korea.* Honolulu: East–West Center Press, 1972.

Harrison, Selig S. *Korean Endgame: A Strategy for Reunification and U.S. Disengagement.* Princeton: Princeton University Press, 2002.

Harrison, Selig S., ed. *Dialogue with North Korea.* Washington, DC: Carnegie Endowment for International Peace, 1991.

Hatada, Takashi. *A History of Korea.* Translated and edited by Warren W. Smith Jr., and Benjamin H. Hazard. Santa Barbara: American Bibliographical Center–Clio Press, 1969.

Henderson, Gregory, and Key P. Yang. "An Outline History of Korean Confucianism, Pt. 1: The Early Period and Yi Factionalism." *Journal of Asian Studies* 18, no. 1 (November 1958): 81–101.

Hunter, Helen-Louise. *Kim Il-song's North Korea.* Westport, Connecticut: Praeger, 1999.

Kim, Han-Kyo. *Studies on Korea: A Scholar's Guide.* Honolulu: University Press of Hawaii, 1980.

Kim, Ilpyong J. *Communist Politics in North Korea.* New York: Praeger, 1975.

Kim, San, with Nym Wales. *Song of Ariran: A Korean Communist in the Chinese Revolution.* San Francisco: Ramparts Press, 1973.

Kim Il Sung. "On the Elimination of Formalism and Bureaucracy in Party Work and the Revolutionization of Functionaries." Pages 421–58 in Kim Il Sung, *Kim Il Sung: Selected Works,* vol. 4. P'yŏngyang: Foreign Languages Publishing House, 1974.

Kim Key-Hiuk. *The Last Phase of the East Asian World Order: Korea, Japan, and the Chinese Empire, 1860–1882.* Berkeley: University of California Press, 1980.

Koh, B.C. "North Korea, 1976: Under Stress." *Asian Survey* 17, no. 1 (January 1977): 61–70.

Korean Workers' Party. Central Committee. Party History Research Institute. *Chosŏn Nodongdang Yoksa Kyojae* [Korea Labor Party History Text]. P'yŏngyang: Chosŏn Nodongdang Ch'ulp'ansa, 1964.

Lankov, Andrei. *From Stalin to Kim Il Sung: The Formation of North Korea, 1945–1960.* London: Hurst, 2002.

Lee, Chae-Jin, ed. *The Korean War: 40-Year Perspectives.* Monograph Series, no. 1. Claremont, California: Claremont McKenna College, Keck Center for International and Strategic Studies, 1991.

Lee, Chong-Sik. *Korean Workers' Party: A Short History.* Histories of Ruling Communist Parties, no. 185. Stanford, California: Hoover Institution Press, 1978.

Lee, Chong-Sik. "Land Reform, Collectivization, and the Peasants in North Korea." *China Quarterly* (London), no. 14 (April–June 1963): 65–81.

Lee, Chong-Sik. "New Paths for North Korea." *Problems of Communism* 26, no. 2 (March–April 1977): 55–66.

Lee, Chong-Sik. "The 1972 Constitution and Top Communist Leaders." Pages 192–220 in Dae-Sook Suh and Chae-Jin Lee, eds., *Political Leadership in Korea.* Seattle: University of Washington, 1976.

Lee, Chong-Sik. *The Politics of Korean Nationalism*. Berkeley: University of California Press, 1963.

Lee, Chong-Sik. "Stalinism in the East: Communism in North Korea." Pages 114–39 in Robert A. Scalapino, ed., *Communist Revolution in Asia*. Englewood Cliffs, New Jersey: Prentice-Hall, 1965.

Lee, Ki-baik. *A New History of Korea*. Translated by Edward W. Wagner, with Edward J. Schultz. Seoul: Ilchokak, 1984.

Lee, Mun Woong. *Rural North Korea under Communism: A Study in Sociocultural Change*. Monograph in Behavioral Science, 62, no. 1. Houston: William Marsh Rice University, 1976.

Lowe, Peter. *The Origins of the Korean War*. 2d ed. Origins of Modern War Series. London: Longman, 1997.

The Military Balance, 2003–2004. London: International Institute for Strategic Studies, 2003.

Nelson, Frederick M. *Korea and the Old Orders in Eastern Asia*. Baton Rouge: Louisiana State University Press, 1945.

O Tae-hyŏng and Yi Hyŏn-bok, eds. *Pulmyŏl ŭi t'ap* [Tower of Immortality]. P'yŏngyang: Munye Ch'ulpansa, 1985.

Oberdorfer, Don. *The Two Koreas: A Contemporary History*. New York: Addison–Wesley, 1997.

Oryun haengsilto [Five Rules of Conduct] 3, 1775.

Palais, James B. *Confucian Statecraft and Korean Institutions: Yu Hyŏng-wŏn and the Late Chosŏn Dynasty*. Seattle: University of Washington Press, 1996.

Palais, James B. *Politics and Policy in Traditional Korea*. Harvard East Asian Series, no. 82. Cambridge: Harvard University Press, 1975.

Republic of Korea. Government Information Agency. Korean Overseas Information Service. *Facts About Korea*. Seoul, 2006.

Republic of Korea. Ministry of Culture and Information. Korean Overseas Information Service. *A Handbook of Korea*. Seoul, 1993.

Rim San Jung. *An Outline of Korean Culture*. P'yŏngyang: Foreign Languages Publishing House, 1979.

Robinson, Michael. *Cultural Nationalism in Korea, 1920–25*. Seattle: University of Washington Press, 1985.

Scalapino, Robert A., and Chong-Sik Lee. *Communism in Korea*. 2 vols. Berkeley: University of California Press, 1972.

Shabshina, Fania I. *Ocherki Noveĭsheĭ Istorii Korei, 1918–45* [Essays from Modern Korean History, 1918–1945]. Moscow: Izdatel'stvo Vostochnoĭ Literatury, 1959.

Sigal, Leon V. *Disarming Strangers: Nuclear Diplomacy with North Korea*. Princeton: Princeton University Press, 1998.

Sohn, Pow-key, Kim Chol-choon, and Hong I-sup. *History of Korea.* Seoul: United Nations Educational, Scientific, and Cultural Organization, Korean National Commission, 1970.

SP's Military Yearbook, 2003–2004. New Delhi: Guide Publications, 2004.

Suh Cheong-soo, ed. *An Encyclopaedia of Korean Culture.* Seoul: Hansebon, 2004.

Suh, Dae-Sook. *Kim Il Sung: The North Korean Leader.* New York: Columbia University Press, 1989.

Suh, Dae-Sook. *The Korean Communist Movement, 1918–1948.* Princeton: Princeton University Press, 1968.

Suh, Sang Chul. *Growth and Structural Changes in the Korean Economy, 1910–1940.* Harvard East Asian Monographs, no. 83. Cambridge: Harvard University Press for Council on East Asian Studies, 1978.

Tsubo, Senji. *Chosen minzoku dokuritsu undo hishi* [Secret History of the Korean National Independence Movement]. Tokyo: Nikkan Rodo Tsushinsha, 1959.

United States. Central Intelligence Agency. *World Factbook.* Washington, DC, 1993.

United States. Central Intelligence Agency. National Foreign Assessment Center. *Korea: The Economic Race Between the North and the South.* ER 78–10008. Washington, DC, 1978.

United States. Department of State. *The Conferences at Malta and Yalta, 1945.* Foreign Relations of the United States. Publication 6199. 2 vols. Washington, DC: GPO, 1955 (reprinted Westport, Connecticut: Greenwood Press, 1976).

United States. Department of State. *North Korea: A Case Study in the Techniques of Takeover.* Publication 7118. Far Eastern Series, no. 103. Washington, DC GPO, 1961.

Wada Haruki. *Kin Nichisei to Manshū kōnichi sensō* [Kim Il Sung and the Anti-Japanese War in Manchuria]. Tokyo: Heibonsha, 1992.

Washburn, John N. "Notes and Comment: Soviet Russia and the Korean Communist Party." *Pacific Affairs* (Vancouver) 23, no. 1 (March 1950): 59–65.

Woo-Cumings, Meredith. *The Political Ecology of Famine: The North Korean Catastrophe and Its Lessons.* Tokyo: Asian Development Bank Institute, 2001.

Yang, Sung Chul. *The North and South Korean Political Systems: A Comparative Analysis.* Seoul: Hollym, 1999.

Chapter 2

Amnesty International. "Democratic People's Republic of Korea: Persecuting the Starving: The Plight of North Koreans Fleeing to China." *Amnesty International Report* (London), December 15, 2000.http://web.amnesty.org/library/Index/ENGASA240042000? open& of=ENG-PRK.

Armstrong, Charles K. *The North Korean Revolution, 1945–1950*. Ithaca: Cornell University Press, 2003.

Banbury, Tony. "World Food Programme Press Conference on the DPRK." *Nautilus Institute, Northeast Asia Peace and Security Network*, March 31, 2005. http://www.nautilus.org/ napsnet/sr/ 2005/ 0528A_Banbury.html.

Becker, Jasper. *Rogue Regime: Kim Jong Il and the Looming Threat of North Korea*. New York: Oxford University Press, 2005.

Breen, Michael. *Kim Jong-il: North Korea's Dear Leader*. Singapore: John Wiley, 2004.

Chamberlin, Paul F. "Cultural Dimensions of Korean Reunification: Building a Unified Society." *International Journal on World Peace* 21, no. 3 (September 2004): 3–42.

Chamberlin, Paul F. "Toward a Unified Korea: Part I: When One People Becomes Two," and "Part II: Transforming Two Cultures Into One." *Good Governance*, November–December 2004, 24–31, and January–February 2005, 36–43. http://www.iifwp.org/programs/ governance/.

Chang, Sehun. "The Urbanization of Provincial Cities Through the Study of the Transformation of Spatial Structure." Pages 21–63 in Wankyu Choi, ed., *Formation and Development of North Korean Cities: Chongjin, Shinyuiju, and Haesan*. Seoul: Hanwool Academy, 2004.

Choe, In Su. *Kim Jong Il: The People's Leader*. P'yŏngyang: Foreign Languages Publishing House, 1983.

Cody, Edward. "N. Koreans Fleeing Hard Lives Discover New Misery in China." *Washington Post*, March 7, 2005.

Cohen, Roberta. "Aid Meant for the Hungry." *New York Times*, May 16, 2002.

Cornell, Erik. *North Korea Under Communism: Report of an Envoy to Paradise*. New York: Routledge–Curzon, 2002.

Cumings, Bruce. *Korea's Place in the Sun: A Modern History*. New York: Norton, 2005.

Democratic People's Republic of Korea. Supremc People's Assembly. "The Citizenship Law of the Democratic People's Republic of Korea." P'yŏngyang, March 23, 1995.

Eberstadt, Nicholas. "Bring Them Home: Why South Korea Should Open its Doors to Refugees from the North." *Weekly Standard*, June 6, 2005, 23–29.

Eberstadt, Nicholas. *The End of North Korea*. Washington, DC: AEI Press, 1999.

Eberstadt, Nicholas. "Leadership and Vision for Korea: Humanitarian Rescue as Prologue to Reunification of a Free Korea." Address to the Kim Koo Academy, Seoul, May 25, 2005.

Eberstadt, Nicholas, and Judith Banister. *The Population of North Korea*. Berkeley: University of California, Institute of East Asian Studies, Center for Korean Studies, 1992.

Economist Intelligence Unit, *Country Profile: North Korea, 2004–5*. London, 2004.

Europa World Year Book, 2004, 2. London: Europa, 2004.

Far East and Australasia, 2004. London: Europa, 2004.

Gershman, Carl. "North Korea's Human Catastrophe." *Washington Post*, April 17, 2003.

"Grand Plan for Construction of P'yongyang." *P'yŏngyang Times*, May 23, 1992.

Haggard, Stephan, and Marcus Noland. *Hunger and Human Rights: The Politics of Famine in North Korea*. Washington, DC: U.S. Committee for Human Rights in North Korea, 2005.

Hawk, David R. *The Hidden Gulag: Exposing North Korea's Prison Camps: Prisoners' Testimonies and Satellite Photographs*. Washington, DC: U.S. Committee for Human Rights in North Korea, 2003.

Holloway, Andrew. *A Year In Pyongyang*. Internet Web site of Aidan Foster-Carter, 2002. http://www.aidanfc.net/a_year_in_pyongyang_1.html (accessed July 6, 2005).

Human Rights Watch. "The Invisible Exodus: North Koreans in the People's Republic of China." *Human Rights Watch* 14, no. 8 (November 2002): 1–36.

Hunter, Helen-Louise. *Kim Il-song's North Korea*. Westport, Connecticut: Praeger, 1999.

Hwang, Jang-yop. *The Problems of Human Rights in North Korea*. Seoul: Network for North Korean Democracy and Human Rights (Nknet), 2000. http://www.dailynk.com/english/keys/2002/lastkeys.php (accessed July 6, 2005).

"In Celebration of Dear Comrade Kim Jong Il's 50th Birthday." *Democratic People's Republic of Korea* (P'yongyang), April 1962, 14–19.

Institute for South–North Korean Studies. *The True Story of Kim Jong Il.* Seoul, 1993.

International Conference on North Korean Human Rights and Refugees. 3d. *Shining the Light of Human Rights on North Korea.* Tokyo, 2002.

International Conference on North Korean Human Rights and Refugees. 4th. *Shining the Light of Human Rights on North Korea.* Prague, 2003.

International Conference on North Korean Human Rights and Refugees. 5th. *Shining the Light of Human Rights on North Korea.* Warsaw, 2004.

Kim, Myong Chol. "Biography of an Infant Prodigy." *Far Eastern Economic Review* (Hong Kong) 119 (March 5, 1982): 30–32.

Kim, Suk-Young. "Revolutionizing the Family: A Comparative Study on the Filmed Propaganda Performances of the People's Republic of China and the Democratic People's Republic of Korea, 1966–1976." Ph.D. dissertation. Chicago: Northwestern University, 2005.

Kim Il Sung. *Kim Il Sung: Selected Works*, vol. 2. P'yŏngyang: Foreign Languages Publishing House, 1964.

Kim Il Sung. "Some Problems Related to the Development of the Korean Language." Pages 346–92 in Kim Il Sung, *Kim Il Sung: Selected Works*, vol. 4. P'yŏngyang: Foreign Languages Publishing House, 1971.

Kim Il Sung. "Theses on Socialist Education." Pages 346–92 in Kim Il Sung, *Kim Il Sung: Selected Works*, vol. 7. P'yŏngyang: Foreign Languages Publishing House, 1979.

Kim Il Sung. *With the Century*, vols.1–6. P'yŏngyang: Foreign Languages Publishing House, 1992–95.

"Kim Il Sung Termed Model for Revering Elders." *Korean Affairs Report*, Washington, DC: Joint Publications Research Service, no. 76367 (September 4, 1980): 11–15.

"Kim Jong Il Cult Worship System Now Rivals Kim Il Sung's in Intensity." *North Korea News* (Seoul), no. 619 (February 24, 1992): 1–2.

Kirk, Jeremy. "N. Korean Defections Strain Ties: Flow of Refugees a Diplomatic Issue for Beijing, Seoul." *Washington Times,* February 11, 2005.

Kwon, Youngmin. "Literature and Art in North Korea: Theory and Policy." *Korea Journal* (Seoul) 31, no. 2 (Summer 1992): 56–70.

Lee, Mun Woong. *Rural North Korea under Communism: A Study of Sociocultural Change.* Monograph in Behavioral Science, 62, no. 1. Houston: William Marsh Rice University, 1976.

Lee, Soon Ok. *Eyes of the Tailless Animals: Prison Memoirs of a North Korean Woman.* Bartlesville, Oklahoma: Living Sacrifice Book Company, 1999.

Macintyre, Donald. "Northern Exposure." *Time Asia* (Seoul), November 4, 2002, 24–29.

Martin, Bradley K. *Under the Loving Care of the Fatherly Leader: North Korea and the Kim Dynasty.* New York: Dunne Books, 2004.

Muntarbhorn, Vitit. "Situation of Human Rights in The Democratic People's Republic of Korea." New York: General Assembly. Sixtieth Session, United Nations, August 29, 2005.

Natsios, Andrew S. *The Great North Korean Famine: Famine, Politics, and Foreign Policy.* Washington, DC: United States Institute of Peace Press, 2001.

Network for North Korean Democracy and Human Rights (Nknet). "Friend of North Korean People: KEYS," vols. 3–21, 2001–5, July 6, 2005. http://www.dailynk.com/english/ keys/2005/ last keys.php.

Noland, Marcus. *Avoiding the Apocalypse: The Future of the Two Koreas.* Washington, DC: Institute for International Economics, 2000.

"No Medical Fees." *P'yŏngyang Times,* August 17, 1991.

Oberdorfer, Don. *The Two Koreas: A Contemporary History.* Reading, Massachusetts: Addison-Wesley, 1997.

Park, Myung-jin. "Motion Pictures in North Korea." *Korea Journal* (Seoul) 31, no. 3 (Autumn 1991): 95–103.

Park, Yong-hon. "Cultural Policy of North Korea." *Vantage Point* (Seoul), no. 8 (August 1979): 1–12 .

Park, Young-soon. "Language Policy and Language Education in North Korea." *Korea Journal* (Seoul) 31, no. 1 (Spring 1991): 28–40.

Paterniti, Michael. "Escape from North Korea: The Flight of the Fluttering Swallows." *New York Times Magazine,* April 27, 2003, 46–51, 62, 112–13.

"Public Education System of the DPRK." *Do You Know About Korea? Questions and Answers.* P'yŏngyang: Foreign Languages Publishing House, 1989.

Pukhan yŏn'gam, 2005 [North Korea Year Book, 2005]. Seoul: Yonhap Nyusu, 2005.

Pyongyang. P'yŏngyang: Foreign Languages Publishing House, 1980.

Rendler, Jack. "The Last Worst Place on Earth: Human Rights in North Korea." Pages 113–29 in Henry D. Sokolski, ed., *Planning for a Peaceful Korea.* Carlisle Barracks, Pennsylvania: U.S. Army War College, Strategic Studies Institute, 2001.

Robinson, Michael. *Cultural Nationalism in Korea, 1920–25.* Seattle: University of Washington Press, 1985.

Rosental, Elisabeth. "Defying Crackdown, North Koreans Stream into China." *New York Times,* June 6, 2002.

Scalapino, Robert A., and Chong-sik Lee. *Communism in Korea.* 2 vols. Berkeley: University of California Press, 1972.

Society to Help Returnees to North Korea (Japan) and Citizens' Alliance for North Korean Human Rights (Korea) and Defense Forum Foundation (U.S.). *Life and Human Rights in North Korea.* vols. 18–37, Seoul, 2000–5.

Suh, Dae-Sook. *Kim Il Sung: The North Korean Leader.* New York: Columbia University Press, 1988.

Suh, Yon-Ho. "The Revolutionary Operas and Plays in North Korea." *Korea Journal* (Seoul) 31, no. 3 (Autumn 1991): 85–94.

Taylor, Robert H., ed. *Asia and the Pacific.* Handbooks to the Modern World. New York: Facts on File, 1991.

United Nations. Commission on Human Rights. *Resolution on North Korea,* April 15, 2003, April 14, 2004, and April 14, 2005. New York, 2005.

United Nations. Department of Economic and Social Affairs. Statistical Division. *Statistical Yearbook, Forty-eighth Issue.* New York, 2004.

United Nations. Department of Economic and Social Information and Policy Analysis. Statistical Division. *Statistical Yearbook, Thirty-eighth Issue.* New York, 1993.

United Nations. Environmental Programme. Regional Resource Centre for Asia and the Pacific. *The National State of the Environment, DPR Korea 2003.* Bangkok, 2003. http://www.rr cap.unep.org/reports/soe/dprksoe.cfm.

United States. Agency for International Development. *Report on U.S. Assistance Provided Inside North Korea.* Washington, DC, May 26, 2005.

United States. Central Intelligence Agency. *The World Factbook, 2007.* Washington, DC, 2007. http://www.cia.gov/library/publications/ the-world-factbook/.

United States. Department of Commerce, Census Bureau. International Programs Center. *International Data Base Population Pyramids (North Korea).* Washington, DC, 2007. http://www.census.gov/ipc/ www/idbpyr.html.

United States. Department of State. *The Status of North Korean Asylum Seekers and the U.S. Government Policy Towards Them.* Washington, DC, March 6, 2005.

United States. Department of State. Bureau of Democracy, Human Rights, and Labor. "Korea, Democratic People's Republic." In *Country Reports on Human Rights Practices for 2002.* Washington, DC, March 31, 2003. http://www.state.gov/g/drl/rls/hrrpt/2002/18249.htm.

United States. Department of State. Bureau of East Asian and Pacific Affairs. Office of Public Communications. *Background Notes: North Korea.* Washington, DC, 2005. http://www.state.gov/r/pa/ ei/bgn/ 2792.htm.

Warren, Rick. *The Purpose Driven Life.* Philadelphia: Miniature Editions, 2003.

"Workers' Houses." *Democratic People's Republic of Korea* (P'yŏngyang), December 29, 1990, 12–13.

Yang, Sung-Chul. *Korea and Two Regimes: Kim Il Sung and Park Chung Hee.* Cambridge, Massachusetts: Schenkman, 1981.

(Various issues of the following publications also were used in the preparation of this chapter: *Chosŏn Sinbo* (Tokyo), http://www.korea-np.co.jp/ pk/, 2006; *Democratic People's Republic of Korea* (P'yŏngyang), 1987–2005; *Far Eastern Economic Review* (Hong Kong), 2003–4; Korea Central News Agency (P'yŏngyang), http://www.kcna.co.jp/item/2003/ 200301/ news 01/17.htm, 2003; *Korea Herald* (Seoul), 1979–2005; *Korea Times* (Seoul), 1979–2005; *Korea Today* (P'yŏngyang), 1987–2005; *P'yŏngyang Times,* 1987–2005; and *Washington Times,* 2006.)

Chapter 3

Babson, Bradley. "Economic Cooperation on the Korean Peninsula." Paper prepared for the Task Force on U.S.–Korea Policy sponsored by the Center for International Policy and the Center for East Asian

Studies, University of Chicago. Washington, DC: Brookings Institution, 2003.

Cha, Victor, and David C. Kang. "Can North Korea be Engaged?" *Survival* 46, no. 2 (Summer 2004): 89–107.

Chung, Joseph S. *The North Korean Economy: Structure and Development.* Stanford, California: Hoover Institution Press, 1974.

Eberstadt, Nicholas. "The North Korean Economy in 2000." Pages 1–24 in James Lister, ed., *The Korean Peninsula in the 21st Century: Prospects for Stability and Cooperation.* Joint U.S.–Korea Academic Studies Series, no.11. Washington, DC: Korea Economic Institute, 2001.

Foster-Carter, Aidan. "North Korea Caves in to the Market." *Asia Times*, August 6, 2002. http://www.asiatimes.com/atimes/Korea/DH06Dgol.html.

Frank, Ruediger. "North Korea: 'Gigantic Change' and a Gigantic Chance." *Nautilus Institute Policy Forum Online.* PFO 03–31. http://www.nautilus.org/fora/security/0331_Frank. html (accessed May 9, 2003).

Frank, Ruediger. "A Socialist Market Economy in North Korea? Systemic Restrictions and a Quantitative Analysis." Master's thesis. New York: Columbia University, 2003.

Goodkind, Daniel, and Loraine West. "The North Korean Famine and its Demographic Impact." *Population and Development Review* 27, no. 2 (June 2001): 219–39.

Heiskanen, Markku. "Eurasian Railways: Key To The Korean Deadlock?" *Nautilus Institute Policy Forum Online.* PFO03–4A. http://www.nautilus.org/fora/security/0232A_Heiskanen.html (accessed January 22, 2003).

Hong, Soon-Jick. "North–South Economic Cooperation." Pages 71–76 in James Lister, ed., *2001 Korea's Economy.* Washington, DC: Korea Economic Institute, 2001.

International Monetary Fund. *Direction of Trade Statistics Yearbook* (annuals 1998–2004). Washington, DC, 1998–2004.

Kim, Woon-Keun, Hyunok Lee, and Daniel A. Sumner. "Assessing the Food Situation in North Korea." *Economic Development and Cultural Change* 46, no. 3 (April 1998): 519–36.

Kim Jong Il. "21 Seginun Kŏchanghan Chŏngbyŏnui Segi, Ch'angjoui Segiida [The Twenty-First Century is a Century of Great Change and Creation]." *Nodong Shinmun* [Workers' Daily] (P'yŏngyang), January 4, 2001.

Korean Resources Corporation. "Korea Mineral Information Service." Seoul, 2005. http://kores.net/.

Lee, Chong-Sik, and Se-Hee Yoo, eds. *North Korea in Transition.* Korea Research Monograph no. 16. Berkeley: University of California, Institute of East Asian Studies, Center for Korean Studies, 1991.

MacKinnon, Rebecca. "Chinese Cell Phone Breaches North Korean Hermit Kingdom." *Yale Global Online.* http://yaleglobal.yale.edu/ (accessed January 17, 2005).

Mansourov, Alexandre Y. "Bytes and Bullets: Impact of IT Revolution on War and Peace in Korea." *Nautilus DPRK Briefing Book,* 2002. http://www.nautilus.org/DPRKBriefing Book/.

Natsios, Andrew S. *The Great North Korean Famine: Famine, Politics, and Foreign Policy.* Washington, DC: United States Institute of Peace Press, 2001.

Noland, Marcus. *Avoiding the Apocalypse: The Future of the Two Koreas.* Washington, DC: Institute for International Economics, 2000.

Noland, Marcus. "Famine and Reform in North Korea." WP 03–5. Washington, DC: Institute for International Economics, 2003.

Noland, Marcus. "Life Inside North Korea." Testimony before U.S. Congress, Senate, Subcommittee on East Asian and Pacific Affairs, June 5, 2003. http://foreign.senate.gov/ testimony/2003/ NolandTestimony030605.pdf.

Noland, Marcus, ed. *Economic Integration of the Korean Peninsula.* Special Report, no. 10. Washington, DC: Institute for International Economics, 1998.

Oh, Seung-yul. "Changes in the North Korean Economy: New Policies and Limitations." Pages 74–76 in *2003 Korea's Economy.* Washington, DC: Korea Economic Institute, 2003.

Paik, Haksoon. "North Korea's Economic Reform and Nuclear Programs, and President Roh's Policy toward North Korea." Paper presented at Brookings Institution. Washington, DC, March 23, 2004.

Park, Kyung-Ae. "The Pattern of North Korea's Track-Two Foreign Contacts." Pages 157–84 in James M. Lister, ed., *The Korean Peninsula in the 21st Century: Prospects for Stability and Cooperation.* Joint U.S.–Korea Academic Studies Series, no. 11. Washington, DC: Korea Economic Institute, 2001.

Park, Suhk-Sam. "Measuring and Assessing Economic Activity in North Korea." Pages 76–83 in James M. Lister, ed., *Korea's Economy, 2002.* Washington, DC: Korea Economic Institute, 2002.

Pomfret, John " Congressional Aides Report High Hunger Toll in North Korea." *Washington Post,* August 20, 1998.

Quinones, Kenneth. "Food Security and Agriculture in the DPRK." Paper presented at the North Korean System at the Dawn of the 21st Century Conference, University of California. Berkeley, 1999.

Robinson, W. Courtland, Myung Ken Lee, Kenneth Hill, and Gilbert Burnham. "Mortality in North Korean Migrant Households: A Retrospective Study." *Lancet* (London) 354, no. 9175 (July 24, 1999): 291–95.

Scalapino, Robert A., and Chong-Sik Lee. *Communism in Korea.* 2 vols. Berkeley: University of California Press, 1972.

Scalapino, Robert A., and Dalchoong Kim, eds. *Asian Communism: Continuity and Transition.* Korea Research Monograph, no. 15. Berkeley: University of California, Institute of East Asian Studies, Center for Korean Studies, 1988.

Scalapino, Robert A., and Hongkoo Lee, eds. *North Korea in a Regional and Global Context.* Berkeley: University of California, Institute of East Asian Studies, Center for Korean Studies, 1986.

Shin, Thae-song, et al. "Bilateral Research Collaboration Between Kim Chaek University of Technology (DPRK) and Syracuse University (USA) in the Area of Integrated Information Technology." Paper presented at the Asian Studies on the Pacific Coast Annual Meeting, Honolulu, 2003.

Smith, Heather. "The Food Economy: The Catalyst for Collapse?" Pages 53–75 in Marcus Noland, ed., *Economic Integration of the Korean Peninsula.* Special Report, no. 10. Washington: Institute for International Economics, 1998.

Smith, Heather, and Yiping Huang. "Achieving Food Security in North Korea." Paper presented at the North Korean System at the Dawn of the 21st Century Conference, University of California, Berkeley, 1999.

Suh, Sang Chul. *Growth and Structural Changes in the Korean Economy, 1910–1940.* Harvard East Asia Monographs, no. 83. Cambridge: Harvard University Press for Council on East Asian Studies, 1978.

United Nations. *International Trade Statistics Yearbook* (annuals 1998–2004). New York, 1998–2004.

United Nations Children's Fund. "DPR Korea, Donor Update." February 28, 2003. www.unicef.org/dprk/DPRK_28_February_2003.pdf.

United Nations Children's Fund. "Nutrition Assessment 2002, D.P.R. Korea," February 28, 2003. http://www.uni cef.org/dprk/ nutrition_assesment.pdf.

United Nations. Food and Agriculture Organization. "North Korea Has Bigger Harvest, but Millions Still Need Food Aid," February 28, 2005. http://www.fao.org/newsroom/en/news/2004/51607/index.html.

World Bank. *Transition Newsletter,* February 25, 2004. www.worldbank. org/transitionnewsletter/janfebmar03/ pgs1-6htm.

Wu, John C. "The Mineral Industry of North Korea." In United States Geological Survey, *Mineral Year Book,* 3. Area Reports: International. Washington, DC, 2005. http://minerals.usgs.gov/ minerals/pubs/country/2005/knmyb05.pdf>; http://minerals.usgs. gov/minerals/pubs/country/ind ex.html#pubs.

Yoon, Deok-ryong. "Economic Development in North Korea: A Possible Time Line for North Korean Transformation." Pages 69–75 in *Korea's Economy, 2002,* vol. 18. Washington, DC: Korea Economic Institute, 2002.

Yoon, Deok-ryong, and Park Soon-chan. "Capital Needed for North Korea's Economic Recovery and Optimal Investment Policy." Pages 1–80 in Kyung-tae Lee, ed., *Policy Analysis 01–08,* Seoul: Korea Institute for International Economic Policy, 2002.

Yoshikawa, Yukie. "The Prospect of Economic Reform in North Korea." In *Nautilus Institute: DPRK Briefing Book,* March 15, 2004. http://www.nautilus.org/DPRKBriefingBook/transition/ 200312 NKecon.html.

(Various Web sites and issues of the following publications also were used in the preparation of this chapter: *Asian Survey,* 1999–2005; *Chosŏn chungang yŏn'gam* [Korean Central Yearbook] (P'yŏngyang), 2001–5; *Chosun Ilbo* (Seoul), 1997–2005; Democratic People's Republic of Korea, Chosun Tongsin [Korea Central News Agency], http://www.kcna.co.jp/, 1998–2005; *Donga Ilbo* (Seoul), 1999–2005; Economist Intelligence Unit, *Country Report: China, North Korea* (London), 1999–2001; Economist Intelligence Unit, *Country Report: North Korea* (London), 2002–5; *Foreign Trade of the Democratic People's Republic of Korea* (P'yŏngyang), 2002–5; Institute of Foreign Affairs and National Security (Seoul), http://www.ifans.go.kr, 2003–5; *International Herald Tribune* (Paris), 2001, 2004; *Jane's World Railways,* 2001–5; *Joongang Ilbo* (Seoul), http://joongangdaily.joins.com, 1997–2005; *Kita Chōsen kenkyū* [Studies on North Korea] (Tokyo), 2003; *Kita Chōsen no keizai to bōeki no tenbō* [North Korean Economic and Trade Prospects], Japan External Trade Organization (Tokyo), 2003–5; Korea Institute of National Unification, http://www.kinu.or.kr; *Korea Times* (Seoul), 1999–2005; *Korea Today* (P'yŏngyang), 2001–5; Korean Overseas Trade

Association, www.kotra.or.kr, 2002–5; *Kŭlloja* [The Worker] (P'yŏngyang), 2002–5; Nautilus Institute, http://www.nautilus.org/, 2001–5; *Nodong Shinmun* [Workers' Daily] (P'yŏngyang), 1998–2005; *People's Daily Online*, http://www.people.com.cn/, 2003–5; *People's Korea* (Tokyo), http://www.korea-np.co.jp/pk, 2002; Republic of Korea, Ministry of Unification, 2005, http://www.unikorea.go.kr/en/; Reuters, http://www.reuters.com/, 2001–5; Sejong Institute Web site (Seongna, South Korea), http://www.sejong.org, 2002–5; United States, Central Intelligence Agency, *World Factbook*, 1997–2005 (current edition at https://www.cia.gov/cia/publications/factbook/index.html); U.S. Open Source Center (formerly the Foreign Broadcast Information Service), translations of North Korean broadcasts available via the National Technical Information Service's World News Connection, http://wnc.fedworld.gov/, 1997–2005; *Vantage Point* (Seoul), 1995–2005; and Yonhap News Agency (Seoul), 1999–2005, http://english.yonhapnews.co.kr/.)

Chapter 4

Cha, Victor. "Contemplating Sanctions." *Comparative Connections* 5, no. 1 (1st Quarter, 2003): 111–18. http://www.csis.org/media/csis/pubs/0301q.pdf.

Cha, Victor. "Ending 2000 with a Whimper, Not a Bang." *Comparative Connections* 2, no. 4 (4th Quarter, 2000): 88–93.

Cha, Victor. "Mr. Koizumi Goes to P'yŏngyang."*Comparative Connections* 4, no. 3 (3d Quarter, 2002): 103–11.

Cho, Sung Yoon. *Law and Legal Literature of North Korea: A Guide.* Washington, DC: Library of Congress, 1988.

Clippinger, Morgan. "Kim Chong Il in the North Korean Mass Media: A Survey of Semi-Esoteric Communications." *Asian Survey* 21, no. 3 (March 1981): 289–309.

A Comprehensive Handbook on Korea: Korea Annual 2004. 41st ed. Seoul: Yonhap News Agency, 2003–4.

Delury, George E., ed. *World Encyclopedia of Political Systems and Parties*, vol. 1. New York: Facts on File, 1983.

Dwor-Frecaut, Dominique. *Korea: Long-Term Decline in the North Korea Premium.* Singapore: Barclays Capital Research, February 27, 2004.

Eberstadt, Nicholas, and Judith Banister. *The Population of North Korea.* Berkeley: University of California, Institute of East Asian Studies, Center for Korean Studies, 1992.

Frank, Ruediger. "North Korea: Gigantic Change and a Gigantic Chance." Nautilus Institute, *Policy Forum Online*. PFO 03–31. http:// nautilus.org/fora/security/ 0331_Frank.html (accessed May 9, 2003).

Global Security. "Leadership Succession." *Democratic People's Republic of Korea*, November 19, 2004. http://www.globalsecurity. org/military/world/dprk/leadership-succession.htm.

Goncharov, Sergei, John Lewis, and Xue Litai. *Uncertain Partners: Stalin, Mao and the Korean War.* Stanford: Stanford University Press, 1993.

Hong, Ihk-pyo. "A Shift Toward Capitalism? Recent Economic Reforms in North Korea." *East Asian Review* (Seoul) 14, no. 4 (Winter 2002): 93–106.

Index Mundi. *North Korea-Government Profile.* Updated 2004. http://www.indexmundi.com/ north_korea.

International Press Institute. "*2003 World Press Freedom Review: North Korea.*" http://www.freemedia.at/wpfr/Asia/norkor.htm#2003.

Joo, Seung-Ho. *Gorbachev's Foreign Policy Toward the Korean Peninsula, 1985–1991 Power and Reform.* Lewiston, New York: Mellen Press, 2000.

Kim Jong Il. *The Great Teacher of Journalists.* P'yŏngyang: Foreign Languages Publishing House, 1983.

Lee, Grace. "The Political Philosophy of Juche." *Stanford Journal of East Asian Affairs* 3, no. 1 (Spring 2003): 105–12.

Linter, Bertil. "Shop Till You Drop." *Far Eastern Economic Review* (Hong Kong), May 13, 2004.

Marx, Karl. *Writings of the Young Marx on Philosophy and Society.* Edited by Lloyd Easton and Kurt Guddat. Garden City, New York: Doubleday, 1967.

Miyazaki, Jamie. "Adam Smith Comes to North Korea." *Asia Times.* http://www.atimes.com/atimes/Korea/EJ22Dg01.html (accessed October 22, 2003).

Noland, Marcus. "Life Inside North Korea." Testimony before U.S. Congress, Senate, Committee on Foreign Relations, Subcommittee on East Asian and Pacific Affairs, June 5, 2003. http://foreignsenate. gov/testimony/2003/NolandTestimony030605.pdf.

Oh, Seung-yul. "Changes in the North Korean Economy: New Policies and Limitations." Pages 74–76 in *Korea's Economy 2003*, vol. 19. Washington, DC: Korea Economic Institute, 2003.

Paik, Haksoon. "North Korea's Economic Reform and Nuclear Programs, and President Roh's Policy toward North Korea." Paper presented at Brookings Institution. Washington, DC, March 23, 2004.

Pang, Hwan Ju. *Korean Review.* P'yŏngyang: Foreign Languages Publishing House, 1988.

Reporters Without Borders. *North Korea: 2004 Annual Report.* http://www.rsf.org/article.php3? id_article=10211&Valider=OK.

Republic of Korea. Ministry of Unification. Information Center on North Korea. "Power Structure of North Korea," 2006. http://unibook. unikorea.go.kr/dataroom/images/ table_d_01.gif.

Rhee, Sang-woo, "North Korea in 1991: Struggle to Save *Chuch'e* Amid Signs of Change." *Asian Survey* 32, no. 1 (January 1992): 56–63.

Staar, Richard F., ed. *Yearbook of Communist Affairs.* Palo Alto, California: Hoover Institution Press, 1988.

Suh, Dae-Sook. *Kim Il Sung: The North Korean Leader.* New York: Columbia University Press, 1988.

United States. Central Intelligence Agency. "North Korea." In *Chiefs of State and Cabinet Members of Foreign Governments.* Washington, DC, June 28, 2006. https://www.cia. gov/library/publications/world-leaders/index.html.

United States. Central Intelligence Agency. *World Factbook, 2006.* Washington, DC, 2006. https://www.cia.gov/library/publications/the-world-factbook/index.html.

United States. Congress. Senate. Committee on Foreign Relations. *North Korea: Status Report on Nuclear Program, Humanitarian Issues, and Economic Reforms.* 108th Cong., 2d sess. Washington, DC: GPO, 2004. http://foreign.senate.gov/testimony/2004/DPRKTripReport.pdf.

Wit, Joel, Daniel Poneman, and Robert Gallucci. *Going Critical: The First North Korean Nuclear Crisis.* Washington, DC: Brookings Institution, 2004.

Yang, Sung Chul. *Pukhan Jungchiron* [North Korean Politics]. Seoul: Pakyoungsa, 1991.

Yonhap News Agency. *North Korea Handbook* (annuals). Translated by Monterey Interpretation and Translation Services. Armonk, New York: Sharpe, 1991, 2000, 2003–5.

Yu, In-taek. "Inter-Korean Relations and Situation Around Korean Peninsula." *East Asian Review* (Seoul) 3, no. 4 (Winter 1991): 21–29.

Yun, Dae-Ho. *North Korea's Foreign Policy.* Seoul: Research Center for Peace and Unification of Korea, 1991.

(Various Web sites and issues of the following publications also were used in the preparation of this chapter: *Chosŏn Yaesul* (P'yŏngyang), 1996;

Chosun Ilbo (Seoul), 1992; Democratic People's Republic of Korea (P'yŏngyang), 2006, http://www.korea.dpr.com; *Europa World Year Book*, 2003–5; *Far Eastern Economic Review* (Hong Kong), 2004; Korean Central Broadcasting Network (P'yŏngyang), 1993; Kyodo News (Tokyo), 1993, http://home.kyodo. jp/index.php?; Naenara Korea Computer Center in the DPRKorea (P'yŏngyang), 2006, http://www.kcckp.net/en/; *Nodong Shinmun* (P'yŏngyang), 2001; *Pukhaneul Woomjikinun Paekeen* [Hundred Persons Who Govern North Korea] (Seoul); *Sankei Shimbun* (Tokyo), 1992; U.S. Open Source Center (formerly the Foreign Broadcast Information Service), translations of North Korean broadcasts available via the National Technical Information Service's World News Connection, http://wnc.fedworld.gov/, 1997–2005; *Wolgan Kyunghyang* [Monthly Journal of the Kyunghyang Press] (Seoul), 1989; and Yonhap News Agency (Seoul), 2004, http://english.yonhapnews. co.kr/.)

Chapter 5

Armstrong, Charles K. *The North Korean Revolution 1945–1950*. Ithaca: Cornell University Press, 2003.

Bermudez, Joseph S., Jr. *North Korean Special Forces*. 2d ed. Annapolis: Naval Institute Press, 1998.

Bermudez, Joseph S., Jr. *Shield of the Great Leader: The Armed Forces of North Korea*. Australia: Allen and Unwin, 2001.

Chŏk chŏnsul [Enemy tactics]. Taejŏn, Republic of Korea: Republic of Korea Army College, 2001.

Chŏk ŭl alcha (I): yŏndaegŭp isang pukkoegun chŏnsulgyori [Understanding the Enemy (I): North Korean Military Tactical Doctrine, Regiment Level and Higher]. Reference Manual 30–7–1. Taejŏn, Republic of Korea: Republic of Korea Army Headquarters, 2000.

Democratic People's Republic of Korea. Ministry of Foreign Affairs. "Letter, dated January 10, 2003 by the North Korean Ministry of Foreign Affairs to the French Presidency of the United Nations Security Council and the States Parties of the Nuclear Non-Proliferation Treaty." Cited in Jean du Preez and William Potter, "North Korea's Withdrawal From the NPT: A Reality Check." Monterey Institute of International Studies, Center for Nonproliferation Studies, April 10, 2003. http://cns.miis.edu/pubs/week/030409.htm.

Feickert, Andrew. "Missile Survey: Ballistic and Cruise Missiles of Foreign Countries." *Congressional Research Service Report for Congress*. RL30427. Washington, DC: Congressional Research Service. Foreign

Affairs, National Defense, and Trade Division, March 5, 2004. http://fpc.state.gov/documents/organization/31999.pdf#search=%22A%20Missile%20Survey%3A%20Ballistic%20and%20Cruise%20Missiles%20of%20Foreign%20Countries%22.

Haggard, Stephan, and Marcus Noland, eds. *The North Korean Refugee Crisis: Human Rights and International Responses*. Washington, DC: U.S. Committee for Human Rights in North Korea, 2006.

Hawk, David. *The Hidden Gulag: Exposing North Korea's Prison Camps: Prisoners' Testimonies and Satellite Photographs*. Washington, DC: U.S. Committee for Human Rights in North Korea, 2003.

Hunter, Helen-Louise. *Kim Il-song's North Korea*. Westport, Connecticut: Praeger, 1999.

Jacobs, Gordon. "North Korea Looks South: Unconventional Warfare Forces." *Asian Defence Journal* (Kuala Lumpur), December 1985, 10–23.

Jeon, Jei Guk. "Kim Jong-il's Ride on the Tiger 'KPA': A Two Pronged Strategy Towards the Military." *Korean Journal of Defense Analysis* (Seoul) 11, no. 1 (Summer 1999): 127–46.

Kaurov, Georgiy. "A Technical History of Soviet–North Korean Nuclear Relations." Pages 15–20 in James Clay Moltz and Alexandre Y. Mansourov, eds., *The North Korean Nuclear Program: Security, Strategy, and New Perspectives from Russia*. New York: Routledge, 2000.

Kim, Kyong-soo. "North Korea's CB Weapons: Threat and Capability." *Korean Journal of Defense Analysis* (Seoul) 14, no. 1 (Spring 2002): 69–95.

Kim, Soo-Am. *The North Korean Penal Code, Criminal Procedures, and Their Actual Application*. Studies Series 06–01. Seoul: Korea Institute for National Unification, 2006.

Lee, Suk Ho. *Party-Military Relations in North Korea: A Comparative Analysis*. Seoul: Research Center for Peace and Unification of Korea, 1989.

Lim, Ŭn. *The Founding of a Dynasty in North Korea: An Authentic Biography of Kim Il-sŏng*. Tokyo: Jiyu-sha, 1982.

Mazarr, Michael J. *North Korea and the Bomb*. New York: St. Martin's Press, 1995.

Minnich, James M. "The Denuclearization of North Korea: A Critical Analysis of the 1994 Agreed Framework." *Korean Journal of Defense Analysis* (Seoul) 14, no. 2 (Fall 2002): 5–28.

Minnich, James M. *The Denuclearization of North Korea: The Agreed Framework and Alternative Options Analyzed.* Bloomington, Indiana: 1st Books Library, 2002.

Minnich, James M. *The North Korean People's Army: Origins and Current Tactics.* Annapolis: Naval Institute Press, 2005.

Minnich, James M. "Resolving the North Korean Nuclear Crisis: Challenges and Opportunities in Readjusting the U.S.–ROK Alliance." Pages 268–309 in Alexander Y. Mansourov, ed., *A Turning Point: Democratic Consolidation in the ROK and Strategic Readjustment in the U.S.–ROK Alliance.* Honolulu: Asia–Pacific Center for Security Studies, 2005.

Moltz, James Clay, and Alexandre Y. Mansourov, eds. *The North Korea Nuclear Program: Security, Strategy, and New Perspectives from Russia.* New York: Routledge, 2000.

Oh, Kong Dan, and Ralph C. Hassig. *North Korea: Through the Looking Glass.* Washington, DC: Brookings Institution Press, 2000.

Paek, Pong. *Minjok ŭi t'aeyang Kim Il Sung Changgun* [General Kim Il Sung the Sun of the Nation], vol. 1. Pyŏngyang: Inmum Kwahaksa, 1968.

Pukhan Yŏn'guso [Institute for North Korean Studies]. *Pukhan Ch'ongram* [North Korea Handbook]. Seoul, 1984.

Republic of Korea. Ministry of National Defense. *Defense White Paper, 1989.* Seoul, 1990.

Republic of Korea. Ministry of National Defense. *Defense White Paper, 1991–1992.* Seoul, 1991.

Republic of Korea. Ministry of National Defense. *Defense White Paper, 1995–1996.* Seoul, 1996.

Republic of Korea. Ministry of National Defense. *Defense White Paper, 1998.* Seoul, 1999.

Republic of Korea. Ministry of National Defense. *Defense White Paper, 2004.* Seoul, 2004.

Republic of Korea. Ministry of National Defense, *Kukpang Paesŏ, 2006* [Defense White Paper, 2006]. Seoul, 2006.

Suh, Dae-Sook. *Kim Il Sung: The North Korean Leader.* New York: Colombia University Press, 1988.

United States. Central Intelligence Agency. *CIA National Intelligence Estimates of Foreign Missile Development and the Ballistic Missile Threat Through 2015.* Washington, DC, 2002.

United States. Central Intelligence Agency. "Report to the U.S. Congress on North Korea's Nuclear Weapons Potential," November 19, 2002. http://fas.org/nuke/guide/dprk/ nuke/cia111902.html.

United States. Congress. Senate. Committee on Armed Services. "Annual Threat Assessment of the Director of National Intelligence for the Senate Armed Services Committee, February 28, 2006." 109th Cong., 2d sess. http://armed-services.senate.gov/ e_witnesslist.cfm?:d=1758.

United States. Congress. Senate. Committee on Armed Services. "Statement of General B. B. Bell, Commander, United Nations Command; Commander, Republic of Korea–United States Combined Forces Command; and Commander, United States Forces Korea before the Senate Armed Services Committee, 7 March 2006." 109th Cong., 2d sess. http://armed-services.senate.gov/ statemnt/2006/March/Bell%2003-07-06.pdf.

United States. Congress. Senate. Committee on Governmental Affairs. "Testimony of R. James Woolsey, February 23, 1993." 103d Cong., 1st sess. Pages 51–56 in *Proliferation Threats of the 1990s*. Washington, DC: GPO, 1993.

United States. Defense Intelligence Agency. *North Korea: Foundations for Military Strength*. Washington, DC, 1991.

United States. Department of Defense. *Proliferation Threat and Response*. Washington, DC: GPO, 2001.

United States. Department of State. Bureau of Democracy, Human Rights, and Labor. "Korea, Democratic People's Republic of." In *Country Reports on Human Rights Practices for 2006*. Washington, DC, March 6, 2007. http://www.state.gov/g/drl/rls/hrrpt2006/ 78 777.htm.

United States. Department of State. Bureau of Public Affairs. "Fact Sheet: Military Expenditures and Arms Transfers 1999–2000." Washington, DC, February 6, 2003.

United States. Department of the Navy. Marine Corps. Marine Corps Intelligence Activity. *North Korea Country Handbook*. Washington, DC, 1997.

Won, Hee. "Pukhanŭi missile sanji: che 2 chayŏnkwa hakwŏn" [North Korean Missile Production Site: 2nd Natural Science Institute]. *Manghyang—talpukcha dongjihoebo* [Nostalgia—North Korean Defectors' Circular], no. 5 (October 1999): 31–32. Quoted in Kim, Kyongsoo, "North Korea's CB Weapons: Threat and Capability," *Korean Journal of Defense Analysis* (Seoul) 14, no. 1 (Spring 2002): 69–95.

Yonhap News Agency. *North Korea Handbook* (annuals). Translated by Monterey Interpretation and Translation Services. Armonk, New York: Sharpe, 1991, 2000, 2003–5.

Zhebin, Alexander. "A Political History of Soviet–North Korean Nuclear Cooperation." Pages 27–37 in James Clay Moltz and Alexandre Y. Mansourov, eds., *The North Korean Nuclear Program: Security, Strategy, and New Perspectives from Russia.* New York: Routledge, 2000.

(Various sources and issues of the following publications also were used in the preparation of this chapter: Associated Press, 2003, http://www.ap.org; *Chosŏn* (P'yŏngyang), 2003; *Chosun Ilbo* (Seoul), 2005–6; *Daily NK* (Seoul), 2006; *Defense News,* 2006; Federal News Service, 2006; *Joongang Ilbo* [Central Daily] (Seoul), 1995, 2005; Korean Central News Agency (P'yŏngyang), 1998, 2003; Kyodo News (Tokyo), 2006, http://home.kyodo.jp/index.php?; *Pukhan* [North Korea] (Seoul), 1999; National Intelligence Service (Seoul), 2005, http://www.nis.go.kr/newindex.htm; *Sisa Journal/Sisa Chŏnŏl* [Weekly News Magazine] (Seoul), 1996; *T'ongil Kyongje* [Unification Economy] (Seoul), 2002; U.S. Open Source Center (formerly the Foreign Broadcast Information Center), translations of North Korean broadcasts available via the National Technical Information Service's World News Connection, http://wnc.fedworld.gov, 2005; *Wall Street Journal,* 2004; *Washington Post,* 2003; and *Wŏlgan Chosŏn* [Monthly Choson] (Seoul), 1990–91, 2005.)

Glossary

Agreed Framework—Signed in Geneva, Switzerland, between the United States and North Korea on October 21, 1994, following talks held between September 23 and October 21, 1994, during which the two sides negotiated an overall resolution of the nuclear issue on the Korean Peninsula. Both sides agreed to four points: to cooperate to replace North Korea's graphite-moderated reactors and related facilities with light-water nuclear-reactor power plants; to move toward full normalization of political and economic relations; to work together for peace and security on a nuclear-free Korean Peninsula; and to work together to strengthen the international nuclear nonproliferation regime.

cadre(s), or *kanbu*—Term for responsible party, government, and economic functionaries; also used for key officials in the educational, cultural, and scientific fields.

Choch'ongryŏn—Abbreviation for Chae Ilbon Chosŏnin Ch'ongyon-haphoe, literally General Association of Korean Residents in Japan. Members of this Japan-based association tend to be supportive of North Korea's foreign policy and have kinship and financial ties to North Korea. Known as Zainichi Chōsenjin Sōrengokai, or Chōsen Sōren, in Japanese.

Ch'ŏllima, or Ch'ŏllima Work Team Movement—Intensive mass campaign to increase economic production inaugurated in 1958; began as Ch'ŏllima Movement (Ch'ŏllima Undong), named after a legendary flying horse said to have galloped 1,000 *li* in a single day; a symbolic term for great speed. Farm and factory workers were exhorted to excel in the manner of Ch'ŏllima riders, and exemplary individuals and work teams were awarded special Ch'ŏllima titles. The labor force was organized into work teams and brigades and competed at increasing production. Superseded in the early 1960s by the Ch'ŏngsan-ni Method (*q.v.*) and the Taean Work System (*q.v.*), and then in 1973 by the Three Revolutions Team Movement (*q.v.*).

Ch'ŏndogyo—Teachings of the Heavenly Way. This indigenous monotheistic religion was founded in the nineteenth century as a counter to Western influence and Christianity. Its Christian-influenced dogma stresses the equality and unity of man with the universe. Formerly Tonghak (Eastern Learning) Movement (*q.v.*).

Ch'ŏngsan-ni Method—A personalized, "on-the -spot" management method or spirit reputedly developed by Kim Il Sung in February 1960 during a visit to the Ch'ŏngsan-ni Cooperative Farm in South P'yŏngan Province. In addition to important material incentives, the method had three main components: party and government functionaries must eschew their bureaucratic tendency of only issuing orders and directives; they must mingle with farmers and uncover and solve their problems through comradely guidance; and they should give solid technological guidance to spur efficient and productive achievement. The method was largely abandoned in the early twenty-first century.

chuch'e, or *juch'e*—Political ideology promulgated by Kim Il Sung. The application of Marxism–Leninism to the North Korean experience based on autonomy and self-reliance popularized since 1955 as an official guideline for independence in politics, economics, national defense, and foreign policy.

Comintern—Short form for Communist International or the Third International, which was founded in Moscow in 1919 to coordinate the world communist movement. Officially disbanded in 1943, the Comintern was revived as the Cominform (Communist Information Bureau) from 1947 to 1956.

Demarcation Line—Established at the thirty-eighth parallel under the Korean War armistice agreement of 1953; marks the actual cease-fire line between North Korea and South Korea.

Demilitarized Zone (DMZ)—The 4,000-meter-wide buffer zone that runs east and west across the waist of the Korean Peninsula for 238 kilometers over land and three kilometers over the sea, dividing it into North Korea and South Korea. The DMZ was created by the armistice in 1953.

exclusionism—Chosŏn Dynasty (1392–1910) foreign policy of isolation adopted after the Japanese invasions in the 1590s.

fiscal year—January 1 through December 31.

gross domestic product (GDP)—A value measure of the flow of domestic goods and services produced by an economy over a period of time, such as a year. Only output values of goods for final consumption and intermediate production are assumed to be included in the final prices. GDP is sometimes aggregated and shown at market prices, meaning that indirect taxes and subsidies are included; when these indirect taxes and subsidies have been eliminated, the result is GDP at factor cost. The word *gross* indicates that deductions for depreciation of physical assets have not been made. Income arising from investments and possessions owned abroad is not included, only domestic production—hence the use of the word *domestic* to distinguish GDP from gross national product (*q.v.*).

gross national product (GNP)—The gross domestic product (*q.v.*) plus net income or loss stemming from transactions with foreign countries, including income received from abroad by residents and subtracting payments remitted abroad to nonresidents. GNP is the broadest measurement of the output of goods and services by an economy. It can be calculated at market prices, which include indirect taxes and subsidies. Because indirect taxes and subsidies are only transfer payments, GNP often is calculated at factor cost by removing indirect taxes and subsidies.

hangul—The Korean phonetic alphabet developed in fifteenth-century Chosŏn Korea by scholars in the court of King Sejong (r. 1418–50). This alphabet is used in both North Korea and South Korea; in North Korea, it is called *chosŏn'gul* and is used exclusively, whereas in South Korea a mixture of the alphabet and Chinese characters is used.

International Atomic Energy Agency (IAEA)—Specialized agency of the United Nations established in 1956, which became effective in 1957, to assist member nations with the development and application of atomic energy for peaceful uses and to foster and monitor a universal standard of nuclear safeguards. Through on-site inspections and monitoring, the IAEA ensures that fissile and related nuclear material, equipment, information, and services are not used to produce nuclear weapons as provided for in bilateral nuclear safeguard agreements between the IAEA and individual member nations of the Nuclear Nonproliferation Treaty (NPT), formally the Treaty on the Non-Proliferation of Nuclear Weapons. In 2007 there were 144 members of the IAEA, not including North Korea.

Kapsan—Name of a political faction that takes its name from a town in Yanggang Province in the Changbai mountain range on the border of Korea and Northeast China (then called Manchuria), where Kim Il Sung's guerrilla army conducted some of its militant activities against the Japanese in the 1930s. Having joined up with the Manchurian-based Northeast Anti-Japanese United Army, surviving partisans from this group fled to the Soviet maritime provinces in 1941. In 1945 this group of Soviet exiles, Kim Il Sung loyalists—the Kapsan faction or Kapsanists—returned to North Korea, where many eventually were elevated to prominence in the national political-military hierarchy.

Kim Il Sung Socialist Youth League—A branch of the Korean Workers' Party. It was originally known as Korea Democratic Youth from 1946 to 1953. At the end of the Korean War (1950–53), it was renamed the Socialist Working Youth League, sometimes given as the Socialist Labor Youth League. In 1994, after the death of Kim Il Sung, the group was given its current name.

national solipsism—Term indicating North Korea's isolationism and its sense that it is the center of the world's attentions.

Nordpolitik, or *pukbang chŏngch'aek*—The name given to the foreign policy pursued in various forms by South Korea since 1988 aimed at improving its diplomatic and economic ties with the former communist nations of Eastern Europe and the Soviet Union.

Organisation for Economic Co-Operation and Development (OECD)—Established in 1960, the OECD took effect in 1961 to promote economic cooperation and development among member countries (in 2008, Australia, Austria, Belgium, Canada, Czech Republic, Denmark, Finland, France, Germany, Greece, Hungary, Iceland, Ireland, Italy, Japan, Luxembourg, Mexico, the Netherlands, New Zealand, Norway, Poland, Portugal, Slovak Republic, South Korea, Spain, Sweden, Switzerland, Turkey, the United Kingdom, and the United States; one member with special status is the European Union—EU) by assisting member governments in the formulation and coordination of policy; and to encourage member-nation support of developing nations.

sŏngbun—Term for a person's socioeconomic or class background, which determines his or her standing with the state.

suryŏng—Ancient Koguryŏ term for "leader," which Kim Il Sung took in 1949 as his highest, and usual, title.

Taean Work System—An industrial management system that grew out of the Ch'ŏngsan-ni Method (*q.v.*). Introduced in December 1961 by Kim Il Sung while on a visit to the Taean Electrical

Appliance Plant, the Taean Work System applied and refined agricultural management techniques to industry. Higher-level functionaries assisted lower-level functionaries and workers in a spirit of close consultation and comradery. Party committees controlled the general management of factories and enterprises and stressed political or ideological work as well as technological expertise. The system allowed for material incentives to production. The system was abandoned in 2002.

Three Revolutions Team Movement—Inaugurated in February 1973 as "a powerful revolutionary method of guidance" for the Three Revolutions—ideological, technical, and cultural—stressed since the early 1960s. Under this method, the Three Revolutions teams were sent to factories, enterprises, and rural and fishing villages for on-the-spot guidance and problem solving in close consultation with local personnel through the 1970s and 1980s.

Tonghak (Eastern Learning) Movement—Refers to an indigenous religious movement founded by Ch'oe Che-u in the early 1860s that brought together elements of traditional Korean and Christian religious beliefs and was the antecedent of Ch'ŏndogyo (*q.v.*).

wŏn—North Korean unit of currency. The North Korean wŏn is divided into 100 chon and has several exchange rates—some for official transactions and others for commercial rates in foreign trade. As of late October 2008, officially US$1=140 wŏn but 2,500–3,000 wŏn or more to US$1 on black market.

yangban—The traditional Korean term for the scholar-official gentry (literally, the two orders or classes) who virtually monopolized all official civil and military positions in the bureaucracy of the late Koryŏ Dynasty (918–1392) and the Chosŏn Dynasty (1392–1910) by competing in a system of civil and military service examinations.

Index

Academy of Defense Sciences, 271
Academy of Sciences, 200, 260
Acheson, Dean, 43, 44
acquired immune deficiency syndrome (AIDS), 126–27
Agreed Framework (1994), 57, 58, 147, 174, 228–30, 261, 262
Agreement on Reconciliation, Nonaggression, Exchanges, and Cooperation (1991), 220–21
agriculture (see also famine; rice; volunteer labor), xxxi, 46–47, 67, 153–57; arable land for, 64, 67, 145, 233; collective farming, 46–47, 143, 154, 155–56; early practice of, 6, 9; inputs for, 100, 145, 154; irrigation for, 154; output of, 64, 145, 153–54, 233; workforce in, 104
AIDS. See acquired immune deficiency syndrome
air combat divisions, 252
air defense, 249
air force aircraft and equipment, 252–53, 272
Air Force Academy. See Kim Ch'aek Air Force Academy
Air Force Command, 240, 242, 250, 252–53
Air Koryo, 150
air pollution, 65–66
airports, 150, 195
air training divisions, 252
air transport brigades, 252
Alaska, 259
Albright, Madeleine, 57–58, 93, 230
Amnok (Yalu) River, 4, 11, 14–15, 62, 64, 167
An Chung-gŭn, 28
An Si Fortress, 10
Andong, 12
Anti-Japanese Guerrilla Army (Han il Yugyŏtae), 237
armed forces (see also individual services): attitudes to, 103; deployment of, 246–57; development of, 237–38; doctrine, strategy, and tactics, 269–70; mission of, 195, 237–38, 241–42, 244–45, 269–70; national command structure of, 238–45; strength of, xxxiv, 245, 247, 249, 252, 253, 254, 256, 280
armistice agreement (see also Military Armistice Commission), xxx, 44–45, 57, 63, 227

armored equipment, 248, 272
Armor Officer School, 262–63
arms exports, 47, 228, 271
arms imports, 238, 252, 258, 260
arms production, 270–72
arms trafficking, 47
Armstrong, Charles K., 79
army. See Korean People's Army
Army Day (April 25), 85
Army Service Decree, 264
arrests, political, 276, 278
artillery: corps, 247; equipment, xxxiv, 247, 248, 249, 254, 272
Artillery Guidance Bureau, 248
artistic expression, freedom of, 216
Asia–Pacific Peace Committee, 176–77
Australia, 3, 173
Austria, 173

Babson, Bradley, 161
ballistic missiles, 226, 229, 230, 257–60; moratorium on testing, 258–59
Banco Delta Asia, xxxv
banking sector, 153, 162–63, 195
Bank of Korea (Seoul), 31, 160
base classes, 19–20, 79–80
Bell, Burwell B. (B.B.), 249, 259
Berlin Wall, 3
Bermudez Jr., Joseph S., 260
biological weapons. See chemical and biological weapons
birth control, 69
birthrate, 67, 99, 105, 130
black market, 160–61, 232, 233
bonds, 162–63
bone-rank system, 9
Bonner, Nicholas, 161
borders, 61–63
border security brigades, 280
Border Security Bureau, 279
Border Security Command, 240, 277, 279–80
Border Security Division (Tenth), 280
Boxer Uprising, 28
Britain (see also United Kingdom), 25, 125
British Broadcasting Corporation, 115

Hwang Jang-yop, 75, 119
Hwangju, 252
Hwasŏng short-range ballistic missile (SRBM), 258, 259–60
hydroelectric power, 65, 147
Hyŏn Ch'ŏl-hae, 241, 245
Hyundai Asan, 167, 176
Hyundai Group, 57, 167, 231

IAEA. *See* International Atomic Energy Agency
ideology (*see also chuch'e*; Marxism–Leninism), 41, 50, 203–8
idu (Korean adaptation of Chinese characters), 11
imports, 46, 48; of food, 66, 69; of oil, 48, 146
Inch'ŏn, 14
income (*see also* wages), 46
independence, xxix, xxxi, 37–38
Independence Club, 26
India, 173
industrialization, xxxii, 35, 46
industrial sector (*see also* construction industry; heavy industry; manufacturing), 32, 35, 40, 136, 145, 161, 233; development of, 32, 35, 46, 137–41; growth of, 46, 145
infant mortality rate, 130
infantry corps, 242, 247
inflation, 159, 171–72, 232
informal sector, 161, 162, 171, 233
ING, 162
Inner Asia, 12
intellectuals, 49–50, 79, 120, 184, 194, 209–10
Interim People's Committee, 40
Inter-Korean affairs, xxix, xxxii, xxxvi, xxxvii, 55, 57–58, 174–78, 218–22, 278
internal security (*see also* security forces), 272–80
International Affairs Department. *See* Korean Workers' Party (KWP)
International Atomic Energy Agency (IAEA), xxxv, xxxvi, 223, 228, 230, 262; Full-scope Safeguards Agreement (1992), 261
International Friendship Exhibition Hall, 76
International Press Institute, 216
International Telecommunication Union, 151
Internet, 151–52, 217; access, 151–52; cafés, 151–52
Interrogation Bureau, 277

invasions, foreign, xxx, xxxi, 10, 11, 14, 21, 22, 23
Investigation Bureau, 277
Iran, 47, 258
Iran–Iraq War, 47
Iraq, 124
irrigation (*see also* agriculture), 47, 154
IRT–2000 thermal research reactor, 260–61
Italy, 25, 173
Itō Hirobumi, 28

Jaisohn, Phillip (Sŏ Chae-p'il), 26
Japan: attitudes to, in Korea, 30, 33; colonization of Korea by, xxix, xxxi, 25, 26, 28, 29, 30–37, 61, 136, 183, 237; defeat of, in World War II, 38, 125; early links with, 9; invasions by, xxxi, 21, 22; language training in, 124; North Koreans in, 215, 225, relations with, xxix, 25, 125, 224–27; role of, in Six-Party Talks, xxix, xxxv, 262; as target, 258
Japanese colonial occupation (1910–45), xxix, 25, 29–37, 237
Japanese Imperial Army, 34, 237
Japanese language, 18
Japanese Red Army, 225
Jehol Diary, 24
Jilin Province (China), 61, 175
Joint Declaration on the Denuclearization of the Korean Peninsula (1992), 221, 223, 261
Joint Nuclear Control Commission, 221, 261
juch'e. See *chuch'e*
judiciary, 201, 275–76
Junior Reserve Officer Training Corps, 256

Kaech'ŏn, 252
Kaesŏng, xxxvi, 12, 24, 57, 150, 166–67, 176–78, 202
Kaesŏng Special Industrial Zone, 166–67, 231; Management Committee, 177
Kamakura shogunate, 14
Kanggye, 260
Kanghwa Island, 14
Kang Kŏn General Military Academy, 263
Kang Sok-ju, 228
Kang Song-san, 140, 184
kangsong taeguk (rich nation and strong army), 189
Kangwŏn Province, 166, 202, 280
Kantor, Arnold, 228

Mount Kŭmgang (Mount Diamond), 57, 117, 167
Mount Kŭmgang Tourist Zone, 167–69, 173–74, 176, 231
Mount Mohyang, 117
Mount Paektu (Paektu-san or White Head Mountain), 7, 62–63, 115, 196
Mu Chŏng, 42, 43
mudang (shamans), 16
Mun Il-bong, 171
Munitions Industry Department. *See* Korean Workers' Party (KWP)
Munson, xxxvi
Musudan-ni launch facility, 258

Naemul (king), 9
Najin, 150, 152, 175, 253
Najin Business Institute, 167
Najin–Sŏnbong, 152, 172, 202; International Trade Zone, 164, 165–67, 231
Naktong River, 9
Namdaemun (South Gate), 24
Nam Il, 38
Namp'o, 65, 110, 150, 175, 201, 202, 253, 254
narcotics trafficking, 54, 227
Narita International Airport (Tokyo), 184, 214
"nation-first-ism," 52–53
National Day (September 9), 85
National Defense Commission (*see also* Guard Command, Second Economic Committee, State Security Department), xxxiii, xxxiv, 183, 188–91, 194, 196, 198–200, 239, 240, 241–42, 244, 246, 265, 270, 276, 277
National Intelligence Service (South Korea), 274, 278
nationalism, 41, 204
nationalization, 40, 137
National Party Congress. *See* Korean Workers' Party (KWP)
national solipsism, 52
natural resources, 144–45, 195
Naval Academy. *See* Kim Ch'ŏng-suk Naval Academy
Navy Command, 240, 242, 250, 253–54
navy equipment and ships, 254, 272
neighborhoods (*dong*), 202
Neo-Confucianism, xxx–xxxi, 16, 21, 41
nepotism, xxxii, 183–84
Netherlands, 173
newspapers. *See* censorship; media

"New Thinking Initiative," 207
NGOs. *See* nongovernmental organizations
Nixon, Richard M., 55
Nodong Chŏngnyŏn (Working Youth), 216
Nodong medium-range ballistic missile (MRBM), 258, 259–60
Nodong Shinmun (Workers' Daily), 43, 171, 186, 207, 216
Noland, Marcus, 172, 224
nongovernmental organizations (NGOs), 173–74
Nordpolitik, 220
North Hamgyŏng Province, 166, 202, 211, 252, 253, 258, 280
North Hwanghae Province, 202
North Kyŏngsang Province, 9
North P'yŏngan Province, 166, 202, 229, 230, 280
Northeast Anti-Japanese United Army, 237–38
Northeast Asia (*see also* Manchuria), xxx, 4, 8, 35–36, 61, 135
Northeast China (*see also* Manchuria), 4, 79
nuclear bomb test, xxxiv–xxxv, 262
Nuclear Nonproliferation Treaty (NPT). *See* Treaty on the Non-Proliferation of Nuclear Weapons
nuclear proliferation, 227
nuclear weapons (*see also* missiles), xxxiv, xxxv, 260–62
nuclear weapons issue, xxix, xxxv, xxxvi, xxxvii, 57–58, 187, 222, 223–24, 226–27, 227–30, 261–62
nullum crimen sine lege (no crime without a law), 274

Oberdorfer, Donald, 70
O Chin-u, 189, 267
O Guk-nyol, 213
oil (*see also* energy sector): imports, 47, 146, 261; shortage of, 65
Okinawa, 259
O Kŭm-ch'ŏl, 252
Old Chosŏn, 6
Olympic Games, 54, 57
Operations Bureau. *See* General Staff Department
Opium War (1839–42), 24
Ŏrang, 252
ordinary cities (*si or shi*), 202
Organisation for Economic Co-operation and Development (OECD), 139
Oriental Development Company, 30–31

Contributors

Victor D. Cha, is Associate Professor of Government and D.S. Song–Korea Foundation Chair in the Edmund Walsh School of Foreign Service, Georgetown University, Washington, DC.

Bruce Cumings is the Norman and Edna Freehling Professor of History at the University of Chicago.

Helen-Louise Hunter is a former National Intelligence Officer for the Far East and the author of *Kim Il-song's North Korea*.

Balbina Y. Hwang is Visiting Assistant Professor, Department of Government, Georgetown University, Washington, DC.

David C. Kang is Associate Professor of Government at Dartmouth College, Hanover, New Hampshire.

James M. Minnich is a Lieutenant Colonel in the United States Army and Director of Policy, Liaison, Operations, and Training, Joint United States Military Affairs Group—Korea, Seoul, South Korea.

Robert L. Worden is the former Chief of the Federal Research Division, Library of Congress, Washington, DC.

Published Country Studies

(Area Handbook Series)

Afghanistan
Albania
Algeria
Angola
Argentina

Armenia, Azerbaijan,
    and Georgia
Australia
Austria
Bangladesh

Belarus and Moldova
Belgium
Bolivia
Brazil
Bulgaria

Burma
Cambodia
Cameroon
Chad
Chile

China
Colombia
Commonwealth Caribbean,
    Islands of the
Congo
Costa Rica

Côte d'Ivoire (Ivory
    Coast)
Cuba
Cyprus
Czechoslovakia

Dominican Republic
    and Haiti
Ecuador
Egypt
El Salvador

Estonia, Latvia, and
    Lithuania
Ethiopia
Finland
Germany

Ghana
Greece
Guatemala
Guinea
Guyana and Belize

Honduras
Hungary
India
Indian Ocean
Indonesia
Iran

Iraq
Israel
Italy
Japan
Jordan

Kazakstan, Kyrgyzstan,
  Tajikistan, Turkmenistan,
  and Uzbekistan
Kenya
Korea, North

Korea, South
Laos
Lebanon
Liberia
Libya

Malawi
Malaysia
Mauritania
Mexico
Mongolia

Morocco
Mozambique
Nepal and Bhutan
Nicaragua
Nigeria

Oceania
Pakistan
Panama
Paraguay
Persian Gulf States
Peru

Philippines
Poland
Portugal
Romania
Russia

Rwanda and Burundi
Saudi Arabia
Senegal
Sierra Leone
Singapore

Somalia
South Africa
Soviet Union
Spain
Sri Lanka

Sudan
Syria
Tanzania
Thailand
Tunisia

Turkey
Uganda
Uruguay
Venezuela
Vietnam

Yemens, The
Yugoslavia
Zaire
Zambia
Zimbabwe